*To Mary
John Kehoe
great-great-grand[daugh]ter
love,
Anne*

THE PASSION OF JOHN KEHOE

AND THE MYTH OF THE "MOLLY MAGUIRES"

ANNE FLAHERTY

Copyright © 2021 by Anne Flaherty

an.flaherty@gmail.com

All rights reserved. Except for brief quotations in printed reviews, no part of this book may be reproduced in any form or by any electronic or mechanical means, including information storage and retrieval systems, without written permission from the author.

Cover art by Bill Engelhardt

Printed in the United States of America

ISBN [pending]

❀ Created with Vellum

*to Annie O'Brien,
who went without
the necessaries of life*

We want you ... to join us against the Reading Railroad ... Because they oppress you, you in turn oppress the men. ... You have not calculated what the poor men of the collieries have lost by these difficulties. We have more labor and risks and losses in the Schuylkill perhaps than anywhere else. You want this burden to rest on the poor men. We cannot submit to it. Starvation may drive us, for it is said this starvation will break through stone walls, but I tell you the workingmen of the coal regions will eat these stones before they submit.

> Grand Council president James Kealy
> Address to coal operators, April 19, 1871

... autocracy or democracy? ... that is what is at stake ...

> President Joseph Biden, March 25, 2021

Love guides the whole design.

> Revised AOH charter, New York and Pennsylvania
> March 11, 1871

CONTENTS

Author's Note	ix
Preface	xvii
Note of Caution	xxiii
1. The Rebuttal	1
2. Wiggan's Patch	29
3. The Copperheads and the Hibernians	43
4. The First Great Contest	93
5. The AOH Caseload: The Members	117
6. A Black Mark on Time's Calendar	175
7. The AOH Caseload: The Officers	187
8. Jug-Handled Justice	215
9. Mary Ann	241
10. The Last Service	275
11. End of the Road	291
12. The Second Great Contest	303
13. The Western Caseload: The WFM	331
14. The Seduction of Theodore Roosevelt	359
15. Two Powerful Movements	389
16. Our Heart's Blood	399
Epilogue	405
Glossary	435
Acknowledgments	451
About the Author	453

AUTHOR'S NOTE

Discussions around the kitchen table of my mother Margaret—great-granddaughter of John Kehoe, hanged as the so-called king of Pennsylvania's "Molly Maguires"—brought me to this history. My mother's mother Eleanor, along with my mother's aunts and uncles, were the children of Kehoe's eldest daughter Margaret. At one family gathering, a late-night discussion of Kehoe's ordeal reached such heights that my father Marty went down to the fuse box and pulled the circuit breaker, effectively calling "lights out" amidst a storm of hilarity.

On one point the great-aunts agreed passionately: Kehoe had been framed. Their family had lived the Gilded Age horror that flowed from the wholesale ceding of state authority to powerful corporate interests. Names they all knew entered the discussion: Allan Pinkerton, founder of the Pinkerton National Detective Agency; James McParlan, Pinkerton's undercover operative and chief prosecution witness during the trials; Franklin Gowen, president and former legal counsel for the Philadelphia and Reading Railroad and self-appointed lead prosecutor in Schuylkill County's "Molly Maguire" trials; Cyrus Pershing, Gowen's handpicked choice for president judge of that county's Court of Oyer and Terminer; Asa

Packer, president of the Lehigh Valley Railroad; and Charles Parrish, president of the Lehigh and Wilkes-Barre Coal and Iron Company.

Both Packer and Parrish were on-again, off-again members of Gowen's Coal Combination, a cartel of railroad and anthracite coal interests described by one historian as "the first industry price-fixing device in U.S. history."[1] In 1876 Packer and Parrish both sent their corporate counsel to prosecute Carbon County's "Molly Maguire" caseload.

Stated simply, Gowen, aided by his industrial and political colleagues, seized the courts for the duration of these trials. For almost a half-decade, district attorneys throughout Pennsylvania's anthracite region disavowed the ethics guiding conflicts of interest and willingly took a backseat to Gowen's handpicked legal teams. Gowen's influence extended even to Pennsylvania's Board of Pardons, a body he helped create as delegate to Pennsylvania's 1873 Constitutional Convention.

On one issue, the great-aunts remained adamant. "It was political," Aunt Marion said of Kehoe's prosecution, striking the table with the flat of her hand. Aunt Madge agreed.

Martin Ritt's film *The Molly Maguires*, with Sean Connery playing Kehoe, further animated the discussion, as did Pennsylvania's posthumous pardoning of Kehoe in 1979, brought about in part through the efforts of our cousin, Joseph Wayne. Even the issuance of Kehoe's posthumous pardon, overseen by attorney John Elliott, did little to sway the historical recording.

In 1998, Oxford University Press published Kevin Kenny's *Making Sense of the Molly Maguires*. Those who knew, and had lived, the history received that volume with mystification, as they had received Wayne Broehl Jr.'s work in 1964 and Ritt's film in 1970. The family also had a copy of a letter written by Kehoe in 1878 from Pottsville Jail. "I would sooner die than swear a wilful [sic] lie on my fellow man," Kehoe's letter said.[2]

My aunt, Ellen Engelhardt, had spent much time in her library in Bergen County, New Jersey, poring over microfilm of the *New York Times*. Like my great-aunts, she held utterly to the conviction that

Kehoe, as with many of the so-called "Mollies," had been innocent of the crimes charged against him. Research by my sister, Susie Flaherty, included discussions with the great-aunts that kept the conversation going.

Examiners of Pennsylvania's "Molly Maguire" conflict fell into two camps. Many believed that Irish mineworkers, driven to desperation, had waged a campaign of terror against mine officials. Others believed that Pinkerton operatives, agents of commercial terrorism in the pay of railroad and coal interests, had orchestrated the murderous reign of terror that drove the early trials.

I dipped into Ellen's files. Intrigued, I took a deeper dive into more extensive research. My search lasted for two decades. What I found astounded me. Very little of this history had been accurately told. Many of the Irishmen charged as "Mollies," as some had noted, were not miners. They were small businessmen, running hotels and taverns. But many were also political delegates. Many had achieved elected office themselves, including five so-called "Mollies," with some miners among them, elected as township school directors. They had sent candidates to federal office, reform politicians who advocated in Washington on behalf of the workingmen. These Irish Catholic civic and community leaders were a very long way from the illiterate Irishmen history had continually served up.

I had one devilishly persistent question: how had this history become so skewed? Specifically, how, over a century and a half, had the truth of these events lain obscured in local newspapers? How had researchers over decades continually ignored most of the evidence that pointed to the innocence of these Irishmen?

As one zipped file folder expanded into boxes, and the boxes into cabinets, I shared my findings with others. To my repeated query, how this history could have received such shabby treatment, my mother finally responded. "They wanted them to be guilty," she said.

That sharpened my focus. It had simply not crossed my mind that these Irishmen had been ethnically scapegoated, not only by their prosecutors and a hostile press, but by historians who had continually mischaracterized the "Molly Maguire" history, and even by almost all sympathetic observers who had reflected upon it. Those observers included Eugene Debs.

As I worked on the last sections of this manuscript, the killing of George Floyd convulsed the country and the globe. The video of a forty-six-year-old Black man, handcuffed and prone, strangling to death under the knee of Minneapolis police officer Derek Chauvin, drew forth a storm of collective outrage beyond anything I had seen in my lifetime. In the midst of a pandemic, demonstrations spread to more than fifty countries. Protestors toppled statues that evoked slavery and colonialism.

One day after Floyd's death, Nobel laureate Bob Dylan, longtime chronicler of U.S. history, spoke with historian Douglas Brinkley. "'It sickened me no end to see George tortured to death like that,'" Dylan told Brinkley. "'It was beyond ugly. Let's hope that justice comes swift for the Floyd family and for the nation.'"[3]

I felt the same. After Floyd's killing, I went back to research that had lain in my files for more than a decade. At the time I collected it, it had seemed too painful to take in. Not for the faint of heart.

A *New York Herald* article from June 1877, written after eleven so-called "Mollies" died on the gallows at Pottsville, Mauch Chunk, and Wilkes-Barre, gave this information: "None of the men had the vertebrae dislocated, but died a lingering death by strangulation, an invariable consequence of using the drop gallows, always resorted to in this State."[4]

That account made it sickeningly clear. Officials for the Commonwealth of Pennsylvania had built gallows for use in the "Molly Maguire" proceedings that were designed to deliberately strangle men to death. At Mauch Chunk, the sheriff and deputies had executed four men at once, all bound in chains. From June 1877 to October 1879, the commonwealth had used those instruments of torture against twenty-one men in five counties. The state-sanctioned depravity had taken place over and over again. Sheriffs had opened their jail yards to crowds of gawkers. Some spectators had brought children.

Of the media's news coverage in general, Dylan said in the

Brinkley interview: "'All we see is good-for-nothing news. And we have to thank the media industry for that. It stirs people up.'" He added: "'Sex and politics and murder is the way to go if you want to get people's attention. It excites us, that's our problem.'"[5]

For years before the coal region trials began, newsmen countrywide had pounded the specter of "Molly Maguireism" into the public mind. Fake news reports of alleged "Molly" outrages had reached south to Virginia, South Carolina, Tennessee, and Louisiana and north to New York and Massachusetts. German newspapers had printed tales of "Die Molly Maguires" for readers in Maryland and Pennsylvania. For years, the image of hordes of Irishmen committing depraved acts of violence had seeped from unnamed sources into the national psyche.

These outlandish tales appeared as the political gains of coal region Hibernians accelerated. Whoever crafted these bizarre tales designed them to inflame. As coal region Hibernians gained political clout, sending preferred candidates to Washington, yellow press headlines of supposed "Molly" outrages appeared within a day or two of the political gains the alleged "Mollies" had helped to secure.

All of the alleged "Molly" defendants belonged to the Ancient Order of Hibernians (AOH). Tales of fictional "Molly" outrages intensified as the order's members grew in influence. In 1871, AOH men in New York and Pennsylvania filed almost identical revised charters with their state legislatures. The charters encouraged brotherly love. A poem in the preamble advised: "Love guides the whole design."[6] Items found in Kehoe's cell on the morning of his execution reinforced these AOH aims. So did statements of innocence given by many of the condemned men.

Other research astounded. At least twelve of the hanged men had been married. At least nine were over the age of forty. Given the times, a number of them may have been grandfathers. The commonwealth had not, as the historical record insisted, executed a group of illiterate young Irish immigrant mineworkers. It had, in many instances, executed older married men, men with large families, men well established in their communities.

Again, the question arose: how had this history become so skewed? Early on, arrows pointed to Allan Pinkerton. Pinkerton operatives had crafted the trial testimony. Pinkerton operatives had delivered the testimony. Pinkerton himself had kept the propaganda mill running by folding McParlan's testimony, and Gowen's prosecution argument, into a dime novel. Called *The Mollie Maguires and the Detectives* and published while trials remained ongoing, the novel, the literary press that produced it, and the caseload that generated it had all helped draw Pinkerton's firm back from the edge of bankruptcy.

Other arrows pointed to the prosecution teams. As with the Pinkertons, a number had charges of illegal activity leveled against them. All were devotees of railroad and coal interests. A number spoke German, easing communication with juries packed with German farmers. Many were skilled in press manipulation. Some had honed these skills in pre-Civil War days. All held nativist views. All were politically hostile to the up-and-coming Irish Catholics. The same year Pinkerton published his book, Francis Dewees, a nephew of one of the lead prosecutors, published another volume. Heavily skewed, it served as the first so-called authoritative account of this conflict.

The actions of some Roman Catholic coal region clergy, and of Archbishop James Frederick Wood of Philadelphia, proved equally troubling. Their conflation of coal region AOH membership with so-called "Molly Maguire" terrorism had helped hang innocent men. Here again, after some time, my mother weighed in. "It was about power," she said.

Kehoe's granddaughters had said: "It was political." I followed the politics. A cursory examination of biographies showed that three successively defeated Democratic gubernatorial candidates, from 1869 to 1875, had roles in the trials: Asa Packer, Charles Buckalew, and Cyrus Pershing. Bitterly disappointed politicians had conducted this caseload. Pershing's court had sentenced many, including Kehoe, to death. In 1872 Kehoe, in another fact routinely overlooked by historians, had placed his name in consideration for Democratic candidate to state assembly. Kehoe's father, Joseph Kehoe, a miner, had served both as constable and supervisor for Mahanoy Township. "Kehoe's father was an important man," my grandmother had said.

Horrors emerged, including Pinkerton actions that smacked of commercial terrorism. Where Pinkerton agents entered, violent death often followed.

In January 1875 Pinkerton operative Robert Linden had procured the explosive "Greek fire" from the federal arsenal at Rock Island, Illinois, for use in a post-midnight raid on the Missouri farmhouse of the family of Frank and Jesse James. Their eight-year-old brother died in the attack. Five months later, Linden entered Pennsylvania's coalfields. After Linden's appearance, six murders took place. They drove the early trials. Seven months after Linden entered the region, in December 1875, a post-midnight raid on a coal region boarding house at Wiggan's Patch left two dead, including Kehoe's pregnant sister-in-law.

Similar horrors marked McParlan's abortive cases against the Western Federation of Miners. These took place three decades after McParlan testified in the "Molly Maguire" trials. Two nearly identical bomb blasts, one in Idaho and one in Oregon, killed two men critical to the western trials: a former Idaho governor whose death provided the cases' fulcrum, and an Oregon sheriff who testified against McParlan's interests. "Molly" historians had routinely overlooked the western caseload, where three stellar defense attorneys, including Clarence Darrow, had effectively discredited McParlan at the end of his career.

News from Fayette County in Pennsylvania's western bituminous region in 1881, two years after the last "Molly" hanging took place, raised the possibility that the Pinkerton agency was not a detective agency at all, but a crime syndicate hired to sabotage organized labor. Linden's 1881 arrests of eight so-called "Molly Maguires," all Irish Catholic mineworkers, have gone unrecorded by historians. In these cases, Linden again claimed that he had "evidence of their connection with a well-organized and dangerous conspiracy, and that he has sufficient testimony to convict the accused."[7] The arrests, one source said, were "due to the detective work of McParlan."[8]

Two fatally tainted sources, Pinkerton and Dewees, guided the writing of the "Molly Maguire" history. The first task toward seeking greater understanding involves challenging previously published works. Chapter 1 of this work does just that.

Anne Flaherty
Saint Leonard, MD

---

1. Wayne G. Broehl Jr., *The Molly Maguires* (Cambridge, MA: Harvard University Press, 1964), 171.
2. John Kehoe to W. R. Potts, circa March 1878, John Kehoe File, M 170.18 MI, Schuylkill County Historical Society.
3. Douglas Brinkley, "Bob Dylan Has a Lot on His Mind," *New York Times*, June 12, 2020.
4. *New York Herald*, June 22, 1877.
5. Brinkley, "Dylan," *New York Times*, June 12, 2020.
6. *Report of the Case of the Commonwealth vs. John Kehoe et al.* (Pottsville, PA: Miners' Journal Book and Jobs Room, 1876), 167.
7. *Butler (PA) Citizen*, August 24, 1881; reprinting *Philadelphia Record*.
8. *Milheim (PA) Journal*, August 25, 1881.

PREFACE

In the introduction for Dover Publications' 1973 reprint of Allan Pinkerton's 1877 dime novel, *The Mollie Maguires and the Detectives*, attorney John Elliott described Pinkerton's narrative as "a biased, self-serving version of the defeat by capital of labor's first effort to organize America's largest mass industry—coal."[1]

Elliott's assessment continued: "Published in 1877 as a sales piece for Pinkerton's strikebreaking talents, it was followed by such spiritually reassuring Pinkerton sequels as *Strikers, Communists and Detectives; Gypsies and Detectives;* and *Professional Thieves and Detectives*."[2]

"Within the book itself," Elliott said, "Pinkerton appears as 'an intelligent and broadminded Scotchman' acting in virtuous partnership with the 'eloquent,' 'brave' and 'gentlemanly' Reading president Gowen. In sharp contrast, striking miners are labeled 'communists' before that slander became fashionable."[3]

Time, Elliott added, had "enhanced the significance of this period piece's invaluable insights into the power and politics of industrial arrogance." Writing in 1973, he observed: "Today, as many concerned Americans, armed with a sense of injustice and aided by a more enlightened judicial climate, challenge institutions to direct their power and purpose to the common good, *The Mollie Maguires and the Detectives* offers a stark reminder that eternal vigilance is indeed the price of liberty. It contains all the ingredients of epic tragedy and holds uncomfortable contemporary parallels. Class struggle, heroes, traitors and death abound in the socio-economic confrontation of John Kehoe, the immigrant Irish labor and political leader, and Franklin B. Gowen, Esq., the relentlessly acquisitive president of the Reading Coal and Iron Company."[4]

Elliott addressed the conflict's political triggers: "As Schuylkill County Ancient Order of Hibernian delegate and elected Democratic high constable, Kehoe represented an ascending Irish political power which embarrassingly defeated Gowen's hand-picked gubernatorial candidate, Judge Cyrus Pershing, in 1875. Ironically, Pershing later presided at Kehoe's trial and pronounced Kehoe's death sentence in 1878, for an alleged crime committed in 1862 without witnesses."[5]

"The Mollie Maguire trials were conceived in an atmosphere of religious, social and economic bigotry," Elliott continued, with defendants' fates "preordained by a rabid press, and by juries which excluded Catholics. Their trials failed to comport with elemental due process. ... The chief witness against the miners was the same resourceful Pinkerton informer James McParlan whom Clarence Darrow later uncovered turning perjured evidence against Big Bill Heywood [sic] and the Western Federation of Miners in Idaho's famous [1907] Steunenberg case. Significantly, none of the twenty hanged miners [in Pennsylvania] were ever apprehended in an act of violence."[6]

The "Molly" hangings, Elliot said, "made the Pinkertons invaluable tools of the pre-Wagner Act industrial princes." Describing Pinkerton's book as a "contrived industrial fable," Elliot observed: "the Protestant Ethic emerges victorious; the miners are hanged; labor is crushed in the Pennsylvania coal fields until John Mitchell, Teddy Roosevelt and the 'Great Strike' of 1902; the pontifical English Archbishop Wood of Philadelphia loses a few of his Irish flock, but then history reveals that good English archbishops were never excited by the mere diminution of their Irish flocks; the coal fields are again safe for citizens of rectitude and wealth; and Pinkerton moves on to the next bloody round of his proficient strike-breaking."[7]

Of Pinkerton's 1877 dime novel, Elliott concluded: "By contemporaneously recording the attitudes and strategies which fueled this brutal period of American industrial expansion, *The Mollie Maguires and the Detectives* offers a seminal historical document of vast importance. Unfortunately, the vast socio-economic-political implications of the Mollie Maguire era have not yet received the objective, widespread scrutiny they deserve. It is the stuff of heroism and high history which should be plumbed by all who would seriously undertake the difficult task of advancing human understanding and social justice."[8]

Six years after Elliott wrote his introduction to the reissue of Pinkerton's book, Pennsylvania's Board of Pardons granted John Kehoe a posthumous pardon. Governor Milton Shapp signed the document. Elliott, a fierce litigator and a native of Girardville, Pennsylvania, home to Kehoe's nineteenth-century Hibernian House, oversaw the legal effort that secured the posthumous pardon. Elliott's brother, attorney Thomas Elliott, along with Kehoe's great-grandson Joseph Wayne and the Pennsylvania Labor History Society, aided the effort.

Over the past two decades, I have corresponded with John Elliott regarding my research into the "Molly Maguire" conflict. Some years ago, he helped me rewrite the following conclusion to an essay I drafted regarding the legal maneuvering that brought about the trials:

> The blatantly unconstitutional judicial lynchings that have forever defined these "Molly Maguire" executions remain an indelible stain on the commonwealth's history. Irish Catholic labor advocates were framed for murder on perjured evidence from the Pinkertons' private detectives who were paid by the anthracite region's most powerful coal and iron company; its president, Franklin Gowen, personally divested Pennsylvania's governor of

his power to pardon. Denied proper habeas corpus proceedings, AOH men stood trial in courtrooms guarded by Coal and Iron policemen. This private Gestapo repeatedly violated fundamental due process as the Reading Coal and Iron Company accused them of perjury, thereby chilling the exercise of fundamental constitutional sixth amendment rights.

Area newspapers also working in concert with Gowen and the coal barons repeatedly and vociferously attacked the AOH defendants as "Molly Maguire" assassins. The commonwealth itself identified the AOH as "the Molly Maguires." AOH defendants faced special prosecutors in the employ of regional railroads and coal and iron companies. They faced judges with ties to those companies; judges who repeatedly denied changes of venue while unconstitutionally declaring these a special "class of cases." Judges statewide, including the Pennsylvania Supreme Court, then established uniquely onerous obstacles that doomed all of the "Molly Maguire" defendants. Most shamefully, Pennsylvania's highest court denied its most vulnerable citizens the fundamental rights of due process and equal protection.

Of the prosecution's legal maneuvering, Elliott concluded: "This fundamental violation of constitutionally protected due process and equal protection leaves an indelible stain on Pennsylvania's jurisprudence."

On February 26, 2021, John drafted a letter to me forwarding a generous contribution toward the publication of this book. He told me: "Your research and writings continue to shine the light of truth on the real history of the Molly Maguires, exposing the false history written by their enemies since 20 Irish Catholic miners were hanged on the perjured testimony of a Pinkerton."

In the same letter, John advised me: "Keep up your great work. Stay healthy and strong in the struggle. Let me know how I can be helpful."

On March 9, I emailed John in response to his acknowledgement of my letter. "Thanks again for your offer of help," I told him. "Once the manuscript is in your hands, if you feel moved to write a foreword, that would be a boon. I'll be in touch soon."

Four days later, John passed away, suddenly, from a heart attack.

I offer this book without its intended foreword, but in the interest, in John Elliott's words, "of advancing human understanding and social justice."[9]

A. F.

---

1. John Elliott, introduction to *The Mollie Maguires and the Detectives* by Allan Pinkerton (1877; repr. New York: Dover Publications, Inc., 1973), i.
2. Ibid.
3. Ibid., i-ii.
4. Ibid., ii.
5. Ibid.
6. Ibid., iii.
7. Ibid., iv.
8. Ibid.
9. Ibid.

NOTE OF CAUTION

This text documents ethnic and class conflict. It contains many disturbing images and references, including use of the "n-word" in the era's political hate speech. These profoundly offensive references help fully characterize the arena in which the "Molly Maguire" prosecutors mounted their caseload.

1
THE REBUTTAL

It is now established that there was no society in America calling itself the Molly Maguires, that this name was tagged to the Ancient Order of Hibernians by the commercial press whose purpose it was to help the coal operators crush all organization in the mining industry; that the Philadelphia and Reading Company hired the Pinkerton spy agency not to save society from a band of terrorists but to spread terror.

Philip Foner, 1947

The Nineteenth-Century Conflict: The Background

From 1877 to 1879, the Commonwealth of Pennsylvania hanged twenty-one Irish Catholic men in its anthracite coal region, and prosecuted at least fifty more. All these defendants, all charged as alleged "Molly Maguires," belonged to the Ancient Order of Hibernians (AOH), a benevolent order chartered in March 1871 with the Pennsylvania state legislature. Many of the defendants were AOH officers.

The black veil of the "Molly Maguire" epithet, laid over much of the conflict's source materials, effectively obscured the writing of this history. The intense intellectual involvement in labor and politics of many AOH men charged as "Mollies," and the religious faith that underpinned their advocacy, have gone unexamined for almost a century and a half. The prejudice that ensured the success of the nineteenth-century trials flows, with few exceptions, through the conflict's entire historical canon.

The wholesale ceding of state authority to corporate interests defined these prosecutions. In 1971, historian Harold Aurand stated the matter succinctly: "'The Molly Maguire investigation and trials marked one of the most astounding surrenders of sovereignty in American history. A private corporation initiated the investigation through a private detective agency, a private police force arrested the supposed offenders, and coal company attorneys prosecuted—the state provided only the courtroom and hangman.'"[1]

James McParlan, an operative for the Pinkerton National Detective Agency, served as the trials' chief prosecution witness. Franklin Gowen, a Democratic Party operative, president and former legal counsel for the Philadelphia and Reading Railroad, and self-appointed lead counsel during the trials, paid for McParlan's services through the railroad's subsidiary, the Philadelphia and Reading Coal and Iron Company. Several AOH men charged as "Mollies" also served as prosecution witnesses. They corroborated McParlan's testimony and subsequently received pardons, or immunity from prosecution.

A long line of chroniclers have characterized Pennsylvania's alleged "Mollies" as violent Irishmen whose brutal tendencies had roots in Ireland. The prosecutors in the "Molly" trials took great pains to promote this theory, and to codify its legitimacy in subsequent histories. The promoters of the trials counted among them many disappointed Democratic operatives, including three successively defeated candidates for the highest office in Pennsylvania.

The White Men Establish the Narrative

The intensely political nature of the "Molly Maguire" conflict has received little scrutiny. Three successively defeated Democratic gubernatorial candidates in Pennsylvania took part in these trials. In 1868, in support of Horatio Seymour's presidential bid, their party chose as its slogan: "This is a White Man's Country; Let White Men Rule."

In 1876, Lehigh Valley Railroad president Asa Packer, defeated in 1869 for Pennsylvania's governorship, sent his corporate counsel Allen Craig to Mauch Chunk to craft prosecution strategy for the "Molly Maguire" trials. Former U.S. and state senator Charles Buckalew, described by one coal region observer as Franklin Gowen's "right hand man" while in political office,[2] lost the race for governor in 1872. Five years later, Buckalew served as a "Molly" prosecutor in Bloomsburg. Cyrus Pershing, president judge of Schuylkill County's Court of Oyer and Terminer, lost the bid for the governor's office in 1875. From 1876 to 1877, Pershing's court condemned more AOH men to death than any other court. Pennsylvania's Labor Reformers, with many AOH men among them, helped defeat all of these candidacies.

In 1871, a correspondent for the *Irish Times* wrote a column from New York directed toward readers in Ireland. In it, he summed up the era's perception of the Irish Catholics transplanted from Ireland to the United States: "It is a fact not known in Ireland how small American politicians think of Irishmen. The idea at your side of the Atlantic is, that there is a brotherhood of sentiment, a sort of alliance—offensive and defensive—between the native Americans and the Irish. No such thing! The Americans, in the main, consider the Irish in no such light. They find them useful as hewers of wood and drawers of water." Of Irish political influence, the correspondent said: "Their vote is wanted for the irrepressible politicians with which this country abounds, and they tolerate them so far; but ... they ... remind me very much of the fox who climbed out of the well on the back of the goats. They certainly reach profit and emolument by the means of the Irish, and, as far as I see, will continue to do so."[3]

A few years before, a New York newspaper called *The Irish People* published similar views. In the paper's discussion of New York's Democratic gubernatorial candidate John Hoffman, an Irish observer described the "'proper place,'" in Hoffman's view, of Irishmen in America: "'we have proved ourselves exceedingly useful in this country in building houses and draining swamps, and cutting down forests ... indeed, we are capital "rail-roaders" and "cannalers," and ... were never intended by God and nature to be anything else ... [but] hewers of wood and drawers of water.'"[4] In May 1877, a coal region publisher baldly expressed the prevailing view of Irishmen as non-white. After the issuance of numerous death warrants in the "Molly Maguire" cases, Thomas Foster's *Shenandoah Herald* advised that "Mollieism" must now take a back seat, "while white men say what shall be done."[5]

The progressive politics of Pennsylvania's alleged "Mollies" threatened not just their prosecutors' nativist and elitist views. They threatened their commercial holdings. British capital backed much of Pennsylvania's hard coal industry. The McCalmont Brothers, a London firm, financed Gowen's railroad and coal enterprises. A number of AOH men charged as "Mollies" embraced Labor Reform Party tenets. These included a strong pro-union stance and a call for the exclusion of British capital from U.S. industry.

Gowen's service as a delegate to Pennsylvania's 1873 Constitutional Convention, including his personal and successful effort to remove the governor's authority to grant pardons, underscores the political cast of the trials. That effort, along with Gowen's wholesale use of Pinkerton operatives to conduct the caseload, underscores the commonwealth's willing abdication of its legal authority to formidable corporate interests.

A shadowy detective agency enabled those interests. In May 1873 Allan Pinkerton, president of the Pinkerton National Detective Agency, stood on the edge of bankruptcy. Pinkerton urged George Bangs, his New York superintendent, to solicit business from Gowen.

Five months later, Pinkerton operative James McParlan entered the coal region undercover. Nine murders followed. These, along with a number of earlier, unsolved murders, formed the basis for the prosecution's "Molly Maguire" caseload. McParlan served as the trials' chief prosecution witness. Several AOH men charged as "Mollies" corroborated McParlan's testimony in exchange for their lives.

The prosecution did not charge defendants as individuals. Instead, it conflated AOH membership with supposed Irish terrorism. The official transcript for John Kehoe's 1876 trial reads "THE COMMONWEALTH *vs.* JOHN KEHOE ET AL., *MEMBERS OF THE ANCIENT ORDER OF HIBERNIANS, COMMONLY KNOWN AS 'MOLLY MAGUIRES.'*"[6]

Politicians Work the Sensational Press

In the decades before the Pennsylvania trials began, widespread sensational press accounts trumpeted the criminality, along with the political influence, of alleged "Molly Maguires" in the United States. In fall 1857, almost twenty years before the trials began, a spate of such coverage arose from Philadelphia. It arose five months after the ordination of James Frederick Wood, an avowed AOH foe, as coadjutor bishop for the Roman Catholic diocese of Philadelphia.

A long history of AOH activity in the United States also predated the trials. In 1836, Hibernians from New York City and Schuylkill County, Pennsylvania, headquarters of the subsequent "Molly" prosecutions, applied to executive members in Ireland and Great Britain for the first U.S. AOH charter. "'You must love without dissimulation, hating evil, cleaving to good,'" the first U.S. charter advised.[7] Over the years the benevolent order, headquartered at first in Pennsylvania and later in New York City, grew in strength, numbers, and influence. At the height of the "Molly" trials, it numbered more than seven hundred thousand U.S. members, and by one official source, more than sixty thousand in Pennsylvania.[8] The New York officers retained their ties with Pennsylvania's coal region officers. In January 1875, the year before his arrest, John Kehoe hosted AOH national officers from New York at his coal region tavern, Girardville's Hibernian House.

Almost two decades before that, on September 23, 1857, a Washington paper published a reprint from the *Philadelphia Sun*. "Who is 'Molly Maguire?'" the article asked. It described "an *alien* organization in this country, sworn to act in determined hostility to the citizens of American birth." The *Sun* claimed that the order arose from the Irish organization known as Ribbonmen, whose members vowed "the stealthy murder of every Protestant who became an object of their hatred." The purpose of the order in the United States, the *Sun* maintained, was "to govern the dominant political party of the Union, by casting its entire power as if it were a single person."[9]

A few weeks later, the venomous coverage reached Pennsylvania's hard coal region. Benjamin Bannan, editor of the *Miners' Journal*, quoted similar coverage from the *Philadelphia Transcript*. Bannan warned readers in Pottsville, future site of nine "Molly" executions, of the secret Roman Catholic association that Democrats were using for political ends. Philadelphia's "Molly Maguires," the *Transcript's* coverage said, "'would march to the polls, almost in regular army'" to cast a solid vote for their preferred candidates.[10] Nativist editors in South Carolina, Tennessee, Missouri, Kansas, Iowa, Indiana, and Ohio picked up the malignant coverage.

Fifteen years later, as coal region AOH men worked to place their candidates in office, coverage of fictional "Molly Maguire" outrages appeared in force. Nativist editors in New Orleans; in Charleston and Columbia, South Carolina; in Knoxville and Nashville, Tennessee; in Virginia, Ohio, New York, and throughout Pennsylvania ran the coverage. In 1874, the same year Allan Pinkerton started a dime novel press with a staff of artists and writers at his disposal, the nativist propaganda accelerated dramatically.

Three days before Pinkerton's undercover operative James McParlan joined a coal region AOH lodge, such coverage appeared in the *Chicago Tribune*, from the city where Pinkerton kept his home office. "THE 'MOLLIE MAGUIRES,'" this headline ran. "Terrorism in the Coal Regions of Pennsylvania—Wholesale Assassination by a Regularly-Organized Band of Outlaws."[11] This inflammatory press appeared at a time of quiet in the coal region, with coal region AOH men actively swaying national political races.

On August 3, 1874, Christopher Donnelly, AOH treasurer for Schuylkill County later imprisoned as a "Molly," served as a delegate to the Democratic convention at Pottsville. Five months after Donnelly's election as an AOH county officer, he delivered thirty-nine votes to the nomination of James Reilly, a young Irish Catholic, to U.S. Congress.[12] Reilly secured the nomination and, in November, the federal congressional seat. The day after Reilly secured the nomination, the *New York Herald* ran fictional coverage. "THE COAL REGIONS," its headline read. "General Prevalence of Riot, Robbery and Murder. BODIES HORRIBLY MUTILATED. Ku Klux Notices Served on Obnoxious Citizens."[13]

As the *Herald* and other papers ramped up their lurid coverage during the 1874 election cycle, rebuttals appeared. From Schuylkill County's Mahanoy City, Father Charles McFadden wrote to deny "the existence of such a society, much less a single member of such an organization as the 'Molly Maguires.'"[14] The *New York Tribune* sent its reporter to investigate. *"STORIES OF MINERS' OUTRAGES DENIED,"* the *Tribune* concluded. "STORIES OF ORGANIZED LAWLESSNESS SAID TO BE WHOLLY UNTRUE—SENSATION TALES OF THE 'MOLLY MAGUIRES.'"[15]

At the height of the "Molly" trials, with newspapers countrywide glutting newsstands with sensational accounts, the *New York Sun* published an article that included Franklin Gowen's summation, as self-appointed lead prosecutor in the trial of Thomas Munley, to a coal region jury. "A SOCIETY OF MURDERERS," the *Sun's* account read. *"THE LEAGUE OF POLITICIANS AND THUGS IN PENNSYLVANIA.* The History of the Molly Maguire Organization from the Time it was Chartered by a Republican Legislature—A Horrible List of Crimes—President Gowen's Testimony."[16]

At the time the *New York Sun* ran this coverage, John Swinton served as chief of the paper's editorial staff. After the "Molly" trials ended, Swinton addressed a group of fellow journalists at a banquet in New York. There, Swinton described all New York pressmen as "'tools and vassals of rich men behind the scenes.'" He added: "'We are intellectual prostitutes.'"[17]

But Gowen's self-serving narrative of alleged Irish terrorism continues to hold sway. As of this writing, the online "Molly Maguire" page for the Library of Congress reference service "Chronicling America" sends researchers to numerous sensational press articles of "Molly Maguire" coverage. The page uses this descriptor: "An Irish secret society known as the Molly Maguires is thought responsible for a string of violent attacks in the Pennsylvania coal fields."[18]

The "Molly Maguire" Prosecutors Amplify the Narrative

During the "Molly Maguire" trials in the late 1870s, the prosecution, along with Pinkerton operative James McParlan, repeatedly pounded the theory of Pennsylvania's "Molly Maguire" terrorism as an outgrowth of dissent in Ireland. For their supposed authoritative text, the prosecution chose the work of Anglo-Irish land agent William Steuart Trench.

Trench described Ireland's alleged "Mollies" in *Realities of Irish Life*, published in 1869. "These 'Molly Maguires,'" Trench said, "were generally stout, active young men, dressed up in women's clothes, with faces blackened, or otherwise disguised ... [they] sometimes smeared themselves in the most fantastic manner with burnt cork about their eyes, mouths, and cheeks. In this state they used suddenly to surprise [rent agents], and either duck them in bog-holes, or beat them in the most unmerciful manner ...the 'Molly Maguires' became the terror of all our officials."[19]

As with the fictional newspaper coverage, Trench's work drew rebuttals. From New Orleans, the *Morning Star and Catholic Messenger* derided "the falsifications and truculency of this agent of Irish landlords."[20] A reviewer for the *Chicago Tribune* scoffed: "If we are to judge of the peasantry of Ireland by his descriptions, every peasant is a Celt in a savage condition, with a stubble-covered face ... and a half-savage, half-sneering smile ... always insolent, insolent, reckless, desperate, intemperate, rebellious, ready to murder his next friend ... making it the prime object of his life not to pay rent or give up his land."[21]

The *New York Herald* said: "Mr. Trench is not only an Irish Protestant, but he is also a 'born aristocrat.' ... evidently one of those Irishmen who have resolved to forgive their Catholic neighbors for the centuries of ill-treatment which they have compelled them to suffer. ... Mr. Trench, however, does not tell us this: Whence arose the necessity for his book."[22]

Seven years after Trench's book appeared, Franklin Gowen told the jury in the trial of alleged "Molly" Thomas Munley: "get a little book called Trench's Realities of Irish Life ... you will find the history of this organization. ... an organized resistance in Ireland to the payment of rents. The malcontents became known as Ribbonmen, and they generally made their attacks upon the agents ... Their object was to intimidate and hold in terror all those to whom they owed money ... As a branch of this society ... sprang the men known as Mollie Maguires."[23]

Special prosecutor Francis Hughes, yet another Democratic operative, also told jurymen of "the Ribbon Men of Ireland ... outrages by beating, by ducking in the bog-ponds, and afterwards by murder. ... inside of that organization ... a body of men known as Mollie Maguires. ... They used to blacken their faces and put on bonnets and frocks, and go out at nights and seize a bailiff or an agent ... if they did not kill him, they would beat him, or duck him ... thus they inspired a feeling of terrorism."[24]

McParlan, chief prosecution witness during the "Molly" trials, restated Trench's theories. The *New York Herald* headlined its account of McParlan's testimony thus: "THE MURDERERS' LEAGUE. DAMNING EXPOSURES OF THE INNER WORKINGS OF THE MOLLIE MAGUIRES—DIABOLICAL INTRIGUES—BARTERING BLOOD."[25] The *New York Times* said of McParlan's testimony: "The Mollie Maguires, he testifies, are a branch of the society known as the Ancient Order of Hibernians. ... a secret, oath-bound association ... the order has its origin and fountain-head in Ireland. ... the bloody purposes of the Mollie Maguires have been grafted upon the Pennsylvania branch of the organization by the men whose crimes have just been exposed. This explanation seems reasonable."[26]

As trials remained ongoing, the prosecution also overtook the writing of the "Molly Maguire" historical canon. The work of Francis Dewees, nephew of prosecutor Hughes, appeared in January 1877, before the first mass executions. Dewees's book, titled *The Molly Maguires: The Origin, Growth, and Character of the Organization*, also referred readers to Trench's *Realities of Irish Life*. Dewees restated Trench's fantasias of cross-dressing, with men's faces blackened "or otherwise disguised, with ... fantastic masks, or with burnt cork about their eyes, mouths, and cheeks. ... the very name of Molly Maguire inspired terror."[27]

The same year Dewees's book appeared, Allan Pinkerton, still in Gowen's employ, published his semi-fictional work *The Mollie Maguires and the Detectives*. Pinkerton's book included Gowen's speech from the trial of Munley, including Gowen's admonition to jurors to "'get a little book called Trench's *Realities of Irish Life*.'"[28]

In 1935, W. E. B. Du Bois said of the skewed writing of U.S. Reconstruction-era history: "It simply shows that with sufficient general agreement and determination among the dominant classes, the truth of history may be utterly distorted and contradicted and changed to any convenient fairy tale that the masters of men wish."[29] The "Molly Maguire" fairy tale has rolled through the history books, mostly unchallenged, for well over a century.

The Academic Discussion, and a Film

In 1892, after the arming of Pinkerton guards at Andrew Carnegie's Homestead steel mill led to violent confrontation and death, Congress stepped forward. The *New York Sun* reported the Senate investigation at Washington. "'These forces,'" Illinois Democrat John Palmer said of the Pinkertons, "'are responsible neither to God nor man, only to those who hire them. ... They ought to be hounded down by such means as are employed against enemies of mankind.'"[30] In March 1893, the federal Anti-Pinkerton Act went into effect, prohibiting the employment of private detectives by the federal government and the District of Columbia. By 1899, more than half of U.S. states or territories had enacted similar legislation.

In 1936, almost six decades after the "Molly" trials ended, historian J. Walter Coleman published *The Molly Maguire Riots: Industrial Conflict in The Pennsylvania Coal Region*. Coleman concluded: "The worst that might be said of the prosecutors of the Molly Maguires is that they entered into a deliberate conspiracy to manufacture evidence with which to convict their enemies, the labor leaders, a charge which, obviously, cannot be proved. ... the conspiracy theory is so far within the realm of possibility that it deserves consideration."[31]

In 1947, historian Philip Foner rebutted all former "Molly Maguire" propaganda. Regarding supposed "Molly" terrorism in Pennsylvania's coal region, Foner said: "It is now established that there was no society in America calling itself the Molly Maguires, that this name was tagged to the Ancient Order of Hibernians by the commercial press whose purpose it was to help the coal operators crush all organization in the mining industry; that the Philadelphia and Reading Company hired the Pinkerton spy agency not to save society from a band of terrorists but to spread terror."[32]

Foner based his conclusions in part on the actions of defense attorney Clarence Darrow. In 1907, Darrow successfully defended officers of the Western Federation of Miners (WFM), including William Haywood, against James McParlan's accusations against them of conspiracies to commit murder. Those accusations included the 1905 bombing death of former Idaho governor Frank Steunenberg. As the Pinkertons had done against AOH men in Pennsylvania, McParlan used perjured testimony backed by perjured corroboration to press his cases against the WFM men.

In the Idaho trial of Haywood, Darrow characterized McParlan as "the chief perjury manufacturer in this case." McParlan, Darrow said, had instructed his prosecution witness Harry Orchard to swear to "a piece of testimony which is as worthless, as crooked, as valueless as any figment that ever went before a jury."[33]

In a 1908 WFM trial in Colorado that flowed from McParlan's accusations, defense attorney Orrin Hilton described the Pinkertons as "'human jackals,'" the "'most abandoned criminal organization of the country.'" Hilton instructed the jury: "'I want to hold up to your gaze the work of the Pinkerton Detective Agency. Don't you know perjury and false witness always follows in its trail?'"[34]

But the efforts of the attorneys in the West, along with Coleman's challenge to investigate the possibility of a conspiracy on the part of the "Molly" prosecution, and Foner's 1947 outright rebuttal of "Molly" propaganda, failed to move the academic needle. In the late 1950s, Dartmouth historian Wayne Broehl Jr. took up the "Molly Maguire" study. In 1964, Harvard University Press published Broehl's *The Molly Maguires*. To craft his work, Broehl relied heavily on prosecution documents, including McParlan's reports and Allan Pinkerton's dime novel. In his acknowledgements, Broehl named four key manuscript collections, including those of the Pinkerton National Detective Agency, the Reading Railroad, and Mrs. George Keiser of Pottsville, Pennsylvania.

Mrs. George Keiser, born in 1886, was the daughter of George Kaercher, the district attorney for Schuylkill County who ceded his role during the "Molly Maguire" trials to Franklin Gowen. Keiser was also the granddaughter of Francis Hughes, another self-appointed prosecutor during the trials. Hughes was the uncle of Francis Dewees, the first "Molly Maguire" chronicler. Through Broehl's lens, the prosecution was again writing the "Molly Maguire" history.

"So very many of the Molly Maguire tactics in the coal fields," Broehl concluded, "stemmed directly from closely similar tactics in Ireland. ... If one were a determinist in his brand of historical philosophy, he could easily conclude that the whole Pennsylvania development had about it a classic inevitability."[35]

Broehl's conclusions swept aside both Foner's assessment from two decades before and the work of three stellar defense attorneys—

Darrow, Hilton, and Edmund Richardson—who in the early 1900s had successfully exposed McParlan's corrupt machinations, and with them the entire Pinkerton courtroom strategy. In Broehl's work, published under Harvard's imprimatur, Pennsylvania's "Molly Maguires" again rose up as transplanted Irish terrorists.

"Broehl has gathered much useful new material and raised important questions," historian Herbert Gutman said in a review published the year after Broehl's work appeared. "But he has not used the material well nor answered the questions adequately."[36] Of Broehl's reliance on Pinkerton sources, Gutman said: "*entire events—including significant meetings and acts of violence and murder—are reconstructed from these Pinkerton sources and nothing else.*"[37] Of Broehl's effort, Gutman concluded: "the entire narrative is unbalanced. It is almost as if one wrote of anti-British agitation in Boston between 1763 and 1776 and relied mainly on reports from British spies, loyalist memoirs, courts of admiralty, and the loyalist press."[38]

As of this writing, the online catalog for Harvard University Press lists Broehl's work for purchase. "The Molly Maguires," its description reads, "were direct descendants of clandestine organizations that proliferated in the Irish homeland and it was this heritage that inspired the vengeful and bloody tactics they employed to gain their social and economic objectives."[39]

Martin Ritt's 1970 film *The Molly Maguires*, based on a screenplay by Walter Bernstein, further clouded the canon. Once again, the alleged "Mollies" were portrayed not as effective political advocates, but as oppressed mineworkers driven to violence through draconian working conditions. "The Molly Maguires," a film review in the *New York Times* said of Ritt's effort, "were a secret society of Irish-American coal miners who in the second half of the 19th century fought by sabotage and murder against their overseers and for better pay in the mines."[40]

Pinkerton intervention colored even Ritt's film. Nine decades after Allan Pinkerton published his dime novel, attorneys representing the Pinkertons exercised control over Ritt's work. Pinkerton representatives demanded, and got, script approval from Paramount.

In December 1968, at a private screening in New York, Pinkerton representatives viewed Ritt's film before its release. In late January 1970, Paramount released the film with "their blessings."[41]

As with Ritt's film, even the views of authors sympathetic to labor, or skeptical of the Pinkertons, fall very short of the mark. Sidney Lens's 1973 *The Labor Wars: From the Molly Maguires to the Sitdowns*, discusses "the martyrs of the Pennsylvania coal fields of the 1870s, the so-called Molly Maguires."[42] Lens quoted Patrick Ford's *Irish World*, that "Molly Maguireism had no more reality than 'fairies or hobgoblins.'" Lens concluded that Ford "hit very close to the truth. ... That a movement so strong ... should have left no records behind, no leaders to share their reminiscences with the public, is inconceivable. The primary source for the Molly Maguire legend was the famous detective, Allan Pinkerton, and his spy, James McParlan, who infiltrated the movement and was the main witness in the trials."[43]

But even Lens's sympathetic treatise argued both sides of the aisle. In one instance, Lens stated: "many if not most, of the illegal acts were instigated by the operators and perpetrated by their agents."[44] Two pages later, Lens said: "Irish miners, now without a union, fought rear guard, guerilla battles—organized within the Hibernians—to rebuild their organization. They were hardly effete, and were no doubt responsible for many of the killings, threats, burnings, and other acts that harried the area in the latter half of 1875."[45] Though Lens recognized the political capability of the Irish in the coalfields in electing "a sizable number of local officials, such as county commissioners, tax collectors, school directors," he named only one alleged "Molly," John Kehoe, as having achieved such elective office.[46]

Lens also resurrected a portion of Eugene Debs's view of the alleged "Mollies." In 1907, the prominent Socialist gave an address titled "The First Martyrs of the American Class Struggle." In it, Debs gave this view of Pennsylvania's alleged "Mollies": "All were ignorant, rough and uncouth, born of poverty and buffeted by the merciless tides of fate and chance. To resist the wrongs of which they and their fellow workers were victims and to protect themselves against the brutality of their bosses, according to their crude notions, was the prime object of the organization of the 'Molly Maguires.' ... It is true that their methods were drastic, but it must be remembered that their lot was hard and brutalizing; that they were the neglected children of poverty, the products of a wretched environment."[47] The five alleged "Mollies" who served as township school directors had escaped Debs's notice entirely. Some had achieved that elective office while continuing to work as coal miners.

In 1997 came J. Anthony Lukas's *Big Trouble: A Murder in a Small Western Town Sets off a Struggle for the Soul of America.* In his discussion of the trials that emanated from Pinkerton superintendent McParlan's arrest of Western Federation of Miners (WFM) officers in Colorado, Lukas reached back for a discussion of Pennsylvania's "Mollies." Lukas described the group's supposed Irish origins: "a secret society called the Molly Maguires had operated in north central Ireland, threatening, beating, sometimes killing English landlords and their agents. ... In Ireland, the bravos who adopted the name disguised themselves by dressing in women's clothing and smearing their faces with burnt cork."[48]

In his discussion of Pennsylvania's so-called "Mollies," Lukas referred glancingly to Irish "tavern keepers with a hand in politics,"[49] but neglected to describe the breadth of those political attainments: election to local office as school directors, tax assessors, tax collectors, high constables, township supervisors, and in at least one instance, overseer of the poor; election to labor union offices; involvement in national movements such as Labor Reform politics; and even the attempt, by "Molly" prosecutors soliciting perjured testimony, to influence the outcome of the 1876 Hayes-Tilden presidential election. Lukas also failed to follow the complete trail of McParlan's eventual unmasking by WFM defense attorneys, in particular the efforts of attorney Orrin Hilton in the 1908 trial at Grand Junction, Colorado.

The work of authors who did come close to the mark, as with Joseph Rayback in *A History of American Labor*, gained little traction.[50] Works with less subtle interpretations, notably Ezra

Heywood's *The Great Strike* from 1878, Anthony Bimba's *The Molly Maguires* from 1932, and Charles McCarthy's *The Great Molly Maguire Hoax* from 1969, received short shrift.[51] Most significantly, no author has ever noted that the two Pinkerton caseloads, against the AOH in the 1870s and the WFM in the early 1900s, thwarted not just labor organization, but two burgeoning political movements.

In 1986, Philip Foner restated his belief that Pennsylvania's coal men had conducted a conspiracy against the AOH men. In a letter to the *New York Times* that described the alleged "Mollies" as, in Eugene Debs's words, "'the first martyrs of American labor,'" Foner said: "Today, many historians agree with Debs and point out that the 20 miners were hanged as part of a conspiracy by mineowners, using the Pinkerton Detective Agency to smash unionism in the anthracite mines."[52]

Rebutting the Most Recent Scholarship

In 1998, Oxford University Press (OUP) published Kevin Kenny's *Making Sense of the Molly Maguires*. Kenny researched this work in pursuance of a doctoral degree with Columbia University. "Kevin Kenny has certainly done historical justice to his fascinating, if elusive, topic," Michael Kazin said in a *Washington Post* review. Of Kenny's conclusions, Kazin said: "Transplanted to Pennsylvania, the Mollies seem to have devolved into a gang of unskilled, Gaelic-speaking laborers that rose and fell with the fortunes of trade unionism."[53]

On its website in 2021, OUP says of the "Molly Maguire" controversy: "Ever since [the executions], there has been enormous disagreement over who the Molly Maguires were, what they did, and why they did it, as virtually everything we now know about the Molly Maguires is based on the hostile descriptions of their contemporaries." Of Kenny's 1998 work, OUP asserts: "this work examines new archival evidence from Ireland that establishes that the American Molly Maguires were a rare transatlantic strand of the violent protest endemic in the Irish countryside."[54] Google Books uses an identical descriptor.[55]

Kenny's work itself posited: "Significant numbers of the Irish immigrants in Pennsylvania came from a preliterate Gaelic culture, marking them off as fundamentally different not only from the Welsh and the English, but also from the people of eastern and southern Ireland ... It was these Irish-speakers, and not the Irish in general, who became 'Molly Maguires' in Pennsylvania."[56] Kenny added: "Because of their language, culture, and customs, they were the archetypal 'wild Irish,' noticeably and ominously different from the mass of Irish immigrants."[57]

Extensive research into coal region newspapers refutes Kenny's theories. It shows many of Pennsylvania's alleged "Mollies" as community leaders: influential businessmen who served in elected office as tax assessors and collectors, high constables, and township supervisors. These Irish American men embraced the opportunities offered by the government of a free republic. At least five Irishmen charged as "Mollies" served as township school directors: Patrick Dolan Sr. in Butler Township, Christopher Donnelly in New Castle, Patrick Hester in Mount Carmel, Cornelius McHugh in Mauch Chunk, and John Slattery in Schuylkill Township.[58]

These Irishmen had names, and they had faces. Hester, who served as school director, tax collector, township supervisor, and overseer of the poor, had four grown daughters. All four served as schoolteachers in their communities.

At the time of his arrest John Kehoe, alleged "King of the Mollies" born in Ireland's County Wicklow, served as AOH delegate for Schuylkill County and high constable of Girardville. "'You will find the leaders of this society the prominent men in the townships,'" Gowen told the jury in the trial of alleged "Molly" Thomas Munley. "'Through the instrumentality of their order, and by its power, they were able to secure offices for themselves.'"[59]

To promote the theory of "the sense of alienation and rootlessness so evident among the Molly Maguires in Pennsylvania," Kevin Kenny's work focused in particular on the western section of County

Donegal.[60] Kenny described this section as "one of the poorest and most isolated places in Ireland and the birthplace of many of the American Molly Maguires."[61]

Again, research in coal region newspapers refutes this theory. The commonwealth executed five natives of County Donegal and imprisoned many more. Executed Donegal men showed deep ties to their adoptive American communities.

Liquor distributor and hotelkeeper Alexander Campbell was born in 1833 in Dungloe, County Donegal. Married and the father of an infant and an unborn child at the time of his arrest, Campbell served the year before his arrest as Democratic Party delegate to Pennsylvania's Carbon County. "Campbell was a well-to-do Irishman," the *Philadelphia Times* said after Campbell's execution, "having risen from the position of miner to that of a bottler of porter and seller of liquors."[62]

In April 1875 miner and tavern-keeper Hugh McGehan, married a month before his arrest as an alleged "Molly," led a peaceful parade of four hundred miners through Tamaqua in Pennsylvania's Schuylkill County. There, during the height of the region's "Long Strike," Donegal-born McGehan, who authored poetry in English but could not read or write, brokered an agreement with area coal operators to supply the town with coal during the ongoing wage dispute between mineworkers and coal operators. "This man," an area paper said after McGehan's arrest, "had since his arrival at Summit Hill always possessed considerable influence over his fellows and among them was always a leader."[63]

Carbon County AOH delegate Thomas Fisher, a third native of Ireland's County Donegal, owned the Rising Sun Hotel in Summit Hill, Pennsylvania. Fisher, a former miner and an older married man, had no children. In 1875 Carbon County's Democratic delegates considered Fisher, a longtime Democratic operative, among prospective nominees for county commissioner. Four months before his arrest as an alleged "Molly," a local paper reported interest in Fisher for county tax collector. The article said: "Tom is a good man and deserves reward at the hands of the party he has long and faithfully served."[64] Fisher's nephew, Joseph Fisher, supported him steadily throughout his legal ordeal. Joseph Fisher served as permanent secretary to Carbon County's Greenback Labor Party.

Thomas Duffy, born in County Donegal, came to the United States as a child. Duffy, as did all of his Donegal-born AOH co-defendants, gave his assertion of innocence in English, not in Gaelic. When asked by Judge Thomas Walker to give any reason why sentence should not be passed upon him, Duffy responded: "'Well, I've got this much to say, that my life has been sworn away by perjury and that I got no justice in this court.'"[65]

As for the County Donegal roots of James Roarity, Roarity's father Columbus wrote to him from Meencorvick shortly before Roarity's hanging at the mass execution at Pottsville. Columbus's letter, written in English from County Donegal, remains one of the most compelling documents in the literature of this conflict.

"'I sit to write to you the last letter that I'll ever write, again, and don't be afraid to meet your doom or your Judge,'" Columbus told his son. Columbus believed James's assertion of innocence. He consoled James: "'I hope, through the intercession of the Blessed Virgin, that you are going to meet with a happy death.'" Of James's family in Ireland, Columbus told him: "'we never stop praying night and day, in hopes still that God will spare you. And so He will and have that place prepared for you that will cause you joy and consolation during eternity ... so keep yourself stout in heart.'"[66]

Regarding alleged "Mollies" serving as union officers, Kenny stated: "Other than [Cornelius] McHugh, no trade union leader was ever indicted for a Molly Maguire crime."[67] Newspaper coverage rebuts this as well. Four additional alleged "Mollies" served as trade union officers.

In March 1872, alleged "Molly" Thomas Fisher served as officer and accounts auditor for the Workingmen's Benevolent Association (WBA) of Carbon County.[68] The same year, alleged "Molly" John Donohue identified himself as president of WBA District 10, Tuscarora. At the same time, Donohue identified alleged "Molly" John Slattery, a Democratic candidate that year for associate judge, as the first WBA president of District 10, Tuscarora. "Mr. Slattery was one of the most active in organizing this district of the W.B.A.," Donohue said of his fellow union officer, "at a time when unionism met with formidable opposition from those whose interest it was to crush it in its infancy."[69]

In 1871, alleged "Molly" Michael Lawler, a fifth union officer, served as delegate to WBA Grand Council proceedings at Mauch Chunk. The *New York Herald* characterized that group as an "Immense Politico-Industrial Organization—A New Power Forming in the Land."[70] The *Shenandoah Herald* said at the time: "Mr. Lawler's devotion to the Union is ... well known ... he is the most outspoken member in the district ... in defending the men he has frequently incurred the displeasure of operators."[71]

But in *Making Sense of the Molly Maguires*, Kenny again pressed the theme of transplanted Irish violence. "Accustomed to oppression," Kenny said of Pennsylvania's alleged "Mollies," "but not to its industrial form, the immigrants responded with a type of violence that had its roots in the Irish countryside."[72] Kenny's work reinforced the specter of imported Irish American terrorism.

In his introduction, Kenny said: "The Molly Maguires themselves left virtually no evidence of their existence, let alone their aims and motivation."[73] On the contrary: along with their record of labor union and political activity, including the election of five union officers and five school directors, Pennsylvania's alleged "Mollies" left behind a state-sanctioned document that they themselves may have authored.

In March 1871 at Harrisburg, Pennsylvania's AOH men filed a revised charter with the state legislature. The same month, New York's AOH officers filed an almost identical revised charter. The revised charter superseded that obtained jointly in 1836 by Hibernians in New York City and Schuylkill County. It defined the order's structure and its administration. At the office of the *Shenandoah Herald*, AOH delegate John Kehoe oversaw the printing of these charters for distribution in Schuylkill County. All AOH initiates, including Pinkerton undercover operative James McParlan, during his sham initiation as "James McKenna" in April 1874, received a copy of the revised AOH charter.

In August 1876, at the height of the "Molly Maguire" trials, the *Philadelphia Times* said of this document: "The constitution book, it is alleged, until lately had printed in it, after the conclusion of the by-laws, the names of the framers of the charter of the organization. The books, as printed at present, contain no such names. It is merely hinted that this is because some of the framers of the charter are at present awaiting trial or sentence for murder."[74]

The language of the revised AOH charter, based on "FRIENDSHIP, UNITY, and TRUE CHRISTIAN CHARITY," is poetic. It is profound. It accords with the trade union philosophy of Pennsylvania's alleged "Mollies" and with their embrace of Labor Reform Party tenets. Drafted by Irishmen who may have witnessed the horrors of Ireland's Great Hunger, the document informed both the Hibernians' aims and their motivation.

The introduction advised: "BRETHREN: It is beyond all doubt that the Supreme Being has placed man in a state of dependence and need of mutual support from his fellow man. Neither can the greatest monarch on earth exist without friendship and society. Therefore, the Supreme Being has implanted in our natures tender sympathies and most humane feeling towards our fellow creatures in distress, and all the happiness that human nature is capable of enjoying must flow and terminate in the love of God and our fellow creatures. So we, the members of this Order, do agree to assist each other, and conform to the following rules ... ." The preamble closed with this poem:

> These laws though human,
> Spring from Love Divine,
> Love laid the scheme—
> Love guides the whole design.

> Vile is the man
> Who will evade these laws,
> Or taste the sweets
> Without sufficient cause.[75]

Along with their constitution and bylaws, Pennsylvania's alleged "Mollies" left behind numerous protestations of innocence. Some of the condemned men, in a faint echo of the 1836 AOH charter urging members to "'love without dissimulation, hating evil, cleaving to good,'"[76] left behind statements of forgiveness for those who had sworn falsely against them.

For those willing to examine the evidence, the charters, biographies, statements, and actions of Pennsylvania's alleged "Mollies," these constitute a substantial record of historical documentation. They illuminate the aims, the motivation, and the abiding faith of the executed Irish Catholic men. They set aside today's descriptions of the so-called "Molly Maguires," along with the film released by Paramount in 1970; the accounts published by Harvard in 1964 and Oxford in 1998; the cross-dressing "Mollies" conjured by William Steuart Trench in 1869, Wayne Broehl Jr. in 1964, Anthony Lukas in 1997, Kevin Kenny in 1998, and Mark Bulik in 2014; the theory of alleged "Molly" violence as a form of "retributive justice" put forth by Anthony Wallace in 1987; Kenny's "archetypal 'wild Irish'" from 1998; and the well-meaning but dangerously erroneous views of Eugene Debs from 1907.[77]

Into the Twenty-First Century

In 1935, W. E. B. Du Bois asked: "What is the object of writing the history of Reconstruction?" He answered: "it is simply to establish the Truth, on which Right in the future may be built. We shall never have a science of history until we have in our colleges men who regard the truth as more important than the defense of the white race, and who will not deliberately encourage students to gather thesis material in order to support a prejudice or buttress a lie."[78]

In July 2020 Eric Foner, holder of the Pulitzer Prize for *The Fiery Trial: Abraham Lincoln and American Slavery*, gave an interview to *ideastream.org*. Titled "Historian Eric Foner Disputes 'Fake History' of Reconstruction Era," Foner's views reinforced Du Bois's earlier observation. Foner gave this assessment of chroniclers' condescending and prejudiced view of Blacks during Reconstruction: "'Too much of the previous literature and much of the old view of Reconstruction ... basically saw Blacks as ignorant and incapable. Therefore, what's the point of studying them?'" Foner observed further: "'Sixteen African-American men served in Congress during Reconstruction. Their views were important. Their speeches were important. Down to even the basic level of government, justices of the peace, school board officials, local commissioners, African-Americans held all sorts of offices in Reconstruction. By and large, they did a very capable job. The idea that they were all ignorant and corrupt is a total myth.'"[79]

Foner's description of the biased view applied by historians to Black men during Reconstruction can also be applied to Pennsylvania's alleged "Mollies," who have been consistently viewed through a similar, distorted lens of prejudice. During the Pennsylvania trials that lasted from 1875 to 1880, the appellation "Molly Maguire" proved lethal. The more than seventy Irish American men arrested under the label in Pennsylvania's hard coal region faced certain imprisonment. Twenty-one faced execution. Numerous others, fearing arrest, fled the region. The label's use, with its concomitant implications of ignorance and corruption, effectively halted historians' inquiries into, and acceptance of, the true biographies of the Irish Catholic men charged under the toxic umbrella.

In 2015, the University of Pennsylvania Press published Leon Fink's *The Long Gilded Age: American Capitalism and the Lessons of a New World Order*. In this work published through a Pennsylvania university Fink, considered a foremost expert in American labor and immigration history, neglected to mention Pennsylvania's "Molly Maguire" conflict at all.

In August 2020 James Grossman, president of the American

Historical Association (AHA), responded to a request from this author regarding academic interest in "Molly Maguire" scholarship. In regard to the AHA member forum, Grossman said: "The Mollies would no doubt attract a narrow constituency given even how many historians bring knowledge/research to the table, but I suspect there would be broader interest in the role of Pinkerton, and how that might have shaped the historiography."[80]

Given the plethora of Irish Studies departments in colleges and universities throughout the United States and Canada, historians' examination of Pennsylvania's "Molly Maguire" conflict—a Gilded Age tone poem that encapsulates the corporate seizure, rooted in ethnic hatred, of legal, judicial, and executive authority—remains strangely deficient. The ongoing failure of scholars to examine the reverberant issues in this late-nineteenth-century political conflict remains inexplicable.

In February 2021, Ireland's president Michael Higgins addressed the ongoing "feigned amnesia" of those academics and journalists who refuse to address the legacy of British imperialism and the impact of colonialism. In published remarks, Higgins called for an "ethical remembering" of the events that led to Irish self-determination and the independent republic of Ireland.[81]

"This is not only to allow us to understand more fully the complexities of those times," Higgins said. "It is also to allow us to recognise the reverberations of that past for our societies today and for our relationships with each other and our neighbours."[82]

Higgins made his remarks in support of Machnamh 100, an initiative formed to foster historical exploration. Based on an ancient Irish concept encompassing reflection, contemplation, meditation, and thought, the initiative's first seminar spoke of "'the Hospitality Necessary in Reflecting on Memory, History and Forgiveness.'" The truth of Pennsylvania's "Molly Maguire" history, buried for almost a century and a half, cries out for the "ethical remembering" of President Higgins's eloquent appeal.

1. Quoted in Kevin Kenny, *Making Sense of the Molly Maguires* (New York: Oxford University Press, 1998), 213.
2. *Mauch Chunk (PA) Coal Gazette*, September 13, 1872.
3. *Irish Times* (Dublin), August 9, 1871.
4. Quoted in *Sunbury (PA) Gazette*, October 3, 1868.
5. *Shenandoah (PA) Herald*, May 2, 1877.
6. *Report of the Case of the Commonwealth vs. John Kehoe et al.* (Pottsville, PA: Miners' Journal Book and Jobs Room, 1876).
7. John O'Dea, *History of the Ancient Order of Hibernians*, vol. 2 (New York: National Board of the AOH, 1923), 885.
8. "National Convention of the A. O. H.," *Boston Pilot*, May 22, 1880: "Prior to the Molly Maguire troubles, the Order of Hibernians had a membership of about 63,000 in Pennsylvania." See also *Philadelphia Times*, August 28, 1876, letter from AOH divisional secretary, William McIntyre of Philadelphia: "There are over 4,000 members in this county ... and over 700,000 in the United States."
9. *American* (Washington, DC), September 23, 1857; reprinting *Philadelphia Sun*, italics in *American*.
10. *Miners' Journal* (Pottsville, PA), October 3, 1857; quoting *Philadelphia Transcript*.
11. *Chicago Daily Tribune*, April 11, 1874.
12. Reported in "Schuylkill County Democracy. Warm Contest over the Congressional Tid-Bit," *Miners' Journal* (Pottsville, PA), August 7, 1874.
13. *New York Herald*, August 4, 1874.
14. Ibid., November 27, 1874.
15. *New York Tribune*, November 24, 1874.
16. *New York Sun*, October 22, 1876.
17. Richard O. Boyer and Herbert M. Morais, *Labor's Untold Story: The Adventure Story of the Battles, Betrayals and Victories of American Working Men and Women* (1955; repr. Pittsburgh: United Electrical, Radio, and Machine Workers of America, 2005), 81.
18. Library of Congress Research Guides, "Molly Maguires: Topics in Chronicling America," https://guides.loc.gov/chronicling-america-molly-maguires.
19. William Steuart Trench, *Realities of Irish Life* (1869; repr. Cambridge: Cambridge University Press, 2011), 67-68.
20. *Morning Star and Catholic Messenger* (New Orleans, LA), March 6, 1870.
21. *Chicago Tribune*, May 23, 1869.
22. *New York Herald*, May 1, 1869.
23. Gowen's argument reported in *Clearfield (PA) Republican*, August 9, 1876.
24. *Commonwealth versus Patrick Hester, Patrick Tully, and Peter McHugh*, Argument of Francis Wade Hughes (Philadelphia: G. V. Town & Son, 1877), 18-19.
25. *New York Herald*, May 9, 1876.
26. *New York Times*, May 14, 1876.
27. F. P. Dewees, *The Molly Maguires: The Origin, Growth, and Character of the Organization* (1877; repr. New York, 1969), 44.
28. Pinkerton, *Mollie Maguires*, 518.
29. W. E. B. Du Bois, *Black Reconstruction in America, 1860-1880* (1935; repr., New York: The Free Press, 1998), xvi.
30. *New York Sun*, August 3, 1892.
31. J. Walter Coleman, *The Molly Maguire Riots: Industrial Conflict in The Pennsylvania Coal Region* (Richmond: Garrett & Massie, 1936), 168.

32. Philip S. Foner, *History of the Labor Movement in the United States*, vol. 1, *From Colonial Times to the Founding of the American Federation of Labor* (1947; repr. New York: International Publishers, 1972), 460.
33. *Wayland's Monthly* (Girard, KS), "Darrow's Speech in the Haywood Case," October 1907, 78.
34. Hilton's argument reported in *Grand Junction Daily Sentinel*, July 14, 1908.
35. Wayne G. Broehl Jr., *The Molly Maguires* (1964; repr., New York: Chelsea House/Vintage, 1983), 361.
36. Herbert Gutman, review of *The Molly Maguires*, by Wayne G. Broehl, Jr., *The Pennsylvania Magazine of History and Biography* 89, no. 2 (1965): 252.
37. Ibid., 251; italics in original.
38. Ibid., 252.
39. Harvard University Press, "The Molly Maguires, Wayne G. Broehl, Jr.," https://www.hup.harvard.edu/catalog.php?isbn=9780674731547.
40. Roger Greenspun, review of *The Molly Maguires*, directed by Martin Ritt, *New York Times*, February 9, 1970.
41. Carlton Jackson, *Picking up the Tab—The Life and Movies of Martin Ritt* (Bowling Green: Bowling Green University Press, 1994), 106.
42. Sidney Lens, *The Labor Wars: From the Molly Maguires to the Sitdowns* (New York: Doubleday, 1973), 7.
43. Ibid., 11-12.
44. Ibid., 25.
45. Ibid., 27.
46. Ibid., 16.
47. *Voices of Revolt*, vol. 9, *Speeches of Eugene V. Debs* (New York: International Publishers, 1928), 76.
48. J. Anthony Lukas, *Big Trouble: A Murder in a Small Western Town Sets off a Struggle for the Soul of America* (New York: Simon & Schuster, 1997), 177.
49. Ibid., 182.
50. See Joseph G. Rayback, *A History of American Labor* (1959; expanded and updated New York: Simon & Schuster, 1966), 132: "The identity of the Molly Maguires has never been proved."
51. One exception does include a discussion of McCarthy and Bimba. See Harold D. Aurand and William A. Gudelunas, Jr., "The Mythical Qualities of Molly Maguire," *Pennsylvania Labor History* 49 (April 1982): 91-103.
52. Philip Foner, "Haymarket Martyrs and the First May Day," *New York Times*, May 27, 1986.
53. Michael Kazin, "A View of Violence," review of *Making Sense of the Molly Maguires*, by Kevin Kenny, *Washington Post*, April 19, 1998.
54. Oxford University Press, "Making Sense of the Molly Maguires, Kevin Kenny," https://global.oup.com/academic/product/making-sense-of-the-molly-maguires-9780195116311?cc=us&lang=en&.
55. Google Books, "Making Sense of the Molly Maguires, Kevin Kenny," My Book.
56. Kenny, *Making Sense*, 37.
57. Ibid., 38.
58. For Dolan, see *New York Sun*, August 25, 1876; for Donnelly, *Pottsville (PA) Standard*, February 19, 1876; for Hester, *New York Sun*, March 25, 1878; for McHugh, *Mauch Chunk (PA) Coal Gazette*, February 27, 1874; for Slattery, *Pottsville (PA) Standard*, June 29, 1872.

59. Gowen's speech quoted in Allan Pinkerton, *The Mollie Maguires and the Detectives* (1877; repr. New York: Dover Publications, 1973), 519. See also *Philadelphia Times*, July 25, 1876.
60. Kenny, *Making Sense*, 36.
61. Ibid., 31.
62. *Philadelphia Times*, June 25, 1877.
63. *Shenandoah (PA) Herald*, March 10, 1876.
64. "Summit Hill and Vicinity," *Mauch Chunk (PA) Democrat*, May 27, 1876. For Kevin Kenny's reference to Thomas Fisher in Democratic politics, see Kenny, *Making Sense*, 291.
65. *Shenandoah Herald*, January 22, 1877.
66. Letter of Columbus Roarty [sic] given in Broehl, *Molly Maguires*, 338-39. See also Kenny, *Making Sense*, 249-50; also chapter 10, 283, this work.
67. Kenny, *Making Sense*, 239.
68. Report of WBA executive board meeting, *Anthracite Monitor* (Tamaqua, PA), March 16, 1872.
69. *Pottsville (PA) Standard* (signed "John Donohoe"), July 6, 1872.
70. *New York Herald*, April 12, 1871. For Lawler's attendance at this council, see *Shenandoah (PA) Herald*, April 13, 1871.
71. *Shenandoah (PA) Herald*, April 27, 1871.
72. Kenny, *Making Sense*, 8.
73. Ibid., 5.
74. *Philadelphia Times*, August 30, 1876.
75. For Pennsylvania's revised AOH charter, see *Commonwealth vs. John Kehoe*, 167-71.
76. O'Dea, *Ancient Order*, vol. 2, 885.
77. For Bulik's views, see Mark Bulik, *The Sons of Molly Maguire: The Irish Roots of America's First Labor War* (New York: Fordham University Press, 2014); for Wallace, see Anthony F. C. Wallace, *St. Clair: A Nineteenth-century Coal Town's Experience with a Disaster-prone Industry* (New York: Alfred A. Knopf, 1987).
78. Du Bois, *Black Reconstruction*, 725.
79. Dan Polletta, "Historian Eric Foner Disputes 'Fake History' of Reconstruction Era," ideastream.org, July 16, 2020, https://www.ideastream.org/news/historian-eric-foner-disputes-fake-history-of-reconstruction-era.
80. James Grossman, email to author, August 28, 2020.
81. Michael D. Higgins, "Empire shaped Ireland's past,"*Guardian*, February 11, 2021, http://www.theguardian.com/commentisfree/2021/feb/11/empire-ireland-century-partition-present-britain-history.
82. Ibid.

2

WIGGAN'S PATCH

Beware of the Mollie Maguires. If you have a brother among them pray for his repentance, but have nothing further to do with him, and remember that he is cut off from the Church. ... These men I tell you, are the scum of their kind; they are not American citizens, but Irishmen, and a disgrace to the name and to their country.

Daniel O'Connor
Pastor, Holy Rosary Roman Catholic Church
Mahanoy Plane, Pennsylvania, December 1875

IN A POST-MIDNIGHT RAID on December 10, 1875, more than forty armed men swarmed into the mining village of Wiggan's Patch in Pennsylvania's hard coal country. John Kehoe's widowed mother-in-law, Margaret O'Donnell, kept a boarding house there. Six or seven of the gang smashed open the back door of the O'Donnell house and surged into the kitchen. In an adjoining bedroom, Charles McAlister lay sleeping with his wife Ellen and their toddler.

"I was in bed when the door was being broken in," McAlister

testified at the habeas corpus hearing. "I got up first and told my wife to lay still, but she got up; as soon as she reached the door leading into the kitchen the first shot was fired; it killed her ... I was standing at the top of the cellar stairway, which is in my room; I ran down into the cellar and got into Mrs. Cassidy's, the next house."[1] McAlister escaped unharmed.

The *Pottsville Standard* said of the shooting of Ellen McAlister: "Before she had time to speak, one of the parties fired, the ball entering the nipple of the right breast. Saying, 'I'm shot,' the unfortunate woman fell dead."[2] At the time of the attack Ellen McAlister, aged twenty-one, was visibly pregnant.

The shooter and one other man pounded up the stairs to the second floor. The gunshot had awakened Margaret O'Donnell, who had leapt out of bed. The assailants met her at her bedroom door. One, reported the *Standard*, "clapped a revolver to her cheek. His companion knocked it up and then gave her a terrible blow upon the right temple, which knocked her down."[3]

The men entered an adjoining bedroom and found a boarder, sixty-five-year old Thomas Murphy. One shooter aimed a revolver at the terrified man. The second swung a lantern in the direction of his bed and said, "'that's an old man, don't meddle with him.'"[4]

The men entered another bedroom and found Charles O'Donnell, James McAlister, James Baird, and John Purcell. They tied Purcell to a bedpost. He told them if allowed to dress, he would go with them. They draped ropes around the necks of O'Donnell, McAlister, and Baird and led them down the stairs and into the yard, where the crowd waited.

On arriving outside, the assailants asked Baird his name. On hearing it, they told him he wasn't wanted. The men's quarry was evidently Kehoe's family.

A gunman, or gunmen, fired two shots. One hit O'Donnell in the breast. The second hit McAlister in the right arm. Both wounded men broke free. McAlister ran toward the woods. O'Donnell ran about eight feet, when a volley of gunfire brought him to the ground.

Murphy, Margaret O'Donnell's boarder, testified subsequently:

"I came down stairs after the mob left; when I came down stairs it was dark; I saw Ellen McAlister lying on her back with her head against the door and the blood running from her breast; she was dead; I saw Charles O'Donnell's body burning outside, across the road; his clothes were burning."[5]

The *Shenandoah Herald* reported the post mortem hearing. It said of the condition of O'Donnell's body: "The head, which had received no less than fifteen bullets and was in a shockingly crushed condition, was tied up in a white cloth. From the hips to the chin the body was crisped, there being no less than the marks of ten balls to be seen and the fire-arms must have been held in such close proximity that the powder had actually roasted the flesh."[6] Other accounts suggested that the mob had set fire to O'Donnell's clothes in an attempt to roast the body.[7] When questioned, Kehoe testified that bullets had entered O'Donnell: "All around his neck and breast; in fact he was all holes."[8]

Margaret O'Donnell subsequently described the scene: "I went down stairs and saw my daughter lying dead. I thought she was in a faint as I saw the child crying over her."[9]

In an editorial titled *"NO MORE 'VIGILANTES,'"* the *Pottsville Standard* said: "The murder of an innocent and unprotected woman and her unborn babe, and the brutal assault on an aged lady, doubtless old enough to be the mother of her assailants, are not achievements that are calculated to reflect credit upon any community."[10]

The morning after the attack Dr. Hermany, the coroner from Mahanoy City, arrived at the house to conduct the post mortem. A coroner's jury of six men accompanied him. To record events Hermany chose not a court reporter, but Thomas Fielders of the *Shenandoah Herald*. The newspaper that had targeted Kehoe repeatedly in calls for vigilantism would be the sole recorder of the first legal hearing of evidence in the Wiggan's Patch murders.

Kehoe's wife Mary Ann lost two siblings in the attack. Ellen McAlister was her sister. Charles O'Donnell was her brother. After the attack, her wounded brother-in-law, James McAlister, fled the scene and the region. Her brother James "Friday" O'Donnell, not mentioned in the initial press reports, also fled the region.

When the coroner's group arrived at Wiggan's Patch, the corpses of both victims lay in the downstairs bedroom. Hermany declared the cause of death in both cases so evident, no post mortem was needed. He called Margaret O'Donnell as the first witness. Fielders reported: "At this moment John Kehoe, of Girardville, entered the room and going to the side of the bed on which lay the dead body of Mrs. McAlister, raised the covering from off the face and kissed it; he then went over and kneeling upon the floor he kissed the face of Chas. O'Donnell, and then standing up he raised his right arm and said, 'Dr. Hermany, this business is going to be settled in another manner.' The doctor requesting him to be silent, he complied."[11]

Later that day Kehoe, Girardville's high constable, made a charge before the local justice of the peace. Kehoe's charge read:

> ... that on the night of December 9th, 1875, or morning of December 10th, 1875, at the township of Mahanoy ... several persons who were armed and disguised, surrounded and broke open the house of Widow O'Donnell and then and there did shoot and kill Charles O'Donnell, and also did shoot and kill Ellen McAlister, also that Widow Margaret O'Donnell received a violent blow of a large revolver on her forehead which nearly deprived her of life; that said blow was given to her by Frank Wenrich, butcher, of Mahanoy City, as he [Kehoe] has been informed, and verily believes that said Frank Wenrich and several others at present unknown to deponent are the persons who did shoot and kill the said Charles O'Donnell and Ellen McAlister.[12]

Kehoe's charge led to Wenrich's arrest. The *Herald* said: "Men at first couldn't believe their ears, as Mr. Wenrich is considered one of Mahanoy City's most respectable citizens."[13]

Margaret O'Donnell identified Wenrich as her assailant in habeas corpus testimony: "*it was him,*" she said, "I have seen him often around the patches; I have known him about nine or ten years;

he is a butcher; I have often bought meat of him; I can point him out here; (does so); to the best of my knowledge I calculate it was him who put the pistol to my face; when I say 'I calculate' I am sure."[14]

Wenrich, the butcher from Mahanoy City, also served as first lieutenant in the Silliman Guards. The Guards, a private militia, had formed a few weeks before the raid on Wiggan's Patch. Edward Silliman, prominent Schuylkill County Republican and president of Mahanoy City's First National Bank, had helped arm the militia and supply it with uniforms.

Cyrus Pershing, having lost his bid for Pennsylvania's governorship the previous month, had retained his seat as Schuylkill County's president judge. Pershing's court ruled that without better testimony than that offered by Margaret O'Donnell, the case would not go to a jury. Wenrich was released. No further charges were brought.

The *Pottsville Standard* asked: "Who but a contemptible craven would have fired that fatal shot at Ellen McAllister, when she came to the door of her room?" It added: "We are scarcely able to account for the fact that one of these brave men didn't put a bullet through the brain of the little infant crying over its dead mother."[15]

News accounts of the O'Donnell household at the time of the raid were mixed. The *Standard's* initial coverage said: "The O'Donnells themselves have not borne the best of reputations; and the house itself was a place of resort for desperate characters."[16] One week later the *Standard* printed an unsigned letter from Mahanoy City. It said: "It has been said through the columns of the press, that this house was the resort of the worst class of people, and that it was a groggery. Allow me to say that such was not the case; there was no drink sold in the house at all, and the O'Donnells were known as respectable, hard working people."[17]

The *Standard's* editor commented: "It is but justice to the bereaved family, to say that the public have been misled by the first dispatches from Mahanoy City, giving the O'Donnell house a bad name. We have been assured, not only by our correspondent, but by at least a dozen other respectable gentlemen, that the O'Donnells have always borne a good name."[18]

At Tamaqua, nine hundred mourners swelled the funeral procession for the burial of the Wiggan's Patch victims. A rumor that gave the wrong time for train departures left five hundred more stranded at Mahanoy City. "The funeral was in every respect conducted in a most orderly and decorous manner,"[19] the *Shenandoah Herald* said.

Nine days after the raid at Wiggan's Patch, Daniel O'Connor, pastor of Holy Rosary Roman Catholic Church at Mahanoy Plane, delivered a sermon. Mahanoy Plane lay within walking distance of Margaret O'Donnell's house.

Thomas Fielders of the *Shenandoah Herald*, sent to record O'Connor's sermon, joined the congregants that Sunday. At the church's doorway, the reporter had encountered so large a crowd crowd he could scarcely make his way through. "The gallery," Fielders later reported, "which is bare even of benches, was closely packed by an attentive body of men. All the pews were occupied to their fullest capacity, as was also almost every foot of standing room."[20]

If locals expected solace that week following the early morning murderous raid, they were disappointed. After O'Connor concluded the service, he held up a document covered with script. The priest told congregants it contained "a formal excommunication of the society known as the Mollie Maguires, otherwise the Ancient Order of Hibernians."[21] On the previous Friday, a week after the raid on Wiggan's Patch, O'Connor had received the document from James Frederick Wood, the archbishop of Philadelphia whose diocese included the anthracite coal region.

In his address to the jury at Pottsville in the trial of alleged "Molly Maguire" Thomas Munley, Franklin Gowen, self-appointed prosecutor and president of the Philadelphia and Reading Railroad, freely admitted his collusion with Wood in the prosecution of the Ancient Order of Hibernian (AOH) men. "Archbishop Wood of Philadelphia was the only confident [sic] I had," Gowen said, "and fully knew the mission of McParlan in this whole matter."[22] Wood's papers confirm that Gowen had confided in Wood. The archbishop's correspondence includes a copy of a memorandum circulated to Gowen in late 1875 by the Pinkerton National Detective Agency. It described various alleged "outrages." The following year, in hopes of securing additional excommunications against AOH men, Wood circulated the Pinkerton memorandum to a number of bishops in Pennsylvania.

Wood's animus against Irish organizations that operated outside the veil of church authority likely predated his relationship with Gowen. In early 1864, Wood had issued a pastoral letter that condemned all secret societies. Those societies condemned by Wood included the Masons, the Odd Fellows, the Sons of Temperance, the Fenian Brotherhood, "and, in addition to these, the 'Molly Maguires,' 'Buckshots,' and others, whose spirit is equally objectionable, and whose names seem to be selected rather to conceal, than to indicate the object of their association."[23]

A Washington paper said of Wood's 1864 pastoral: "His attention was called to the subject by the spread, in power and influence, of a society known as the Fenian Brotherhood."[24] The following year both Wood and John Purcell, the archbishop of Cincinnati who had officiated at Wood's consecration as bishop, issued "cards" condemning the Fenians, an activist brotherhood that sought Ireland's independence from England.[25]

A decade later, news of Wood's excommunication of the AOH throughout the Archdiocese of Philadelphia, including Pennsylvania's hard coal region, flowed over the country. A "dead stillness," Fielders later reported, prevailed throughout O'Connor's church as the priest read Wood's statement. O'Connor then offered his own comments: "In regard to the affair at Wiggan's patch, you were struck by the fact that a woman had been shot. Whenever you meet a Molly and he describes to you in pathetic language how O'Donnell was shot down ... how his murderers placed their weapons against his body and fired, completely riddling him, how a woman was killed, do not allow any of those facts to influence you or to lead you to sympathize with him ... whether the man received one bullet or a hundred it is all the same. He belonged, or was suspected of belonging, to the Mollie Maguires."[26]

O'Connor concluded: "These men, I tell you, are the scum of their kind; they are not American citizens but Irishmen, and a disgrace to the name and to their country. ... do not show sympathy for these men for they are cut off from all connections with the church. Let them fight their own battles for you have a conscience and they have none. They are scum and a disgrace to us as Irishmen and American citizens."[27]

Coal region congregants had heard this language before. The year before O'Connor read the archbishop's statement of excommunication, a second coal region priest, Daniel McDermott, had delivered a slanderous indictment of both the AOH and the Emerald Benevolent Association (EBA). McDermott had titled his discourse, delivered in July 1874 at New Philadelphia, "The Church & Forbidden Societies."

A few months after McDermott delivered his screed, the *Freeman's Journal* in New York gave it more than six columns of print. The following week, the paper followed up with a document titled "Declaration of Seven Pastors." Seven additional coal region pastors had stepped forward to libel the AOH as a murderous organization. Their statement claimed that despite the AOH constitution and bylaws: "Men of notoriously infamous character ... have not only been admitted to membership, but elected to offices, and actually control the Society in many places." Point eight of their ten-point statement, sent by them to James McMasters for publication in the *Freeman's Journal*, said: "Evidence sufficient to convince the most skeptical has come to light that works forbidden by the Commandment, *Thou shall not kill*, are traceable to the A. O. H."[28]

On October 17, 1874, one week after the *Freeman's Journal* published the pastors' declaration, Wood published McDermott's discourse in full in the *Catholic Standard*, the Catholic newspaper printed in Philadelphia with Wood's support. In his publication of McDermott's discourse, Wood included the pastors' statement, whose signers had expanded to eight coal region priests. "We invite special attention to this discourse," the *Standard* said. "Its subject is of vital importance. It carries with it, too, not only the weight, which is due to the character of the Rev. Priest who delivered it ... but, also, the additional weight due to its having been adopted ... by eight other highly respectable and most worthy Priests."[29]

McDermott's discourse dismissed out-of-hand the state sanction that legislative charters granted benevolent societies. "Catholics," he said, "have organized associations without any ecclesiastical sanction, but simply empowered by a charter granted by a State Legislature, by which they are authorized to extend their organization over a State or over the country. These societies ... sought not to obtain *first* the approbation of the Church and then the recognition of the State, in order to secure their civil rights. ... they have constituted themselves above, or at least independent of, Church authority."[30]

Of the threat to clerical authority posed by the societies' free membership, McDermott said: "The priest's usefulness, if not entirely destroyed, is greatly impaired, the authority of the Church in him is defied, order is subverted." He asked: "Are they the ministers of God, or are they the ministers of Satan? This rejection of the authority of the Church is the beginning of evil, the great sin, the great danger, and in this the A. O. H. and the E. B. A. dwell."[31]

McDermott condemned all association with these societies as "an apostasy." He condemned the coal region society of "the *Molly Maguires*, a society rendered infamous by its treachery and deeds of blood." He linked the AOH to the supposed "Mollies," saying: "When it became impossible any longer to bear the odium of being called a 'Molly Maguire,' application was made to the State Legislature for a charter for the A. O. H."[32]

Two years before undercover Pinkerton operative James McParlan recited Allan Pinkerton's nativist propaganda in Judge Pershing's courtroom at Pottsville, McDermott delivered it at New Philadelphia: "The *Hibernians*, even the respectable ones (?) [*sic*], as a body and organization have sympathized with and aided murderers *after the fact*, have contributed to their defence not only by money, but by suborning witnesses—have gone so far as to barter the votes of the A. O. H. for the pardon of felon members."[33]

Decades later, McDermott told a reporter that Wood had personally written the introduction to McDermott's discourse for the *Catholic Standard's* publication. The archbishop had then "sent copies of that issue of the paper to every priest and bishop in the United States, Canada and Australia."[34]

Fourteen months after Wood's global circulation of McDermott's condemnation, O'Connor read Wood's pastoral letter at Mahanoy Plane. Wood's 1875 order of excommunication identified the AOH as a terrorist society. Wood's list of "evil associations" included the Masons, the Odd Fellows, the Sons of Temperance, the Fenian Brotherhood, and "the Mollie Maguires, otherwise the Ancient Order of Hibernians, or the Buckshots."[35]

That the coal region clergy under Wood's authority had a vendetta against the AOH had become apparent. After O'Connor read Wood's pastoral letter, telegrams went out from Shenandoah to points all over the country. In Washington D.C., in Chicago, in New York, in New Orleans, in Ohio and Oregon, in Nevada and Maine, news editors told readers of the formal excommunication of Pennsylvania's coal region society of "the 'Molly Maguires,' otherwise the Ancient Order of Hibernians."[36]

Wood directed pastors throughout Pennsylvania's anthracite region to read his order of excommunication to their congregations. The *New York Tribune*, the *Chicago Tribune*, and the *Catholic Standard* printed it in full.[37] The *New York Times* and the *Shenandoah Herald* printed both Wood and O'Connor's statements in their entirety.[38]

On Christmas Day the *Chicago Tribune*, published from the city where Allan Pinkerton kept his home office, printed an editorial headlined "MOLLIE MAGUIRISM AND THE CHURCH." The column gave the same argument Pinkerton's undercover operative McParlan would give in trial testimony the following year. "The Mollie Maguires," the *Tribune* said, "are but the imitators of the Irishmen who in their own country associated themselves under the name of the Ancient Order of Hibernians. Both are associations for the purposes of assassination. One is a band organized to kill landlords, landlords' agents, rent-collectors, evictors, etc.; the other is an association to apply the same theory of [assassination] to mine-owners and anti-strikers. Terrorism and blood-letting are the tenets of Mollie Maguirism, and the members are bound by oath to protect each other, and swear out the innocence of every one who is apprehended."[39]

A few months before the "Molly Maguire" showcase trials began, with Franklin Gowen as self-appointed lead prosecutor, the dispersal by the national press of Wood's pastoral letter made Gowen's trial argument for him. It achieved what nativist politicians had attempted for decades. In the minds of a credulous public, a supposed terrorist society in Pennsylvania's coal region and the AOH, a legally sanctioned Irish Catholic benevolent order based on the premise "Love guides the whole design,"[40] were now one and the same.

Over the next half-decade, the cry of "Molly Maguire" terrorism against Pennsylvania's AOH men would cause the arrest of more than seventy defendants in Pennsylvania's anthracite region and more than two dozen in its bituminous region. It would send twenty-one Irish Catholic men to the gallows in five hard coal counties. It would devastate families and communities. It would decimate the organizing power of the AOH. And it would place the AOH lodges that survived the purge under the rule of the clergy.

An additional factor complicated the relationship in the 1870s between Pennsylvania's AOH and the commonwealth's Roman Catholic clergy. In late March 1876, the *New York Herald* published a brief account of AOH news from Pittsburgh, home to the AOH state delegate. "This is a very strong Catholic organization hereabouts," the report said, "and, in fact, all over the country."[41]

The account told of the upcoming AOH national convention at New York City, scheduled to begin on March 28. It also mentioned the conflation, by Wood and Tobias Mullen, bishop of Erie, of AOH membership with supposed "Molly Maguire" terrorism. The account said: "Ill feeling has been engendered by this clerical onslaught, and the matter, it is said, is to be brought before the Convention by delegates from this end of the State, who will ask that hereafter all moneys of the Order be withheld from Church purposes."[42]

If Pennsylvania's AOH followed through on its threat to withdraw funds from the Catholic Church, no notice of this action has come to light. Less than two weeks after the *Herald* published its notice, newspapers gave wide coverage to the supposed confession of James Kerrigan, a notorious prosecution witness in the "Molly Maguire" trials. Kerrigan's statement also conflated AOH membership with "Molly Maguire" terrorism. Used against numerous AOH defendants, it corroborated McParlan's testimony in every particular.

At the time of Pennsylvania's "Molly Maguire" trials, the United States was a young country, absorbed in self-invention. Less than twenty years before the trials began, U.S. Senator James Henry Hammond of South Carolina gave an infamously racist speech on the floor of the Senate. Later known as the "mudsill theory," Hammond's address encapsulated the viewpoint of many on how the young country should be established. It said:

> In all social systems, there must be a class to do the menial duties, to perform the drudgery of life. That is, a class requiring but a low order of intellect and but little skill. Its requisites are vigor, docility, fidelity. Such a class you must have, or you would not have that other class which leads progress, civilization, and refinement. It constitutes the very mud-sill of society and of political government; and you might as well attempt to build a house in the air, as to build either the one or the other, except on this mud-sill. Fortunately for the South, she found a race adapted to that purpose to her hand.[43]

Thirteen years later, an Irish correspondent reporting from New York City observed that Americans, and especially politicians, considered Irish Catholics useful "as hewers of wood and drawers of water."[44] The Irish Catholic men who gathered under the AOH banner sought social and professional advancement. The Protestant industrialists and politicians who conducted the "Molly Maguire" caseload believed in Hammond's division of classes. To build fortunes quickly, they needed industrial serfs. They viewed Irish

Catholics as non-whites, fit for society's "mudsill" role. In Pennsylvania's coal region the clergy who led the parishes, including the Irish Catholic priests under Wood's authority, also demanded subservience from their parishioners.

In the 1870s Irish Catholic men in the United States sought ascendancy in part through the auspices of the AOH. In Pennsylvania's coal region, the order helped them attain numerous local offices, and helped send their preferred candidates to state and national office. Not content to remain as hewers of wood, drawers of water, or mineworkers, these Irish Catholic men hoped, in John Kehoe's words, for "the elevation of their members."[45] In their quest to attain their desired role in U.S. society, they directly challenged, politically and socially, the very men who most desired their subjugation. The thwarting by AOH men of the political ambitions of their Copperhead opponents provided the fulcrum for the "Molly Maguire" trials that followed.

---

1. *Shenandoah (PA) Herald*, December 18, 1875 (Charles McAlister is incorrectly identified as "James McAlister" in this coverage).
2. *Pottsville (PA) Standard*, December 18, 1875.
3. Ibid.
4. Ibid.
5. *Shenandoah (PA) Herald*, December 18, 1875.
6. Ibid.
7. *New York Times*, December 11, 1875; see also *New York Herald* and *Pottsville Standard*, same date.
8. *Shenandoah (PA) Herald*, December 18, 1875.
9. Ibid.
10. *Pottsville (PA) Standard*, December 18, 1875; italics in original.
11. *Shenandoah (PA) Herald*, December 18, 1875.
12. Ibid.
13. Ibid.
14. *Pottsville (PA) Standard*, December 18, 1875; italics in original.
15. Ibid.
16. Ibid., December 11, 1875.
17. Ibid., December 18, 1875.
18. Ibid.
19. *Shenandoah (PA) Herald*, December 18, 1875.
20. Ibid., December 25, 1875.
21. Ibid.
22. Gowen's address printed in the *Clearfield (PA) Republican*, August 9, 1876.

23. Pastoral of Archbishop James Frederic [sic] Wood, 19 January 1864, Accession 1520, Box 979, Hagley Museum and Library.
24. *Evening Star* (Washington, DC), February 3, 1864.
25. *Alexandria Gazette* (Washington, DC), March 2, 1865.
26. Ibid.
27. Ibid.
28. *Freeman's Journal* (New York), October 10, 1874; italics in original.
29. Signers of the pastor's statement included Michael Sheridan of Ashland, Joseph Bridgman of Girardville, Edward T. Field of Centralia, Joseph Koch of Shamokin, D. O'Connor of Mahanoy Plane, Henry F. O'Reilly of Shenandoah, Thomas Quinn of Pottsville, Hugh J. McManus of Pottsville, and D. I. McDermott of New Philadelphia.
30. *Catholic Standard* (Philadelphia), October 17, 1874.
31. Ibid.
32. Ibid.; italics in original.
33. Ibid.; italics in original.
34. *Evening Public Ledger* (Philadelphia), August 15, 1916.
35. *Shenandoah (PA) Herald*, December 25, 1875.
36. *New York Herald*, December 22, 1875. For variants of this report, see (same date): *Chicago Tribune*; *Eureka (NV) Daily Sentinel*; *New Orleans Bulletin*; *Pioche (NV) Daily Record*; *Portland (ME) Daily Press*. See also: *Evening Star* (Washington, DC), December 21, 1875; *New Northwest* (Portland, OR), December 24, 1875; *Highland News* (Hillsborough, OH), December 30, 1875.
37. *New York Tribune*, December 23, 1875; *Chicago Tribune*, December 24, 1875; *Catholic Standard* (Philadelphia), December 25, 1875.
38. *New York Times*, December 23, 1875; *Shenandoah (PA) Herald*, December 25, 1875.
39. *Chicago Tribune*, December 25, 1875.
40. *Report of the Case of the Commonwealth vs. John Kehoe et al.* (Pottsville, PA: Miners' Journal Book and Job Rooms, 1876), 167.
41. *New York Herald*, March 26, 1876.
42. Ibid.
43. "Africans in America, Part 4. 'The "Mudsill" Theory,' by James Henry Hammond," PBS, https://www.pbs.org/wgbh/aia/part4/4h3439t.html.
44. *Irish Times* (Dublin), August 9, 1871.
45. *Shenandoah (PA) Herald*, June 9, 1876.

3

THE COPPERHEADS AND THE HIBERNIANS

D—n the governor! If he don't hang Kehoe, we will hang him!

Franklin Gowen to Father A. J. Gallagher
Philadelphia, ca. May 1878

A NUMBER of Pennsylvania's Ancient Order of Hibernian (AOH) men hanged as "Molly Maguires" showed ties to the era's Labor Reform Party efforts. AOH divisional secretary James Carroll was hanged at Pottsville on June 21, 1877, as an alleged "Molly Maguire." Five years before, the *Mauch Chunk Coal Gazette* had run the notice "Nominations by the Labor Reform Party at Nesquehoning," Carroll's home at that time. Members, the paper said, had "met at the home of Jas. Carroll last Saturday evening" and unanimously nominated a township ticket. The notice said: "All the candidates pledged themselves to support the principles of the Labor Reform Party."[1]

AOH bodymaster, or divisional president, Patrick Hester was hanged at Bloomsburg on March 25, 1878, for an alleged "Molly

Maguire" crime. Seven years before that Richard Trevellick, president of the National Labor Union (NLU), had travelled to Northumberland County in Pennsylvania's hard coal region on behalf of the NLU, the first U.S. national labor federation. In September 1871, in Sunbury, Trevellick and Hester met together in the office of C. A. Reimensnyder, an attorney, labor sympathizer, and editor of the *Democratic Guard*. Hostile local newsman Emanuel Wilvert of the *Sunbury American* called out Reimensnyder's "genial friends, Messrs. Pat Hester and Trevelick [sic]." Wilvert said of the NLU's aims: "it is the intention to use the organization as a political machine to elevate themselves into power." Of the interest of Irish Catholics in NLU affiliation, Wilvert said: "the Irish Catholic members, who have long since affiliated ... are now making every effort to secure power everywhere, and are fast ruining every party they affiliate with. We would caution all against those who give themselves over to that element, of the dangerous results that will follow by placing them in power."[2]

Wilvert's hostility, and that of other coal region nativists, had other roots. Five months before Hester met with Trevellick at Sunbury, alleged "Molly Maguires" Michael Lawler and Cornelius McHugh joined in Grand Council proceedings at Mauch Chunk. The *New York Herald* characterized that April 1871 council, advocating for peaceful settlement of wage disputes, as "A New Power Forming in the Land." The *Herald* reported the exhortation of one delegate in attendance: "'Let us repudiate politics and elect workmen. We can go to the workshop or the mine and select men who will make better and more honest laws than all the politicians in the country.'"[3]

The following year, in August 1872, AOH delegate John Kehoe, hanged at Pottsville in December 1878, placed his name in consideration for Democratic candidate to Pennsylvania's state assembly. By 1874, Kehoe's political ties reached to the U.S. Capitol, with an initiative that directly threatened railroad interests nationwide.

During his incarceration, Kehoe noted from Pottsville Jail that he and U.S. Congressman John Killinger had once been "Good old friends."[4] In January 1874, Killinger offered a bill on the floor of Congress that called for cooperative ownership of the U.S. railway system. The *Shenandoah Herald* said of Killinger's proposed bill: "It strikes an effective blow against the Railroad Monopolies of the land, and is in the true sense of the term a people's measure."[5] In 1876 Pennsylvania state representative John Morgan, a second friend of Kehoe's, "a practical miner from Schuylkill county," and a warm friend of labor, strenuously backed measures to ensure mine safety practices through the Bituminous Ventilation Bill.[6]

In taverns run by AOH officers, in union halls, in Pennsylvania's state capital, and even in Washington DC, AOH men later charged as "Mollies" challenged the interests of Pennsylvania's coal and railroad men. The coal and railroad men leaned on state and national legislatures to promote their interests. The clash of the two ideologies produced fatal results.

Strands of nativism and pro-slavery advocacy defined the ideology of the Protestant politicians who mounted Pennsylvania's "Molly Maguire" caseload. Asa Packer, Franklin Gowen, Francis Hughes, Charles Buckalew, Cyrus Pershing, and Francis Dewees, chronicler of the first "Molly Maguire" history, all nurtured white supremacist leanings in the decades before the trials began. In speeches with rhetoric devised to inflame, in camp meetings that rivaled Klan rallies, and in Democratic Party resolutions so outrageous they engaged the attention of Abraham Lincoln's secretary of state, the men who would later hang Irish Catholics on gallows in five Pennsylvania counties showcased their racist and elitist tendencies.

The nativism of the "Molly" prosecutors collided with the religious and political advocacy of Pennsylvania's AOH men. In 1836, Irish Catholics from Pennsylvania's Schuylkill County had joined with Irishmen in New York City to secure the first U.S. AOH charter from Great Britain. The charter advised members: "'You must love without dissimulation, hating evil, cleaving to good.'" Based on

"FRIENDSHIP, UNITY, AND TRUE CHRISTIAN CHARITY," the document called for the extension of hospitality to any "emigrant brother that may land on your shores."[7]

As detailed above, during the early 1870s, many AOH men charged as "Mollies" embraced Labor Reform Party tenets. By 1876, the year of Pennsylvania's showcase "Molly Maguire" trials, the AOH had become a powerhouse. The benevolent order numbered more than sixty thousand members in Pennsylvania and more than seven hundred thousand throughout the United States. The order had grown in the face of long-simmering hostility against Irish Catholic immigrants.

In 1857, two decades before the trials began, an athletic anti-Irish-Catholic propaganda campaign targeted political operatives in the AOH stronghold of Philadelphia as "Molly Maguires." Newspapers all over the country spread the taint of the ethnic slur. In scope and vitriol, this earlier campaign foreshadowed the "Molly Maguire" press coverage that accompanied the famous trials nineteen years later.

In fall 1857, with Know Nothings still smarting from the defeat of their presidential candidate Millard Fillmore, an unnamed player initiated the weeks-long offensive. The smear campaign against Philadelphia's Irish Catholic politicians began five months after James Frederick Wood, an avowed foe of both the AOH and the Fenian Brotherhood, was ordained coadjutor bishop of Philadelphia. The campaign coincided with the onset of the Panic of 1857 and petered out as banks reopened. It raised the phantom of "Molly Maguire" agitation and tied it to election fraud. Nativist editors used it to re-energize the Know Nothing Party.

The *Philadelphia Sun* led the charge. It told of "an *alien* organization in this country, sworn to act in determined hostility to the citizens of American birth." Per the *Sun*, terrible oaths and secrecy characterized this "Molly Maguire" association, "whose sworn purpose was to deprive the American born of a fair voice and place in the affairs of the nation." The *Sun* described the order's alleged ties to Ireland's eighteenth-century Ribbonmen, when almost "every hedge and ditch contained an assassin, who leveled his gun at the passing Protestant, or treacherously pierced him with a pitchfork, or a scythe fastened to a long pole."[8]

From these Irish roots, the nativist propaganda ran, sprang the alleged American "Molly Maguires," whose braggart members now boasted of lodges "'in every city, town, village and hamlet in the United States,'" and whose call could "'arouse every inmate of every cabin in the Union.'" In the country's towns and large cities, the *Sun* warned, "Molly" reigned supreme. The order's main object? To "govern the dominant political party of the Union, by casting its entire power as if it were a single person ... They are sworn to move in a body, whether it be to control Democratic nominations or to secure profitable places for their fellows."[9] American-born citizens must rise to put down this noxious order overseen by Jesuits and sworn to act in concert in all elections.

From Philadelphia, the venom flowed outward. In Washington DC, *The American* reprinted the *Sun's* account in full. "Who is 'Molly Maguire?'" *The American's* headline asked. "What her Purpose [sic]—and who are her Supporters?"[10] In Missouri, the *Glasgow Weekly Times* spoke of "calling a convention of *true* Democrats to crush out the 'Molly Maguires,' who are looked upon as a kind of foreign 'know nothing' order."[11] From Clearfield, Pennsylvania, the *Raftsman's Journal* repeated the charge.[12] Word spread west to Ohio, Indiana, Illinois, and Iowa, and south to South Carolina and Tennessee.[13]

Tennessee's *Clarksville Chronicle* gave the supposed secret signal of this Irish American order whose members already claimed too many political offices: two green lanterns mounted to sway over gatherings.[14] In Ohio, the *Meigs County Telegraph* reported "much indignation" among Protestant Democrats against the supposed order.[15] Steubenville's *True American* said of the "Mollies": "They are solemnly sworn against every American by birth, whether he belongs to the Democratic party or not. ... Thus the Democrat of American birth finds himself in the hands and in the power of a secret order of foreign Catholics, a thousand fold more dangerous to Democracy than the dreaded Know Nothings." The *True American* urged strict allegiance to the Know Nothings, "the only party that can effectually check Catholic usurpation."[16]

The *White Cloud Kansas Chief* agreed with the *True American* in a call for a resurgence of the American Party. The *Chief* predicted the rising up of "the American spirit ... with double the strength it ever possessed" to remove the foreign influence from U.S. politics.[17]

In Pottsville, Pennsylvania, future site of nine so-called "Molly Maguire" hangings, *Miners' Journal* editor Benjamin Bannan reprinted the noxious coverage. In Bannan's newsprint, coal region residents read for the first time of the dangers of "Molly Maguire." Notorious for his anti-Irish bias, Bannan described the alleged "Mollies" as "a secret Roman Catholic association, which the Democracy is using for political purposes."[18]

"The Philadelphia *Transcript*," Bannan told readers, "says this association commenced in Boston and now extends all over the country, controlling all the nominations of the Democratic party in our cities and in some portions of the country. The association is exciting a good deal of feeling among the American born Democrats, many of whom even talk of a Convention to rid themselves of the Association."[19]

The accusation of the dangers of Irish Catholic political strength lingered after the anonymous 1857 Know Nothing propaganda campaign launched in Philadelphia. The campaign played directly into the ethnic hatred that characterized the Know Nothing oath: "I will not knowingly vote for, appoint or elect any person of foreign birth, or a Roman Catholic, to any office in the local or general administration of the American government; and I ... will use all the means in my power to counteract and destroy the influence of foreigners and Roman Catholics in the administration of the government of the United States, and in any and all parts thereof, both local and general."[20]

Whoever authored the 1857 nativist propaganda campaign, it lodged the "Molly Maguire" demon firmly within the U.S. political consciousness. In the ensuing two decades, other events ran in tandem with the propaganda campaign. During this time, the Democratic politicians who prosecuted the "Molly Maguire" caseload showcased their nativist political stripes.

Francis Hughes Calls for Pennsylvania's Secession – 1861-1862

In October 1862, the *Lewistown Gazette* advised Pennsylvania's Democrats to "look around and see in whose company you are in." Francis Hughes, the *Gazette* reported, had "attended the democratic convention last year with a resolution in his pocket for Pennsylvania to secede from the Union and join Jef. Davis's cutthroat confederacy."[21] In 1858 Hughes, a long-time Pottsville attorney dubbed by the *Miners' Journal* "the great thunderer of Democracy in this County,"[22] had headed a meeting of Schuylkill County Democrats. Future "Molly" prosecutor Hughes had worked up his audience, the *Journal* said, "to the highest point by his eloquence, and sprung upon it a series of resolutions, Pro-Slavery in character, for its adoption."[23]

By 1860, Hughes's racist views had congealed. While serving as a delegate to the national Democratic Convention at Charleston, South Carolina, Hughes and his fellow delegates "took some pains to look into the condition of the slaves, and were surprised and pleased at finding them, generally, well dressed, well fed, contented and happy."[24]

In July 1862, delegates to Pennsylvania's Democratic state convention at Harrisburg named Hughes permanent president. They named Hughes's nephew, Francis Dewees, as a second permanent officer. The convention's ninth resolution, adopted unanimously on July 4, declared: "That this is a Government of white men, and was established exclusively for the white race; that the negro race are not entitled to and ought not to be admitted to political or social equality with the white race, but that it is our duty to treat them with kindness and consideration, as an inferior and dependent race ... ."[25] In Coudersport, an editor charged Hughes's sympathizers with "Negro-Phobia," a disease that destroyed the mind.[26]

Following the convention, Hughes authored the address of Pennsylvania's Democratic State Central Committee. In August, he delivered the speech to a fervid crowd in Philadelphia.

Hughes's committee speech, a paean to slavery and the Confederacy, addressed "the virus of Abolitionism," an ideology based upon "a misguided sentimentality in regard to the servitude of the negro race in the Southern States," which sentimentality "[swallowed] up all true feelings of patriotism." Northern abolitionists, Hughes claimed, were "determined that the white population of the South shall be exterminated or held in subjugation." By use of the Underground Railroad and other devices, abolitionists "deprive the slaveholders of the South of that property to which the Constitution and laws of his States, as well as those of the United States, guarantee protection." Hughes declared abolitionism "in the highest degree criminal and disloyal" and called for its eradication. Its spirit, he claimed, "seems now to brood over us like some evil genius, that would control us to our destruction."[27]

Hughes forwarded both his Fourth of July speech and his state committee address to Lincoln's secretary of state, William Seward. The gist of these addresses, Hughes assured Seward, reflected the sentiments of at least three hundred thousand men in Pennsylvania and more than one million throughout Pennsylvania, New Jersey, New York, Ohio, Indiana, and Illinois. Hughes hoped to stimulate Seward to promote a policy through President Lincoln's administration "to put down the demon of Abolitionism."[28]

Seward responded to Hughes's outrageous request. He reminded Hughes of the ongoing civil war, a conflict that would determine the nation's life or death. He advised Hughes that though he himself would not dictate the course others should pursue, if he, like Hughes, were at liberty to serve his country in his own way, "I could make an appeal to Democrats and Republicans, Abolitionists and slaveholders in behalf of our distracted country that would bring the whole people at once under arms, and send treason reeling back into the den of darkness from whence it sprung."[29] A Chicago newsman who applauded Seward's handling of Hughes said: "Mr. Hughes' association with the democracy is after the style of Lucifer with the angels who did not rebel."³⁰

Controversy followed controversy. In late September, Christopher Loeser, an attorney who knew Hughes well, sent detailed correspondence to the *Miners' Journal* in Pottsville "to give the people such facts as will enable them to determine for themselves, whether Hughes is ... trying to have the Union restored or to have the rebels succeed, the States divided, and a Southern Confederacy established."³¹

Among the statements curated by Loeser, Schuylkill County resident David Lomison stated that in 1861, Lomison had traveled by train in the same car that carried Hughes to Pennsylvania's Democratic Convention. Lomison had overheard Hughes declare to another traveler that as a delegate to the convention, Hughes would offer a resolution "'that Pennsylvania secede from the Union, and join herself with the South, and leave Rhode Island, and Connecticut, and Massachusetts, and them d—d little petty States, to subsist on their codfish and Plymouth rock.'"³²

Pottsville resident Jerome Boyer also told of Hughes's determination to introduce his secessionist resolution at Harrisburg in February 1861. Hughes's nephew John Hughes, a Confederate, told Boyer that he had read Hughes's statement several times, and advised him not to offer it. Judge Charles Hegins told Boyer that Hughes had given his resolution to Hegins to read. "'I advised him,'" Hegins said, "'for God's sake, not to offer it, as it would kill him politically, forever.'" General J. Y. James told Boyer that after he read Hughes's "'d—d treasonable resolution,'" he had gotten "'so d—d mad that I shook my fist and swore that if he attempted to offer that resolution, either in committee or Convention, that I would pitch him and his resolution headforemost out of the window.'"³³

Hughes responded to Loeser's outing of his "'d—d treasonable resolution'" by offering it for publication. Should the Confederacy succeed in its aims, Hughes's resolution stated, *"should the fifteen Slaveholding states ... successfully establish another Confederacy,"* then Pennsylvania, as a member of this new alliance, could become that body's "'*great Manufacturing workshop,*'" and Pennsylvania's cities "'*the great commercial depots and Distributing points for this Confederacy, and her wealth, population, and glory, be promoted in a degree unparalleled in the history and prosperity of any people!*'"[34]

Inflamed editors raced their opinions to print. The *Raftsman's Journal* condemned Hughes's "determination to drag Pennsylvania out of the Union and to attach her to the bloody despotism of the Slaveholding traitors."[35] The *Philadelphia Press* declared Hughes "'the champion of the Southern traitors ... the enemy of the Union.'"[36] A Lewisburg paper declared Hughes's actions "rank Treason."[37] Rumors of the secessionist tendencies of northern Democratic Party leaders, including Hughes, reached London, where journals speculated on their intent "to encourage and help the rebels."[38]

From Pottsville in Schuylkill County, Hughes's bailiwick and future site of nine so-called "Molly Maguire" hangings, Hughes's fellow Democrats responded differently. Less than two months after news of Hughes's secessionist resolution broke, a Wyoming County paper reported: "The Democrats of Schuylkill county have resolved to purchase, by contribution of a dollar to each person, a silver service, to be presented to Hon. F. W. Hughes for political services as chairman of the Democratic State Committee."[39] Two months later, Pennsylvania's Democrats bestowed on Hughes "a magnificent portrait of himself, painted by John Keenan, of Philadelphia, and presented by a committee of Democrats of his State as a testimonial of their appreciation of his service in the defence [sic] of constitutional rights."[40]

The same fall that Schuylkill County's Democrats rewarded Hughes for his political service, they elected Franklin Gowen as their district attorney. The following year Gowen and Hughes, two self-appointed lead prosecutors during the "Molly" trials of the subsequent decade, again shared the political field. In October 1863, at a Democratic mass meeting in Sunbury, Northumberland County, Hughes mounted a wagon to address the crowd at the town's square. He still backed the cause "that no true Jackson or Jefferson democrat could sustain."[41] Gowen held forth from a second wagon parked before one of the town's residences. "We listened to him a short time," the *Sunbury American* said of Gowen, "but heard enough to convince us that Frank's disease was deeply seated and incurable. His tongue was as copperish as an old fashioned penny used in greening pickles."[42]

Four months after the Civil War ended, Gowen's name appeared on a roster of proposed speakers for a political camp meeting to be held near Orangeville at Megargell Grove, on the west end of Nob Mountain. The Columbia County event, a showcase for white supremacy, lasted three days. Charles Buckalew, a third lead prosecutor during the "Molly Maguire" trials, served as its primary organizer.

Pennsylvania's Democrats Convene on Nob Mountain – 1865

In August 1865, four months before Confederate veterans in Tennessee formed the first lodge of the Ku Klux Klan, Democrats in Pennsylvania's Columbia County held a camp meeting on Nob Mountain. "Some of the best speakers of Pennsylvania and New York will be in attendance to discuss the issues," the *Star of the North* advised readers in Bloomsburg. It urged all to fill covered wagons with three days' rations and make the trek to Nob Mountain "to revive your health, to revive your pleasures, and … to revive and strengthen your Democratic principles, and draw you to a more sincere respect of the old Constitution—the bulwark of our liberties."[43]

The roster of eight prospective speakers for the three-day extravaganza included Franklin Gowen, sitting district attorney for Schuylkill County and future chief prosecutor during the "Molly Maguire" trials. A correspondent from Harrisburg chronicled the "Democratic Camp Meeting, got up by Senator Buckalew and the gallant Democracy of Columbia county."[44] A decade later, Charles Buckalew would also serve as a prosecutor during the "Molly" trials.

"The grounds lay in an elegant wood," the Harrisburg correspondent said, "finely shaded and well calculated for such an occasion. To the north stands the majestic Nob Mountain, like a sentinel, stern and defiant."[45]

The event's first meeting took place on Tuesday, August 29. Democratic Party members from Columbia County, future site of three so-called "Molly Maguire" executions, drove in with their wives and children. Tents housed the families. Speakers addressed the crowd from a stand decorated with bouquets arranged by the wives.

Attendance on day one proved much larger than expected. Democrats had traveled in from Philadelphia, Harrisburg, Reading, Williamsport, Lewisburg, and Bradford; and from Carbon, Montour, Northumberland, Schuylkill, Sullivan, and Wyoming counties. Buckalew opened the gathering with prayer. He lauded the presidential inaugural given by Thomas Jefferson, and asked the crowd what course they thought their party should follow.

Attendance on Wednesday, August 30, proved even larger. A cornet band headed delegations from Danville and Bloomsburg. A Bloomsburg minister opened proceedings with "an impressive and appropriate prayer to the Throne of Grace."[46] Day two's festivities closed with song, led by the choir director of Bloomsburg's Lutheran Church and performed by twenty girls dressed in red, white, and blue.

"A Darkey Ditty," performed by Iram Derr and sons, opened Wednesday's evening meeting. Sung to the tune of "De Floating Scow," the song called for all jolly Democrats to lend an ear to denounce the "precious crew" of abolitionists: Wendell Phillips, Hiram Wilson, Benjamin Wade, Salmon Chase, and Charles Sumner. The fourth stanza included these lines: "And all their torchlight followers got / The darkey on the brain; / Oh! if they could the n———r free, / They would not ask any more."

"But when the darkey gets a vote," another stanza ran, "An equal he will be; / And Phillips, Sumner, Chase & Wade, / Will ask his wench to tea." The ditty's last stanza advised:

> Then comes the last, the grand finale,
> There is but one step more;
> Miscegenation is the word
> By which they seek for power;
> Oh! give them but the darkey wench,
> And they will ask no more;
> Oh! give them but the darkey wench,
> And they will ask no more.[47]

Campfires burned for three days. On Thursday evening, the Derr family sang "The Mountain to the Meeting." The Goddess Liberty, they advised, had long ruled the region, "While Democrats securely held / A hand upon the helm."

> "Yes I have seen," the Nob rejoins
> In accents loud and clear;
> "Your strife for laws and white-men's rights,
> Kept up from year to year;
> And I have seen the stalwart sons
> Of Old Columbia stand
> Before the brazen throat of power,
> A small undaunted band.[48]

A Bloomsburg paper ran a column headed "Nob Mountain Items." It said: "Rarely has any popular gathering in the interior of the State been more extensively noticed or attracted more of public favor. It was just the right thing, at the right time, and in the right place." The column noted Gowen's lack of attendance due to pressing professional duties. Though Gowen's absence "was regretted, there was no failure in speech-making and the programme of exercises was substantially executed."[49] Victor Piollet, who would later intertwine with Gowen politically, held the audience entranced for an hour with his discussion of the consequences of abolition mismanagement. "So I need not be mistaken," the former Civil War colonel said, "when I speak of men; I mean white men."[50]

Just before Piollet spoke, John Freeze, author of "A Darkey Ditty" and "The Mountain to the Meeting," read the resolutions from Pennsylvania's recent Democratic state convention. The convention's sixth resolution, cheered the week before by Democrats at Pennsylvania's House of Representatives in Harrisburg, stated:

> That the effort now making ... to force negro suffrage on the States against the will of the people and contrary to existing laws, is ... a high crime against the Constitution ... a deliberate and wicked attempt to put the States of the Union ... under the domination of negroes, to Africanize a large portion of the country, and degrade the white race, morally and socially as well as politically, to the low level of the black. We will not ... surrender the destinies of the country into the hands of negroes, nor put ourselves under their guardianship, nor give up to them the political privileges which we inherited from our fathers, and we exhort our brethren in other States to take up the same attitude and maintain it firmly.[51]

From Williamsport, a Democratic editor feared that Nob Mountain's proceedings could breed fanaticism. He deemed the gathering "'ill-timed and improper,'" and speculated that the young men behind its organization sought to control Pennsylvania's Democratic Party.[52]

Asa Packer's Failed Bid for the U.S. Presidency – 1868

Three years after Pennsylvania's Democrats gathered at Nob Mountain, the *Raftsman's Journal* declared that the 1868 Democratic National Convention, scheduled at New York's Tammany Hall, would be "the Copperhead National Convention."[53] For the first time since the Civil War had severed the country, southern politicians would join with their northern brethren to select their party's presidential nominee. Less than two months before the convention opened, impeachment proceedings against party leader President Andrew Johnson had almost removed Johnson from office. One issue would unite this seemingly disparate band of delegates: their hatred of federal-government-backed Reconstruction policies that sought equality for the newly freed slaves.

So many prospective candidates crowded the field, some papers refused to predict outcomes. Four months before the convention opened, an observer from Delaware declared Democratic delegates "depressed, out of spirits, and almost hopeless." He spoke of the need on the ticket for "some quiet old gentleman unheard of or forgotten who has no record and no enemies." Though with little hope for success, "Old Asa Packer, the Lehigh Valley millionaire, is suggested as an available man of this kind."[54]

Packer, a self-made millionaire originally from Mystic, Connecticut, had started out in the canal trade and moved on to railroads. A member of Pennsylvania's state assembly in 1842, Packer had served as an associate judge in Carbon County from 1843 to 1844. In 1853, he assumed the presidency of the Lehigh Valley Railroad and began a four-year stint as Pennsylvania's federal representative to the Thirty-fourth and Thirty-fifth Congresses. In 1856, Packer declined renomination to federal office. Two decades later, he would help mount Carbon County's "Molly Maguire" trials.

From south of Pittsburgh, a newsman observed in mid-June 1868: "The one-horse Democratic papers of Pennsylvania are trying to raise an undercurrent in favor of Judge Packer as the Democratic nominee for President."[55] As the Fourth of July convention approached, the *New York Sun* reported that Packer sought only "a complimentary vote and will doubtless get it."[56] From Philadelphia, the *Telegraph* described the railroad president as "Asa Packer, the modest."[57]

On the convention's third day, the *Telegraph* reported: "All the influences of Pennsylvania, particularly the Germans, are now in favor of Packer."[58] Packer's supporters, pressing on through a debilitating heat wave, made up a card to sway the unknowing and the unconvinced. The card reminded convention delegates that "as went Pennsylvania so always went the Union." It characterized Packer as "a sound, conservative, practical statesman, of enlarged views, pure integrity and mature judgment. ... a representative man of the great industrial, business and improvement interests of the country." It told of Packer's strength in New York, New Jersey, "and far into the West."[59]

In "Hot Weather—A Touch of Tophet in Tammany Hall," the *New York Herald* reported the terrific heat. Though the sufferings of the city's builders, street pavers, ditch diggers and dockworkers had been terrific, those sufferings were "as nothing compared to the torture, trials and temptations of the sweltering democracy, crowded, packed and struggling in the Convention at Tammany Hall."[60]

On the convention's first ballot, George Washington Woodward, associate justice to Pennsylvania's Supreme Court, placed Packer's name in consideration. The entire Pennsylvania delegation gave Packer its vote through fourteen ballots. On day five, the delegation left the hall to consult in private. "She [Pennsylvania] was gone an unconscionably long time," the *New York Sun* reported, "at least, so it seemed to the sweltering throng who sat and stood gasping for breath during her absence." When the delegation returned, it again held to Packer. The *Sun* said: "The whole assembly screamed with laughter."[61]

On July 11, the *New York Herald* reported the "Last Scene of the Convention Farce." Delegates and spectators crammed Tammany Hall, where stars-and-stripes bunting decorated the rotunda's frescoed dome. Outside, thousands of spectators thronged the street. Brilliant outdoor lighting, the playing of bands, and the firing of cannon added to the mayhem. Inside, on day seven of a now contentious and raucous gathering, delegates finally settled on Horatio Seymour, former governor of New York, for president; and for vice-president Francis Blair Jr. of Missouri, a former major general in the Union Army.

Seymour accepted the nomination and endorsed the party platform. Blair did the same. Then Blair gave the aim of the Democratic ticket: "We make this contest for the restoration of those great principles of government which belong to our race." To cheers and applause, Blair restated the party's theme "to prevent the people of one race from being exiled from their homes—exiled from the government which they formed and created for themselves and for their children, and to prevent them from being driven out in exile or trodden under foot by an inferior and a semi-barbarous race."[62]

On the platform outside, Colonel Yeger of Mississippi called for the country's salvation. To cheers, Yeger asked listeners "whether this was to be a white man's government or a black man's government." J. R. Fellows of Arkansas followed Yeger. Fellows asked: "Would the North permit the necks of white men to be loaded with the chains placed by a radical Congress in the hands of the negro?"[63] Campaign badges for the Seymour-Blair ticket asserted: "This is a White Man's Country. Let White Men Rule."

Glimmers of Packer's sympathy with the Confederate cause had arisen earlier in the decade. In June 1862, Cleveland's *Morning Leader* reported a dispatch from Mauch Chunk, home to Packer's Italianate villa on a hill overlooking the town. The dispatch read: "This morning's train brought to our quiet town Senator Starke, Vallandigham, and others of the same stripe. They were guests of Asa Packer."[64] Midway through the Civil War, Packer had entertained under the roof of his Pennsylvania coal region mansion both U.S. Congressman Clement Vallandigham, leader of the northern Copperhead faction, and Mississippi's Peter Starke, a state senator whose commission as a Confederate Army colonel began four months before he dined with Packer at Mauch Chunk.

During Packer's 1868 presidential bid, the *Daily Press* noted from Portland, Maine: "The only account of him we are able to find is in Lanman's Dictionary of Congress, where his biography is given with more than Spartan brevity."[65] The following year, Packer's bid for Pennsylvania's governorship expanded the public's knowledge of his biography, and his elitist aims. From Clearfield, the *Raftsman's Journal* described Packer, during the Civil War: "Hobnobbing with the arch traitor Vallandigham, in his palatial residence, Mauch Chunk." The Clearfield editor said of Packer: "He is the meanest of all aristocrats—a rich parvenu. He believes that capital should own labor, and would vote for slavery—black or white—tomorrow, if by doing so, he could fasten it upon the working classes."[66]

Asa Packer's Failed Bid for Pennsylvania's Governorship – 1869

On November 3, 1868, Republicans Ulysses S. Grant and Schuyler Colfax beat the Democratic presidential "White Man's" ticket of Seymour-Blair by more than three hundred thousand popular votes. Grant swept the Electoral College vote with more than two hundred to Seymour's eighty.

Republican newspapers celebrated the win. "Total Overthrow of the Democracy. FINAL DEFEAT OF THE CONFEDERATE ARMY," a report said from Wisconsin.[67] From Philadelphia, the *Telegraph* exulted: "VICTORY! WHICH MEANS PEACE! RECONSTRUCTED AT LAST."[68] Newsmen in Indiana, New Orleans, and West Virginia declared Grant's presidential victory a second Appomattox.[69]

Democratic sheets deplored Grant's win. In Bloomsburg, from the county that hosted the Nob Mountain meeting, an editor said of state majorities for Grant: "Africa has not yet been heard from, but it can be safely counted for Grant."[70] From Cambria County, home to Cyrus Pershing, future president judge in Pennsylvania's "Molly Maguire" trials, the *Cambria Freeman* reprinted a rant from the *New York Democrat*. "Not Beaten!" the *Freeman's* headline ran. "No, never!" the *Democrat* said. "Then stand to your arms, white men of America! ... The grand, heroic, old Democratic party, ever the party of the country, of the Constitution, of Liberty! is not dead."[71]

Asa Packer mounted his gubernatorial campaign in this divisive and divided electoral field. From Clearfield, the *Raftsman's Journal* said of Packer's bid for the governorship: "His money obtained him the nomination. He is a railroad king and a millionaire ... the very leader of the aristocracy of wealth in Pennsylvania."[72] The *Harrisburg Telegraph* declared Packer "the Great Mogul and purse holder of the party."[73]

The *Reading Times* averred Packer had amassed his wealth "by *grinding the faces of the poor.*"[74] The *Harrisburg Telegraph* declared the railroad president, loathed by his canal workers, "the most unpopular man among the miners that could have been chosen."[75] "Judge Packer has grown immensely rich on the toil of the poor," the *Telegraph* said, "and has always made it a point to purchase that toil at the lowest figure."[76]

Packer faced a formidable challenger in Republican John Geary, who sought a second term in office. A Civil War general whose son had died in his arms at the Battle of Wauhatchie, Geary's support of the eight-hour workday underscored his grasp of labor's hardships.

The *Mauch Chunk Gazette* sounded Geary's call for Carbon County's workingmen, with many Irish Catholics among them: "If you have always voted the Democratic ticket, think twice before you go to the polls ... ... and you will cast your ballot for a man who will not be influenced in his official course by a great railway or large capitalists."[77]

A miners' strike in Luzerne County further challenged Packer's bid. "A strike like this among democratic voters in the coal regions," the *New York Herald* predicted, "if allowed to continue, will elect Geary ... by an immense majority, and sink Packer down a political shaft so deep that it will be difficult ever to rescue him therefrom."[78] Three weeks later, as the campaign accelerated, a fire at Luzerne County's Avondale Colliery claimed the lives of one hundred and ten mineworkers, boys and men. A rescue party spent two days locating and removing bodies.

The *Raftsman's Journal* reported the recent rejection by Pennsylvania's Democratic legislators of a bill providing for mine-safety inspections. "These Democrats opposed it," the *Journal* said, "simply because it entailed additional expense on the operators."[79] Geary visited Avondale and attended funeral services. He inspected the ravaged mine to bring his findings before state legislators at Harrisburg.

In an address given to state representatives four months later, Geary described the horrors. None of the mineworkers who entered the shaft that day, Geary said, "anticipated danger as they descended the fatal shaft; not one supposed that he was entering a tomb in which he was doomed to be buried alive. But the Destroying Angel hovered over them, and the shaft, constructed principally of combustible materials, having become ignited from some cause yet undetermined, was soon a sheet of flame, and huge burning timbers came tumbling from above, choking up with fire and smoke the only avenue of escape." The mineworkers met death, Geary said, "clasped in each other's arms."[80]

Of the mine owners, Geary said: "The mines in many cases are constructed and managed in the most selfish and parsimonious manner, the owners exacting the largest amount of profit from them, from the [least] possible outlay; consequently some of them, like that of Avondale, are nothing but underground man-traps, without any other outlets than wooden chimneys, and these constantly liable to become blazing volcanoes, through which escape is impossible. The lives of so useful a class of men as our miners, should not and must not be permitted to be thus sacrificed upon the altar of human cupidity."[81]

Geary described the challenges the mineworkers faced from unsafe ventilation, from the continual threat of collapse of mine roofs and walls, from the ongoing threat of combustion from the flammable gas called "firedamp." He urged legislators to enact laws to secure "competent inspectors" throughout the region. He declared Pennsylvania's mining system "worse than that of any other country, whilst our mining interests are unequalled by those of any other part of the world."[82]

On October 12, 1869, five weeks after the Avondale tragedy, Geary defeated Packer by almost five thousand votes, securing his second term as Pennsylvania's governor. The *New York Tribune* said of the vote in the anthracite coal region: "The men who dig Coal have had trouble the past season—they have felt the heavy hand of Power—they ... know little of Gov. Geary, who lives far away but they know Asa Packer—know how he made his Twenty Millions—and they could not feel that he was their man. Hence the result."[83] In this bellwether election, the mineworkers, with many Irish Catholics among them, were swinging their votes from the Democrats to the Republicans.

Two years after Geary defeated Packer, a *Herald* reporter interviewed Packer at the Astor House in New York. The reporter informed the railroad president "that the miners, at a secret meeting to which a Herald reporter was the only person admitted, had concluded in future to vote for no party man, but for him only who would find himself to befriend the laborer and under no condition to give his influence to any act that was calculated in the remotest degree to deprive the laboring man of any of his rights."[84]

The reporter observed: "Mr. Packer, from former bad experience —the miners' vote defeated him for Governor—does not seem to have much faith in this class of our population. He thinks they are treacherous in the extreme, and that any candidate who places his dependence on them builds his house on the sand."[85]

The following month, a *Herald* reporter interviewed Geary at Harrisburg. The two discussed the Labor Reform Party movement that was sweeping the land. "'Yes;'" Geary told the reporter, "'there are from 100,000 to 150,000 of them. Thus far they have, as a general thing, gone with the republican party. They have saved our elections several times in this State. In [1869] they supported me against Asa Packer.'" Geary added: "'They are strong enough, if they choose, to have a party of their own and to elect their own men, or to compel some one of the parties to nominate men who will take care of their interests.'"[86]

After Packer's defeat, Schuylkill County's Labor Reformers pushed on with their efforts. During Geary's second term, at the urging of miners in Mahanoy City, Geary authorized a legislative investigation into Franklin Gowen's abrupt rise in railroad freight rates, an investigation whose scope included Packer's Lehigh Valley Railroad. After Geary authorized the investigation, Packer answered a subpoena to appear before the state Judiciary Committee. The "treacherous" miners challenged Packer twice: through the ballot box and through investigations conducted by Pennsylvania's legislature.

Asa Packer's Advocates Descend Into Hate Speech

After the defeat of the presidential "White Man's" ticket, Packer did not openly parade the white supremacy of the 1868 Democratic national campaign. But during Pennsylvania's Democratic gubernatorial convention in 1869, a delegation of young men, numbering about seventy-five, rode into Harrisburg to cheer for Packer. They descended from cars of the Philadelphia and Reading Railroad "sporting white cotton gloves, white duck vests, and white silk hats."[87] Silk badges on their coats declared them members of the Asa Packer Association of Philadelphia.

The young Philadelphians who supported Packer displayed their racism subtly. Other, open, displays from that era broadcast racist views so casually, and delivered a venom so poisonous, their recounting horrifies modern readers. This casual, horrifying, racism on plain view in Pennsylvania's coal region in the 1860s helped both desensitize the region and galvanize it for the next decade's public strangulations of alleged "Molly Maguires," when anti-Irish, anti-Catholic fervor overtook for a time the widespread animus displayed against recently emancipated Blacks.

At least two coal region Democratic organs that lauded Packer's candidacies openly aired their vitriol against the recently emancipated slaves. During Packer's race for governor, the *Columbian* in Bloomsburg described Packer as one of the Democrats' "men of National character."[88] The month before, in February 1868, the same paper trafficked in hate speech when it gave a supposed humorous account of a "COLORED CUSS" addressing Alabama's state assembly. "N——rs is sumbody," the *Columbian's* fiction ran. "We'se gwine to yoccupy de land—we'se gwine to hab our forty acres ob land and a pair ob mules—we'se gwine to play gemplum ... for de bottom rail am on top!"[89]

In June 1868, also from Bloomsburg, the *Democrat* lauded Packer's "unquestioned integrity, and moral character of the very highest grade."[90] Six weeks before that, the paper published a column that ran:

"N—r! n—r! n—r! ... He stands forth the chief object of Black Republican sympathy ... He is the big dish at the feast. ... the main issue and all the side issues ... It is n—r *a la mode*, fricasseed n—r, fried n—r, stewed n—r, baked n—r, with n—r sauce, roasted n—r, boiled n—r, hashed n—r, raw n—r — n—r around the festive board, n—r up stairs, n—r in the garret, n—r down stairs, n—r in the kitchen, n—r in the parlor, n—r in the wood-pile, n—r on the fence, n—r as a man and brother, n—r in and out of Congress, and n—r on the brain!"

The column, featured on the *Democrat's* front page, asked: "Good Lord! Is there nothing!—no rights—no interest—no country for white men?"[91]

Hate speech, however venomous, did not help Packer's cause. After two successive defeats, he exited the political spotlight and returned to railroad administration. Six years after Packer's failed run for the governorship, his corporate attorney and private counsel, Allen Craig, helped craft prosecution strategy in Carbon County's "Molly Maguire" trials. Observers credited Craig, a hunting companion of Packer's son Harry, with "developing the legal theories for the prosecution team."[92] Craig's efforts helped convict numerous Irish Catholic defendants as alleged "Mollies." The defendants counted among them many Labor Reformers, including a number who likely helped bring about Packer's electoral defeats.

Charles Buckalew's Secessionist Thugs at Harrisburg – 1863

In 1868 the *Nashville Union and Dispatch* described Pennsylvania's U.S. Senator Charles Buckalew as another of a number of "able men" who could "adorn the position" of U.S. president.[93] A lifelong resident of Columbia County, Buckalew, a future "Molly" prosecutor, served as county prosecutor from 1845 to 1847. From 1851 to 1858, he served as state senator. In 1858, President James Buchanan appointed Buckalew resident minister of Quito, Ecuador. Buckalew filled the post until 1861.

In 1863, the *New York Tribune* described Buckalew's election to the U.S. Senate at a time when state legislators, not the general electorate, elected federal senators. Secessionists, the *Tribune* reported, were determined that Buckalew would fill the position of U.S. senator from Pennsylvania. To ensure that end, they chartered a train in Philadelphia and sent a thousand roughs armed with pistols and bowie knives "to intimidate and control the Legislature." Late on the night of their arrival at Harrisburg, the hired roughs roamed the streets, armed, drunken, and singing. One song threatened to hang Abe Lincoln from a sour apple tree. When finally exhausted, the ragtag faux army commandeered hotel lobbies and slept on chairs and settees, wrapped in coats and shawls. An unnamed judge told the New York reporter that the men who came in via chartered car "had indictments hanging over them, and belonged to the scum of low life in Philadelphia."[94]

Before the convention opened, a legislative resolution passed during a night session had disarmed the military force that protected the legislative body. It had authorized the sergeant-at-arms, a Philadelphia dance-hall keeper "more notorious than popular," to swear in "a force of special constables of his own selection."[95]

The *Tribune* reporter said: "I have been assured by men whose judgment is authority, that several Democratic members voted for Buckalew with great reluctance, and were influenced to do so by bodily fear for their personal safety, knowing they were watched with wolfish eyes by men who had been hired to whip refractory members into the harness."[96] A Republican in the chamber, an iron manufacturer, offered to bring in an additional thousand men to protect legislators while the vote was taken. A prominent but unnamed Democratic editor assured the *Tribune* reporter that no Democrat who voted for Simon Cameron, the Republican choice, would have left the capital building alive.

The Democratic caucus nominated Buckalew on the sixth ballot. Of the candidate's Confederate sympathies, the *Tribune* reported: "He is unmeasured in his abuse of Republicans and Abolitionists, while he touches Secessionism as tenderly as old Izaak Walton did the frog he carried in his mouth for bait, biting gently for fear of injuring the creature."[97]

From Cleveland, the *Morning Leader* reported "Mob Law in Harrisburg—How a United States Senator was Elected."[98] From Indiana, the *Evansville Journal* repeated the remark of an unnamed Democratic editor that no man who voted for Cameron "would have been permitted to leave the Capitol alive." The Evansville paper concluded: "That, we presume, is the Constitution as it is."[99]

Charles Buckalew's Record of Racist Elitism

Two and a half years later, in late August 1865, Democrats in Pennsylvania's Columbia County held their outdoor camp extravaganza at Nob Mountain. As event coordinator, Charles Buckalew opened the first meeting with prayer. With God and the Constitution as his themes, Buckalew directed the election of officers and delivered an address "reiterating his faith in Democratic principles."[100]

On day two at Nob Mountain, Captain Charles Brockway picked up the theme. Confined in a Confederate prison when Lincoln signed the Emancipation Proclamation, Brockway declared "the sufferings of imprisonment were nothing compared to the mental torture on finding the high and noble cause for which I enlisted debased by being made a struggle for giving freedom to a few degraded negroes."[101]

Brockway had served as Buckalew's private secretary during Buckalew's appointment as minister to Quito. At Nob Mountain, Brockway displayed a letter written by Buckalew during his diplomatic service. Brockway, who had copied the letter while acting as Buckalew's secretary, did not identify its recipient. Buckalew's letter condemned "the mixing of distinct races," a practice that had inflicted on Spanish colonies in the New World "all the curses of hybridism." The practices of intermarriage, Buckalew said, "have produced monstrous evils ... in Spanish America, there is neither purity of blood nor organization of labor, without which no people can be energetic, virtuous and prosperous."[102]

The same year that Buckalew organized "Buckalew's Camp Meeting" on Nob Mountain, he wielded considerable power as a minority member of the heavily Unionist U.S. Senate. Buckalew consistently voted with the minority who refused to grant civil rights to Blacks.

In 1864, Buckalew voted with the opposition against the repeal of the Fugitive Slave Act. A few days after voting "Nay" to the Civil Rights Act of 1866, Buckalew, as head of a group of Pennsylvania men, joined a throng at the White House who jostled for time with the president. Andrew Johnson granted Buckalew's delegation an audience.[103] Two days later, Johnson vetoed the Freedman's Bureau Bill, designed to aid former slaves.

In late winter 1866, Pennsylvania's Democratic state convention echoed Buckalew's views. Among numerous resolutions, delegates agreed: "That the white race alone is entitled to the control of the Government of the Republic, and we are unwilling to grant to negroes the right to vote." The same set of resolutions tendered thanks to Buckalew for his "patriotic support of the President's restoration policy."[104] A Bloomsburg editor declared that Buckalew knew "that the Democratic party honored and adored him, stood by him in the dark days of tyranny and Lincoln despotism."[105]

Late October 1866 found Buckalew campaigning on behalf of Democrats for the governor's race in Pennsylvania. In Susquehanna County, Buckalew met up with Franklin Gowen to address the party faithful. A few days later, Buckalew traveled to Pottsville, where Gowen lived, to address a throng estimated at fifteen to twenty thousand strong. On the floor of the U.S. Senate, Buckalew argued against suffrage for Negroes and women "because it would corrupt and degrade elections."[106]

In 1867 and 1868, Buckalew again met behind closed doors with President Johnson. In 1867, Buckalew urged the adoption of the minority system of representation being debated at the British Parliament in London, because "the majority principle in vogue worked unjustly and unfairly."[107] A few years later, the Harrisburg correspondent of a Philadelphia paper said of Buckalew's ongoing cheerleading for the convoluted plan: "Buckalew believes that free voting should be reduced to vulgar fractions, and that suffrage should depend upon an intricate knowledge of addition, multiplication, subtraction, simple and compound division, and simple fractions."[108]

In 1867, Buckalew voted nay with four others to Charles Sumner's bill declaring that neither race nor color could disqualify office seekers in the District of Columbia. On Johnson's impeachment, Buckalew served on the committee that notified Chief Justice Salmon Chase of the pending trial. Buckalew continued to meet with the president during the ongoing trial. In mid-May, a Stroudsburg paper declared Buckalew "one of the High Priests of Democracy."[109]

September 1868 found Buckalew stumping for the "White Man's" Democratic presidential ticket of Horatio Seymour and Francis Blair. Buckalew's speeches on their behalf declared the Freedmen's Bureau, among other measures, "a departure from the grants of power in the Constitution of the United States."[110]

October 1868 found Buckalew presiding over a Democratic meeting at Bloomsburg. It included a torchlight parade with five hundred wagons. A float caricatured the Freedmen's Bureau, whose "chief was continually occupied in paying out greenbacks to indolent darkeys, much to their satisfaction."[111]

In 1869, Buckalew's U.S. Senate term expired. By April, he had resumed the practice of law at Bloomsburg. In July, he presided over the Democratic state convention that nominated Asa Packer for governor and Cyrus Pershing for justice of Pennsylvania's Supreme Court. "The agony is over," the *Raftsman's Journal* said of that convention. "The mountain has labored and brought forth a couple of very small mice."[112]

In late August 1869, Pennsylvania's Democrats nominated Buckalew for state senate. "Ex-United States Senator C. R. Buckalew, not satisfied with culminating his political career in the United States Senate, has again entered the arena and proposes to begin over again, commencing on a small scale," the *New York Herald* reported.[113] Buckalew served as state senator until 1872, when he ran for Pennsylvania's governor. "Charles R. Buckalew is acknowledged to be the attorney of the Reading railroad [sic] Company," a coal region newspaper said of Buckalew's 1872 gubernatorial candidacy. "He was their agent while in the Senate, and Frank Gowen's right-hand man generally."[114]

Charles Buckalew's Failed Bid for Pennsylvania's Governorship – 1872

In 1872 the *Northumberland Democrat*, a long-time foe of Irish Catholic politicians, union men, and all Labor Reformers, defined Pennsylvania's upcoming gubernatorial contest. In 1869 Pennsylvania's Labor Reformers, with many Irish Catholics among them, had helped re-elect Governor John Geary and defeat Asa Packer. "If there are any little, weak-kneed, mistaken policy managers," the *Democrat* said three years later, "any wise, little, superficial tricksters, any foxy little gentlemen who always get very cunning in election matters, their services will not be needed in Reading ... the people want honest, solid qualifications ... if the little wrigglers are to give us another babies' platform and another set of Shamocrats to run on some popular breeze which is to blow dust into everybody's eyes, and elect somebody upon side issues ... then sensible people may as well stay away from Reading and from the polls."[115]

A coal region paper said of Charles Buckalew's candidacy: "The thirty or forty thousand anthracite miners and laborers are a unit ... against the Democratic party for putting such an uncompromising foe to labor upon the ticket."[116] "No body in this county seems anxious to take any stock in Buckalew," a Danville paper said from Montour County. "He is not a favorite even among the Democracy."[117] From Northumberland County came this observation: "We have the assurance of his neighbors that Buckalew is very unpopular at his home among his own people ... He has no sympathy with the workingmen, and in fact, none in common with the mass of the people."[118] In early June, the *New York Herald* reported: "About two weeks since Thomas A. Scott, of the Pennsylvania Railroad, received intelligence that Buckalew was the Reading Railroad candidate; that Franklin B. Gowen, President of this road, a young man of decided ability and vaulting ambition that has not as yet over-reached itself, for reasons of his own, had determined to press the nomination of Buckalew."[119]

Despite the warnings of Buckalew's alliance with Gowen, John Siney, president and founder in 1868 of the Workingmen's Benevolent Association (WBA), the anthracite mineworkers' union, endorsed Buckalew in 1872 as a Labor Reform gubernatorial candidate. Siney's reasons for so doing remain obscure. But Schuylkill County's Labor Reformers rejected Siney's choice.

In his race for the governor's chair, Buckalew faced Republican candidate John Hartranft. An attorney and Civil War general born in Pennsylvania's Montgomery County, Hartranft had studied civil engineering at Union College in New York. Stints as a civil engineer for a coal region railroad and deputy sheriff at Norristown preceded Hartranft's military and legal career. In 1865, as provost marshal at Arsenal Penitentiary in Washington D.C., Hartranft had signaled the executioner in the hangings of the four alleged conspirators in the Lincoln assassination. A Democratic Party member early in his career, Hartranft had shifted his allegiance to the Republicans. From 1866 to 1873, Hartranft served as Pennsylvania's auditor general under Pennsylvania's Republican governor, John Geary.

Amidst the tumult of the Hartranft-Buckalew contest, one Danville editor consulted political stock gamblers and scouted barn roofs for weathervanes to gauge the political wind. Criticism of Hartranft's opponent abounded. "He is eminently selfish and at the shrine of his ambition would sacrifice his best friend," the *Bloomsburg Republican* said of Buckalew.[120] A Tionesta editor reprinted this notion: "Buckalew, with his heel upon humanity and his broad back turned toward the sun."[121] From Sunbury, the *American* declared: "All know that Mr. Buckalew is ... run in the interest of English capitalists."[122]

Even Buckalew's friends gave him tepid endorsements. "It is generally known that he was not our choice, but since the honor has been conferred upon him, let us close up the ranks and elect him by a handsome majority,"[123] a Democratic editor said from Bloomsburg.

"Register," the *Sunbury Gazette* urged Northumberland County's voters in September 1871. "Every opponent of the Irish supremacy in this county should make it a point to examine the list and see if he is registered. ... If the full vote is brought out the result will be a complete overthrow of that faction which is attempting to bind our county hand and foot to the Irish power."[124]

The *Gazette's* admonition came six months after Pennsylvania's Ancient Order of Hibernian (AOH) men, with Patrick Hester prominent among them, had filed their revised charter with the state legislature at Harrisburg.[125] Hester, executed seven years later as an alleged "Molly Maguire," served as AOH delegate for Northumberland County.

The filing of the revised AOH charter in March 1871 corresponded with an upsurge in Labor Reform Party activity, from James Carroll's hosting of a convention at his home the following year, to John Kehoe's involvement with U.S. Congressman John Killinger and state assemblyman John Morgan, to Hester's alliance with Richard Trevellick, head of the National Labor Union. The Hibernians' urge toward reform and recognition of the workingmen's plight dovetailed with the profound language of their 1871 AOH charter. "Love guides the whole design," that charter's preamble advised.[126]

"'War, absolute war,'" a *New York Herald* reporter described politics in Pennsylvania, and throughout the country, in October 1872. Less than two weeks before the gubernatorial election, the reporter visited Pottsville in Schuylkill County to check the coal region's electoral pulse. En route to "this land of fire and smoke," the reporter had met William Forten, son of African American abolitionist James Forten. William Forten was traveling to Reading to encourage votes for Hartranft.[127]

The *Herald* reporter said of Pottsville's Welsh and Irish miners, "they are intelligent workers, perhaps, but withal men of low instincts, greatly given to indulgence in animal passions ... not difficult of approach by political thimble-riggers and cunning wire-pullers." While Schuylkill County had gone for Democratic candidate Asa Packer in 1869, the reporter cautioned that "THESE WILD LABOR REFORMERS may change these figures entirely." Though the reporter had no doubt Buckalew would poll a majority in the region, "there is also a very strong republican feeling."[128]

Through late September and early October, the race intensified. On September 20, Democratic operatives sent word to the *New York Herald*: "Buckalew will come to Philadelphia with 20,000 majority."[129] Less than a week later, U.S. senator Simon Cameron, Pennsylvania's leading Republican, spoke with the *Herald* and predicted at least a fifteen-thousand-vote majority for Hartranft.[130]

In early October, from Alexandria, Virginia, the *Gazette* told of a Republican source in Washington predicting "the overwhelming success of Buckalew on Tuesday week."[131] On October 8, 1872, though Pennsylvania's Democrats had "'moved heaven and earth' to place [Buckalew] before the people in his brightest colors,"[132] Democrats gave up the fight at eight in the evening. Gowen's preferred candidate had suffered a devastating loss.

"PENNSYLVANIA!!" the *Evening Star* reported from Washington. "The Republicans Sweep the State!"[133] A few days later, from Wheeling, came news of "The Great Victory in Pennsylvania."[134] A coal region paper reported "The Largest Vote Ever Cast and the Greatest Republican Victory Every Known!!!"[135]

After the electoral bloodbath, disappointed Democrats raised cries of fraudulent votes, rounders, and repeaters. The accusations centered on Philadelphia, where Hartranft had claimed a twenty-thousand-vote majority.

Total votes cast in Pennsylvania's gubernatorial race in 1872, the year after the AOH obtained its state charter at Harrisburg, went from 576,508 in 1869 to 654,891 in 1872, an increase in three years of more than seventy-eight thousand votes. Votes cast in the combined AOH strongholds of the western bituminous region (including Pittsburgh); in the five counties in the anthracite region; and in Philadelphia, went from 101,127 for Republican candidate John Geary in 1869 to 134,773 for Republican candidate Hartranft in 1872, an increase of more than thirty-three thousand votes. Hartranft's majority statewide beat even the most generous estimates. While Geary had won in 1869 with fewer than five thousand votes, Hartranft's majority in Pennsylvania in 1872 totaled more than thirty-five thousand.[136] The AOH stronghold vote, with many Labor Reformers among them, had helped place Hartranft in the governor's chair.

For the second time in three years, the labor vote had helped wrest the governorship from Pennsylvania's Democratic candidates, men with ties to railroad and coal interests. Like railroad president Asa Packer, Buckalew, Franklin Gowen's "right-hand man," had suffered a bruising defeat.

Growing AOH Influence Generates a Pushback

Charles Buckalew and Franklin Gowen met again in 1873 as Democratic delegates, when both helped revise Pennsylvania's state constitution. Decisions made behind closed doors in Philadelphia included revocation of the governor's pardoning power and the restructuring of Schuylkill County's court system. Both issues would weigh directly upon the upcoming "Molly Maguire" trials, where both Gowen and Buckalew would serve as prosecutors.

Events included other menacing harbingers. From 1872 to 1875, when Hartranft sought reelection, sensational press accounts of so-called "Molly Maguire" outrages spread over a wide swath of the country, from Mississippi to South Carolina to Richmond to Washington to Baltimore, throughout Pennsylvania, including accounts in German, and north to New York and Boston. The Confederate sympathies of a number of Pennsylvania's Democrats likely influenced the southern press campaign.

Both failed Democratic gubernatorial candidates—Buckalew and Asa Packer—were skilled in press manipulation, as was their Democratic colleague Francis Hughes. While in the U.S. Senate, Buckalew had helped form a committee that prepared summaries of Senate proceedings for press distribution. In 1860, Packer had bought out the *Democrat* at Mauch Chunk and imported an editor from Philadelphia to promote pro-Confederacy views. In 1862, an outraged newsman in Lewistown had spoken of Hughes's proposal, while chairman of the Democratic State Committee, recommending that each county raise a "'poor fund'" to "pay for the publication of such articles as *he* might furnish, thus virtually placing the whole of the self-styled democratic press under the control of that demagogue."[137]

Yet more dramatic events helped inveigle coal region residents into belief in so-called "Molly Maguire" terrorism. In May 1873, Allan Pinkerton, on the verge of bankruptcy, advised his men to go to Gowen and "suggest some things."[138] Pinkerton had no doubt that Gowen would give them work. Five months later, Pinkerton operative James McParlan entered the coal region undercover. After McParlan's appearance, nine murders took place. The same month that McParlan entered the region, the *Boston Pilot*, that city's Roman Catholic diocesan newspaper, ran correspondence from the coal region that conflated Ancient Order of Hibernian (AOH) membership with "Molly Maguire" terrorism. The *Pilot's* willingness to publish such nativist propaganda underscores the clergy's growing uneasiness over the rising, expanding influence of the AOH.

Three days before McParlan's initiation into the AOH, the *Chicago Tribune*, published from the city that housed Pinkerton's headquarters, accused coal region AOH officers, including John Kehoe's predecessor, Bernard Dolan, as "Molly Maguire" terrorists. In 1874, as part of his plan to save his struggling business, Pinkerton started a dime novel press. Three years later, he published *The Mollie Maguires and the Detectives*. Pinkerton's nativist propaganda helped convince many, including coal region juries in five anthracite counties, of the existence of "Molly Maguire" terrorists.

Throughout this period, despite the published libels against them, coal region AOH men accelerated their political activity. In August 1874 Christopher Donnelly, serving as an AOH officer in

Schuylkill County with John Kehoe, helped secure the nomination of James Reilly to U.S. Congress. Sensational press accounts of fictional "Molly" outrages, including accounts from Pottsville, site of Reilly's nominating convention, accelerated. Circulation of fictional accounts continued after Reilly's election to Congress.

In 1875, when Hartranft sought reelection as Pennsylvania's governor, the Democratic politicians who would control the "Molly Maguire" caseload had one candidate left to offer. Votes from AOH strongholds would help determine the outcome of this contest as well.

In Pennsylvania's anthracite region, electoral politics would intertwine with Labor Reform advocacy and a spate of coal region murders. The mix would leave two of Kehoe's relatives, including a young pregnant mother, dead in a murderous early morning raid at Wiggan's Patch. Following the attack, the actions of coal region clergy under the direction of Philadelphia's archbishop, James Frederick Wood, would bolster Gowen's Pinkerton agenda of alleged "Molly Maguire" terrorism. The judicial authority of Cyrus Pershing, the Democrats' third successively disappointed gubernatorial candidate and president judge during the "Molly" trials, would hover malignantly over all of these disturbing events.

Cyrus Pershing's Treacherous Political Trajectory – 1856-1872

In July 1869, the *Raftsman's Journal* in Clearfield gave an unvarnished opinion of Cyrus Pershing's legal abilities. Pershing's ambition to Pennsylvania's Supreme Court bench fired the paper's opposition. This "third-rate, Cambria county lawyer," the paper said, was "a 'poor stick' out of which to make a Supreme Judge, and fortunately for the honor of the State, there is not the slightest prospect of his election."[139]

Two months later, the Clearfield paper again assessed Pershing's abilities. He had, it said, delivered two political speeches at Clearfield, both "intensely Copperhead—and as shallow as a summer mud-puddle." Pershing's professional inability made him "about as fit for Judge of the Supreme Court as a two days old pup is for watch dog."[140]

In Somerset, the *Herald and Whig* described Pershing as "'a third or fourth-rate country lawyer, enjoying a plodding business as a scrivener and general county counsel.'"[141] A Bedford County editor called Pershing's nomination for justice "one of the most unpardonable blunders ever committed by a political party." This candidate, unsuited for the bench, had one merit only, "even in copperhead eyes ... his bitter partisanship."[142]

"He is a poor lawyer," the *Raftsman's Journal* said in mid-August 1869, "having no love for, or pride in his profession, and is utterly unqualified, in every respect, for Judge of the Supreme Court."[143] Pershing's poor reputation reached even to the Midwest. The *Chicago Post* reported Pennsylvania's Democratic press "in a muss" over the spelling of the candidate's name, "some, in accordance with the 'eternal fitness of things,'" spelling it "Perishing."[144]

Pershing's embrace of nativism surfaced in 1856, when he served for a few months as an interim editor in Johnstown. That year, Millard Fillmore launched his third-party bid for the U.S. presidency through the Know Nothing Party. In March, Pershing published an editorial titled "A Picture of Know-Nothingism." In it, this future judge of dozens of Irish Catholics in the so-called "Molly Maguire" cases called for the merging of the Know Nothing Party into mainstream politics. "Its spirit," Pershing said, "—and we admit that there is a good deal that is peculiar and laudable, too, in its spirit—would have been better spent if infused into other parties to correct their motives and their action." Without such infusion, Pershing observed, the Know Nothing movement would never reach "the highest place in the nation."[145]

More than a decade after Pershing endorsed the laudable spirit of Know Nothingism, Pennsylvania's Democratic State Central Committee endorsed Pershing's "'ability and high character.'"[146] A Bedford editor, unconvinced, warned that the election of "the partisan pettifogger Pershing" to Pennsylvania's highest court would transform it "from a tribunal of justice to a mere machine for partisan purposes."[147] From Philadelphia, the *Telegraph* urged voters "to avoid the calamity of the election of a fifth-rate lawyer to the Supreme Bench."[148]

Despite Pershing's endorsement by the *Cambria Freeman* as an "upright, incorruptible man,"[149] Pershing lost the race for Pennsylvania's Supreme Court justice by four thousand votes. He returned to private practice and his office on Franklin Street in Johnstown above Benton's Hardware Store.

From that office, Pershing had not simply drawn wills and conveyed properties for Johnstown's residents. Pershing had also served for two decades as resident counsel for the Pennsylvania Railroad. Pershing, Cambria County's four-term Democratic state representative, was also corporate attorney for Thomas Scott's Pennsylvania Railroad.

Three years after Cyrus Pershing's unsuccessful run for justice of Pennsylvania's Supreme Court, the self-professed nativist ran for office again. Pershing's unexpected bid in 1872 for president judge of Schuylkill County, site of more so-called "Molly Maguire" trials than any county in Pennsylvania, generated a bizarre split among that county's Democratic, Republican, and Labor Reform parties. Engineered by Franklin Gowen, Pershing's run for Schuylkill County's judgeship raised a smell as high as the highest game.

One hundred and eighty miles separated Pershing's hometown of Johnstown in Cambria County from Pottsville, county seat for Schuylkill County. In July 1872, Pershing placed his name in consideration for president judge of a county he had never seen. From June 1877 to January 1879, Pottsville would mount, under Pershing's authority, nine so-called "Molly Maguire" executions.

J. Walter Coleman, writing in 1936 of Schuylkill County's 1872 judgeship race, said that both Gowen, president of the Philadelphia and Reading Railroad, and Thomas Scott, president of the Pennsylvania Railroad, had secured Pershing's cooperation as "a worthy candidate from a county outside the coal region."[150] In early July 1872 three Schuylkill Democrats, including alleged "Molly Maguire" Edward Monaghan, Shenandoah's high constable, protested that Pershing's friends "had influenced men, by the use of liquor, to sign the election petition. The signers were shocked to find that they were inviting a corporation counsel to become a candidate to oppose Judge Ryon."[151] The *Shenandoah Herald* observed that if Pershing secured the office of judge, "'then Frank Gowen and Tom Scott can ... rejoice in the fact that they have gained a victory for corporate monopolies, which insures the final and complete overthrow of labor and private capital in the Schuylkill coal region.'"[152]

In a baffling move, John Siney once again sided with the railroad men against the interests of his own union members. On August 13, 1872, at the county Labor Reform convention at Woll's Tavern in Pottsville, Siney offered Pershing's name in consideration for Schuylkill County's president judge. After an "acrimonious and exceedingly personal debate," the Labor Reformers fell in with Siney's endorsement.[153] They chose Pershing, a life-long Democrat, as their candidate for the judgeship.[154]

The *Pottsville Standard* dubbed the Woll's Tavern convention "SINEY'S CIRCUS." Its proceedings, the *Standard* said, did not strengthen the cause of Labor Reform, but created a "marketable organization ... to attain the balance of political power in this county, always holding itself ready to join hands with the highest and best bidder."[155]

Two delegates from Kline Township bolted Siney's convention. In a signed card to the *Pottsville Standard*, they declared it "a trick and a fraud upon the Labor Reform Party," with the nominations of the "paid agents of corporations" made "through the lavish use of money." "We wash our hands of the whole thing," they concluded, declaring Siney's convention "a diabolical fraud against the rights of the laboring man."[156] The same day this card was published, Pershing wrote to Siney from Johnstown to formally accept the Labor Reformers' nomination.

Mahanoy City's Labor Reformers also rejected Siney's convention. In a published resolution, they said they could neither endorse its proceedings nor accept its ticket.[157] A few days later, Schuylkill County's Republican Party endorsed Pershing. Pershing now ran under two unfamiliar banners: those of Republicans and Labor Reformers. A correspondent to the *Pottsville Standard* who signed himself "Glan." heard Pershing's speech in Reilly Township and declared it "one tirade of bombastic falsehoods." All honest men should "beware of this leech," this "fanatical, malicious hypocrite."[158]

The *Pottsville Standard* declared Schuylkill County's judgeship race between Pershing and Democratic incumbent James Ryon "a pot-house brawl, as disgusting as it is degrading."[159] Ryon, an Irish Presbyterian and one-term state representative, had risen to Schuylkill County's bench in 1862. His commercial interests included banking, insurance, and canals. The Democrats' endorsement of Ryon for a second term alienated some delegates at Pottsville. "Many German Democrats," the *Miners' Journal* said, "declare themselves highly disgusted with the Convention of Monday."[160]

In late August, in a twist of historic irony, the *Pottsville Standard* published its alphabetical list of Democratic candidates in the order in which nominations would be made. Two names separated that of Cyrus Pershing for president judge from that of John Kehoe for state assembly.[161] "The growing Irish Catholic power in the Democratic Party manifested itself most perceptibly during the 1872 county Democratic convention," historians William Gudelunas and William Shade said of the convention that placed Kehoe's name in consideration. "The Irish were no longer just following. They now demanded a major share of the leadership in the Democratic Party of Schuylkill County."[162] The alarm shown by Schuylkill County's German Democrats at Irish political ascendancy presaged the ethnic conflict that roiled the "Molly Maguire" trials. "There was too much of a German slaughter there," the *Miners' Journal* concluded of the August 1872 convention proceedings.[163]

The fall 1872 campaign rolled on. Pershing, hedging his bets, continued to advertise his legal services from his office at Johnstown. From Clearfield County, just north of Pershing's home county of

Cambria, a paper applauded Pershing's nomination by Schuylkill's workingmen. The Clearfield editor reprinted the opinion of the *Mountain Voice* in Johnstown. It declared Pershing a candidate "learned in the law, upright and honorable in character, and spotless in reputation."[164]

On October 8, 1872, Pershing secured the office of president judge of Schuylkill County's criminal court by a three-thousand-plus vote majority. Of the more than eighteen thousand votes cast in the race, Pershing secured almost sixty percent of total votes cast.[165]

Siney's endorsement of Pershing as a Labor Reformer helped secure the win. The *Pottsville Standard* observed: "John Siney finds it up hill work explaining how the Democratic Labor Reformers were sold out."[166] Three decades later, Alexander McClure observed that it was "largely through [Franklin Gowen's] political ingenuity that Judge [Ryon] was defeated in 1872, and Judge Pershing chosen to succeed him.'"[167] On December 10, 1872, three years to the day before the murderous raid against Kehoe's family at Wiggan's Patch, Pershing took his seat on the bench of Schuylkill County's court.

From his seat on the judge's bench, Pershing watched as Schuylkill County's Irish Catholic politicians made dramatic gains from 1872 to 1875. In 1874, the county's Ancient Order of Hibernian (AOH) men selected Kehoe as county delegate and Christopher Donnelly as treasurer. Earlier that year, U.S. Congressman John W. Killinger, a Republican and "Good old [friend]"[168] to Kehoe, had introduced his bill on the floor of Congress calling for cooperative ownership of the U.S. railway system, with as few as ten men working in concert to own and operate a railway.

In November 1874, AOH efforts at Pottsville's Democratic nominating convention helped send James Reilly, a young Irish Catholic, to U.S. Congress. Under AOH leadership, Schuylkill's Irish Catholics were no longer political followers. They were sending their candidates, irrespective of party, to the nation's capital.

The following year marked another political bellwether in Schuylkill County. Pershing's bid for Pennsylvania's governorship fused the region's warring elements. Ethnic hatred, political jealousy, industrial machinations backed by British capital, Pinkerton agitation that ensured nine murders, and sensational press agitation that inflamed so-called vigilantism united in a face-off against Hibernian political advocacy. The response to the Hibernians' belief in the power of electoral action against massively wealthy industrial interests encapsulates, in one tragic narrative, the history of the U.S. Gilded Age.

The Last Failed Bid: Cyrus Pershing for Pennsylvania's Governorship – 1875

In 1875 Cyrus Pershing, in a ploy to win Pennsylvania's governorship, again coopted the workingmen's political agenda. In September, Francis Hughes crawled back from political exile to secure Pershing's candidacy at Erie. The *Sunbury American* declared the convention's three-day struggle "characteristic of political tricksters ravenous for office."[169]

The *New York Herald* declared the convention one of "political tramps and vagabonds," engineered by the worst of the commonwealth's Democrats.[170] "Nobody thought of him as a candidate," the *Herald* said of Pershing, "but the inflation triumph was his triumph also."[171] From Washington, the *National Republican* reported how "THE KEYSTONE DEMOCRACY" had "FONDLED THE RAG BABY" of paper currency.[172]

The *New York Tribune* declared Pershing's supporters at Erie a "howling mob."[173] Hughes served as chairman to the committee on resolutions. Through Hughes's influence Pershing, in a transparent grab at the workingmen's vote, adopted the Greenback Labor Reform platform that advocated paper currency. "Mr. Hughes was the personal champion of the successful candidate," the *Scranton Republican* said, "and he may well feel elated at his victory over the discomfited clans that went down, one after the other, as the banner of Pershing, in the hands of Hughes, swept by degrees to the front."[174] The *Somerset Herald* declared Pershing "the mere creature of accident ... a political hybrid with hard money principles on a rag money platform, 'conceived in sin and born in iniquity.'"[175]

From Pershing's hometown, an editor ridiculed both Pershing's platform and the man himself. "'He is a cunning, close-mouthed little man, who can worm himself into more places, say less, do less, and make more money by this course than any man on the continent,'" the *Johnstown Tribune* said. "'Here he is considered very thin material.'"[176] From Lancaster, the Naval Office organ reminded voters that during the Civil War, Pershing's support of the Southern cause "'was so intense ... that he shut his windows to avoid seeing the Union soldiers pass his house.'"[177] From Harrisburg, the *Telegraph* called Pershing, former counsel for the Pennsylvania Railroad, "an easily bribed and purchasable tool of that Colossal Corporation."[178]

Hughes, whose convictions blew with the political wind, had changed his own views on the currency question to capture the desired electorate. During the Civil War, Hughes had declared that the day would come when a bushel of greenbacks would not buy a bushel of potatoes. A decade later, on a soft money platform, he predicted a hundred-thousand-vote majority for Pershing.

At Pottsville, Hughes's ploy to seduce the labor vote worked again when *The Workingman*, the organ of the mineworkers' union, invited the fox into the henhouse. The mineworkers' standard-bearer declared that support for Pershing should come from the National Labor Union, the Industrial Congress of the United States, the farmers' Grange lodges, the Harrisburg Anti-Monopoly Convention, the Cincinnati Farmers' and Workingmen's Conference, "and all other bona fide laboring-men's organizations in the land."[179] The platform at the Erie Convention, that paper declared, had honored the workingmen's principles.

A month later, the *Harrisburg Telegraph* described Pershing as the "tool" of railroad presidents Asa Packer and Franklin Gowen. The same column reported a speech given at York by Hendrick Wright, chairman of Pennsylvania's Democratic State Central Committee, showing the determination of the Democrats under Hughes. Wright said of the commonwealth's Republican administration: "'I would sooner see this country torn asunder and reduced to a howling wilderness; I would rather see the people beggared, aye sooner see your children starving and your men and women driven to suicide for want of bread, than to see the present administration again at the head of this Government!'"[180]

From the anthracite region, Carbon County's Labor Reform Party endorsed Pershing's 1875 gubernatorial nomination, and that of Victor Piollet for state treasurer, "because we believe them to most fully represent the views of the Anti-Monopoly party."[181] But at Pottsville, one influential group remained unconvinced. There, in the fall of 1875, Ancient Order of Hibernian (AOH) men would meet with Republican Party operatives to help defeat Pershing, the favored political son of Hughes and Franklin Gowen.

Evidence of John Kehoe's campaign work in 1875 for the re-election of Pennsylvania's Republican governor John Hartranft against Cyrus Pershing surfaced in late 1878, a few weeks before Kehoe's execution for an alleged "Molly Maguire" crime. After Pershing's nomination at Erie on September 9, 1875, both Kehoe and his fellow AOH member John Slattery met at the home of Republican operative Joshua Sigfried in Pottsville. The men discussed the upcoming election. Three years later, Sigfried described Slattery as "a Democratic politician of much influence among the Irish," and Kehoe as "another influential leader among the Irish Democrats." Both Hibernians had advised Sigfried they would do "all they could" against Pershing, "even without getting a cent towards their expenses."[182]

In trial testimony given in 1876, Slattery said that Kehoe's task was to write to AOH officers statewide to secure support for Hartranft. AOH membership around that time numbered more than sixty thousand Irish Catholic men in Pennsylvania.[183]

In mid-October 1875 Bernard Dolan, who preceded Kehoe as Schuylkill County's AOH delegate, gave the Hibernians' rationale for backing Republican candidate John Hartranft against Pershing.

Dolan's correspondence gives further insight into the ongoing spinning of Irish Catholic votes, traditionally Democratic, toward the Republicans.

A few weeks before Hartranft's re-election, Dolan asked a local editor "under what obligations are we to the Democratic party, that we should blindly support an adventurer on the Democratic ticket in preference to a man who has been tried in private life, on the battle field, and in public life … The day is past when party ties bound men to vote as was dictated to them by the hireling of railroad corporations, or corrupt moguls of political combination." Of the Hibernian vote, Dolan said the order's men went to the ballot box "unprejudiced and unbiased, [to] vote for … men who will devote their time to secure the welfare of the Commonwealth, and assuage the sufferings of the poor laboring class, who they consider their brothers in toil."[184]

In late September 1875, that good feeling accompanied Hartranft to Luzerne County, where miners crowded the Central Hotel to shake the candidate's hand. Hartranft arrived at noon, as the men left the mines for their dinner hour. "Dirty and all blackened with coal as they were," a reporter said, "these laboring men crowded to the hotel and insisted on the freeman's right of shaking hands with the Governor."[185] Hartranft enjoyed the press of potential voters, and left with a hand blackened with coal dust.

Francis Hughes's ploy to cast sitting judge Cyrus Pershing as a friend to labor failed with the Hibernians. On November 2, 1875, Pershing did well in the anthracite region, a testament to Hughes's seduction of the workingmen's vote there. But Hartranft carried the state by more than twelve thousand votes. In the combined AOH strongholds of Pittsburgh, the western bituminous coal region, the northeastern anthracite coal region, and Philadelphia, Hartranft bested Pershing by more than fourteen thousand votes.[186]

"In October 1875, it was feared and courted by both political parties," Hughes's nephew Francis Dewees wrote from Pottsville of the AOH two years after Pershing's defeat.[187] Less than a year after Pershing's defeat, in an argument given in a showcase "Molly Maguire" trial, Franklin Gowen said of the AOH: "'I have seen this organization wield a political power in the State which has controlled the election of a great Commonwealth.'"[188]

A number of conflicts from 1871 to 1875 showcased the Hibernians' ongoing challenges to Gowen's railroad and coal interests. In two legislative investigations at Harrisburg, the region's anthracite mineworkers hoped to show Gowen that "'that they, and not the great railroad and other corporations that have assumed it, are the rightful sovereigns in this state.'"[189] Gowen would answer these challenges alternatively, with both an iron fist and a velvet glove. With his burnished rhetoric, he would seduce state legislators. With his starvation wages and his "restless, arbitrary ambition,"[190] he would smash the mineworkers' union.

---

1. *Mauch Chunk (PA) Coal Gazette*, February 23, 1872.
2. *Sunbury (PA) American*, September 9, 1871. The precise extent of Hester's, and AOH, involvement with Trevellick and the NLU remains unknown.
3. Statement of delegate Charles Foley, *New York Herald*, April 12, 1871.
4. John Kehoe to W. R. Potts, ca. March 1878, John Kehoe File, M 170.18 MI, Schuylkill County Historical Society.
5. *Shenandoah (PA) Herald*, January 10, 1874.
6. *National Labor Tribune* (Pittsburgh), March 4, 1876. For Morgan's attendance at Kehoe's Board of Pardons hearing in Harrisburg, see *Miners' Journal* (Pottsville, PA), April 12, 1878.
7. John O'Dea, *History of the Ancient Order of Hibernians*, vol. 2 (New York: National Board of the AOH, 1923), 885.
8. *American* (Washington, DC), September 23, 1857; italics in original, reprinting *Philadelphia Sun*.
9. Ibid.
10. Ibid.
11. *Glasgow (MO) Weekly Times*, October 8, 1857; italics in original, reprinting *Intelligencer*.
12. "A New Secret Order—The 'Molly Maguire,'" *Raftsman's Journal* (Clearfield, PA), October 14, 1857.
13. For Indiana, see "News Items," *Marshall County Republican* (Plymouth, IN), November 12, 1857; for Iowa and Illinois, see *Weekly Ottumwa (IA) Courier*; reprinting *Chicago Journal* dated November 19, 1857; for South Carolina, see "A New Secret Order," *Yorkville (SC) Enquirer*, November 5, 1857.
14. *Weekly Clarksville (TN) Chronicle*, October 16, 1857.
15. *Meigs County Telegraph* (Pomeroy, OH), October 27, 1857.
16. *True American* (Steubenville, OH), November 4, 1857.
17. *White Cloud (KS) Kansas Chief*, November 19, 1857.
18. *Miners' Journal* (Pottsville, PA), October 3, 1857.

19. Ibid. See also Kevin Kenny, *Making Sense of the Molly Maguires* (New York: Oxford University Press, 1998), 7.
20. "Know-Nothingism. Revival of the Native American Party in This City and State," *New York Herald*, October 6, 1873.
21. *Lewistown (PA) Gazette*, October 1, 1862.
22. *Jeffersonian* (Stroudsburg, PA), January 7, 1858; reprinting *Miners' Journal* (Pottsville, PA).
23. Ibid.
24. *Newbern (NC) Weekly Progress*, May 8, 1860.
25. *Columbia Democrat and Bloomsburg (PA) General Advertiser*, July 12, 1862.
26. *Potter Journal* (Coudersport, PA), July 16, 1862.
27. *Star of the North* (Bloomsburg, PA), August 20, 1862 (Hughes's address given in full).
28. Ibid., August 27, 1862; italics in original; quoting Hughes's letter dated August 11, 1862.
29. Ibid.; Seward's letter, dated August 19, 1862, given in full.
30. *Chicago Tribune*, September 1, 1862; reprinting *Chicago Post* dated August 29, 1862.
31. *Raftsman's Journal* (Clearfield, PA), October 8, 1862; reprinting *Miners' Journal* (Pottsville, PA) dated September 27, 1862.
32. Ibid.
33. Ibid.
34. Ibid.; italics in original.
35. Ibid.
36. Ibid.; quoting *Philadelphia Press* dated October 2, 1862.
37. *Union County Star and Lewisburg (PA) Chronicle*, October 3, 1862.
38. Reported in *Daily Intelligencer* (Wheeling, WV), October 21, 1862.
39. *North Branch Democrat* (Tunkhannock, PA), November 12, 1862.
40. *Council Bluffs (IA) Bugle*, January 21, 1863.
41. *Sunbury (PA) American*, October 10, 1863.
42. Ibid. The term "copperish" refers to Gowen's Copperhead tendencies, or his support, as a northern Democrat, for the Confederate cause.
43. *Star of the North* (Bloomsburg, PA), August 23, 1865.
44. Ibid., September 13, 1865; reprinting *Patriot and Union* (Harrisburg, PA).
45. Ibid.
46. Ibid., September 6, 1865.
47. Ibid.
48. Ibid.
49. *Columbia Democrat and Bloomsburg (PA) General Advertiser*, September 9, 1865.
50. Ibid.
51. "Democratic State Nominations," ibid., September 2, 1865.
52. *Star of the North* (Bloomsburg, PA), August 30, 1865; quoting *Williamsport (PA) Democrat*. For Charles Buckalew's remarks to Columbia County Democratic Party meeting at Bloomsburg in August 1865, see Robert M. Sandow, *Deserter Country: Civil War Opposition in the Pennsylvania Appalachians* (New York, 2009), 140.
53. *Raftsman's Journal* (Clearfield, PA), March 11, 1868.
54. *Delaware Tribune* (Wilmington, DE), March 12, 1868.
55. *Waynesburg (PA) Republican*, June 17, 1868.

56. *New York Sun*, June 29, 1868.
57. *Evening Telegraph* (Philadelphia), July 3, 1868.
58. Ibid., July 6, 1868.
59. *New York Herald*, July 6, 1868.
60. Ibid.
61. *New York Sun*, July 9, 1868.
62. *New York Herald*, July 11, 1868.
63. Ibid.
64. *Cleveland Morning Leader*, June 6, 1862 (from dispatch dated June 3, 1862, Mauch Chunk).
65. *Portland (ME) Daily Press*, July 7, 1868.
66. *Raftsman's Journal* (Clearfield, PA), September 29, 1869.
67. *Watertown (WI) Republican*, November 4, 1868.
68. *Evening Telegraph* (Philadelphia), November 4, 1868.
69. See *Evansville (IN) Journal*; *New Orleans Republican*; *Wheeling Daily Intelligencer*, November 4, 1868.
70. *Bloomsburg (PA) Democrat*, November 11, 1868.
71. *Cambria Freeman* (Ebensburg, PA), November 12, 1868; reprinting *New York Democrat*.
72. *Raftsman's Journal* (Clearfield, PA), July 21, 1869.
73. *Harrisburg Telegraph*, August 31, 1869.
74. *Sunbury (PA) American*, August 28, 1869; italics in original, reprinting *Reading (PA) Times*.
75. *Harrisburg Telegraph*, September 9, 1869.
76. Ibid., September 20, 1869.
77. *Raftsman's Journal* (Clearfield, PA), September 29, 1869; reprinting *Mauch Chunk (PA) Gazette*.
78. *New York Herald*, August 19, 1869.
79. *Raftsman's Journal* (Clearfield, PA), September 15, 1869.
80. Geary's address given in *Columbian* (Bloomsburg, PA), January 14, 1870.
81. Ibid.
82. Ibid. See also Kenny, *Making Sense*, 128.
83. "A Word to Pennsylvania," *New York Tribune*, October 18, 1869.
84. *New York Herald*, June 9, 1871.
85. Ibid.
86. Ibid., July 25, 1871.
87. *Evening Telegraph* (Philadelphia), July 14, 1869.
88. *Columbian* (Bloomsburg, PA), March 20, 1868.
89. Ibid., February 28, 1868.
90. *Bloomsburg (PA) Democrat*, June 3, 1868.
91. Ibid., April 15, 1868; italics in original.
92. For this assessment of Craig, see John P. Lavelle, *The Hard Coal Docket: One Hundred and Fifty Years of the Bench and Bar of Carbon County* (Lehighton: Times News, 1994), 130.
93. *Nashville Union and Dispatch*, June 26, 1868.
94. *New York Daily Tribune*, January 14, 1863.
95. Ibid.
96. Ibid.
97. Ibid.
98. *Cleveland Morning Leader*, January 16, 1863.

The Copperheads and the Hibernians | 89

99. *Evansville (IN) Daily Journal*, January 19, 1863.
100. *Star of the North* (Bloomsburg, PA), September 6, 1865.
101. For Brockway's speech, see *North Branch Democrat* (Tunkhannock, PA), September 20, 1865.
102. Ibid. Buckalew's letter, written from Quito, was dated December 26, 1858.
103. "White House," *Evening Star* (Washington, DC), February 17, 1866.
104. *Columbia Democrat and Star of the North* (Bloomsburg, PA), March 14, 1866.
105. Ibid., March 21, 1866.
106. *Evening Telegraph* (Philadelphia), December 13, 1866.
107. *Evansville (IN) Journal*, July 12, 1867.
108. *Evening Telegraph* (Philadelphia), April 8, 1871.
109. *Jeffersonian* (Stroudsburg, PA), May 14, 1868.
110. *Bloomsburg (PA) Democrat*, September 16, 1868.
111. Ibid., October 14, 1868.
112. "The Two P's.," *Raftsman's Journal* (Clearfield, PA), July 21, 1869.
113. *New York Herald*, October 11, 1869.
114. *Mauch Chunk (PA) Coal Gazette*, September 20, 1872.
115. *Northumberland County Democrat* (Sunbury, PA), February 23, 1872.
116. *Mauch Chunk (PA) Coal Gazette*, June 28, 1872.
117. *Sunbury (PA) American*, June 29, 1872; reprinting *Danville (PA) American*.
118. "Buckalew at Home," *Sunbury (PA) American*, July 20, 1872.
119. *New York Herald*, June 1, 1872.
120. *Sunbury (PA) American*, June 29, 1872; reprinting *Bloomsburg (PA) Republican* dated June 13, 1872.
121. *Forest Republican* (Tionesta, PA), October 2, 1872; reprinting *Commercial*.
122. *Sunbury (PA) American*, October 5, 1872.
123. Ibid.; reprinting *Bloomsburg (PA) Republican* dated June 13, 1872 quoting *Democratic Sentinel* (Bloomsburg, PA).
124. *Sunbury (PA) Gazette*, September 23, 1871.
125. In a discourse condemning the AOH, Rev. Daniel McDermott gave an oblique (and hostile) reference to two unnamed AOH men who helped file the AOH charter at Harrisburg. These two unnamed men included AOH officer Patrick Hester of Northumberland County, incarcerated in 1872 by Judge William Rockefeller on a charge of "riot" for burying an AOH member in St. Edward's Catholic cemetery at Shamokin against the wishes of the pastor, Father Joseph Koch. For McDermott's discourse against the AOH, including the quote against Hester, see "The Church and Secret Societies," *Catholic Standard* (Philadelphia), October 17, 1874: "A man, who afterwards acknowledged the iniquities of the society to the Bishop of Philadelphia, and promised to abandon it (a promise which was not kept) and another leader [Patrick Hester], now serving out a term of imprisonment for exciting a riot against a priest for carrying out the Bishop's instructions in regard to this society, were the worthy (?) Catholics who lobbied the charter through the Legislature." See also "The Church & Forbidden Societies," *Freeman's Journal* (New York), October 3, 1874.
126. *Report of the Case of the Commonwealth vs. John Kehoe et al.* (Pottsville, PA: Miners' Journal Book and Job Rooms, 1876), 167.
127. *New York Herald*, October 1, 1872.
128. Ibid.
129. Ibid., September 20, 1872.
130. Ibid., October 8, 1872.

131. *Alexandria Gazette*, October 1, 1872.
132. *New York Herald*, October 7, 1872.
133. *Evening Star* (Washington, DC), October 8, 1872.
134. *Wheeling Intelligencer*, October 10, 1872.
135. *Mauch Chunk (PA) Coal Gazette*, October 11, 1872.
136. For election results, see "The October Election. Official Returns Complete," *Cambria Freeman* (Ebensburg, PA), October 28, 1869; and "Pennsylvania. The Official Vote for Governor," *Jeffersonian* (Stroudsburg, PA), October 24, 1872.
137. *Lewistown (PA) Gazette*, October 1, 1862; italics in original.
138. Allan Pinkerton to George Bangs, 18 May 1873, Box 47, Folder 7, Pinkerton's National Detective Agency Records, Manuscript Division, Library of Congress, Washington, DC.
139. *Raftsman's Journal* (Clearfield, PA), July 21, 1869.
140. Ibid., September 29, 1869.
141. *Bedford (PA) Inquirer*, August 6, 1869; quoting *Herald and Whig* (Somerset, PA).
142. Ibid., August 13, 1869.
143. *Raftsman's Journal* (Clearfield, PA), August 18, 1869.
144. *Bedford (PA) Inquirer*, August 20, 1869; reprinting *Chicago Post*.
145. *Johnstown (PA) Echo*, March 5, 1856.
146. Address reported in the *Evening Telegraph* (Philadelphia), September 22, 1869.
147. *Bedford (PA) Inquirer*, September 24, 1869.
148. *Evening Telegraph* (Philadelphia), September 28, 1869.
149. *Cambria Freeman* (Ebensburg, PA), October 7, 1869.
150. J. Walter Coleman, *The Molly Maguire Riots: Industrial Conflict in The Pennsylvania Coal Region* (Richmond: Garrett & Massie, 1936), 68.
151. Letter of James Duffy, Edward Monaghan, and F. Neuman, *Shenandoah Herald*, July 8, 1872; discussed in Coleman, *Molly Maguire Riots*, 69, n. 89.
152. *Shenandoah Herald*, September 5, 1872; quoted in Coleman, *Molly Maguire Riots*, 68.
153. *Pottsville (PA) Standard*, August 17, 1872.
154. Ibid.
155. Ibid.
156. Ibid.
157. Ibid., September 7, 1872 (resolution dated September 3, 1872).
158. Ibid., October 5, 1872 (letter dated October 1, 1872, New Mines).
159. Ibid., August 24, 1872.
160. *Miners' Journal* (Pottsville, PA), August 28, 1872.
161. *Pottsville (PA) Standard*, August 24, 1872.
162. William A. Gudelunas Jr. and William G. Shade, *Before the Molly Maguires: The Emergence of the Ethno-Religious Factor in the Politics of the Lower Anthracite Region, 1844-1872* (New York: Arno Press, 1976), 120.
163. *Miners' Journal* (Pottsville, PA), August 28, 1872.
164. *Clearfield (PA) Republican*, August 28, 1872; reprinting *Mountain Voice* (Johnstown, PA).
165. See "Schuylkill County Election Returns—Official," *Miners' Journal* (Pottsville, PA), October 12, 1872.
166. *Pottsville (PA) Standard*, October 19, 1872.
167. Alexander K. McClure, *Old Time Notes of Pennsylvania*, vol. 2 (Philadelphia: John C. Winston Co., 1905), 434.

168. Kehoe to Potts, ca. March 1878. In this letter, Kehoe told Potts: "I will write a long letter to John W. Killinger him & me used to Be Good old friends."
169. *Sunbury (PA) American*, September 17, 1875.
170. *New York Herald*, September 11, 1875.
171. Ibid., September 10, 1875.
172. *National Republican* (Washington, DC), September 10, 1875.
173. *New York Tribune*, September 10, 1875.
174. *Scranton (PA) Republican*, September 14, 1875.
175. *Somerset (PA) Herald*, September 22, 1875.
176. *Forest Republican* (Tionesta, PA), September 15, 1875; quoting *Johnstown (PA) Tribune*.
177. *Clearfield (PA) Republican*, September 22, 1875; quoting *Lancaster (PA) Examiner*.
178. "How $500 Changed Pershing's Views," *Harrisburg Telegraph*, September 16, 1875.
179. *Clearfield (PA) Republican*, September 29, 1875; reprinting *Workingman*.
180. *Harrisburg Telegraph*, October 27, 1875.
181. *Cambria Freeman* (Ebensburg, PA), October 29, 1875.
182. Sigfried's assessment given in *Philadelphia Times*, November 27, 1878; reprinting *Philadelphia Press*.
183. Per account in *Boston Pilot*, May 22, 1880, of AOH national convention, Philadelphia: "Prior to the Molly Maguire troubles, the Order of Hibernians had a membership of about 63,000 in Pennsylvania."
184. Dolan's letter printed in the *Miners' Journal* (Pottsville, PA), October 13, 1875.
185. *Sunbury (PA) American*, October 1, 1875; reprinting *Philadelphia Press*.
186. "Pennsylvania Official—1875," *Cambria Freeman* (Ebensburg, PA), November 12, 1875.
187. F. P. Dewees, *The Molly Maguires: The Origin, Growth, and Character of the Organization* (1877; repr., New York: B. Franklin, 1969), 228.
188. Gowen's speech in the trial of Thomas Munley quoted in *New York Sun*, July 29, 1876.
189. Ibid., February 22, 1875.
190. From interview with John Kehoe, *Philadelphia Times*, June 27, 1877.

4
THE FIRST GREAT CONTEST

His [Franklin Gowen's] arbitrary action soon brought on what is well known as "the long strike" in 1874 and 1875. It was, indeed, a long and bitter contest—a desperate hand-to-hand battle between capital in the purse of one man and labor scattered and weakened by suffering.

John Kehoe to Cathcart Taylor
Pottsville Jail, June 1877

TWO SEMINAL CONFLICTS bookended the anthracite miners' plight that helped drive Pennsylvania's "Molly Maguire" prosecutions: its Long Strike of 1875 and its Great Strike of 1902. Both, to borrow John Kehoe's phrase, were "long and bitter" contests. Both showed the miners' need for the union in the face of dangerously inhumane working conditions. Both saw the clash of the coal operators' elitism against the union's ideology of fair rights for all. Echoes of both conflicts reverberate throughout U.S. political discourse.

An earlier skirmish that included three groups predated, and presaged, the Long Strike of 1875. In it, Franklin Gowen, President of the Philadelphia and Reading Railroad, united with other coal and railroad interests to challenge the aims of the Workingmen's Benevolent Association (WBA), the regional mineworkers' union that included a number of alleged "Molly Maguires" among its members. All of the alleged "Mollies" belonged to the Ancient Order of Hibernians (AOH), an Irish Catholic benevolent order. This early clash between Gowen and the WBA and AOH men played out through the winter and spring of 1871, during the second term of Pennsylvania's Republican governor, John Geary.

On the appointment in April 1869 of Gowen as president pro tem of the Philadelphia and Reading Railroad, the *Columbian* said from Bloomsburg: "Mr. Gowen is a young gentleman of decided talent, and from his acquaintance with the duties of the office and the interests of the coal-trade, as well as from his conciliatory manner, it is believed that [his] administration will be popular and satisfactory to all parties."[1] Under this delusional prediction, Gowen began his railroad career.

Born in Philadelphia in 1836, Gowen was the son of an Episcopalian Irish immigrant father and a mother of German descent. For a short time as a young boy, he attended school with his older brothers at Mount St. Mary's in Emmitsburg, Maryland. He left Mount St. Mary's for Beck's Boys Academy in Philadelphia. At age thirteen, Gowen left school to work for a Lancaster County merchant. From there, he moved to anthracite coal retailing with his brother Thomas in Shamokin, Northumberland County. Then came a partnership in a Mount Laffee coal mine north of Pottsville, an enterprise that dissolved into bankruptcy; then the reading of law in the office of Pottsville attorney Benjamin Cumming. In 1860, Gowen joined the bar of Schuylkill County. He opened his own law office. In 1862, voters elected Gowen district attorney for Schuylkill County, a position he held for two years. In 1864, Gowen accepted the appointment of head legal counsel for the Philadelphia and Reading Railroad. In 1869, he became president pro tem, replacing Charles Smith, who was in poor health at the time.

In 1870, Gowen accepted the railroad's presidency outright. The annual report for 1869, at the end of Smith's conservative stewardship, listed a gross income for the company at just over eleven million dollars, with profits at 3.2 million dollars. At the time, the railroad enjoyed a virtual monopoly over the transportation of anthracite coal from the Schuylkill region. But it had no control over production. If the union or the coal operators called a suspension, the Reading's cars sat idle.[2]

Less than two years into Gowen's tenure as Philadelphia and Reading president, the *Anthracite Monitor* refuted the *Columbian's* rosy prediction of Gowen's popularity with all. The *Monitor* served as the organ for WBA. The union men's paper said that while some viewed Gowen as "a great lawyer and a shrewd, far-seeing business man," what really characterized the railroad president was his willingness "to bolster a weak cause by willfully distorting and misrepresenting facts." Of Gowen's monopolistic aim, "the absorption of all the coal lands of this country by the Reading road," the *Monitor* concluded: "He is doubtless a crazy man."[3]

The *New York Herald* reprinted the *Monitor's* view. The *Herald* concurred with the *Monitor*, at least on Gowen's willingness to distort facts. Four days after the *Herald* reprint, Gowen appeared before the Judiciary Committee of the Pennsylvania Senate. At issue was his abrupt, and draconian, tripling of coal region freight rates. Six other coal carrying and mining interests, including three Scranton concerns as well as Asa Packer's Lehigh Valley Railroad and Charles Parrish's Lehigh Coal and Navigation Company, joined in Gowen's ploy in spring 1871 to cripple the anthracite region's independent coal operators.

The concerted plan on the part of the railroad interests to drive the smaller coal operators out of business, thereby weakening the mineworkers' union, intersected with an ongoing strike by the WBA for an increase in wages. Neither the miners nor the small coal men could operate under Gowen's stranglehold freight rates. Governor

John Geary of Pennsylvania, who authorized the senate investigation, said: "'I mean that the workmen shall have justice if there is a law compelling it in the State, and I hold it is the duty of the Executive to protect labor, even before capital, for that can protect itself.'"[4]

The challenge to Gowen's action that led to the senate investigation came from the precise group that Gowen esteemed the least: Schuylkill County's Irish Catholic mineworkers. On March 11, 1871, in the midst of the mineworkers' strike, the *New York Herald* published an article datelined March 9, 1871. It originated from Mahanoy City, an Irish Catholic stronghold in Schuylkill County. "The miners," the article said, "finding their hopes of success from every quarter frustrated, turned, as a last resort, to Governor Geary. They waited until the carrying companies had increased their tolls to such a fearful and unheard of rate that they violated their charters (in the estimation of the miners) and then preferred formal charges against these companies and induced Geary to institute an official inquiry."[5] Mahanoy City, site of the mineworkers' existential challenge to Gowen's railroad company, served as home at that time to future AOH delegate John Kehoe, and to Kehoe's father and two grown brothers. Kehoe, a former miner, kept a tavern. His father and brothers, all mineworkers, were probable WBA men.

An article printed a few weeks before by the *New York Sun* had described the efforts of Mahanoy City's miners on behalf of the poor of the Eastern cities. Concerned that the ongoing strike for higher wages would entail a higher cost of coal to consumers, the WBA men had offered a resolution. "The Mahanoy City branches," the *Sun* reported, "are proposing to resume work for two days without charge to GET OUT COAL FOR THE POOR."[6]

On March 8, 1871, the legislative proceedings against Gowen and his fellow railroad men opened at Harrisburg. The following week, the *New York Herald* headlined the "Farcical Character of the Proceedings," conducted by the "Judiciary Whitewashing Legislative investigating [sic] Committee." Of the question of abrogation of railroad company charters, the *Herald* said: "It is plain to the most superficial observer that the investigation is a farce ... the end has already been determined upon ... Those who are posted will tell you that the railroad men have 'fixed' the committee, and the investigation is just as sure to result in the discomfiture of the miners as if it was written on the walls."[7]

"Money Power of the Railroads Overcoming Legislative Honesty," the *Herald* said in the same report. "The railroad men have the game in their own hands ... Gowen, who was summoned merely as a witness, assumes alternately the character of plaintiff, counsel and defendant with perfect impunity, instead of trying the main question at issue, whether the railroads have or have not violated their charters."[8]

Central to Gowen's game was the introduction into the public conversation of alleged terrorism by union men. The WBA leadership, Gowen told the senate committee, had been "seduced ... by some few politicians" into believing that could control the coal industry. Gowen said: "There has never been, in the most despotic government in the world, such a tyranny, before which the poor laboring man has to crouch like a whipped spaniel before the lash, and dare not say that his soul is his own. ... I say there is an association which votes in secret, at night, that men's lives shall be taken, and that they shall be shot before their wives, murdered in cold blood, for daring to work against the order.'" He added: "'the only men who are shot are the men who dare to disobey the mandates of the Workingmen's Benevolent Association.'"[9]

A violent incident at Mount Carmel in Northumberland County five days before Gowen gave his first testimony to the senate committee gave credence to Gowen's claim. The attempted bombing of a boarding house frequented by non-union workers, along with the shooting death of George Hoffman, a boarder at the house, had aroused the coal region. "THE MOUNT CARMEL MURDER," a *New York Herald* headline ran six days after the attack. "The 'Molly Maguires' on the War Path. THE 'DEVILS' OF THE MINES."[10]

The WBA offered a five-hundred-dollar reward for information on the attack's perpetrators. Whoever launched the fatal raid at Mount Carmel, it included a killing that precipitated no arrests and no seeming investigation. Its timing played beautifully into Gowen's campaign against the WBA.

The facts of Pennsylvania's "Molly Maguire" caseload, along with those of other Pinkerton caseloads, suggest that in addition to being professional con men, late-nineteenth-century operatives of the Pinkerton National Detective Agency were also commercial terrorists, hired to commit violence to further their clients' industrial aims. Gowen's relationship with the agency dated to early 1870. New York journalist John Swinton, who attended the 1875 Anti-Monopoly Convention at Harrisburg, observed years later that "Pinkertons were used not only as strikebreakers and spies but as *agents provocateurs*, deliberately creating violence which was often used to discredit the labor movement and frame up and imprison its members."[11]

The same week that Gowen gulled the senate legislative committee, Pennsylvania's AOH men, including alleged "Molly Maguire" Patrick Hester and possibly other coal region AOH officers, also traveled to Harrisburg on organizational business.[12] On March 10, 1871, AOH men oversaw the filing of revisions to their benevolent order's charter. On March 11, Pennsylvania's legislature instituted the new document. The same week, Hibernians in New York City filed an almost identical revised document with their state legislature.

The language of the revised AOH charter, filed in March 1871, dovetailed with the willingness of Mahanoy City's miners to work without pay the previous month to help supply coal to the poor. The charter's introduction advised: "Brethren: It is beyond all doubt that the Supreme Being has placed man in a state of dependence and need of mutual support from his fellow man. ... Therefore, the Supreme Being has implanted in our natures tender sympathies and most humane feeling towards our fellow creatures in distress, and all the happiness that human nature is capable of enjoying must flow and terminate in the love of God and our fellow creatures."[13]

AOH men later charged as "Mollies" moved in other potent arenas that spring. At Mauch Chunk, future site of Carbon County's seven "Molly Maguire" hangings, WBA delegates with at least two "Mollies" among them met in Grand Council proceedings to urge arbitration for the settlement of strikes. In this gathering, described by the *New York Herald* as an "Immense Politico-Industrial Organization—A New Power Forming in the Land," delegates also discussed the election of workingmen to political office.[14]

The *Shenandoah Herald* said of Grand Council delegates: "A majority of the members of the present Council are young men, and are certainly, as a whole, the most intelligent and respectable body of representative miners we have ever seen together ... from their earnest, serious bearing it is very evident that they appreciate the responsibilities attending their position."[15]

The *New York Herald* continued to disparage Gowen's credibility. Of Gowen's performance before the 1871 legislative investigation, the *Herald* said: "He, within the rest of the railroad men, are making the whole matter a good joke, and haven't the least apprehension of its ultimate result. ... His great endeavor is to fasten upon the miners. The charges of murder and conspiracy at first made against them, [have been] amply disproved."[16] The *Herald* concluded: "The investigation is considered by disinterested parties one of the most barefaced frauds that has [ever] characterized the Pennsylvania Legislature."[17]

Some weeks later, as the miners' strike continued, Gowen's company made a wage offer to the WBA men. They declared it "'a trap, a snare, and a delusion,'" one that bore "'on its face the impress of the mind of that wily schemer, F. B. Gowen.'"[18]

"He will be welcomed home by his many friends," the *Miners' Journal* said from Pottsville six months later, after Gowen's return from a European sojourn, "not solely on account of his prominent connection with one of the most important railways in the country, but because he has won by his courtesy and social qualities the esteem and approbation of those who have had the pleasure of personal intercourse with him."[19]

The following year, the *Mauch Chunk Coal Gazette* said: "Gowen is regarded by the men in every region (but especially in Schuylkill) as the man who is, more than all others, responsible for all the ills of the miner. He has been the persistent opponent of the men at every step. Instead of compromising, he has wanted to crush ... he has no feeling, no sympathy for the poor man."[20]

Seven months later, a *New York Sun* reporter spoke with urban coal dealers, in Philadelphia and elsewhere, about Gowen's ongoing plan for monopolization of the country's coal trade. "Mr. Gowen's power is too great to be resisted," the reporter said. "They [the coal dealers] aver that his insatiate greed for the company's welfare will not stop until he had national or ENTIRE CONTROL OF THE COAL MARKETS throughout the whole country."[21]

A year later, the *New York Times* characterized Gowen's coal cartel as "the well-known and unscrupulous 'Philadelphia and Reading Railroad combination.'"[22] The year after that, as Gowen's influence intensified, the *Columbian* at Bloomsburg spoke of Gowen's "huge but elegant monopoly." It wished, the paper said, "to call public attention to what is being done by powerful corporations to crush the spirit and absolutely control the great laboring interest of the country."[23]

In April 1875, an unnamed correspondent to a Danville paper reflected on the legislative chicanery in 1871 that had helped bring Gowen's "illegitimate bantling,"[24] the Laurel Run Improvement Company, into its current incarnation as the Philadelphia and Reading Coal and Iron Company. The paper said of the correspondent: "The writer was a member of the Legislature at the time and ... predicted that this act was the germ of a monster which in time would crush out every private coal operator in the Schuylkill valley, and after that, reduce the operative to the condition of a serf."[25]

By 1875, four years after its inception, the Philadelphia and Reading Coal and Iron Company had, with the use of borrowed capital, acquired one hundred thousand acres of anthracite coal lands. But Gowen had built his house on sand. By the end of 1875, the Philadelphia and Reading subsidiary's bonded debt totaled more than sixty million dollars.

In late winter 1875, in their second effort in four years, Schuylkill County's mineworkers again helped initiate a legislative investigation into Gowen's company charter. The 1871 investigation had dealt with freight rates. The 1875 investigation struck at the heart of Gowen's plans for control of the hard coal trade. It threatened the right of the Philadelphia and Reading Railroad to own and mine coal land under its charter.

The paper trails left by Pinkerton operatives' reports, however carefully culled, hint at some uncomfortable truths. "The Legislature of Pennsylvania," Allan Pinkerton wrote in 1877, "listening to the repeated demands of the dissatisfied and the call of the Anti-Monopoly Convention ... in 1875 appointed a committee to investigate the affairs of the Philadelphia and Reading Company."[26] Pinkerton also noted the attendance at the Harrisburg convention of AOH member and alleged "Molly Maguire" Michael Lawler, WBA delegate from Schuylkill County.[27] In March 1875, the so-called "Mollies" entered Pennsylvania's legislative halls to challenge Gowen directly.

Gowen's seduction of the 1875 legislative committee proved even more persuasive than his 1871 courtroom performance. He hosted the second committee at Atlantic City, where he provided state legislators with lavish hotel accommodations that included visits to brothels. "The allegations were abandoned," Pinkerton concluded of the legislative challenge to Gowen's company.[28]

In April 1875 John Smythe, a coal region physician, wrote a letter to the *Boston Pilot*. Smythe deplored "the cunning" of Gowen in "ruining the small operator and starving the miner."[29] Two years later, Gowen challenged the Brotherhood of Locomotive Engineers, a national union that included a number of his employees. Union officers described Gowen's published challenge of them "not the truth, but a plausible tissue of falsehoods."[30] Five weeks after that, the *Tamaqua Courier* described Gowen as "a cold blooded tyrant, a merciless task master."[31]

A few weeks after that, five days before the mass hangings of six AOH men in the jail yard at Pottsville, a Lehighton paper published an interview of Gowen. Given to the *London World* during Gowen's trip to England, the interview described Gowen's plans to secure his company's mortgage after his expenditure of fifty million dollars to purchase anthracite coal lands. Of Gowen's character, the London paper said: "he is unquestionably a man of the highest integrity."[32]

Six days after the mass hangings at Pottsville, John Kehoe, incarcerated for alleged "Molly Maguire" crimes, spoke to a Philadelphia reporter from Pottsville Jail. "'Let me tell you who Gowen is,'" Kehoe told the reporter. "'His whole course as president of the Reading road has shown him to be a man of restless, arbitrary ambition, with such grasping tendencies that no obstacle, however sacred, was ever allowed to interpose between him and his end.'"[33]

In January 1875, at the onset of Pennsylvania's Long Strike, union officer and editor of the *Pottsville Workingman*, C. Ben Johnson, said of preparations by Schuylkill County's mineworkers: "'In almost every little hut or cabin ... will be found several barrels of flour, a half or whole hundred of bacon, or a hog or two, a tub of sourkrout, a few pounds of tobacco, and such like necessaries and sundries. With these and a resolution not to succumb as long as there is hope left, they will set themselves down and quietly abide the result.'"[34]

By the end of 1874 Franklin Gowen, president of the Philadelphia and Reading Railroad and Philadelphia and Reading Coal and Iron Company, had organized Schuylkill County's remaining independent coal operators into the Schuylkill Coal Exchange. The pooling system controlled the county's production and distribution of anthracite. Throughout the autumn of 1874, regional operators organized under Gowen's Coal Combination had stockpiled enough hard coal to see them through a long work stoppage.[35]

Their coal stockpile safely in hand, operators in the Schuylkill, Lehigh, and Wyoming regions announced wage cuts. From Wilkes-Barre, in the Wyoming region, the *Chicago Tribune* reported: "there is a powerful spirit of opposition rife, and the men may determine upon a strike at any moment. At a large and enthusiastic meeting of the miners last night they were advised to oppose the corporations at any risk, and to live on corn-meal, if necessary, rather than accept the reduction to starvation wages."[36]

In early January the *Workingman's* editor wrote to the *Philadelphia Press* to plead the mineworkers' case. Gowen's profits, Johnson said, "must be made good at enormous cost to the consumer on the one hand, and by reducing the miners to a state of semi-starvation on the other."[37] By early January 1875, mineworkers had suspended production in the Schuylkill and Lehigh coal regions, from Pottsville to Mahanoy City to Hazleton. The following week, the *New York Sun* said: "The general feeling is that there will be a great strike."[38]

Almost three decades after the strike's end, Joseph Patterson, secretary for the Executive Board of the Workingmen's Benevolent Association (WBA) in Schuylkill County during that turbulent time, addressed an audience at Pottsville's Historical Society. "What did the Union do for miners?" Patterson asked his audience in 1908. The union collected dues, he told them, and distributed funds to the injured and disabled. In a region that had no hospitals, it sent men out to nurse those injured in the mines. It served as a watchdog for fair wages and resolved grievances between mineworkers and operators. It lessened frictions among the different nationalities "and brought them together, to more generous relations, and a recognition ... that they were brothers and ought to work with and for each other. It educated the miner into a state of watchfulness as to what affected the market price of labor, and how demand and supply bore on his relation to his employer. It made him more independent by giving him the backing of organized friends." Finally, it "did positively" increase the mineworkers' wages.[39]

In mid-January 1875, striking miners at Hazleton issued a circular. They asserted: "'the people at large will at least see that our demands are reasonable, and that the refusal to accede is rather based on the tyranny and force of capital than on fair and equitable dealing.'" The strikers added that under six years of union protection: "'We have learned to live; we have learned to send our children to school instead of making them work in tender youth, to assist their fathers to earn bread for the family.'" They entreated the coal operators: "'Gentlemen, be just; consider the poor families of your workmen; consider that you are rich and we are poor; consider the future; consider eternity, and we are not afraid that you will speak any more about reducing the wages of your laborers.'"[40]

Two months into the strike, anti-monopolist and WBA officer John Shanahan of Mount Carmel described its necessity. "'We have to do hard, dangerous work,'" Shanahan said in Patrick Ford's *Irish World*, "'and we should not be asked to do that work and want one-fourth the common necessaries of life.'"[41]

Added to that, some miners, notably Irish Catholic mineworkers who had lived the consequences of Ireland's Great Hunger, feared the corrosive influence that a large influx of British capital into regional industry could have on the anthracite region's wellbeing. In their view, British financial policy had played a substantial role in the death of one million in Ireland and the forced emigration of two million more. Irish workingmen in the United States feared similar inhumane treatment from U.S. industries backed by British capital, with excessive rates of interest that would inevitably undercut the workingmen's wages. Their people had starved once under absentee British rule. They did not want it to happen again.

In April 1875, John Siney sought help for Pennsylvania's striking miners at the Industrial Congress of the United States, held in Indianapolis. Workingmen's delegates there adopted a unanimous resolution condemning the anthracite mineworkers' wage cut offered by the "combination of six monster coal-mining and carrying corporations" organized under Gowen. Those corporations, the delegates observed, would impoverish their mineworkers "by the fact that to make themselves monopolies they have borrowed and invested many millions of British capital, on which they are pledged to pay rates of interest which are excessive, onerous, and oppressive; and, whereas, the effect of the success of their schemes will be a practical repetition of the effect of what is known in history as 'Irish absenteeism.'"[42]

Parties on both sides described the conflict in terms of war. "'This is not a war on the part of the company against the price of coal, it is directly against our organization,'" John Welsh, president of Schuylkill County's WBA, said of the Philadelphia and Reading Coal and Iron Company.[43] The *Harrisburg Patriot* called the struggle "a war between corporate power on the one side and the rights of men upon the other, to which the general public is a party in interest."[44] The *Sunbury American* said it was "from the first ... a struggle for supremacy."[45] Midway through the strike, the *New York Herald* described the conflict: "Two wild, thoroughbred chargers, the one Capital, the other Labor, await the sound of the official bugle before they dash on their reckless course to win or to lose."[46]

John Kehoe, in an interview from his cell at Pottsville Jail two years after the strike ended, described Gowen's obliteration of independent coal operators to create the Philadelphia and Reading's vast monopoly. Kehoe, too, raised the specter of British absenteeism. "'He ... began the work of absorbing all the collieries in the county,'" Kehoe said of Gowen. "'British gold was poured into his coffers.'"[47] At the strike's beginning, Gowen had privately revealed his policy to Benjamin Bannan, editor of the *Miners' Journal* at Pottsville. No compromise, Gowen told Bannan, "would be made with the union if the mines were shut down for two years."[48]

In early April 1875, amidst accusations of violence on both sides, including newspaper accounts of supposed "Molly Maguire" outrages, Gowen sent his superintendent John Wooten to Harrisburg to request that the governor send troops to the region. The *New York Herald* reported Gowen's demands. One of Gowen's dispatches warned: "'The bandits will disperse when the *posse comitatus* [sic] is at hand, but after they leave the bandits will emerge from their holes and continue their depredations.'" A second dispatch predicted "fearful destruction of property and probable loss of life" if troops failed to appear.[49]

As requested, Governor Hartranft sent the state militia to Hazleton, including two regiments of infantry and a battery of artillery. The *New York Herald* accused Luzerne County's sheriff of relying upon "mere rumors and sensational telegrams" as an excuse for demanding troops. "There is a very deep condemnation of Sheriff

Kirkendall on all hands," the *Herald* reported.[50] Two military companies sent to Schuylkill County were disbanded and stripped of their arms when they were found fraternizing with the striking miners.

Of the regional violence, a WBA officer from Hazleton told Hartranft: "The demonstrations and ... raids lately made in this Region were instigated by some of the bosses, and while we are sorry that only few men have taken part in this foolishness, yet we deem the presence of the military unnecessary and this association has at all times obeyed the law, and denounced any and every riotous or foolish demonstration."[51]

A Philadelphia reporter who visited the coal region noted that Gowen's company officers "and the operators generally go in no fear of bodily harm at all, and smile placidly at the idea of being made targets of by the terrible 'Mollie Maguires.'" The reporter believed that "the Company will fight the thing to the bitter end; it has money, power—so have the men, only the latter is of a different kind."[52] A *New York Tribune* reporter also visited the region. He found "more at stake than the question of wages. It is a struggle for the mastery." The conflict, he said, was "a battle between the men and their employers, with no deserters on either side."[53] WBA officer Hugh McGarvey, rejecting fictional stories of miners' outrages, said miners would preserve the peace, "'resolved to see whether they can be forced to work for rich capitalists for too little to live and too much to starve upon.'"[54]

In late April, the *New York Tribune* discussed the main challenge to the striking miners' success.[55] Only the lower regions had entered the strike. In the northernmost Wyoming region encompassing Scranton and Wilkes-Barre, operators had continued to mine coal and ship it to market. The refusal of the northernmost mineworkers to strike helped further the Coal Combination's aim to shatter the union.

As the strike wore on, union men at Hazleton reminded area residents of its origins. In May, four thousand strikers marched in the annual WBA parade. Thousands of women and children looked on from the sidelines. McGarvey, mounted on horseback, led the marchers. Four aides rode alongside. A carriage transporting speakers followed behind.

Behind the speakers' carriage came a horse-drawn wagon. It carried two rows of boys. One side held boys who were "clean, neatly dressed and made ready for the school." A banner above their heads read: "'Our boys as they should be.'" The other side held boys with blackened faces and ragged clothing. A banner above their heads read: "'Our boys as they are.'"[56]

A second wagon carried men who had been injured in the mines. Their banners read: "'Crippled but not Pensioned,'" "'We gave our bodies for the public good.'"[57]

The striking miners carried banners. "'Peace Must Prevail,'" one said; "'Our Cause is Just,'" a second. Others advised: "'A Poor Way of Picking Up an Education, Picking Slate,'" "'The Boys of To-day will be Our Future Citizens,'" and "'Our Calling Robs the Cradle and the School.'"[58]

The conflict tightened. "SYMPATHY WITH THE MINERS," the *Philadelphia Times* reported. "Mass Meeting of Philadelphia Workingmen in Independence Square."[59] From the main stand James Wright, a co-founder with Terence Powderly of the Knights of Labor, denounced the Philadelphia and Reading Railroad. Wright charged that Gowen's companies "had impoverished the miners, and had such potent powers that they controlled even the legislative bodies of the State, to the detriment of the laboring masses."[60]

The coal operators remained adamant. In New York, dealers for Gowen and Charles Parrish assured the *New York Tribune* that their companies would never yield to the miners' demands. Parrish set the fans in his mines running, a sign that his mineworkers would soon resume work at the wages he offered.

Inexorably, the strike wound down. Despite support from the Industrial Congress, the miners' larders emptied. In the Schuylkill region, individual operators at Mahanoy City resumed operations after mineworkers accepted a wage reduction. The *New York Herald* predicted that all of Schuylkill's miners would soon bow to the operators, and the Lehigh district would follow. "The monopolists are holding them with a hand of iron," the *Herald* said, "and can hardly be expected to relinquish the grasp, now that the end is apparently so near at hand."[61] In late May, the *Herald* said that the miners had made a good fight, "and their five months' resistance to the encroachments of the six combined gigantic coal companies must go upon the record as an epoch in the history of the miners' strikes in this State."[62]

On June 1, 1875, with the strike collapsing, a group of from three to five hundred mineworkers who refused to give up marched fifteen miles southwest from Hazleton to Mahanoy City to intimidate the miners there who had agreed to come to terms. The marchers from Hazleton camped in the woods overnight. The next morning, they traveled from colliery to colliery, convincing mineworkers to walk off the job and swelling their ranks with additional marchers.

The morning after that, on June 3, several hundred men gathered at West Shenandoah Colliery to urge Gowen's mineworkers to walk out. A posse of Coal and Iron Police, armed with rifles and led by Pinkerton operative Robert Linden, met the crowd and dispersed it before the marchers could act. During the strike's last days, the upheaval in Schuylkill County helped turn public sympathy away from the mineworkers.

Years later, a newspaper account gave credence to the belief that coal operators had encouraged violence to drain sympathy from the mineworkers' cause. Almost three years after the fact, an act of industrial terrorism brought Pinkerton operative James McParlan's name to the fore. This industrial sabotage had taken place near Mount Carmel, more than fifteen miles west of Mahanoy City and thirty miles southwest of Hazleton. On June 3, 1875, miners at William Schwenk's colliery had been at work for two days, having accepted reduced wages. In the evening, an unknown crowd of men had rushed Schwenk's breaker, the massive wooden structure used to crush coal, and set it on fire.

Almost three years later, the *Philadelphia Times* reported the arrests of eight alleged "Mollie Maguires" for complicity in the burning of Schwenk's Mount Carmel breaker. "McParlan, the detective, was with the rioters then, ostensibly the worst of the gang," the

Times reported. "After rioting all day, but committing but few outrages, about thirty of the most daring went to Schwenk's colliery and after setting it on fire deliberately sat down and played cards while it burned to the ground."[63]

By the second week of June 1875, the mineworkers faced defeat. "Unconditional surrender is now the ultimatum of the great corporations," the *New York Herald* reported from Wilkes-Barre, "and the miners must either submit to the companies' terms or step down and out of their little houses within the next ten days."[64]

The miners memorialized the end of the Long Strike in a poem. "Well, we've been beaten," they said, "beaten all to smash; And now, sir, we've begun to feel the lash, / As wielded by a gigantic corporation, / Which runs the commonwealth and ruins the nation."[65]

As for the union, "It's gone up where the gentle woodbine twineth." The union lamp, the miners said, "no longer shineth."[66]

From Danville, Thomas Chalfant of the *Intelligencer* warned of the dangers inherent in the destruction of the mineworkers' right to associate. Chalfant declared this "an American right, and dark will be the day to the United States when that right cannot be enjoyed. Our liberties then will have rotted away beneath our feet."[67]

News accounts reinforced the urgent need for union advocacy and legislative reform, especially for mine safety. In March, the *New York Tribune* reported from Wilkes-Barre, where miners still worked the Epsy mine. "To-day," the *Tribune* said, "a miner named Anthony Rotham was smothered by falling dirt in this mine, and it will be closed until his funeral has taken place."[68]

On May 13, 1875, the Hanover Colliery near Wilkes-Barre closed its doors for the day. The temporary stoppage honored John Rignari. "The deceased," an account said, "who leaves a wife and four children, was crushed to death by a heavy fall of rock from the roof."[69]

Pennsylvania's bituminous coal region shared the dangers. In late June, two miners at the Eureka mines in Washington County suffered injuries from a fall of slate. One escaped with a broken arm. The second was badly crushed and not expected to live.[70]

In a column published around the same time, the *New York Herald* said: "Every day has brought its casualty, involving the death of one or more unfortunates, and last Saturday six men were hurried into eternity, at one time, in the shaft of No. 2 mine of the Susquehanna Coal Company at Nanticoke. This horrible sacrifice of human life in one industry leads to the suspicion that the mine owners are in some way neglectful of the well being of those who work for them."[71]

Accounts of injuries continued. Months later, the *Mauch Chunk Democrat* listed a roll call of those with fractured limbs and those killed by falls of coal. On December 21, 1875, William Richards, age twelve, was killed by a breaker roller at Woodside. "It is supposed his foot slipped on the chute while leaving his work at quitting time," the mine inspector's account read. "The rollers were covered over and a piece of plank about 4 x 18 inches was in front of the chute, just allowing room for coal to slide into the rollers, and we presume this piece broke when he slid against it, causing room for his legs to go through, and the rollers caught them, pulling him with such force as to lift the covering up, causing instant death."[72] Rollers designed for the breaking of coal had crushed the body of a twelve-year-old boy.

By 1877, two years after the union's defeat, wages had dropped to less than half those paid in 1869, when the WBA was in its ascendancy. The hard coal miners' hopes of sending their boys to school had given way to hopes of buying food sufficient to send them to slate-picking rooms.

In April 1877, two months before the first mass hangings of alleged "Mollies" at Pottsville and Mauch Chunk, the *Pittsburg* [sic] *Commercial* said of a report from Pottsville detailing local conditions: "A terrible tale of suffering and starvation among miners in Schuylkill county is told ... by a mine superintendent, who knows whereof he speaks. He tells of miners going to work with empty dinner kettles, not liking to expose their poverty, who seek solitude during the dinner hour for fear their real condition should become known to their fellow workmen."[73]

Men striking for better wages in Luzerne County in September

1877 fared little better. They told a *New York Sun* correspondent that if they had to starve, they would do it aboveground. A *Sun* headline read: "Dry Bread, Mush, and Potatoes—Meat an Almost Unknown Luxury." The reporter noted that upon "excellent authority ... a very prominent capitalist" had given his views on strikes in general and workingmen's wages in particular. The unnamed industrialist said: "'My policy in managing laboring men is to keep them so poor that they cannot strike.'"[74]

In late June 1877, Henry Pleasants, chief engineer at Gowen's company office at Pottsville, described the condition of Gowen's Irish mineworkers. Pleasants wrote to George De B. Keim, the company's pro tem president, less than a week after the first mass hangings. "The Irish are very poor," Pleasants said, "and having given their last dollar towards the defence [sic] and burial of the Mollies, are left without enough to eat. Men go to work in the mines with only a crust of bread in their dinner cans. They blame our Company for the hanging of innocent men and their hatred of the Company is very great at present."[75]

In early July 1877, a correspondent who signed himself "Vigilantibus" wrote to the *Boston Pilot* from Mahanoy City. A few weeks before, the commonwealth had executed six Hibernians on the gallows at Pottsville, twelve miles to the south. "During the war and afterwards," the correspondent said, "when the coal-heavers had a union, their wages were sufficient to support themselves and their families." Two years after the union's breakup, the men worked for starvation wages, "scarcely able to keep body and soul together, and the coal operators ... squeeze the very vitals and existence out of these poor men, that they may fill their own exchequer, many of these miners trembling upon foot for want of food, and unable to go to work. This is a pretty state of things under the Stars and Stripes." The Irish mine laborers, "the Hewers of Wood and the Drawers of Water," were paid the least, and suffered the most. Vigilantibus concluded: "This state of things was not known previous to the monopoly of the Philadelphia & Reading Railroad Co., in getting possession of nearly all the coal mines in Schuylkill County, and

Generalissimo Gowen has made desolation desolate in these regions."[76]

In a column published in late May 1877, the *New York Sun*, surprisingly, corroborated Vigilantibus. "*THE READING RAILROAD'S DISTRESS*," this headline ran. Gowen's scheme of monopolization of Pennsylvania's hard coal trade, balanced on just a few hundred thousand dollars of borrowed English capital, had started to collapse. The miners' fear of "absenteeism" in Pennsylvania's coal region had come to pass. Gowen's mine supervisors now squeezed "the utmost amount of work ... out of the half-starved miners, until it is safe to assert that as much work is got out of one of them as used to be done by two men in times when they were able to feed themselves well." Some of the region's best miners, per the *Sun*'s correspondent, "are now working [two] weeks for the price of a barrel of flour."[77]

Of Gowen's business plan, the *Sun* said: "Wherever you look in these regions you behold the evidences that the corporation experiment, so far as combining the mining and carrying of coal is concerned, is a total failure. It has a tendency to ruin and crush out two most useful classes of people, the workingmen and business men, and create a most hated petty aristocracy."[78]

Of Gowen's English stock and bondholders, the *Sun* said: "If the man who wrote up the evils of 'Irish Absenteeism' were to come here he would find material enough for a grand blast on 'American Absenteeism.' He would find that the foreign bond and stock holders are getting the cream of our great natural wealth, and that the Reading Company alone, when it meets its obligations, pays an amount annually to its foreign creditors and stockholders equaling $1.50 for every man, woman, and child in Pennsylvania, and for which no return is afterward received ... American interests are now being entirely subordinated to the foreign."[79]

In 1878, an unnamed miner summed up his feelings in a letter to a friend. The letter included a poem. A reference in the miner's poem from that long-ago day located Pennsylvania's anthracite region in the "West." It closed:

> If in exchange for the labor of a day
> You wish to have an honest fair day's pay;
> If you do wish to have just rights among
> Those of freedom of action, speech and
>   tongue;
> If you do wish to have a fair supply
> Of wholesome food, be buried when you die
> With decent rites—by this I mean at least
> Sufficient to distinguish man from beast,
> Stay where you are, or, if you must go hence
> Go East, go North, go South, no
>   consequence,
> Take any one direction, you'll be blest
> Sooner with what you seek than coming
>   West.
> In short, if you wish to enjoy God's bounty,
> Go anywhere except to Schuylkill County.[80]

---

1. *Columbian* (Bloomsburg, PA), April 23, 1869.
2. For Gowen and suspensions, see Wayne G. Broehl Jr., *The Molly Maguires* (Cambridge, MA: Harvard University Press, 1964), 109-110.
3. *New York Herald*, March 12, 1871 (printing advance copy of editorial published in *Anthracite Monitor* (Tamaqua, PA) on March 11, 1871).
4. Quoted in *Shenandoah (PA) Herald*, March 23, 1871.
5. *New York Herald*, March 11, 1871.
6. *New York Sun*, February 27, 1871.
7. *New York Herald*, March 17, 1871.
8. Ibid.
9. Testimony of Franklin Gowen, *Session of 1871. Miscellaneous Documents, Read in the Legislature of the Commonwealth of Pennsylvania, During the Session which commenced at Harrisburg the 3d of January, 1871* (Harrisburg: B. Singerly, 1871), 1531. See also Kevin Kenny, *Making Sense of the Molly Maguires* (New York: Oxford University Press, 1998), 146.
10. *New York Herald*, March 9, 1871. The attack at Mount Carmel appears factual. It does not appear to have been investigated or prosecuted. No arrests were made. It did not feature in the subsequent "Molly Maguire" caseload.

11. Richard O. Boyer and Herbert M. Morais, *Labor's Untold Story: The Adventure Story of the Battles, Betrayals and Victories of American Working Men and Women* (1955; repr. New York: United Electrical, Radio, and Machine Workers of America, 2005), 69; italics in original.
12. The discourse of Rev. Daniel McDermott obliquely (and sarcastically) identified Hester as one of two "worthy (?) Catholics who lobbied the charter through the Legislature." See chapter 3, 89, n. 125.
13. AOH charter given in *Report of the Case of the Commonwealth vs. John Kehoe et al.* (Pottsville, PA: Miners' Journal Book and Job Rooms, 1876), 167.
14. *New York Herald*, April 12, 1871.
15. *Shenandoah (PA) Herald*, April 13, 1871.
16. *New York Herald*, March 18, 1871.
17. Ibid., March 17, 1871.
18. Quoted in Marvin W. Schlegel, *Ruler of the Reading: The Life of Franklin B. Gowen* (Harrisburg: Archives Publishing Company of Pennsylvania, 1947), 31; originally published in *Anthracite Monitor* (Tamaqua, PA), April 29, 1871.
19. *Miners' Journal* (Pottsville, PA), November 4, 1871.
20. *Mauch Chunk (PA) Coal Gazette*, June 28, 1872.
21. *New York Sun*, January 15, 1873.
22. *New York Times*, January 8, 1874.
23. "Monopoly vs. Labor," *Columbian* (Bloomsburg, PA), January 8, 1875.
24. Ibid.
25. "The Struggle Between Capital and Labor," *Danville (PA) Intelligencer*, April 9, 1875.
26. Allan Pinkerton, *The Mollie Maguires and the Detectives* (1877; repr., New York: Dover Publications, Inc., 1973), 346.
27. Ibid., 258. Pinkerton identifies Michael Lawler here as "Muff Lawler."
28. Ibid., 350.
29. J. J. Smythe, M.D., letter to editor, *Boston Pilot*, April 10, 1875.
30. *Philadelphia Times*, April 27, 1877.
31. *Tamaqua (PA) Courier*, June 2, 1877.
32. *Carbon Advocate* (Lehighton, PA), June 16, 1877; reprinting *London World*.
33. Ibid., June 27, 1877.
34. *New York Tribune*, January 8, 1875; reprinting *Pottsville (PA) Workingman*. The *Workingman* was published previously under the name *Anthracite Monitor* (Tamaqua, PA).
35. At that time, the Coal Combination, along with the Philadelphia and Reading Railroad, included the Delaware and Hudson Railroad, under Thomas Dickson; the Delaware, Lackanna and Western Railroad, under Samuel Sloan; the Lehigh Valley Railroad, under Asa Packer; the Pennsylvania Coal Company, under George Hoyt; and the Wilkesbarre Coal and Iron Company, under Charles Parrish and Edward Clark.
36. *Chicago Tribune*, January 6, 1875.
37. *New York Tribune*, January 8, 1875; reprinting *Philadelphia Press*.
38. *New York Sun*, January 12, 1875.
39. Joseph F. Patterson, "Old W.B.A. Days," *Publications of the Historical Society of Schuylkill County*, 2: 376-77.
40. *New York Tribune*, January 13, 1875.
41. *Irish World* (New York), March 13, 1875.
42. *Chicago Tribune*, April 23, 1875.

43. *Philadelphia Times*, April 2, 1875.
44. *Cambria Freeman* (Ebensburg, PA), June 4, 1875; reprinting *Harrisburg Patriot*.
45. *Sunbury (PA) American*, June 4, 1875.
46. *New York Herald*, April 15, 1875.
47. *Philadelphia Times*, June 27, 1877.
48. Marvin W. Schlegel, *Ruler of the Reading: The Life of Franklin B. Gowen* (Harrisburg: Archives Publishing Company of Pennsylvania, 1947), 64.
49. *New York Herald*, April 3, 1875.
50. Ibid., April 11, 1875.
51. M. J. Heeney to John Hartranft, 8 April 1875, Box 5, Folder 2, Roll 4640; RG-10, Records of the Office of the Governor. Pennsylvania State Archives, Harrisburg.
52. *Philadelphia Times*, April 3, 1875.
53. *New York Tribune*, April 5, 1875.
54. *New York Herald*, April 14, 1875.
55. *New York Tribune*, April 27, 1875.
56. Parade description given in *New York Herald*, May 11, 1875.
57. Ibid.
58. Ibid.
59. *Philadelphia Times*, May 17, 1875.
60. Ibid.
61. *New York Herald*, June 1, 1875.
62. Ibid., May 27, 1875.
63. *Philadelphia Times*, April 13, 1878. In an additional example of Pinkerton instigation of violence during the Long Strike, McParlan's reports describe the actions of the Butler brothers, Patrick and John. Both masqueraded as AOH members. In trial testimony Patrick Butler admitted "that he was frequently employed on detective services by the Pinkerton Agency" (see *Miners' Journal*, Pottsville, PA, November 23, 1877). A McParlan report from late April 1875 discussed the Butlers' "pulling up of the tracks" of the Lehigh Valley Railroad, an act of industrial sabotage. At the AOH county convention, also per McParlan's report, Kehoe had knowledge of the Butlers' actions, and had "informed them at the convention, that if they committed any more such depredations they would be expelled for life from the organization." See James McParlan, operative report, ca. 29 April 1875, Box 1001, Reading Railroad Molly Maguire Papers, Hagley Museum and Library.
64. *New York Herald*, June 10, 1875.
65. George Gershon Korson, *Minstrels of the Mine Patch: Songs and Stories of the Anthracite Industry* (Philadelphia: University of Pennsylvania Press, 1938), 225.
66. Ibid.
67. "The Great Struggle," *Danville (PA) Intelligencer*, April 16, 1875.
68. *New York Tribune*, March 25, 1875.
69. *Chicago Tribune*, May 13, 1875.
70. *Somerset (PA) Herald*, June 30, 1875; reprinting *Uniontown (PA) Standard*.
71. *New York Herald*, June 29, 1875.
72. *Mauch Chunk (PA) Democrat*, January 15, 1876.
73. *Pottsville (PA) Chronicle* description of suffering given in *Pittsburg [sic] Commercial*, April 10, 1877.
74. *New York Sun*, August 4, 1877.
75. Henry Pleasants to George de [sic] B. Keim, 27 June 1877, Letterbook of Henry Pleasants, Reading Anthracite Company Collection, Pottsville, PA.
76. *Boston Pilot*, July 14, 1877.

77. *New York Sun*, May 30, 1877.
78. Ibid.
79. Ibid.
80. *Publications of the Historical Society of Schuylkill County*, vol. 4 (Pottsville, Pennsylvania: Historical Society of Schuylkill County, 1914), 184.

5

THE AOH CASELOAD: THE MEMBERS

You must love without dissimulation, hating evil, cleaving to good.

First U.S. AOH charter, 1836

… self-preservation is the first law of nature.

Michael Lawler
Prosecution witness and AOH bodymaster, 1876

Now the State wants this Jury to say that if this man McParland says that a human being shall live, he shall live; that if this man McParland says that a human being shall die, he must die. That is all they want in this case.

Clarence Darrow
Defense counsel, trial of Stephen Adams, 1907

On October 27, 1873, undercover Pinkerton operative James McParlan entered Pennsylvania's hard coal region under the alias "James McKenna." After McParlan's arrival, serial murders terrorized coal region residents. From September 1874 to September 1875, when the commonwealth's so-called "Molly Maguire" arrests began, nine murders took place in four hard coal counties: Carbon, Luzerne, Northumberland, and Schuylkill. A number of these, along with a number of older, unsolved murders, formed the basis of the "Molly Maguire" caseload. Three murders in the latter part of 1874—those of political operative John Reilly at Wilkes-Barre, Mayor George Major at Mahanoy City, and mine superintendent Frederick Hesser at Shamokin—gave warning signs of the conflict to follow.

Franklin Gowen, former legal counsel for the Philadelphia and Reading Railroad, assumed that railroad's acting presidency in 1870. In December 1871, through shady legislative maneuvering, Gowen formed the Philadelphia and Reading Coal and Iron Company as a subsidiary of the Philadelphia and Reading Railroad.[1] Through the Coal and Iron Company, Gowen eventually hired more than twenty Pinkerton operatives to conduct the "Molly Maguire" caseload. The Coal and Iron Company also employed its own private police force.

In 1873, Gowen hired McParlan to investigate the Ancient Order of Hibernians (AOH) in Pennsylvania's anthracite region. An international Irish Catholic benevolent order, the AOH was active at the time in Canada, Great Britain, Australia, and the United States. McParlan traversed the coal region undercover. As "James McKenna," he visited innumerable AOH lodges and compiled copious lists of officers and members, along with their home addresses.

Arrests of AOH men for alleged "Molly Maguire" crimes began in September 1875. Robert Linden, another Pinkerton agent in Gowen's employ, used McParlan's lists to draw up arrest warrants. Coal and Iron police employed by both Gowen's company and Charles Parrish's Lehigh and Wilkes-Barre Coal Company made the arrests. Arrests included more than seventy AOH men and a number of Irish Catholic witnesses who offered defense testimony. Prosecutors linked to railroad and coal interests charged these defense witnesses with perjury. A number served jail sentences, including fifteen-year-old Kate Boyle, a niece of one of the defendants.

Linden's authority also extended to Pennsylvania's newly crafted Board of Pardons, a board Gowen helped create as a delegate to Pennsylvania's 1873 Constitutional Convention. Two years before the "Molly" trials began, the revised constitution, ratified on December 16, 1873, by a large majority of Pennsylvania's voters, gave the new Board of Pardons, not Pennsylvania's governor, the power to authorize pardons in criminal cases. Pennsylvania's sitting governor, John Hartranft, consequently exercised limited authority over the "Molly Maguire" caseload.

Coal region residents, along with a wide public, learned of McParlan's identify in early May 1876, when defense counsel for AOH defendants cross-examined the detective. At Pottsville, alleged "Molly" defendants faced Cyrus Pershing, Gowen's hand-picked candidate for president judge of Schuylkill County's Court of Oyer and Terminer.

Schuylkill County's criminal court had disbanded on December 1, 1875, ten days prior to the raid on Wiggan's Patch. The court's disbandment had resulted from a "future amendment" to Pennsylvania's 1873 Constitutional Convention, where Gowen had served as a special delegate. The "future amendment" abolished the Court of First Criminal Jurisdiction for the counties of Dauphin, Lebanon, and Schuylkill and stipulated that "all causes, and proceedings pending therein in the county of Schuylkill shall be tried and disposed of in courts of Oyer and Terminer and Quarter Sessions of the Peace of said county."[2] As of December 1, 1875, Gowen's political collaborator, Pershing, controlled the outcome of Schuylkill County's criminal caseload.

To pursue Pennsylvania's "Molly Maguire" caseload, railroad and coal interests seized the police power through use of their own private forces and the instatement of numerous deputy sheriffs. They seized the executive power through their removal of the governor's power to grant pardons and the creation of the new pardon board, a board advised on the "Molly Maguire" caseload by Pinkerton operative Linden. In Schuylkill County, these men seized the judicial power both through Gowen's electioneering in 1872, which brought Pershing from Cambria County to serve as a judge, and through Gowen's stint at Pennsylvania's 1873 Constitutional Convention that restructured Schuylkill's court system. District attorneys in numerous counties routinely yielded their seats at the prosecution's table to these powerful, self-appointed, self-interested prosecutors.

Pennsylvania's industrial interests had good reason to desire the removal of the AOH from the political playing field. From 1869 to 1875, three successive Democratic gubernatorial candidates in Pennsylvania—Asa Packer, president of the Lehigh Valley Railroad; Charles Buckalew, former U.S. senator and Gowen's legislative wingman; and Pershing— had suffered defeat, partly at the hands of the Labor Reform Party. In late fall 1875 these badly bruised candidates, along with other influential Democratic Party operatives, helped Gowen fashion the commonwealth's "Molly Maguire" caseload. Packer sent his corporate counsel, Allen Craig, to Carbon County to craft trial strategy. Buckalew served as a prosecutor in Columbia County. Pershing served as president judge in Schuylkill County.

For the trials' supposed historical background, the prosecution relied on the work of Protestant Irish estate agent William Steuart Trench. Prosecutors also relied on the written reports of McParlan, and on scripts drafted from those reports by Linden, and possibly others.

Prosecutors tried men of mostly lower social standing first. Then they moved up to influential Hibernians who served as community leaders. The most prominent trials took place in Schuylkill County's Court of Oyer and Terminer, where Gowen's Coal and Iron police patrolled Pershing's courtroom.

The trials made abundant use of prosecution witnesses. These included influential Hibernian leaders who testified to escape their own prosecution. Under this carefully engineered system, Pennsylvania executed twenty-one so-called "Molly Maguires" in the anthracite coal region and imprisoned at least fifty more.

Pinkerton use of false testimony backed by perjured corroboration helped secure executions in five Pennsylvania hard coal counties from 1877 to 1879. Swayed by McParlan's testimony and the nativist propaganda of the press and the prosecution, juries in Carbon, Columbia, Luzerne, Northumberland, and Schuylkill counties helped place ropes around the necks of twenty-one Irish Catholic men and strangle them to death. At least twelve of the hanged men were aged thirty or older. Of these, at least three were aged fifty or older. The condemned men left behind at least forty-two children and an unknown number of grandchildren.

In Pennsylvania's western bituminous coal region, a similar Pinkerton scheme conducted during the same time frame failed almost absolutely. From 1878 to 1881, arrests of numerous Irish Catholic men as alleged "Mollies" in Allegheny, Fayette, and Westmoreland counties yielded few incarcerations and no executions.[3] In the eastern trials, Gowen's charisma and mesmeric force seduced jurors and district attorneys alike. Once Gowen secured the early verdicts of "guilt," similar verdicts followed easily.

In Pennsylvania's eastern coal region, the Pinkerton scheme incorporated sensationalist press coverage that broadcast cartooned images, in print and illustrations, of supposed "Molly Maguire" terrorism. Three books bolstered this campaign: *Realities of Irish Life* by Trench; *The Molly Maguires: The Origin, Growth, and Character of the Organization* by Francis Dewees, nephew to "Molly" prosecutor Francis Hughes; and Allan Pinkerton's *The Mollie Maguires and the Detectives*, made available to the public shortly before the first mass executions, while Pinkerton remained in Gowen's employ. All three books strengthened the image of "Molly Maguire" terrorism in the public mind.

During the trials, the myth of "Molly Maguire" terrorism sprang primarily from two sources: Trench's book, published in 1869, and the testimony of Pinkerton operative McParlan, given in 1876. The claims of both remain influential today. When aligned against the biographical facts of Pennsylvania's Hibernians convicted as "Molly Maguires," against the political agenda that drove the trials, and against McParlan's eventual unmasking thirty years later by defense counsel in Colorado and Idaho, the claims of Trench and McParlan invite disbelief, if not ridicule.

Three decades after McParlan testified in the "Molly" trials, he resurrected the Pinkerton script for use against the Western Federation of Miners (WFM). In Rathdrum, Idaho, in 1907, Clarence Darrow cross-examined the now-famous detective. Under Darrow's interrogation, courtroom spectators laughed at McParlan's shopworn Pinkerton fantasias trotted out thirty years after Pennsylvania's "Molly Maguire" trials.

By mid-1875, Franklin Gowen had decimated Pennsylvania's Workingmen's Benevolent Association (WBA), the regional mineworkers' union of the hard coal fields. But Gowen had not yet broken the rising power of the AOH. In the anthracite region, the order's men had achieved widespread success in local office, with at least five alleged "Mollies" elected as school directors, two as high constables, three as township supervisors, one as tax assessor, and one tapped as prospective tax collector for Carbon County. Before Gowen's evisceration of the WBA, at least five alleged "Mollies" had served as union officers.

AOH men embraced Labor Reform Party tenets. These included the proposed plan of John Kehoe's "Good old friend," U.S. Congressman John Killinger, for cooperative ownership of the U.S. railway system. In summer 1873, Schuylkill County's Labor Reformers chose alleged "Molly" John Slattery as a prospective senatorial nominee. In 1874, AOH efforts helped send James Reilly to Congress. In 1905, Alexander McClure said of Pennsylvania's alleged "Mollies": "The political power of this organization became next to absolute in Schuylkill County, and that domination lasted for a number of years."[4]

The AOH based its political ideology on tenets of Christian brotherhood. Its first U.S. charter, secured through the efforts of Irish Catholic men in New York City and Schuylkill County, advised members: "'You must love without dissimulation, hating evil, cleaving to good.'"[5] A clause from Pennsylvania's revised AOH 1871 constitution read: "Brethren: It is beyond all doubt that the Supreme Being has placed man in a state of dependence and need of mutual support from his fellow man ... has implanted in our natures tender sympathies and most humane feeling towards our fellow creatures in distress, and all the happiness that human nature is capable of enjoying must flow and terminate in the love of God and our fellow creatures." A poem from that charter's preamble advised: "Love guides the whole design."[6]

These profound sentiments helped swell AOH membership. By the mid-1870s, the order numbered more than sixty thousand men in Pennsylvania and more than seven hundred thousand nationwide. In the commonwealth's industrial regions, AOH tenets of cooperative ownership and advocacy for fair wages and safe working conditions threatened the industrialists' agenda of absolute control.

The leaders of the commonwealth's railroad and coal industries needed the subjugation of an underclass to achieve their commercial ends. In Pennsylvania in the 1870s, that meant Irish Catholics.

John Kehoe in particular challenged this caste system. In 1875, from his office as Schuylkill County's AOH delegate during a time of violent regional upheaval, Kehoe described the order as "a chartered organization, recognized by the commonwealth, and composed of men who are law-abiding and seek the elevation of their members." He added: "nothing can be more unjust than to charge the order with any acts of lawlessness."[7]

To break up this tightly woven, disciplined movement of social, political, and industrial reform, Gowen needed a countervailing strategy—a successful challenge to this benevolent order based on profound ideology.

After Allan Pinkerton solicited the "Molly Maguire" caseload from Gowen, Pinkerton's undercover operatives surged through Pennsylvania's eastern coalfields. Archived reports from the detective agency note more than twenty undercover men, most identified only by initials, assigned to Gowen's "Molly Maguire" operation.

"Pinkerton has now received a hundred thousand dollars from the coal-owners," D. J. Browne, a fallen-away Pinkerton operative, said in 1876. *"He has had men down there running saloons and in every capacity, yet not one has found out anything except* MacParlan [sic]."[8] In Massachusetts, an AOH member wrote to the *Boston Pilot* of McParlan: "Paid swearers will swear for pay, especially perjured ones ... I would not hang a fly on his oath."[9]

In August 1876, in an early "Molly" trial, defense attorney James Ryon said of McParlan, "he came here well supplied with money, and, with a shrewdness scarcely equaled, he has plotted all this deviltry, and carried it out to a most successful issue, because he succeeded in killing every man against whom his plans were formed."[10] In the same trial, defense attorney Martin L'Velle called McParlan "the emissary of death."[11]

James Kerrigan and Daniel Kelly, two corrupt AOH men, helped assure the success of Pennsylvania's "Molly Maguire" caseload. With the combined testimony of McParlan, Kelly, and Kerrigan, the commonwealth's prosecutors cut a swath of destruction across the hard coal region. The first trial, that of Michael Doyle for the murder of John Jones, set the template for future trials. It showed the extremes of the AOH defense strategy, whose counsel swerved wildly from passionate advocacy to treachery; the frightened bewilderment of the young AOH defendants; and the lengths to which the prosecution would go to secure the all-important first verdict of "guilty of murder in the first degree."

James Kerrigan joined the AOH in the early 1870s at Alexander Campbell's Columbia House in Tamaqua. In 1868 Campbell, at age thirty-five, had emigrated from Ireland's County Donegal to Pennsylvania's coal region. Within two years, Campbell had worked his way from mine laborer to miner to hotel owner. In 1875 Campbell, by then the father of a young family, served as delegate from Summit Hill to Carbon County's Democratic convention. Less than ten years after emigrating to Pennsylvania's coal region, Campbell had realized the American dream.

Kerrigan, born near Tuscarora in Schuylkill County, worked in area mines. The father of four, he drank and caroused. In trial testimony, he admitted abusing his wife. "I did use to give her some trouble," Kerrigan said, "but a good beating don't hurt a woman once in a while."[12]

Kerrigan spent time at Campbell's Columbia House bar. Campbell's acceptance of this suspect initiate into his AOH lodge remains a mystery. Within a few years of his AOH initiation, Kerrigan would be a self-confessed killer.

The details of Kerrigan's crimes unfolded gradually. At two in the morning on July 6, 1875, the wife-beater shot and killed police officer Benjamin Yost while Yost extinguished a gas lamp on a Tamaqua street. Two months later, Kerrigan's involvement in the murder of mine superintendent John Jones helped set the "Molly Maguire" juggernaut rolling.

Of Yost's murder, the *Pottsville Standard* said: "His death aroused the most intense excitement among his immediate friends and the citizens generally, and if his murderers could have been identified, they would doubtless have been strung up at the same lamp post at which Yost met his death."[13] As part of a citizens' committee formed to determine Yost's murderer Daniel Shepp, a brother-in-law of Yost's wife, and Michael Beard, a Tamaqua hotel owner, hired the Pinkertons to investigate.

Less than five weeks after Yost's murder, Welsh miner Gomer James was shot and killed at Glover's Grove in Schuylkill County while tending bar at a picnic for the Rescue Hook and Ladder Company. The assassin cut through the revelers, leveled a revolver at James, shot him dead, and disappeared back into the crowd.

On the same day that James was shot, August 15, 1875, a murder took place in Girardville. An assailant targeted Justice of the Peace Thomas Gwyther as Gwyther stepped out onto the porch of his office to deliver an arrest warrant after a bar fight. Gwyther, like James, fell dead on the spot. AOH delegate John Kehoe, Girardville's high constable, arrested a suspect on a warrant issued by a local squire. The *Pottsville Standard* said of Kehoe's subsequent actions: "While on the way to the justice's office, the constable and his prisoner were surrounded by an excited crowd, who brandished revolvers and knives, and threatened to take the latter's life. Another tragedy was only prevented by the coolness and courage of the officer of the law."[14]

Two weeks later, at seven in the morning on September 1, Thomas Sanger, inside colliery boss at S. M. Heaton and Co., left his house for work. William Uren, a miner who boarded with Sanger, walked out with him. A group of five men approached Sanger and asked him about work in the colliery. Sanger told them there was no work to be had. The men opened fire, striking Sanger six times. An assailant's bullet hit Uren in the groin.

The attack on Sanger and Uren took place before a large group of mineworkers, men and boys gathered in groups awaiting the opening of the day's work. Both Sanger and Uren received fatal wounds. "There can be no doubt," the *Miners' Journal* said, "that the death of Sanger had been decreed in some of those devilish conclaves of ruffians this country once knew so much about ... The assassins were strangers, imported to do the killing, and they chose their own time."[15] Sanger, an Englishman and a Mason, left a wife and six children. His youngest child was one month old.

The murder of Welsh mine superintendent John Jones followed two days later, at seven in the morning on September 3. The attack at the Lansford train depot five miles northeast of Tamaqua took place almost, as defense counsel Daniel Kalbfus said, "in the presence of a train full of passengers."[16] Two gunmen shot at Jones as he walked to work. When hit, he staggered toward the brush that lined the path. The men fired again. Jones struggled ten or fifteen feet up the hill. The assassins, intent on murder, pursued and fired a third time. Then they turned and fled.

With the recent murders of Yost, James, Gwyther, Sanger, and Uren in Schuylkill County, Jones's early morning murder inflamed locals almost into a lynch mob. The murder of this Welshman, father of seven, Mason, and mine superintendent for the Lehigh and Wilkes-Barre Coal Company ignited Tamaqua.

Samuel Beard, a young law student and the brother of hotel-keeper Michael Beard, witnessed Jones's murder at Lansford. Someone, perhaps Samuel himself, telegraphed news of the shooting to Tamaqua. Then Samuel returned to Tamaqua. There, with a friend, he took a spyglass to Odd Fellows Cemetery, on a hillside west of town.

The two men positioned themselves at the cemetery and waited. Sometime after noon, Kerrigan stepped out onto a footpath on the opposite hillside and waved his handkerchief. Defense counsel Kalbfus later said of Kerrigan, "he stood upon the hillside and waved his handkerchief, as much as to say, I am the man who did the killing."[17]

By their own account, mineworkers Edward Kelly and Michael Doyle, two young AOH men from twenty miles southeast in Schuylkill County, had arrived at Tamaqua by train "about noon" on the day of Jones's killing, five hours after the murder took place.[18] The young Irishmen, both dressed in dark suits, had met in Pottsville early that morning and taken the train together. Both were seeking work. They stopped at Tuscarora for a drink at a hotel and then traveled on to Tamaqua. Both later told a reporter, from their separate jail cells, that Kerrigan was a stranger to them. Their involvement with Kerrigan had consisted solely of asking him about local prospects for work.

If Kerrigan colluded with McParlan in the killing of Jones and the framing of Kelly and Doyle for Jones's murder, Kerrigan and McParlan had ample opportunity to refine their plans. McParlan's expense reports left a trail. The undercover Pinkerton operative expensed items in Tamaqua from August 12 through August 28. On five occasions between August 12 and August 27, McParlan claimed expenses for drinks with James Kerrigan. McParlan also remained in close contact with Pinkerton operative Robert Linden, claiming expenses for meetings with Linden on three occasions between August 16 and August 26.[19]

McParlan left Tamaqua on August 28 and returned to the town on September 2, the day before Jones's murder. He remained for three days. On September 4, per his expense sheet, he left Tamaqua for Mahanoy City. Both McParlan and Kerrigan were in Tamaqua on the morning of Jones's murder.

McParlan's status as a faux divisional AOH secretary in Schuylkill County gave him access to news, including travel plans, of fellow Hibernians. Telegraphs could flash this news instantly. Kerrigan's meeting with the two young Irishmen, traveling by train and on foot seeking work in their good suits, does not appear accidental. After meeting Kelly and Doyle, presumably near the train depot at Tamaqua, Kerrigan had led them up the mountainside to the spring. From there, he had signaled to Samuel Beard with his handkerchief.

Samuel Beard caught Kerrigan's signal and returned to Tamaqua. With his brother Michael and fellow townsmen, they formed a party of twenty or twenty-five men. The posse advanced up the mountain, where Kerrigan remained in position. When they arrived at the spring, they demanded the names of Kerrigan's companions. Both young men complied.

"Those men did not act as murderers," defense counsel Kalbfus said of Kelly and Doyle at Doyle's trial. "When they were stopped upon the highway for it they would not halt until told that their d---d hearts would be blown out."[20] One of the posse, a Welshman from Summit Hill, told a reporter that one of the Irishmen said to his captors: "'You are a nice set of men for arresting a fellow when he is looking for work.'"[21]

The posse marched Kelly, Doyle, and Kerrigan back down the mountain. They marched them through the streets of Tamaqua, where hundreds of townspeople had gathered. At Doyle's trial, defense counsel Lin Bartholomew described the suspects' march through town: "three men were arrested and taken through the main street of the borough of Tamaqua, where they were seen by everybody, their descriptions were circulated, and the next day published in the papers both in this county and Schuylkill county."[22] Newspaper gave descriptions of both Doyle's hat and Kelly's cap.

The posse marched the prisoners, amidst shouts for lynching, to the jail in Tamaqua. At the jail, they were stripped and searched. Officials secured the men in separate cells to question them. Then they placed Kelly and Doyle in a room together, "and the parties who had seen the shooting were brought in, one at a time, to identify them as being or not being the men who committed the murder."[23] Kerrigan, who "seemed to think that the precaution of keeping him in a cell was altogether unnecessary," remained hidden from view.[24]

Of the hundreds who saw the prisoners' march through Tamaqua, one hundred and twenty-two would serve as prosecution witnesses against Doyle. "To be marked by all these men," Bartholomew said, "these prisoners were placed upon an open track when they were taken to jail and they were kept in the prison and had the hat and the cap placed on their heads until the very boys on the streets could have drawn their pictures with a piece of chalk."[25]

Kalbfus said of the copious trial testimony against Doyle: "I say to you again that the slouch hat may hang Doyle but not the evidence. The same story told by all. How did you know him so and so? By his slouch hat; by his slouch hat, always the same answer to the same question." Every witness, Bartholomew said, "who came on the stand had the [description] pat."[26]

Six days after the arrest of Kelly and Doyle, the *Miners' Journal* published a report. An unnamed individual from Tamaqua had confirmed the finding of badges under the lapels of the suit coats of Kelly and Doyle. The badges bore the initials "A. O. H. ... the initials of that brotherhood known as the Ancient Order of Hibernians." The Pottsville paper added: "The reader is left to form his own conclusions."[27]

McParlan, still undercover, continued to file reports with his Pinkerton supervisors. On October 20, seven weeks after Jones's murder, with the trials of Kelly and Doyle pending, McParlan reported of AOH defense counsel, Lin Bartholomew and federal Congressman James Reilly: "Bartholomew and Reilly are confident of success and say they do not fear the result no matter how many witnesses the commonwealth may have."[28] On November 25,

McParlan repeated the assessment: "Lin Bartholomew and James B. Reilly ... are both confident of success."[29]

But sometime during the trials of Kelly and Doyle, their defense counsel's advocacy turned to treachery. Threatened, intimidated, or bought, the attorneys abandoned their clients. "THE DEFENCE [sic] HAVE NO CASE, AND OFFER NO TESTIMONY IN REBUTTAL," the *Mauch Chunk Democrat* reported after the commonwealth closed in Doyle's trial. The "surprise of all present," the *Democrat* said, "can hardly be described."[30]

During Kelly's subsequent trial, attorney Bartholomew's betrayal became especially pronounced. "Hon. Lin. Bartholomew virtually abandoned the case on Saturday," the *Democrat* reported in early April. "He was in the Court House but a short time on that day and yesterday he did not put in an appearance at all. This practical desertion of his client in the hour of extreme peril is variously commented upon, and in all cases to Mr. B.'s disparagement."[31]

The previous October, Bartholomew had argued strenuously for a change of venue in the cases of Kelly and Doyle and, at that time, Kerrigan. Then, Bartholomew had described "an influential combination ... [that] had passed witnesses and parties interested in this case along the line of railway free of charge, that their police had been working in concert with all parties interested in the conviction of the prisoners, and that everything which was possible to be done toward the conviction of the men was done."[32]

Later events helped explain Bartholomew's betrayal of his AOH clients. In August 1879, two months before the last "Molly Maguire" hanging took place, a local newspaper reported a summer sojourn to Europe by Franklin Gowen.[33] In Paris, Gowen was joined by Bartholomew and his traveling companion George Kaercher, district attorney for Schuylkill County during the "Molly Maguire" trials. In a letter to his father Kaercher, who was Gowen's law student before his election as district attorney, described the Paris rendezvous. The railroad magnate had treated the two lawyers to a fine dinner, and Bartholomew had spoken "'of the old Pottsville life ... when the old coterie ... made merry in the days that are gone.'"

Gowen, Kaercher added, "'heartily enjoyed the recollections of those days.'"[34]

The day after the group met for dinner in Paris, Gowen prepared a tour itinerary for the two Pottsville attorneys. They should, Gowen wrote to Kaercher, allow forty-three days from Paris to Munich "to do everything comfortably."[35] He mapped their route from Cologne to Coblenz to Biebrich, by Rhine boat, to Wiesbaden to Frankfurt to Heidelberg to Baden-Baden to Regi-Kulm, on Switzerland's Lake Lucerne, where they must not miss the sunrise. He suggested they visit the Castle of Chillon by lake transport. They should not miss the organ at Freiburg Cathedral, nor the illumination of Switzerland's Geissbach Falls. A week later, before returning to the States, Gowen wrote to Kaercher: "I write to wish you & Lin a very delightful time on your continental trip."[36] When Bartholomew returned to Pottsville from Europe, a local biographer noted: "His fellow citizens, of all shades of politics, united in giving him a public reception, which amounted to an ovation."[37]

One last source helps explain the defection of defense counsel in the trial of Doyle. James McParlan's friendship with Kerrigan, stated the work of author Francis Dewees in 1877, "caused him [McParlan] to be consulted upon every step taken for the defense." In particular, McParlan "consulted with Mulheran, a young lawyer,—an Irishman, —who went to Mount Laffee for the purpose of looking up the witnesses for the 'alibi' to be set up for Doyle and Kelly."[38]

McParlan sat through Doyle's trial at Mauch Chunk with every appearance of chagrin. He arranged his interviews with Pinkerton operative Linden, also present in the courtroom, "with skill and care." Dewees related: "Day by day, the exact position of the defense is disclosed, and night after night [it is] reviewed, discussed, and guarded against in General Albright's office."[39]

Other corrupt influences contaminated the prosecution's team. Carbon County's district attorney Edward Siewers, who years later would defraud his own mother,[40] willingly ceded his legal authority to railroad and coal interests. The checkered career of former Civil War general Charles Albright, counsel for the Lehigh and Wilkes-

Barre Coal Company, included reports from 1854 of Albright's scamming, in a fraudulent Kansas property scheme, of residents of Ebensburg, Pennsylvania.[41]

After the arrest of Michael Doyle and Edward Kelly for the murder of John Jones, newspapers made the prosecution's argument for them. The day after Jones's murder the *Shenandoah Herald* said of the murderers of Thomas Sanger and William Uren, "the men who committed the outrage ... belong to an organization formed for the sole purpose of committing such outrages as our whole region has teemed with during the last year ... the next man caught indulging his taste for blood will meet with the mercy he deserves—time to say his prayers and a rope."[42] A few weeks later, the *Herald* told readers: "There is an association of fiends in human shape in your midst. ... what is required of us all, of every man ... [is] to put his shoulder to the wheel and do all in his power and strain every nerve to wipe out that foul blot upon the good name of our country—the association known as the Mollie Maguires."[43]

The *New York Herald* said: "It is not doubted that there exists in the coal regions an excellently organized band of ruffians, called 'Molly Maguires' by some, who meet and select victims. Certain men are then deputed to slay these victims. A good deal of cunning is evinced, by the fact that men are always sent from one locality to another to commit the murders."[44] From Delaware came the report of assassinations of mine bosses, whose fate "is sealed by a secret society known as the Mollie Maguires."[45]

The *New York Times* amplified the vicious clamor. "A secret society known as the 'Molly Maguires' seeks to control all matters in connection with the management of the mines," it said. "The Molly Maguires are a well-organized body, and rarely betray each other or turn State's evidence. ... When the death-warrant is issued, the assassin or assassins are selected by lot, and the person or persons to whom such lot falls must, under pain of death, execute the commands of his lodge."[46]

In late January 1876, the trial of Doyle for the murder of Jones set the template for upcoming "Molly Maguire" trials. Real estate scam artist Charles Albright, counsel for Charles Parrish's coal company, served as prosecutor. A pamphlet published later that year giving Albright's argument in the Yost trial noted: "Charles Parrish, Esq., President of the Lehigh and Wilkesbarre Coal Company, determined to spare neither effort nor money to bring the murderers of John P. Jones to punishment, and demonstrate, if possible, that the power and majesty of the law were supreme."[47] Of Kelly and Doyle's arrest, Albright told Doyle's jury: "These two badges were found upon them ... those letters A. O. H. ... denote that it belongs to a society of Irishman." Albright added, "that society was admitted in argument and there are ramifications of old country organizations."[48]

Prosecutor Francis Hughes held aloft Kelly and Doyle's AOH badges for the jury to see. Irishmen could band for fellowship, Hughes said, "but there are large numbers of Irishmen who, to use the language of Father O'Connor, are the very scum not only of their race but of creation. ... this crime belonged to an organization that upon a requisition will commit murder."[49] Prosecutor Allen Craig of the Lehigh Valley Railroad said: "I am satisfied that these men were the hired assassins of some organization, and it must have been for the purpose of mutual recognition that they carried these badges."[50]

In 1994 John Lavelle, senior judge for the Court of Common Pleas in Carbon County, published *The Hard Coal Docket: One Hundred and Fifty Years of the Bench and Bar of Carbon County*. Of jury selection during the trials, Lavelle observed: "In October of 1875, a pool of jurors had been selected for the 'Mollie' trials in a way which violated their constitutional rights to a jury of their peers. Subtly but surely, the scales of justice had already been tipped against them."[51] Lavelle and a team of researchers examined the ethnicity of six hundred and forty prospective jurors whose names were placed in the jury wheel for Carbon County's trials. Of those six hundred and forty men, two were of Irish descent.

A number of prospective jurors did not speak fluent English. The *Shenandoah Herald* gave the account of those questioned in Doyle's trial. William Bloss, the first juror, said he could understand English "well enough to understand the evidence of the witnesses." Bloss took his seat in the jury box. Joel Strohl, cross-examined by defense counsel, said: "I understand most of what is said; don't write or read English or do business in English; am all Dutch ... don't always understand what is said ... it depends upon how high a word is whether I understand it or not."[52] Strohl, too, took a seat.

In Kelly's trial, counsel made no pretext of a full knowledge of English as a prerequisite for "Molly" jurors. Elias Koons said "that he didn't know English to any extent." Koons was sworn. Gabriel Gilger had "no scruples; at least he didn't object to hanging a man (his English was defective) ... he was sworn, and took the fourth seat." Reuben Snyder, described by the *Shenandoah Herald* as "a dumb Dutchman," took the sixth seat.[53]

Coal and Iron policemen for the Lehigh and Wilkes-Barre Coal Company secured the arrests of Kelly, Doyle, and Kerrigan. On the day of Jones's murder, they marched the prisoners from the jail at Tamaqua to the train depot. They guarded the handcuffed prisoners on their trip from Tamaqua to Mauch Chunk Jail via "a flat car ... the engine steaming off amid hideous yells."[54] They transferred the prisoners to the jail at Mauch Chunk, a massive freestone structure that fronted Broadway, located a half-mile up the hill from the courthouse. A sheet of boiler iron lined the jail's massive front door. A wall of stone, more than twenty feet high, surrounded the structure. A mounted cannon aimed its muzzle at the fortress-like structure. Three additional cannon inside stood "ready for an emergency."[55] The jail's first floor, surrounded by cells, included an indoor hall where executions could be staged.

After depositing their charges at Mauch Chunk Jail, six of Parrish's policemen tramped through town in uniform. While they patrolled the courtroom's aisles during the trials, former Civil War general and swindler Albright prosecuted in his dress uniform, sword dangling by his side.

Throughout his incarceration Doyle, born in Schuylkill County twenty-seven years before on George Washington's birthday, believed his country's laws would protect him. On his arraignment for the murder of Jones, Doyle threw himself "upon God and his country."[56] After defense counsel deserted him and German-speaking jurors convicted him, Doyle remained in Mauch Chunk Jail awaiting execution. In mid-March, he spoke to a reporter. Doyle drew the reporter's attention to his legs, cuffed and chained. "'You see I am chained and would like to let the people know it,'" Doyle said. "'I have to sleep in my clothes, and think that it's rather hard on a fellow.'"[57]

Doyle drew sketches to decorate his cell walls, including likenesses of himself and his fellow prisoners. A former militia member himself, he depicted a company of soldiers carrying the Stars and Stripes. On one wall, he hung the American flag.

A few days before Christmas, a reporter visited the jail. "'Doyle is just getting a bath,'" the keeper told him. The reporter, waiting, heard the rush of bare feet along the corridor. Looking out, he saw Doyle racing from one end to the other. Doyle ran until exhausted. "'This is the first run I have had since I came in here,'" Doyle told the reporter. "Poor unfortunate," the reporter said, "confined in jail for over fifteen months and shackled for almost a year, what a relief that short run must have been to him."[58]

The reporter interviewed Doyle in his cell. By this time, the young Irishman had drawn a sheaf of self-portraits. He asked the reporter to critique them, for, he said, "'you can tell better than I can whether they look like me, for I can't see myself.'" Doyle read the reporter one of his poems, written for the Christmas season. In one stanza, he mused: "For the time will come again, I hope, / And perhaps it will come soon, / If we only take things in good faith, / The flowers again will bloom."[59]

Doyle continued to hold out hope for a second trial. "Looking at me," the reporter said, "with his soul in his eyes he said: 'Do you think that they would hang an innocent man. I am as innocent of the death of that man ... and was no more near Summit Hill that day ... than—

you were ... I can prove my whereabouts on that day, still if I have to die I am prepared.'"[60]

Doyle's parents visited him at Mauch Chunk Jail the month of his arrest. The *Shenandoah Herald* described them as "very respectable people ... who left a very favorable impression on all who conversed with them."[61] On the morning of Doyle's execution, his family arrived at the jail with an express wagon to bear his remains home. "The old man is almost in his dotage," the *Chicago Tribune* said. "One of the sons was prepared to lay out his brother's remains."[62]

On January 27, 1876, the evening before defense counsel in the trial of Michael Doyle defected from the case, James Kerrigan made "a confession." In its density, its complexity, its bizarre hyperbole, it resembled the fantasias James McParlan would spin in Idaho thirty years later for Harry Orchard's attack against the Western Federation of Miners.

Kerrigan gave his statement from his cell at Mauch Chunk Jail. Prosecutor Charles Albright was among those who heard the tale.

A few weeks later, the *Shenandoah Herald* ran the headline "JUSTICE!! THE MOLLIES EXPOSED!!! One of the Prisoners at Mauch Chunk Makes a Confession." The accompanying article said: "On Friday evening, January 28th, a conversation was held in Mauch Chunk jail that, if known to the world, would have made hundreds in this county tremble as they never before did before. ... Not many listened to what passed in that prison cell, but those who were present will never forget the frightful nature of the disclosures, or the manner in which they were made."[63]

A week after Kerrigan gave his statement, the commonwealth arrested six AOH men. "DEATH TO THE MOLLIES," the *Philadelphia Times* headline ran. "Murder Will Out—The Assassins of F. B. Yost in Jail—Where Will the Lightning Strike Next?"[64]

On the afternoon of February 18, a closed carriage pulled up at the courthouse in Mauch Chunk. Kerrigan emerged, under guard. A second carriage arrived bearing Alexander Campbell, AOH treasurer for Storm Hill. Campbell, charged with the murder of John Jones on Kerrigan's word, entered the courthouse for his habeas corpus hearing under heavy guard.

Throughout the hearing, Campbell remained shackled between two Coal and Iron policemen, with eight or ten more, poised for action, stationed about the courtroom. Campbell, the *Mauch Chunk Democrat* said, "is a young man of rather prepossessing personal appearance, and looked anything but the hardened criminal he is represented to be."

Albright questioned Kerrigan. Kerrigan responded, the *Democrat* said, "in a low and somewhat husky voice, but answered with promptness, and as though he had his lesson by heart, and could repeat it backward or crosswise if he should be required to do so."[65] The *Shenandoah Herald* said Kerrigan testified "like one who knows that his only salvation is in going forward and that for him there is no return."[66] After Kerrigan completed his memorized testimony, the court denied Campbell's application for bail.

Kerrigan's work had just begun. From Mauch Chunk, he boarded a special train to Pottsville. On February 19, the day after Campbell's hearing, Judge Cyrus Pershing presided over the habeas corpus hearing for James Boyle, James Carroll, Thomas Duffy, Hugh McGehan, and James Roarity, all charged on Kerrigan's word with the murder of Tamaqua police officer Yost.

At the Pottsville hearing, Kerrigan recited the specifics of his conspiracy theory regarding Yost's murder. He described, the *Shenandoah Herald* said: "Who had wanted the job done, what amount of money had been paid for the work ($10), who had done the deed, in fact told everything he knew about the affair ... and implicated beyond, we think, hope of escape the five men charged with the murder."[67]

Moving from the specific to the general, Kerrigan made the statement the prosecution most wanted to hear. "'The one object of the society,'" Kerrigan said of the AOH, "'is murdering, burning and beating, and when a man once becomes a member he is afraid to leave for fear of getting a bullet in him.'" Of the "Molly" defendants' collective demeanor, the *Herald* observed: "All five of the men are fine looking specimens of manhood and not at all like the men whom one would expect to find charged with murder."[68]

A week before Kerrigan's turn as prosecution witness at the Pottsville hearing, the *Shenandoah Herald* reported the arrests, by Gowen's Coal and Iron policemen and Pinkerton Robert Linden, of Charles McAlister and Thomas Munley for the murders of Thomas Sanger and William Uren. McAllister's wife Ellen had been killed at the raid on Wiggan's Patch.

"Munley is the oldest of four sons," the *Herald* said, "has a wife and three children and has been considered by the majority of people who knew him, a very quiet, unassuming sort of man." Munley's father called on Squire Davidson to ask if he could see his son at Pottsville Jail. "'He is as innocent as I am,'" Munley's father told the squire. He spoke of the hardship of employing defense counsel. "The old man is to be pitied in his distress," the *Herald* said, "and has always been a quiet citizen."[69]

Six months later, Gowen used the trial of Munley, the "very quiet, unassuming" father of three, to broadcast his most famous trial speech. "CRUSHING THE MOLLIES," the *Philadelphia Times* headline ran. "THE SLAYER OF SANGER CONVICTED. Mr. Gowen's Great Speech—Mollie Maguireism and Its Frightful Crimes —The End of its Terrible Reign at Hand."[70]

The *Shenandoah Herald* reported Munley's sentencing. Judge Green asked the prisoner, "'what have you to say why sentence should not be pronounced upon you?'" Munley responded: "'I haven't much to say; only that I'm as innocent of the crime I am charged with as any man in the world. I never shed any man's blood. I've lived in Gilberton for eleven years, and never raised my hand against a man; and why my life should be sworn away I don't know.'" The *Herald* added: "Munley cried while speaking and continually wiped his eyes."[71]

Through the spring of 1876, reporters interviewed the alleged

"Molly" prisoners at Mauch Chunk Jail. Edward Kelly, aged twenty when arrested, showed a newsman a ticket saved from a Fourth of July ball given by the Keystone Guards. Kelly, a guard member, had served as floor manager. Kelly, like Doyle, hung the American flag on the wall of his cell. And like Doyle, Kelly wrote poetry. "'Tis always best," one poem concluded, "to live in hope, / Than die in dark despair."[72]

Less than a year later Kelly, aware of the parade of fellow Hibernians who had been arrested, charged with murder, and used as prosecution witnesses against their fellows to secure their own pardons, offered his own "confession." Kelly's statement corroborated Kerrigan in every particular.

A reporter asked Alexander Campbell's view of Kelly's statement. Campbell replied: "'He hears of the "squealers" who are being pardoned on every hand, and he no doubt thought, why cannot I save my life, if I can do so by telling a tale that will correspond with Kerrigan's story. Life is sweet, and I tell you that some men will do anything, even to the imperilling [sic] of their immortal souls, to save it ... if it be God's will that we die, the people of this county and the coal region will find out, when it is too late, that our lives have been sacrificed to prejudice, and through the perjury of men who are less men than devils.'"[73]

Kerrigan used his stay at Mauch Chunk Jail to prepare for his most important presentation: that of prosecution witness during the Yost trial. The *Mauch Chunk Democrat* said of Kerrigan: "He has become quite a dandy in his tastes lately, having shaved off his whiskers and obtained a piece of looking-glass, which has been placed in a convenient position for him to admire his fair proportions of feature."[74]

The upcoming trial of the AOH defendants for the murder of Yost would show both the paucity of the commonwealth's "Molly Maguire" cases and the eagerness of regional jurors to convict Irish Catholic men of capital crimes. The commonwealth's use of Kerrigan to corroborate Pinkerton operative James McParlan in every particular would become a mainstay of Pennsylvania's "Molly Maguire" trials.

On April 5, 1876, the jury in the trial of Edward Kelly convicted the young Irishman of the murder of John Jones. The same day prosecutors released, for publication, James Kerrigan's confession made in late January at Mauch Chunk Jail. "THE MOLLY MAGUIRES," the *New York Herald* reported the next day. "THE ORDER IDENTICAL WITH THE ANCIENT HIBERNIANS."[75] From Richmond, the *Daily Dispatch* reported "An Infamous Secret Society." Its operations, the *Dispatch* said, "are carried on under a charter granted to the Ancient Order of Hibernians."[76] The *New York Times* used similar copy.

"THE MOLLY MAGUIRES," a Stroudsburg paper reported. "Expose [sic] of the Notorious Cabal. ... THE SECRET ORDER OF HIBERNIANS."[77] The *Mauch Chunk Democrat* gave Kerrigan's statement in full. It included this assertion: "The purposes of the 'Mollie Maguires' or A. O. H. is to kill people, beat them and burn down buildings. The notion is that it is to protect workingmen, but really they are all of the most hardened villains in the places where they reside." Kerrigan elaborated on the supposed trading of murders by AOH officers: "If any man wants such a thing done they inform the head man, known as body master or president, and he calls a meeting; two or three men are usually appointed to do such work; it is the Ancient Order of Hibernians who do it."[78]

Within a week of the publication of Kerrigan's statement, the *Shenandoah Herald* reported "we are pleased to notice that all the leading papers of the country are taking the matter up, and from this time forward the whole press will be united in a crusade against 'Mollieism.'" On the same day, a second *Herald* column said: "Our work is nearing its consummation ... all respectable papers in this section of the State are hand in glove with justice, and will, we hope, remain so."[79]

An unnamed mechanic wrote to the *Irish World* in New York to protest the worst of the sensational press. He said: "There are people living outside the coal regions who are foolish enough to believe every word contained in those stories; yet the organization known as the Molly Maguires is a myth, and the bloody tales told of it are gotten up in the interest of capital, whose object is to keep Irish workingmen and those of other nationalities at enmity with each other."[80] The *Mauch Chunk Democrat* described Kerrigan's "Squeal of the Squealer. Something Like a Romance. Truth Stranger Than Fiction."[81]

The *Philadelphia Times* cautioned: "the public elsewhere will not be prepared to believe that a widespread and influential society, which has usually been considered entirely respectable, contains within itself a carefully-perfected system by which arson and assassination are planned and committed with almost perfect impunity ... it will require something more than the statement of one confessed murderer to convince people generally that the Ancient Order of Hibernians is everywhere an association of assassins as reckless of human life as the Carbonari of Italy."[82]

On May 6, 1876, George Kaercher, district attorney for Schuylkill County, addressed the jury in the trial of four Yost defendants. He would, he told listeners, reveal the details of confessions made by defendants James Carroll, Hugh McGehan, and James Roarity to James McParlan, an undercover operative employed by the Pinkerton National Detective Agency. McParlan had infiltrated the benevolent society, Kaercher told the packed courtroom. McParlan had obtained the confidence of the AOH men and "been initiated into their most profound mysteries."[83]

McParlan told defense counsel Lin Bartholomew of his alleged cultivation of Pennsylvania's AOH men: "I ... told them different tales. Sometimes I told them I shot a man; sometimes I told them I counterfeited money ... the stories were all lies."[84] McParlan's court testimony was also a lie. More than two years before, he had advised his Pinkerton supervisors of a weeklong church mission to be held at Pottsville, Pennsylvania, in January 1874. His report from that time said: "The operative intends attending this mission closely as he will meet with all the M.M.'s and the fact of his attendance will gain for him more friends and confidence than all else."[85] McParland first cultivated Pennsylvania's alleged "Mollies" not in area saloons, with tales of blood and thunder, but at a weeklong Roman Catholic church mission at Pottsville.

At least two AOH men charged in the murder of Yost on the word of McParlan and Kerrigan shared qualities of vibrant leadership. After the arrest of Yost defendant McGehan in March 1876, the *Shenandoah Herald* described him as "rather a fine looking fellow with an unmistakably Irish cast of countenance." McGehan had married just weeks before his arrest. During the Long Strike of 1875, at age twenty-three, McGehan had led a peaceful parade of four hundred miners through Tamaqua. Midway through the parade, he had met with the town's coal operators and brokered an arrangement for provision of coal to the town during the ongoing strike. "This man had since his arrival at Summit Hill always possessed considerable influence over his fellows and among them was always a leader," the *Herald* noted in March 1876.[86]

The *New York Sun* said of McGehan's co-defendant James Carroll: "His people are well off, and of good social position."[87] Carroll, owner of Tamaqua's Union Hotel, supported Labor Reform Party activities. Carroll's wife Anne, the mother of four, was the cousin of John Kehoe's wife Mary Ann. The *New York Times* said of Carroll: "His father is a very respectable man, who has lived many years in this section, and has the good will of every one."[88]

Franklin Gowen and Francis Hughes, self-appointed prosecutors in the Yost trial, staged events to produce maximum drama. As Kaercher finished his speech the courtroom audience, already stunned, heard the rattle of chains. That Saturday morning had brought the arrests of eleven new alleged "Mollies" on warrants drawn by Pinkerton operative Robert Linden. As courtroom spectators awaited McParlan's arrival, Gowen's Coal and Iron policemen led the new prisoners past the courthouse and into the jail.

The *New York Times* reported: "Eleven were arrested to-day, among them being Jack Kehoe, the reputed leader of the band, all charged with complicity in the various murders that have recently disgraced this region. Their arrests, together with the court proceedings, have thrown the whole region into excitement."[89] The new prisoners included Patrick Dolan Sr., AOH bodymaster, or head officer, for the Big Mine Run division, and school director for Butler Township; and miner Michael O'Brien, AOH bodymaster for Mahanoy City, husband, and father of eight. "I was acquainted with him for several years as a resident of Mahanoy City," a petitioner wrote to Pennsylvania's Board of Pardons on O'Brien's behalf, "during which time he bore an excellent reputation as a peaceable and law abiding citizen."[90]

The new prisoners, dubbed the "chain gang,"[91] included miner Michael Lawler, AOH bodymaster for Shenandoah, WBA delegate for Schuylkill County's District Five, Democratic delegate for Schuylkill County, husband, and father of six. Three months before his arrest, Lawler had been elected an election judge for Shenandoah's First Ward. Five years before, as part of the *New York Herald's* "New Power Forming in the Land,"[92] Lawler had served as union delegate to Mauch Chunk's Grand Council proceedings, where he advocated arbitration for peaceful settlement of strikes. At Pottsville one month later, he had served as one of four WBA signatories to the agreement with the Anthracite Board of Trade accepting arbitration by umpire for peaceful settlement of wage disputes. "The meeting was pleasant and satisfactory to both parties," the *Philadelphia Press* reported, "and the agreement insures steady work for the remainder of the year."[93]

The new prisoners also included miner Christopher Donnelly, AOH treasurer for Schuylkill County, father of a large family, Democratic delegate for Schuylkill County, and delegate to Schuylkill's Labor Reform Party. Three months before his arrest, Donnelly had been elected school director for New Castle Township. In 1874, at Schuylkill's Democratic Party convention, Donnelly had delivered thirty-nine votes to the nomination of James Reilly to U.S. Congress. Reilly subsequently won the election. Reilly also served as one of the defecting defense counsel in the "Molly Maguire" trial of Michael Doyle.

And, as the *New York Times* noted, the new prisoners included tavern keeper John Kehoe, AOH delegate for Schuylkill County. The father of five, a Democratic hopeful in 1872 to Pennsylvania's state assembly, Kehoe had secured a second term as Girardville's high constable in February 1876, three months before his arrest.

The habeas corpus hearing for the new prisoners took place the Tuesday following their arrests. The *Philadelphia Times* said: "It was a melancholy and humiliating sight for the citizens of this county to see eleven persons, some of whom had enjoyed both social and political influence, handcuffed and chained together, being taken from the court house to prison, guarded by a strong force of police and followed by their weeping wives and mothers."[94]

As Kerrigan's testimony had remanded Hibernian defendants to Mauch Chunk Jail, McParlan's testimony remanded Gowen's new batch of prisoners to Pottsville Jail. "MOLLY MAGUIRE MURDERS," the *New York Herald* said. "TERRIBLE REVELATIONS OF A PINKERTON DETECTIVE WHO ATE AND SLEPT WITH THE CUTTHROATS FOR MONTHS—REWARDS FOR ASSASSINATION."[95]

To secure the new defendants' incarceration, Gowen charged them with conspiracy to murder William and Jesse Major, two murders that had not taken place. Gowen also charged them with conspiracy to murder a notorious local rough, William "Bully Bill" Thomas, a murder that had failed in execution. In addition, Gowen charged defendants with conspiracy to reward AOH men for the commission of murder. Per McParlan's testimony, all of these conspiracies to commit murder, assign murder, and reward men for murder had arisen from an August 1875 convention of AOH officers held at Tamaqua, at the house of James Carroll.

"A JAIL FULL OF ASSASSINS," the *New York Sun* said. "EIGHTEEN MOLLY MAGUIRES WHO ARE LIKELY TO BE HANGED. Fresh Arrests Made Yesterday—The Trial of the Yost Murderers Begun in Pottsville. Excitement in the Mining Regions."[96]

Before Gowen tried the new batch of defendants, he needed four verdicts of guilt in the Yost trial. Kerrigan's wife Fanny would almost topple that effort, along with the balance of Gowen's entire "Molly Maguire" caseload.

On May 17, 1876, defense counsel in the trial of four AOH defendants for the murder of Tamaqua police officer Benjamin Yost[97] called the wife of James Kerrigan to the stand. "She is a fresh-complexioned, and rather pleasant-faced woman," the *Shenandoah Herald* said of Fanny Kerrigan, "and about twice the size of Jimmy, for whom, if we are to judge from what she will endeavor to prove, she has the most SOVEREIGN CONTEMPT."[98]

Fanny Kerrigan told attorney John Ryon that at four in the morning on July 6, 1875, two hours after Yost's murder, she had let her husband into the house. Kerrigan had left their house the evening before around dusk. She had seen him leave the house "with a pistol in his hand, and he was loading it." Fanny testified further: "I was in bed, and I came down and let my husband in … he wasn't home between dusk and four in the morning; I let him in; the door was locked; he had his boots in his hand, and HE SAID HE SHOT YOST."[99]

On cross-examination by Franklin Gowen, Fanny Kerrigan testified that she had given statements regarding her husband's role in Yost's murder to both Squire O'Brien at Tamaqua and Lin Bartholomew at Pottsville. She had stopped visiting Kerrigan at Mauch Chunk Jail after he implicated others in Yost's murder. "I didn't go to see him, for why should I go to see a man guilty of such a crime as that of Yost's murder?" she asked Gowen. She had remained with Kerrigan after the murder, because "if I disclosed him he would have shot me; I went to see him in jail several times after I knew that he had killed Yost; he threatened me, and said that he would blow my brains out."[100]

On cross-examination by Charles Albright, Kerrigan's wife testified that she had stopped visiting Kerrigan in jail after he "tried to drag innocent men in for his crime." She had contacted Bartholomew to give her statement because "the Lord wouldn't allow that weight to remain on my poor soul."[101]

Ryon advised the jury: "The Commonwealth having proved that Kerrigan threatened to take the life of this witness if she ever disclosed the fact of his killing Yost, we propose to prove that when he came home on the morning of the 6th of July Kerrigan told her that HE KILLED YOST, and that he did it because every time he got drunk Yost beat him, and put him in the lock-up, and that if she ever told on him he would kill her."[102]

Fanny Kerrigan remained on the witness stand for almost three and a half hours. The *Shenandoah Herald* concluded: "Mrs. Kerrigan occupied the stand till almost half-past twelve o'clock, and left it feeling not altogether satisfied in her own mind as to whether she had been of much assistance to the prisoners or not. We think she has."[103] Fanny Kerrigan's testimony was crucial to Gowen's campaign. He needed first-degree murder convictions in Yost to push the upcoming trials of the region's AOH leaders.

Later that afternoon Levi Stein, a juror in the Yost trial, took ill. The next day, Stein began to spit blood. On May 24, one week after Fanny Kerrigan testified, Stein died. "His death will cause a very great delay in the trial," the *Philadelphia Times* said, "which cannot be resumed until July."[104]

Fanny Kerrigan never again raised testimony against her husband. Bribed, persuaded, or threatened, her service as a "Molly Maguire" defense witness ended with the first Yost trial.

Before the second Yost trial began at Pottsville, prosecutors tried Alexander Campbell at Mauch Chunk for the murder of John Jones. Prosecutors again called Kerrigan and James McParlan as their main witnesses. The prosecution entered McParlan's detective reports into evidence.

Self-appointed lead prosecutor Francis Hughes petitioned the court to allow Kerrigan to testify: "'if we shall show that there are five thousand "Mollie Maguires" in Schuylkill county; if we shall show you that in Carbon—the small county of Carbon—there are six hundred, and that in Luzerne county there are two thousand five hundred, and that of all the leaders of these ruffians in the coal regions Aleck Campbell is the worst, and that we will prove this by our witnesses, will he not be admitted?'"[105]

"We have been discreet in your selection," Hughes told the jury, "and the gentlemen on the other side have complimented us in this respect." Of Campbell's affiliation with the AOH, Hughes said: "This prisoner is a 'Mollie Maguire.' We have proved that society a murderous organization; that the penalty of their vengeance is death."[106]

The Pinkerton trading-of-murders theory took center stage in Campbell's trial. Kerrigan and McParlan alleged that Campbell's grudge against Jones arose from Jones's blacklisting of AOH men, including Hugh McGehan. Campbell, they alleged, a prosperous businessman, husband and father and Democratic delegate, had provided men for the shooting of Yost in return for the provision of murderers for Jones.

Allen Craig, counsel for Asa Packer's Lehigh Valley Railroad, told the jury: "This organization of bandits have the power of murdering, plundering, and killing. ... An organization of this kind has no ground to be among a civilized people, and I want no court or jury to naturalize it."[107]

Craig continued: "If you allow this organization to live and be a power among us, you will have to leave, I will have to leave, and my friends on the other side will HAVE TO LEAVE ALSO. Are we to allow them to ruin our beautiful country by their terror-striking actions? Or are we to allow them to kill you or me with impunity? Are we to allow them to still further disgrace this beautiful anthracite coal region, which by its productions [sic] gives impetus to rolling mills and furnaces all over the country?"[108]

The prosecution in Campbell's trial also used Kerrigan and McParlan's testimony to further inflame ethnic tensions. Craig praised McParlan as "A CELEBRATED DETECTIVE." Of Campbell, Craig told the jury: "Campbell said, as the evidence proved,

'Don't put one ball in him, but put four or five into the Welsh bugger.'"[109]

Hughes extolled the Pinkerton agency as "a noble institution." Of McParlan, Hughes said, "during the thirty-nine years of practice I have had at the bar I have never seen a more intelligent man, or a man possessing the noble qualities he does, go upon a witness stand."[110]

Defense counsel Daniel Kalbfus advised the jury that if they did not believe McParlan and Kerrigan, they must acquit Campbell. Of McParlan's credibility, Kalbfus said: "His testimony all writers admit, is of the most dangerous character. ... who is McParlane [sic]? He is a detective. What nerved Brutus to slay Ceasar [sic]? ... Why did Booth kill Lincoln? ... ambition, that which threw Satan over the walls of heaven." Of Kerrigan's testimony, Kalbfus said: "I would not ask a jury to convict the vilest wretch in my country by the evidence of James Kerrigan. ... He has no soul; he is a wreck of total depravity."[111]

The jurors in the Jones trial convicted Campbell of first-degree murder. The Irishman heard the verdict without flinching. "CAMPBELL CONVICTED," the *Shenandoah Herald* headline ran. "THE DEATH-KNELL OF "MOLLIEISM.""[112]

At Pottsville later that week, the retrial of the four Yost defendants began. Despite Fanny Kerrigan's damning testimony in the first Yost trial, she failed to take the stand during the second trial. Kerrigan and McParlan again took turns as prosecution witnesses.

Defense counsel John Ryon advised the jury: "This case rests almost solely upon the evidence of James Kerrigan and James McParlane [sic]." Of Kerrigan's contention that ten dollars, split three ways, had been allocated for the killing of Yost, Ryon told the jury, "you wouldn't return a verdict for thirty-one cents upon the evidence of Kerrigan, a creature of the most savage instincts."[113]

Of McParlan's collusion with Kerrigan, Ryon said: "Why it was the easiest thing in the world to work this case up, and so much time had [McParlan] on his hands that he courted—who? Kerrigan's sister. It ought to have been consummated and wouldn't it have made a happy family? James and James, oh, yes, they ought to be taken and hung up in a cage together."[114]

Lin Bartholomew, reverting once again to an impassioned defense, said of Kerrigan: "Character! character! what can I say of this despicable wretch, this curse let loose from hell, a confessed murderer, a participant in the most fearful of crimes. He has never been called to the bar of justice for the murder of Jones, and I say that he can never be tried, but will be let loose once more to feed upon the blood of his fellows." To convict the defendants upon the word of Kerrigan and McParlan, Bartholomew concluded, "would be a MONSTROUS THING."[115]

Charles Albright, once again in Civil War dress uniform, traveled in from Carbon County to help prosecute the Yost trial. "You have heard during the trial," he advised the jury, "that an organization has been in existence which has imperiled the lives of all of us who inhabit the coal region." If the jury failed to convict in this instance, Albright concluded, "I doubt if this class of men will be found guilty." He slyly assured jurors: "Remember that you do not execute these prisoners, you merely RETURN YOUR VERDICT and even when this court shall pass upon your verdict, the end may not have come for there is the supreme court."[116]

"The prisoners are each and all of them 'Mollie Maguires,'" Francis Hughes said. "They belong to that order, which, under the mask of the name of the Ancient Order of Hibernians, has committed crimes." Hughes exhorted: "If it is necessary to hang five hundred or a thousand 'Mollies' at the end of a rope to restore peace and quietness, why let us try THE SURGICAL OPERATION." He added, "affairs are situated so that it must be either 'Mollie Maguires' and anarchy, or that 'Mollie Maguires' MUST BE EXTERMINATED, not only in the coal regions, but I wish I could say throughout the world."[117]

At half past seven on the evening of July 22, the jurors retired to deliberate. Defense counsel once again abdicated before a verdict was returned. George Kaercher, county district attorney, suggested ringing the courthouse bell to summon Ryon and Bartholomew. Judge Pershing told Kaercher that the defendants' attorneys were well aware of the time that court was to reconvene. In their stead,

Pershing appointed Pottsville attorney Ramsay Potts, John Kehoe's friend who was seated among the spectators, to act as counsel on behalf of the four defendants awaiting the verdict.

Kaercher asked that jurors give their verdicts individually. Forty-eight times, courtroom spectators heard the judgment "guilty of murder in the first degree." As the last juror spoke the verdict for the last time, the courthouse bell tolled the last stroke of eleven.

On August 28, 1876, the four Yost defendants, along with Thomas Munley, received their sentences. "SENTENCE OF DEATH," the *Shenandoah Herald* reported. *"THE ASSASSINS AT LAST TO RECEIVE THEIR DESSERTS."* All five Irishmen protested their innocence. The *Herald's* headline sensationalized even Judge Green's statement: "'You Shall be Taken to the Jail and Thence to the Place of Execution, to be Hung by the Neck Until You are Dead! Dead! Dead! And may God have Mercy on Your Souls!'"[118]

The same day the *Shenandoah Herald* reported the completion of Kerrigan's testimony in the Yost trial, it ran an adjoining column. "THE PICNIC," this article announced. *"A DAY OF ENJOYMENT AND FEASTING IN THE WOODS.* The Successful Work of the Shenandoah Rifles—Visiting Guests—Beautiful Grounds, and a Display of Good Taste."[119] Three military companies and three bands would take part. These included the Grandville light infantry and its cornet band, the Pennsylvania cornet band and a Tamaqua militia, and, from Mahanoy City, the Citizens' Cornet Band and the Silliman Guards. Frank Wenrich, the first lieutenant in the Silliman Guards named in the murder of the young pregnant mother at Wiggan's Patch, would help lead the day of enjoyment and feasting.

With the conviction of the Yost defendants on the testimony of James Kerrigan and James McParlan, Franklin Gowen had a clear field to press his "Molly Maguire" caseload. "NINETY-SEVEN MURDERERS," a *New York Sun* headline exaggerated a week after the verdict came in. "THE CONDEMNED MOLLY MAGUIRES HOPING FOR A RESCUE."[120]

Gowen's intent to use the upcoming "Molly Maguire" trials as a political megaphone soon became apparent. Less than a week after securing convictions in Yost, Gowen circulated his prosecution argument, delivered during the trial of Thomas Munley, in pamphlet form. "The argument is a powerful one," the *Carbon Advocate* said from Lehighton, "and puts the Mollie Maguires into a light, from which they will be glad to hide. Mr. Gowen has been untiring in his effort to put down lawlessness in the Coal Regions, and he is slowly but surely accomplishing his great end."[121]

On the same day, the *New York Sun* ran a column headlined "Murderers as Political Agents." The article alerted the press and the public "that the most extensive and desperate body of organized incendiaries, thugs, and assassins ever known on this continent has for several years been used as a part of the Republican organization in Pennsylvania." The *Sun*, too, quoted Gowen's speech. "The Reading Railroad Company," it editorialized, "finding that the State authorities would not protect the community from this gigantic combination, took the matter into their own hands, employed detectives, made arrests, collected evidence, and the President of the corporation, Franklin B. Gowen, appeared in the court room and conducted the prosecutions against some of the ruffians who had been engaged in the work of assassinating peaceable citizens."[122]

Gowen's attempt to smear Pennsylvania's Republican Party through the "Molly Maguire" trials reached full bloom in October 1876, less than three weeks before the U.S. presidential election. First, Gowen sought to paint national AOH officers as criminals. To do so, he used the trial testimony of Patrick Butler.

Gowen's assault against AOH officers in New York had three aims: the crippling of national AOH support for coal region defendants, the destruction of the order's national reputation, and the annihilation of its political influence.

As with James Kerrigan, the acceptance of Patrick Butler into a coal region AOH lodge remains a mystery. Born in Ireland in the mid-1840s, Butler emigrated with his family to Quebec in the early 1850s. At age eighteen, Butler took up residence in Schuylkill County. A decade later, Dennis Donnelly initiated Butler into the AOH division at Raven Run. Within a year, Butler was bodymaster of both the Raven Run and the Lost Creek divisions.

In trial testimony given in November 1877, Butler claimed little interest in his Roman Catholic heritage. Though initiated on August 15, 1873, a Catholic day of obligation, Butler had no knowledge of the date's significance. "Very seldom I go to church," he told defense counsel in the trial of Dennis Donnelly.[123]

During the same trial, Butler admitted to being a Pinkerton informer. More than three years before, during the region's Long Strike, John Kehoe, AOH delegate for Schuylkill County, had been informed of Butler's predilection, along with Butler's brother John, for violence. During the Long Strike, the Butler brothers had claimed responsibility for sabotage along the railroad tracks on the Lehigh road. "Kehoe had informed them at the [county AOH] convention," McParlan had advised his supervisors at the time, "that if they committed any more such depredations they would be expelled for life from the organization."[124]

Sixteen months later, on August 19, 1876, Butler testified in one of Gowen's many Pottsville trials. It became known as the Hurley reward conspiracy trial. "THE 'BOSS' SQUEALER," the *Shenandoah Herald* reported. "PAT. BUTLER'S STORY THE MOST ASTOUNDING YET TOLD." The press had been alerted to Butler's upcoming testimony. "The reporters straightened up," the *Herald* said, "as something good was expected of Patrick and it came."[125]

Butler told defense attorney John Ryon that at the county AOH meeting held at Tamaqua on August 25, 1875, Kehoe had instructed Butler, along with McParlan, to form a committee to determine who should be rewarded for the murder of Gomer James, and how much the reward should be. Butler named numerous AOH men as members of this committee, which had supposedly met on Mahanoy Mountain near Shenandoah. As members of this alleged murder committee, Butler included two AOH township school directors: Christopher Donnelly and Patrick Dolan Sr.

When Ryon concluded his examination of Butler, some in court suspected more to come. "Metaphorically speaking," the *Herald* said, "there had been lightening in the air all day ... but none of the uninitiated had the faintest idea of where it was going to strike."[126]

District Attorney George Kaercher handled Butler's cross-examination. Kaercher asked Butler, "What has become of Michael Doyle?"[127] Kehoe, Butler told Kaercher, had spoken with Butler after Kehoe's return from New York's national AOH convention. Butler alleged that Kehoe had informed Butler that he had taken Michael Doyle, a Hibernian, with him to New York. Butler then gave Kehoe's supposed statement to the New York officers: "'Gentlemen, this man has committed a crime, and if you don't help him he will go up.'" New York's national AOH board, Butler alleged, had honored Kehoe's request and given Doyle one hundred dollars to flee the country.[128]

In cross-examination Butler depicted various murder schemes allegedly plotted by AOH men, but never carried out. He hinted, but gave no details, of a nefarious failed scheme by AOH men at Jackson's Patch, in Schuylkill County. "Such a scene is not equaled in the history of the world," the *Cambria Freeman* said of Butler's testimony.[129] "In all the annals of crime," a Delaware paper said, "there has not been more deliberate, cruel, cold blooded and in all respects infamous murders than those brought to light in the prosecutions of the Mollie Maguires."[130]

The *Philadelphia Times* said: "The evidence of Patrick Butler, one of the body masters of the Ancient Order of Hibernians, ought to be enough to sink the whole order in shame and disgrace. It shows that the national body has knowingly voted money to defeat the ends of justice." Butler's testimony, the *Times* claimed, showed conclusively "that the whole organization of the Ancient Order of Hibernians, from the National Board down (and we may fairly infer also the higher body known as the 'Board of Erin' in England, Scotland and

Ireland) are a band of criminals, who perpetrate crimes and shield criminals from justice."[131]

"Murder in Its Most Horrible Form," a *Reading Eagle* headline ran. "DEATH CONCOCTED, PLANNED AND CARRIED OUT—CHARGES OF AN ENTIRE ORGANIZATION LEAGUED TO KILL AND AID CRIMINALS."[132]

After hearing Butler's testimony, the jury in the Hurley conspiracy trial deliberated for fifteen minutes before convicting all defendants. Gowen's "Molly Maguire" juggernaut was now unstoppable. Irish Catholic school directors, if they belonged to the AOH, could now be convicted of mountaintop murder conspiracies on the word of Pinkerton operatives.

Gowen's ploy to decimate AOH membership by portraying the order as criminal worked. A week after Butler testified, the *Chicago Tribune* reported from Philadelphia: "Since the Ancient Order of Hibernians has been openly charged with [collusion] with the Molly Maguires, many conscientious and respectable members have been quietly disconnecting themselves from their divisions."[133] The proposed plan of national AOH officers to secure a five-dollar contribution from each of the country's six thousand AOH divisions to be used as a defense fund for Pennsylvania's coal region defendants also evaporated with Butler's testimony.

Less than a month after Butler accused national AOH officers of criminality, someone who signed himself "Butler," probably Patrick Butler's brother John, wrote to Gowen from Lost Creek. Among other items, "Butler" told Gowen of a boast made by James Kerrigan to Fenton Cooney, McParlan's one-time landlord, that Kerrigan himself was the man who shot Yost.

"Butler" informed Gowen that Cooney had made his statement in "Butler's" presence, in the office of defense attorney Ryon. Cooney had met Kerrigan in Tamaqua after a funeral, and the two had discussed Yost's murder. Kerrigan, the letter-writer told Gowen, had asked Cooney of the murder: "was it not a good Job. Cooney said it was then Kerrigan said i [sic] am the man that shot Yost."[134]

Five AOH defendants, convicted of Yost's murder, were hanged at Pottsville on June 21, 1877. All five defendants were convicted on Kerrigan's testimony, though Kerrigan had told his wife, and boasted to Cooney, that he was the man who shot Yost. Kerrigan's testimony brought him emoluments along with immunity from prosecution. Asked by defense counsel in a later trial where he had gotten new clothes while imprisoned, including a beaver topcoat he wore in a freezing courtroom, Kerrigan replied: "'The tailor fetched 'em; I had to have new clothes; my old ones were worn out showing men the roads to commit murder.'"[135]

Others who assisted the "Molly" prosecution fared well. Four months before the June 1877 executions, authorities released Patrick Butler from Pottsville Jail on his own recognizance. "The reason for this leniency," the *Shenandoah Herald* said, "is because of the service Butler has been to the commonwealth in the late trials."[136]

Two months before the executions took place Charles Albright secured Kerrigan's release from Mauch Chunk Jail under the "two-term" rule. As more than two full terms of court had elapsed since Kerrigan's indictment with no prosecution mounted against him, Albright won his point.

After his release, Kerrigan served as a prosecution witness in additional "Molly" trials. In all, his testimony secured the executions of ten AOH defendants: James Boyle, Alexander Campbell, James Carroll, Michael Doyle, Thomas Duffy, Edward Kelly, James McDonnell, Hugh McGehan, James Roarity, and Charles Sharpe. Kerrigan's testimony in the Thomas and Major trials secured two terms of imprisonment for John Kehoe, and left the public with the implication of Kehoe as a violent leader of violent men.

"This unmitigated, unholy villain," defense counsel Lin Bartholomew characterized Kerrigan in the second Yost trial. Bartholomew concluded: "no man with a soul would hang a dumb brute upon the testimony of such a thing as Kerrigan."[137]

Precisely when Michael Lawler decided to collude with the Pinkertons against his fellow AOH members remains a mystery. Born in Ireland in 1838, by 1871 Lawler had become a power in Schuylkill County. In April 1871 he attended, as a WBA delegate, Mauch Chunk's Grand Council proceedings. In May, Lawler served as one of four signatories to the articles of arbitration that arose from the council's proceedings. At the time, the *Shenandoah Herald* spoke of Lawler's "devotion to the Union," and of his outspoken defense of the workingmen against the interests of the coal operators.[138]

Lawler, a miner and father of six, kept a tavern in Shenandoah. In 1872, under John Kehoe's sponsorship, he joined the AOH there. Kehoe moved from Shenandoah to Girardville, and Lawler became bodymaster for Shenandoah's AOH division. Lawler's upward political trajectory also continued. In February 1875, he was elected tax assessor for Shenandoah's East Precinct. In March 1875, he served as a miners' delegate to the Harrisburg Anti-Monopoly Convention. In September 1875, he served as delegate to Schuylkill County's Democratic convention. In February 1876, he was elected "judge" for Shenandoah's First Ward, a post that likely involved oversight of elections.

Lawler's relationship with undercover Pinkerton operative James McParlan remains murky. After McParlan entered the coal region in late 1873, McParlan cultivated Patrick Dormer, commissioner of Schuylkill County from 1867 to 1873 and AOH member of a St. Clair lodge. In September 1873, a month before McParlan entered the region, Labor Reformers in convention at Pottsville named Dormer as a prospective senatorial nominee. By the time McParlan first rendezvoused with Dormer in mid-January 1874 at Dormer's Sheridan House in Pottsville, Dormer's fellow AOH members had begun to suspect Dormer's loyalty. Rumors afloat said that Dormer had broken with the AOH to join with the Protestant Odd Fellows.

McParlan first met Lawler at Dormer's hotel bar. Within three months of their meeting, Lawler had initiated McParlan into the AOH division at Shenandoah. Lawler then, in his own words, "took passage for Europe."[139] On Lawler's return from Europe, Frank

McAndrew had become Shenandoah's AOH bodymaster and McParlan, undercover as "McKenna," its secretary. Though Lawler sought membership in the Mahanoy City AOH division of William Callaghan, Callaghan rebuffed him. As a prosecution witness in Lawler's trial, McParlan testified that Lawler had told McParlan "that he had presented his card to Callaghan and that he had been refused admittance on the ground that he was giving information to the coal and iron police."[140]

Shortly before Lawler's arrest as an alleged "Molly," rumors arose of Lawler's connections with the Masons, an organization, in the coal region at that time, hostile to Irish Catholics. John Kehoe evidently believed the rumors. Kehoe had told Callaghan that Lawler, "a bad man," had plans to join the Masons.[141]

Whatever Lawler's relationship with the Odd Fellows, the Masons, the Coal and Iron police, the Pinkertons, or the prosecution's conspiracy against the AOH, in September 1876 he became an effective prosecution witness. Arrested on May 6, 1876, and charged in the murders of Thomas Sanger and William Uren, Lawler's court case began on September 20, 1876. Newspapers hereafter changed the spelling of his name, routinely referring to him as "Lawlor."

Rumors that Lawler had defected to the prosecution began in late July. An unnamed observer told the *Pottsville Standard* that he had seen Franklin Gowen, with his stenographer, leaving Pottsville Jail.[142] "There is no doubt," the *Shenandoah Herald* said, "that Lawler talked to Mr. Gowen, and, perhaps, talked to him to the extent of forty pages of manuscript, as some say."[143]

Lawler appeared in court on September 20 without counsel to defend him. District Attorney Kaercher noticed attorneys Mason Weidman and Martin L'Velle in court, and tried to corral them to Lawler's defense. Both protested. Kaercher told them "that they would not experience much trouble in the case, as they would probably discover after holding an interview with their client."[144] The following day, L'Velle asked to be relieved from the case, and the court appointed Charles Brumm to assist Weidman. "This case promises to be short and sweet," the *Shenandoah Herald* said, "and will therefore be interesting."[145]

McParlan served as the primary prosecution witness in Lawler's trial. Once again, the Pinkerton agent testified to the broad criminality of the AOH. Lawler, in a turn calculated to shock listeners, backed up McParlan's allegations. The *Chicago Tribune* said of Lawler's testimony: "He confirmed McParlan in even minute particulars, and went beyond him in painting the almost incredible savageness of his former associates."[146]

On cross-examination by Kaercher, Lawler confirmed Patrick Butler's hints of alleged terrorism at Jackson's Patch. Lawler outlined an alleged scheme of arson, never carried out, supposedly formed by two hundred AOH men against the small mining village. The *Chicago Tribune* said: "The programme was to set fire to the houses ... and either burn the inmates or shoot them down as they tried to escape from the flames."[147]

On the supposed details of the murders of Sanger and Uren, Lawler corroborated former prosecution witnesses with great precision. "THE 'MUFF' SQUEALS. *THE CAT OUT OF THE BAG AT LAST*," the *Shenandoah Herald* reported. "Michael Lawlor, Ex-Body-Master, on the Stand Telling all he Knows—He Corroborates McParlan and Pat. Butler in Every Particular."[148]

Lawler's testimony grabbed national headlines. "THE MOLLY MAGUIRES," the *New York Herald's* account ran. "A TERRIBLE REVELATION BY MICHAEL LAWLOR—DETAILS OF A DESIGN TO BURN HOUSES AND MURDER WOMEN AND CHILDREN—RECIPROCAL MURDERS."[149]

Gowen also used Lawler's testimony to open doors to allegations of political corruption. The *New York Sun* said: "The horrible confession of Lawlor, that it was designed by the Mollies to burn houses in Jackson Patch ... excites no astonishment here. Believing themselves backed by the Republican leaders of Pennsylvania, and trusting in their political influence, the Mollies hesitated at no atrocity. The greatest interest is felt here as to whether Hartranft will or will not be frightened into pardoning Simon Cameron's old supporters."[150]

Lawler's trial ended in a mistrial, with ten jurors for conviction and two for acquittal. His retrial two months later ended in conviction. In February 1877, Lawler was taken to Bloomsburg in Columbia County to testify against Patrick Hester et al. in the Alexander Rea murder trial. In July 1877, Lawler was released from Pottsville Jail on his own recognizance. In November 1877, he testified in court at Pottsville against AOH defendant Dennis Donnelly.

By October 1878, Lawler had received three small cash payments expensed through the reports of Pinkerton operative "G. E. I."[151] By late 1878 Lawler, a former leading light of union advocacy in Schuylkill County, was an acknowledged Pinkerton collaborator.

On cross-examination in the case of Dennis Donnelly, Lawler told counsel "self-preservation is the first law of nature."[152] Gowen's coal company, as it did for Patrick and John Butler, looked after Lawler's interests. "Please give Muff Lawler work as miner at Indian Ridge Colliery," Gowen's superintendent Henry Pleasants wrote to district superintendent John Reese in July 1877, "because it is important that all the men who turned State's evidence should remain in the region and not be driven away by fear of the mollies [sic] or for lack of work."[153] Lawler, by now universally known as "Muff Lawlor" for a breed of game hens that he raised, had gone from setting the terms of arbitration for the union's negotiations with coal operators to becoming a supplicant, through perjured testimony, for work at Gowen's collieries.

After Lawler's trial testimony in September 1876, Gowen's human chess game continued. The fall from grace of influential AOH Tuscarora member John Slattery, lodged at that time in Pottsville Jail, would be spectacular.

The same day that Michael Lawler's trial ended in a mistrial, four more "Molly Maguire" defendants came to the bar. The charge was conspiracy to murder William and Jesse Major, two murders that never took place.

On May 6, 1876, Pinkerton operative Robert Linden issued arrest warrants for eleven men in the Major case. Other arrests for the supposed Major conspiracy followed. The testimony of James Kerrigan fueled all these arrests. They included at least seven men who had held elected office: Michael Lawler as precinct tax assessor; Christopher Donnelly and Patrick Dolan, Sr. as township school directors; John Kehoe and Ned Monaghan as high constables; and Charles Mulhearn and John Slattery as township supervisors.

Slattery's career spanned labor, business, and politics. A native of Cape Breton, Nova Scotia, Slattery had emigrated to the United States in 1850. In 1864, he moved to Tuscarora, in Pennsylvania's Schuylkill County. "He is a man of considerable intelligence," author Francis Dewees said of Slattery in 1877, "and married to a good wife, the daughter of the Widow Kelly, for many years favorably known as the mistress of a hotel in New Philadelphia." Dewees described Slattery's mother-in-law as a "woman of influence" who controlled the politics of Blythe Township in Schuylkill County.[154]

Slattery, a storekeeper, held numerous elected offices, including school director, tax collector and assessor, auditor, postmaster, and treasurer of the school fund. In 1871, he narrowly lost an election for associate judge of Schuylkill County. The *Philadelphia Times* said of Slattery's defeat, "it was only by the strenuous efforts of a number of Independent Democrats, who nominated a candidate and prevailed on the Republican Convention to adopt their nomination, that this county was spared the shame of seeing a Mollie Maguire on the bench of their court."[155]

In 1872, when Slattery ran for the office of register, John Donohue, then president of the Workingmen's Benevolent Association (WBA) District No. 10 local in Tuscarora, lauded Slattery both as a candidate and as a fellow WBA officer. "Mr. Slattery," Donohue said, "was one of the most active in organizing this district of the W.B.A. at a time when unionism met with formidable opposition from those whose interest it was to crush it in its infancy."[156] Like Slattery, Donohue became caught in the net of "Molly Maguire" arrests.

Slattery joined the AOH at Tuscarora in March 1872. Donohue, bodymaster for the division, initiated his fellow labor union officer. In September 1873 at Pottsville, Labor Reformers named Slattery as a prospective senatorial nominee.

Slattery's first clue that Gowen intended him as a "Molly Maguire" target came in February 1876, in habeas corpus testimony given by Kerrigan against defendants in the Yost trial. There, Kerrigan testified that Slattery, who had almost secured an associate judgeship, "'gave [Hugh McGehan] $10 to burn down Barney O'Hare's barn and afterwards gave him more to go to the school house and beat him, and if Barney did not leave then he was to get a bullet.'"[157] In April 1876, a wider broadcast of Kerrigan's accusations alleged that Slattery had paid Alexander Campbell to burn O'Hare's property.

In late June 1876, Slattery served as a defense witness in Campbell's trial. The *Mauch Chunk Democrat* gave a clipped summary of Slattery's testimony: "never paid one cent for the procurement of somebody to burn a barn. Never heard of the design against the lives of the Majors. ... Never knew of propositions made to burn out or kill people.... Never offered $5.00 to have the Majors shot. Never heard of a proposition, in meeting or convention, to have people shot or murdered." Of the purpose of the AOH, Slattery testified "we contributed toward the support of the sick and burial of the dead."[158]

In Gowen's widely broadcast speech from the trial of Thomas Munley, given a few weeks after Slattery denied all allegations of AOH criminality, Gowen added Slattery to the list of AOH men he called out for special mention. "When McParlane [sic] took that stand," Gowen said, "... I felt as if I could go to Jack Kehoe, the county delegate of the Ancient Order of Hibernians, and high constable of Girardville, and tell him that his reign was over ... I felt as if I could go to John Slattery, who ran for judge, and say to him, it would have been better for you had you never been born than that I had known you."[159]

Less than a week after Gowen taunted Slattery from a Pottsville courtroom, the Coal and Iron Police arrested the storekeeper at

Tuscarora "on a charge of arson committed several years ago."[160] Kerrigan made the allegations that prompted Slattery's arrest.

At Pottsville, Slattery was released on five thousand dollars bail. A month after his release, the *Shenandoah Herald* reported: "SLATTERY ARRESTED. *HIS BONDSMAN SURRENDERS HIM AND HE IS LODGED IN JAIL.* Another Charge Against Him—Conspiracy to Murder the Majors."[161] Slattery's bondsman had traveled to Pottsville to request the cancellation of Slattery's five-thousand-dollar bond. The bondsman suspected that Slattery had plans to flee the region, as the Irishman had recently sold, at a loss, his horse, wagon, and harness to his brother at Hazleton. Linden obtained the warrant for Slattery's arrest and transferred him to Pottsville Jail.

Five weeks later Slattery, along with three co-defendants, appeared in Pottsville on trial for conspiracy to murder William and Jesse Major. "SLATTERY CONFESSES," the *Shenandoah Herald* reported. "*HE ALSO MAKES A CLEAN BREAST OF IT*. He says the Organization of the Ancient Order of Hibernians is a Criminal One—His Testimony Creates Great Excitement."[162] Regarding the alleged murder plot against the Majors, Slattery corroborated Kerrigan in many particulars, including the fact that the alleged plan for murder had been discussed on June 1, 1875, at a Mahanoy City meeting of county AOH bodymasters called by Kehoe.

"Didn't you go to Mahanoy City with a crowd to attend a labor reform meeting?" an AOH defense attorney asked McParlan that same week, in yet another "Molly" trial. "Didn't they hold several labor reform meetings in Shenandoah?" McParlan stuck to his story of the AOH as a murderous club. The Pinkerton steadfastly denied all knowledge of Labor Reform Party meetings called by AOH officers.[163]

With Slattery's courtroom appearance, spectators had again been alerted to expect sensational testimony. "He left the table at which he had been sitting," the *Philadelphia Times* said, "trying from a feeling of shame to withdraw himself from public gaze by covering his face with his hands, and took his place on the elevated witness-stand and in a low voice told his story." Of Slattery's discourse, the paper said:

"He was very much moved while testifying, with great difficulty repressing the tears, which seemed determined to flow."[164]

Prosecutor Francis Hughes asked Slattery to explain the nature of the AOH. "It is criminal," Slattery responded, adding, "the practice of the organization was to commit crime and afterward aid criminals."[165] Prosecutors also brought in Charles Mulhearn, Slattery's co-defendant and former colleague as township supervisor, to corroborate both Slattery and Kerrigan.

In the September 1876 trial of Slattery and three co-defendants, defense counsel once again sabotaged the case. They solicited no testimony from defendants. They did not address the jury. Judge David Green instructed the jurymen and they retired to deliberate. They returned a short time afterward, finding Slattery guilty as charged. One month later, Gowen's Coal and Iron police escorted Slattery from Pottsville Jail to the courthouse at Mauch Chunk, where he testified against his former union colleague, John Donohue.

Slattery's testimony at Pottsville prepared him for his presentation at Mauch Chunk. At Mauch Chunk, Slattery testified that his wife had persuaded him to tell all he knew of the AOH and its workings. His testimony, the *New York Herald* said, "will produce throughout the State a very great sensation."[166] Self-appointed prosecutor Hughes, frustrated for more than a decade in political contests where the AOH had wielded a potent influence, finally had his day in court.

Slattery, on close questioning by Hughes, "said the A. O. H. from Maine to the Gulf is a criminal organization which does not hesitate at bribery, fraudulent voting, falsifying electoral returns or murder. He knew personally that the National Board in New York had contributed money to assist a Schuylkill county murderer to escape from this country to Ireland."[167]

Slattery affirmed Patrick Butler's allegations of criminality against national AOH officers. On re-direct, Slattery told Hughes: "I have it from the county delegate [John Kehoe] that the national board contributed funds to get a murderer out of this country."[168]

Slattery gave his testimony at Mauch Chunk less than three

weeks before the country's upcoming presidential election between Samuel Tilden and Rutherford B. Hayes. Hughes's questioning veered widely from the case at hand, that of the trial of John Donohue for the murder of Morgan Powell. "Was the Ancient Order of Hibernians," Hughes asked Slattery, "or the 'Mollie Maguire' organization ever used as a means to gain a desired end politically?" Slattery replied: "Yes, sir; last fall when Judge Pershing ran against Governor Hartranft for the governorship the 'Mollie Maguires' worked hard for Hartranft that they might get a friend in the government who would stick to them when they were in need."[169]

There followed a volley of testimony from Slattery that confirmed every whisper, every nuance, every rumor ever raised against the AOH as a corrupt political arm of Pennsylvania's Republican Party. Slattery testified that in fall 1875, a few weeks before Pennsylvania's gubernatorial election, he and Kehoe had met with two prominent local Republican operatives: D. C. Henning and Joshua Sigfried, a former Civil War Union officer. To help secure Governor John Hartranft's re-election Sigfried and Henning, per Slattery's testimony, had promised the AOH men cash for votes, with an implied promise of pardons from the governors' office for incarcerated AOH men; specifically, for Schuylkill County commissioners who had been convicted of fraud in Cyrus Pershing's court at Pottsville. Slattery alleged further that Judge James Ryon, a Democrat and defense counsel in numerous "Molly Maguire" trials, had been present when this transaction took place. Slattery claimed that an aide to Hartranft at Harrisburg had "carried a fund of money to Luzerne county for the purpose of securing the Mollies' vote of that county for Hartranft, and that a much larger fund was sent to Pittsburg [sic], the headquarters of the A. O. H. in Pennsylvania, to be used for the same purpose."[170]

Donohue's defense counsel raised no objection to Hughes's continued questioning of Slattery. It rested with Judge Samuel Dreher to stop the flow of irrelevant and prejudicial allegations. Dreher, a first-generation American of German descent, served as president judge of Pennsylvania's forty-third judicial district, comprising Monroe and Carbon counties. In former "Molly" trials, Dreher had shown no mercy to AOH men, routinely dismissing motions for change of venue and the quashing of unfair jury pools. Hughes's strategy tested even Dreher's limits. "Gentlemen, we are certainly drifting from this case," he cautioned prosecution counsel. A short time later, Dreher said: "Gentlemen, we must now put a stop to this. We will interfere. We are about to adjourn."[171]

By then, the damage had been done. Hughes and Gowen had gotten their press. The *Philadelphia Times* said: "Slattery's testimony fully vindicates Mr. Gowen's assertion in his speech on the trial of Thomas Munley for the murder of Uren and Sanger, in which he charged that persons holding high office in Pennsylvania had bargained with members of the Mollie Maguire organization to secure the votes of these outlaws for Republican candidates."[172] Slattery's testimony placed men of all political stripes in Pennsylvania on notice. All could be used as target practice in Gowen's "Molly Maguire" trials. Further, Slattery's allegations of votes for pardons tied the hands of Pennsylvania's Governor Hartranft for all alleged "Molly Maguires" on trial. If Hartranft dared consider authorizing pardons or requests for commutation of sentence, charges of corruption would forever stain his political legacy.

In 1873, as a delegate to Pennsylvania's Constitutional Convention, Gowen had led the effort to remove the power of the governor to grant pardons and cede that power to a new four-man pardon board. The only authority left to the governor was the signing of pardons, and of death warrants. With Slattery's testimony, Gowen secured a further guarantee that Hartranft would exercise no authority to stay the judicial bloodbath taking place in the commonwealth's coal region. In all, Hartranft would sign twenty death warrants in Pennsylvania's "Molly Maguire" caseload. Governor Henry Hoyt would sign the final warrant, that of Peter McManus in Northumberland County.

"Grand Expose [sic] of Radicalism," the *Daily Gazette* reported from Wilmington, Delaware, after Slattery's testimony at Mauch Chunk. "Murder, Robbery and Bribery. Hartranft and the Molly

Maguires." Slattery's revelations, the *Gazette* said, "fully confirm the allegation of Mr. Gowen that certain persons high in office had made a corrupt bargain with the Mollies for their votes."[173]

The *Harrisburg Patriot* said: "Mr. Gowen has made good his terrible accusation that he knew of meetings between republican leaders and the chief of the Molly Maguires." It asked: "what penalty shall a sound public opinion inflict on the republican leaders who have sought and found in this foul combination the prop and stay of their political supremacy in Pennsylvania?"[174]

"GOWEN'S CHARGES PROVEN," the *Columbian* reported from Bloomsburg. "In the face of these facts how can any decent Republican longer act with a party that deliberately buys up a band of cut-throats."[175]

"MORE REPUBLICAN INFAMY," the *Wheeling Daily Register* said. "Buying Up an Oath-Bound, Murderous Gang. The Cash Down Paid for the Votes of the 'Mollie Maguires.' How Pennsylvania was Carried. The Disgrace of American Politics."[176] The *New York Herald*, reporting from Pottsville, said: "The excitement here over [Slattery's] revelations of last Saturday has not subsided, and they are being used to influence the coming election."[177]

In New York, Charles Dana's *Sun* openly exulted. "MURDERERS FOR ALLIES," it said. "*THE CARRYING OF THE KEYSTONE STATE FOR HARTRANFT.* Combination with the Murderous Molly Maguires—The Votes of the Order Purchased with Money and Pardons—A Thunderbolt Sent Against the Cameron Ring."[178]

The *Philadelphia Times*, under Alexander McClure, voiced the nativists' characterization of the AOH as a criminal organization: "Sigfried and Slattery both knew just the quality and quantity of votes to be delivered by the agreement, and that they were the men known as Mollie Maguires was well understood by both the contracting parties. It was a square purchase for the votes of a lawless, murderous band of men, and the money was paid and the votes delivered."[179]

Slattery's testimony threw Schuylkill County politics into disarray. "The Republicans of this county now throw up the sponge," the *New York Sun* reported. The *Sun* also relayed the mood of Schuylkill County's Democrats, no longer constrained by the progressive politics of regional AOH Democrats: "buoyant, jubilant, hopeful, [they] seem to think that another powerful blow has been struck for Tilden, Hendricks and Reform."[180]

With Slattery's testimony at Mauch Chunk, additional convictions of influential AOH men based on testimony crafted in Allan Pinkerton's fictional narrative factory rolled forward with ease. In December 1876, prosecutors brought Slattery forth to testify against Thomas Fisher, AOH delegate for Carbon County and well-known Democratic Party operative; and against Patrick McKenna, AOH bodymaster for Storm Hill and Democratic delegate for Carbon County. Both were charged with the 1871 murder of Morgan Powell.

At Pottsville Jail, officials placed Slattery in a cell with fellow prosecution witnesses Patrick Butler and Michael Lawler. There, the three former AOH men had ample opportunity to perfect their trial testimony. All three would go on to offer further prosecution testimony in additional "Molly Maguire" trials.

On July 16, 1877, less than a month after the first mass hangings at Pottsville and Mauch Chunk, Judge Green discharged Lawler, Slattery, and Mulhearn from Pottsville Jail. They left town together "on the first train in very jubilant spirits."[181] In 1878, Slattery returned to his post of township supervisor.

In September 1878, John Kehoe's defense counsel argued before the Board of Pardons on behalf of Kehoe's request for commutation of sentence. Anthony Campbell, Kehoe's counsel, "scouted the idea that Jack Kehoe was to be saved from the gallows in consideration of services rendered the republican party." Kehoe, Campbell argued, "might to-day be a free man had he given his consent to fully implicate men high in authority in negotiating for the purchase of the Mollie Maguire vote in the year 1875." Slattery, Campbell argued further, "owed his liberty to perjured testimony, connecting the governor and the secretary of the commonwealth with the alleged transaction."[182]

That same month, the *Chicago Tribune* published an article headlined "PENNSYLVANIA. POLITICIANS PULLING AT THE HANGMAN'S ROPE."[183] Samuel Garrett, a second defense attorney for Kehoe, gave the details for this account to the *Tribune* reporter.

Slattery, Garrett told the *Tribune*, "was willing to 'squeal' against his associates," but the prosecution had orders from Philadelphia, where Gowen and Allan Pinkerton had offices, to keep Slattery from the witness stand "until he would consent to SWEAR THAT GOV. HARTRANFT WAS IMPLICATED in the purchase of Mollie Maguire votes." As a prosecution witness, Slattery had accused Hartranft's associates, but had not implicated Hartranft directly. Slattery "received his reward for thus swearing," the *Tribune's* account said, "by not being sentenced."[184]

The account continued: "Overtures were then made to Kehoe's wife to have her induce Jack to swear that Hartranft was directly implicated in buying the Mollie vote. She was told that, IF SHE COULD GET JACK TO TESTIFY TO THIS it would help him and things would be made easy for him. Kehoe refused point blank, and even denied Slattery's statement. In fact, he refused to testify to anything of the kind. This made Gowen mad, and he has pursued Jack vindictively, has made every effort to convict him, and now has the rope around his neck."[185]

On December 18, 1876, Judge Dreher denied alleged "Molly" John Donohue's motion for a new trial and sentenced him to death. Dreher asked Donohue, convicted in part on Slattery's testimony, "'have you anything to say as to why sentence should not be passed upon you?'" Donohue responded: "'the men who swore my life away, swore it away for money or to save their own necks. Every one of them swore falsely, your honor, but I don't know that talking is going to do my case any good, and I have nothing else to say.'"[186]

Alexander Campbell, another target of Slattery's testimony, received two sentences of death in two separate trials, those for the murders of Jones and Powell. In March 1877, Campbell spoke with a reporter from Mauch Chunk Jail. Campbell laid his right hand on his heart as he spoke: "'here's a man who has been convicted by the most godless perjury, but who will go to his doom, if it be God's will, without faltering, knowing that the Great Judge will overrule the rulings of the Court that sentenced me to a double death.'"[187]

---

1. For this discussion, see Marvin W. Schlegel, *Ruler of the Reading: The Life of Franklin B. Gowen* (Harrisburg: Archives Publishing Company of Pennsylvania, 1947), 33-36.
2. For disbandment of Schuylkill's criminal court, see Alice Allen, ed., *Pennsylvania Manual*, Article XVIII, Future Amendments, Section 11 (Harrisburg, PA: Commonwealth of Pennsylvania, 1947), 55.
3. Pennsylvania's western "Molly Maguire" caseload has not yet received scholarly treatment. For this author's research, see *From John Kehoe's Cell*, "Pennsylvania's 'Molly Maguires': The Surprising Western Caseload," http://mythofmolly-maguires.blogspot.com/p/pennsylvanias-molly-maguires-surprising.html. See also epilogue, 417.
4. Alexander K. McClure, *Old Time Notes of Pennsylvania*, vol. 2 (Philadelphia: John C. Winston Co., 1905), 433.
5. John O'Dea, *History of the Ancient Order of Hibernians*, vol. 2 (New York: National Board of the AOH, 1923), 885.
6. *Report of the Case of the Commonwealth vs. John Kehoe et al.* (Pottsville, PA: Miners' Journal Book and Job Rooms, 1876), 167.
7. Kehoe's letter, written to the *Shenandoah (PA) Herald* on October 10, 1875, was published in that paper on June 8, 1876.
8. *Irish World* (New York), June 3, 1876; italics in original.
9. Correspondent "M. J. G.," *Boston Pilot*, September 30, 1876.
10. *Commonwealth vs. Kehoe*, 207.
11. Ibid., 193.
12. *Mauch Chunk (PA) Democrat*, April 8, 1876 (trial of Edward Kelly).
13. *Pottsville (PA) Standard*, July 10, 1875.
14. Ibid., August 21, 1875. The Gwyther case was never prosecuted.
15. *Miners' Journal* (Pottsville, PA), September 2, 1875.
16. *Shenandoah (PA) Herald*, February 5, 1876.
17. Ibid.
18. For Doyle and Kelly's statement, see *Mauch Chunk (PA) Democrat*, September 11, 1875.
19. For McParlan's meetings with Kerrigan, see James McParlan, expense reports, 12 August 1875, 20 August 1875, 22 August 1875, 24 August 1875, 27 August 1875, Box 1001, Reading Railroad Molly Maguire Papers, Hagley Museum and Library, Wilmington, DE; for McParlan's meetings with Linden, ibid., 20 August 1875, 26 August 1875.
20. *Shenandoah (PA) Herald*, February 5, 1876.
21. *Mauch Chunk (PA) Democrat*, September 11, 1875.
22. *Shenandoah (PA) Herald*, February 5, 1876.
23. Ibid., September 11, 1875.
24. Ibid.

25. Ibid., February 5, 1876.
26. Ibid.
27. *Miners' Journal* (Pottsville, PA), September 9, 1875.
28. James McParlan, operative report, 20 October 1875, Box 1001, Reading Railroad Molly Maguire Papers, Hagley.
29. Ibid., 25 November 1875.
30. *Mauch Chunk (PA) Democrat*, January 29, 1876.
31. Ibid., April 4, 1876.
32. *Shenandoah (PA) Herald*, October 23, 1875.
33. *Sunbury (PA) Gazette*, August 8, 1879.
34. For Kaercher's letter, see Marvin W. Schlegel, *Ruler of the Reading: The Life of Franklin B. Gowen* (Harrisburg: Archives Publishing Company of Pennsylvania, 1947), 276.
35. Ibid., 277.
36. Ibid.
37. *History of Schuylkill County, Pa.* (New York: W. W. Munsell and Co., 1881), 296.
38. F. P. Dewees, *The Molly Maguires: The Origin, Growth, and Character of the Organization* (1877; repr., New York: B. Franklin, 1969), 231.
39. Ibid., 232.
40. See epilogue, 426.
41. See chapter 8, 221.
42. *Shenandoah (PA) Herald*, September 4, 1875.
43. Ibid., September 18, 1875.
44. *New York Herald*, September 4, 1875.
45. *Morning Herald* (Wilmington, DE), September 6, 1875.
46. *New York Times*, September 8, 1875.
47. *The Great Mollie Maguire Trials in Carbon and Schuylkill Counties, Brief Reference to Such Trials, and Arguments of Gen. Charles Albright and Hon. F. W. Hughes in the case of the Commonwealth vs. James Carroll, James Roarity, Hugh McGehan, and James Boyle* (Pottsville, PA: Chronicle Book and Job Rooms, 1876), iv. See also Kevin Kenny, *Making Sense of the Molly Maguires* (New York: Oxford University Press, 1998), 214.
48. *Shenandoah (PA) Herald*, February 5, 1876.
49. Ibid.
50. Ibid.
51. John P. Lavelle, *The Hard Coal Docket: One Hundred and Fifty Years of the Bench and Bar of Carbon County* (Lehighton, PA: Times News, 1994), 291.
52. *Shenandoah (PA) Herald*, January 22, 1876.
53. Ibid., March 31, 1876.
54. *Mauch Chunk (PA) Democrat*, September 4, 1875.
55. *Shenandoah (PA) Herald*, September 25, 1876.
56. Ibid., February 5, 1876.
57. Ibid., March 17, 1876.
58. Ibid., December 27, 1876.
59. Ibid.
60. Ibid.
61. Ibid., September 25, 1875.
62. *Chicago Tribune*, June 22, 1877.
63. *Shenandoah (PA) Herald*, February 12, 1876.
64. *Philadelphia Times*, February 5, 1876.

65. *Mauch Chunk (PA) Democrat*, February 19, 1876.
66. *Shenandoah (PA) Herald*, February 26, 1876.
67. Ibid., February 19, 1876.
68. Ibid.
69. Ibid.
70. *Philadelphia Times*, July 13, 1876.
71. *Shenandoah (PA) Herald*, August 28, 1876.
72. *Mauch Chunk (PA) Democrat*, April 4, 1876.
73. *Shenandoah (PA) Herald*, March 7, 1877.
74. *Mauch Chunk (PA) Democrat*, April 4, 1876.
75. *New York Herald*, April 6, 1876.
76. *Daily Dispatch* (Richmond, VA), April 7, 1876.
77. *Jeffersonian* (Stroudsburg, PA), April 13, 1876.
78. *Mauch Chunk (PA) Democrat*, April 8, 1876.
79. *Shenandoah (PA) Herald*, April 14, 1876.
80. *Irish World* (New York), April 8, 1876.
81. *Mauch Chunk (PA) Democrat*, April 8, 1876.
82. *Philadelphia Times*, April 6, 1876.
83. Ibid., May 8, 1876.
84. *Shenandoah (PA) Herald*, May 12, 1876.
85. James McParlan, operative report, 20 January 1874, Box 1001, Reading Railroad Molly Maguire Papers, Hagley.
86. *Shenandoah (PA) Herald*, March 10, 1876.
87. *New York Sun*, June 23, 1877.
88. *New York Times*, June 24, 1877.
89. Ibid., May 7, 1876.
90. Andrew Courey to Pennsylvania Board of Pardons, 5 June 1880, Christopher Donnelly Clemency File, Folder 1, RG-15 – 13-1139, Department of Justice Records, Pennsylvania Historical and Museum Commission, Harrisburg.
91. The *New York Sun* used this descriptor on October 17, 1876, when reporting the sentencing hearings.
92. *New York Herald*, April 12, 1871.
93. "The End of the Coal Strike—The Articles of Arbitration," *Philadelphia Press*, May 12, 1871.
94. *Philadelphia Times*, May 10, 1876.
95. *New York Herald*, May 10, 1876.
96. *New York Sun*, May 7, 1876.
97. Defendants included James Boyle, James Carroll, Hugh McGehan, and James Roarity. Before the second Yost trial, Thomas Duffy, also charged, demanded a separate trial.
98. *Shenandoah (PA) Herald*, May 26, 1876.
99. Ibid.
100. Ibid.
101. Ibid.
102. Ibid.
103. Ibid.
104. *Philadelphia Times*, May 25, 1876.
105. *Shenandoah (PA) Herald*, June 30, 1876.
106. Ibid., July 3, 1876.
107. Ibid., July 1, 1876.

108. Ibid.
109. Ibid.
110. Ibid., July 3, 1876.
111. Ibid., July 1, 1876.
112. Ibid., July 3, 1876.
113. Ibid., July 19, 1876.
114. Ibid. Ryon referred here to McParlan's relationship with Mary Ann Higgins, the sister of Fanny Kerrigan.
115. Ibid., July 24, 1876.
116. Ibid., July 22, 1876.
117. Ibid., July 24, 1876.
118. Ibid., August 28, 1876.
119. Ibid., July 15, 1876.
120. *New York Sun*, July 30, 1876.
121. *Carbon Advocate* (Lehighton, PA), July 29, 1876.
122. *New York Sun*, July 29, 1876.
123. *Evidence in the Case of Dennis Donnelly* (Philadelphia: Allen, Lane & Scott's Printing, 1878), 319.
124. James McParlan, operative report, ca. 29 April 1875, Box 1001, Reading Railroad Molly Maguire Papers, Hagley.
125. *Shenandoah (PA) Herald* August 21, 1876.
126. Ibid.
127. Kaercher referred here to a second Michael Doyle (not Michael J. Doyle, convicted and executed for the murder of John Jones).
128. *Shenandoah (PA) Herald*, August 21, 1876.
129. *Cambria Freeman* (Ebensburg, PA), August 25, 1876.
130. *Morning Herald* (Wilmington, DE), August 28, 1876.
131. *Philadelphia Times*, August 21, 1876.
132. *Reading (PA) Eagle*, August 21, 1876.
133. *Chicago Tribune*, August 26, 1876.
134. Butler to Franklin Gowen, 17 September 1876, Reading Railroad Molly Maguire Papers, Hagley.
135. *Shenandoah (PA) Herald*, December 14, 1876 (trial of Thomas Fisher).
136. Ibid., February 5, 1877.
137. Ibid., July 24, 1876.
138. Ibid., April 21, 1871.
139. *Case of Dennis Donnelly*, 233.
140. *Shenandoah (PA) Herald*, September 22, 1876.
141. Testimony of Michael Lawler, ibid., September 23, 1876.
142. *Shenandoah (PA) Herald*, July 31, 1876; includes reprint of *Pottsville Standard* column.
143. Ibid.
144. *Shenandoah (PA) Herald*, September 21, 1876.
145. Ibid.
146. *Chicago Tribune*, September 25, 1876.
147. Ibid.
148. *Shenandoah (PA) Herald*, September 22, 1876.
149. *New York Herald*, September 23, 1876.
150. *New York Sun*, September 24, 1876.

151. G. E. I., expense reports, 12 August 1878, 11 September 1878, 18 October 1878 (cash amounts totaling $65.00), Reading Railroad Molly Maguire Papers, Hagley Museum and Library.
152. *Case of Dennis Donnelly*, 236.
153. Henry Pleasants to John Reese, 24 July 1877, Letterbook of Henry Pleasants, Reading Anthracite Company Collection, Pottsville, PA.
154. Dewees, *Molly Maguires*, 149.
155. *Philadelphia Times*, September 25, 1876.
156. *Pottsville (PA) Standard*, July 6, 1872.
157. *Shenandoah (PA) Herald*, February 26, 1876.
158. *Mauch Chunk (PA) Democrat*, July 1, 1876.
159. *Shenandoah (PA) Herald*, July 13, 1876.
160. *Carbon Advocate* (Lehighton, PA), July 22, 1876.
161. *Shenandoah (PA) Herald*, August 18, 1876.
162. Ibid., September 23, 1876.
163. *Shenandoah (PA) Herald*, September 27, 1876 (trial of Edward Monaghan).
164. *Philadelphia Times*, September 25, 1876.
165. *Shenandoah (PA) Herald*, September 25, 1876.
166. *New York Herald*, October 23, 1876.
167. Ibid.
168. *Commonwealth vs. John Donahoe* [sic], Roll 6080, p. 327. Carbon County Trial Transcripts; RG-47, Records of County Governments. Pennsylvania State Archives.
169. *Shenandoah (PA) Herald*, October 23, 1876.
170. *Philadelphia Times*, October 23, 1876.
171. *Commonwealth vs. John Donahoe* [sic], p. 346.
172. *Philadelphia Times*, October 23, 1876.
173. *Daily Gazette* (Wilmington, DE), October 24, 1876.
174. *Harrisburg Patriot*, October 24, 1876.
175. *Columbian* (Bloomsburg, PA), October 27, 1876.
176. *Wheeling Daily Register*, October 28, 1876.
177. *New York Herald*, October 25, 1876.
178. *New York Sun*, October 24, 1876.
179. *Philadelphia Times*, October 23, 1876.
180. *New York Sun*, October 24, 1876.
181. *Columbian* (Bloomsburg, PA), July 20, 1877.
182. *Harrisburg Patriot*, September 4, 1878.
183. *Chicago Tribune*, September 7, 1878.
184. Ibid.
185. Ibid.
186. *Carbon Advocate* (Lehighton, PA), December 23, 1876.
187. *Catholic Standard* (Philadelphia), March 17, 1877; reprinting *New York World*.

6

A BLACK MARK ON TIME'S CALENDAR

The business of the New York journalist is to destroy the truth, to lie outright, to pervert, to vilify, to fawn at the feet of Mammon, and to sell his race and his country for his daily bread.

John Swinton
Former *New York Sun* and *New York Times* editor, ca. 1880

I am sorry to state that since the advent of the Daily Herald it has done more to create a spirit of antagonism among the citizens of Mahanoy Valley than ever the lifetime of any editor can undo. Now, Mr. Editor, I am loth to say anything detrimental about any citizen of the county; but, can the editor of the Herald justly deny that many of the "coffin notices" which have appeared in the Herald, were manufactured in the sanctum of the Herald? ... Did he not take advantage of affairs in Schuylkill to gain notoriety and circulation for his Molly Maguire sheet?

John Kehoe to editor, *Miners' Journal*, 1875

176 | THE PASSION OF JOHN KEHOE

IN PENNSYLVANIA'S COAL REGION, before and during the "Molly Maguire" trials, nativist editors methodically stoked ethnic hatred. Their rhetoric harshened an already coarsened public discourse and sensibility. Editors throughout the country joined in this nativist campaign. Chief among the progenitors of the toxic national discourse was Thomas Nast, cartoonist for *Harper's Weekly*.

[insert illus]

Nast's cartoon of Lady Liberty grasping a whip labeled "Law" to subdue an Irish knife-wielding ape appeared in late July 1871, after an Orange Parade in New York City devolved into violence. More than sixty people were killed, a number of them Irish Catholics.

Two months later, Nast followed with the cartoon captioned "The Usual Irish Way of Doing Things." Nast's ape-like Irishman astride a barrel of gunpowder, waving an upturned bottle of rum and brandishing a shillelagh, left readers with no doubt of Nast's, or Fletcher Harper's, estimation of their fellow New Yorkers of Irish Catholic descent.

[insert illus]

Nast's virulent cartoons appeared the same year that Ancient Order of Hibernian (AOH) officers in Pennsylvania and New York filed almost identical revised charters for their benevolent order with their respective state legislatures. The action reflected the growing social and political influence of Irish Catholics in the country's two most populous states.

Four years after Nast's cartoons appeared, *Frank Leslie's Illustrated Newspaper* sent its artist, Joseph Becker, to Pottsville, Pennsylvania. Becker traveled the coal region as anthracite mineworkers gathered in advance of the Harrisburg Anti-Monopoly Convention, where they would challenge the right of Franklin Gowen's company to own and mine coal land under its charter. Months before any arrests took place, Becker gave the public its first glimpse of so-called "Molly Maguire Prisoners," along with a supposed "coffin notice."

[insert illus]

Descriptions of Irishmen, especially alleged "Molly Maguires," as less than human also proliferated in Pennsylvania's coal region before the "Molly" trials began. In October 1875, a column in the *Shenandoah Herald*, supposedly from a correspondent who identified himself as "A Miner," called on area residents "to stamp out of the midst of us these animals that prowl about and infest our domiciles." The *Herald's* editor, who probably authored the letter, echoed the exhortation, rousing the citizenry to "the wrong which they suffer by allowing such a body of assassins to live in their midst, a body of hounds who murder without warning, like snakes in the grass, as they are."[1]

As arrests moved forward, numerous publications referred to the Irish Catholic defendants as prey. "JUSTICE!!" the *Shenandoah Herald* said after the arrests of the defendants in the Yost trial. "THE MOLLIES EXPOSED!!! ... CLOSING IN ON THE GAME!"[2]

"DRAWING IN THE NET," the *Mauch Chunk Democrat* said at the close of Edward Kelly's trial at Mauch Chunk.[3] The *New York Herald* said of the mass arrests of May 6, 1876: "So well was the affair managed that no alarm was given until all the birds were caged."[4]

In August 1876, the *New York Sun* reported: "Three more Mollies were bagged yesterday."[5] From Ebensburg, Pennsylvania, on the same day, came the announcement "ANOTHER MOLLIE CAGED."[6] A few months later, the *Mauch Chunk Democrat* ran the headline "Exterminating the Mollies."[7] Three decades later James Ford Rhodes, in a discourse on the Pennsylvania conflict, mentioned the town of Tuscarora, "where there was a nest of Molly Maguires."[8]

Editors also indulged in barbs tinged with sadism. On the arrest of John Slattery by Pinkerton operative Robert Linden and his deputy, both in Franklin Gowen's employ, the pseudo-officers of the law "gathered the smiling John into their fond embraces."[9] On the arrival of Slattery at Mauch Chunk Jail with two other defendants, John Donohue "was the only one of the trio that wore steel ornaments."[10]

Certain Hibernian defendants, bewildered and terrified at receiving sentences of death, thanked the courtroom judges. When Judge Samuel Dreher sentenced Donohue, the father of eight, to death, the *Mauch Chunk Democrat* said, "we think he [Donohue] rather departed from the recognized rules of politeness in not thanking Judge Dreher for the boon conferred."[11]

After James McDonnell's arrest in January 1878, newsmen routinely referred to him as "the hairy man." By April 1878, with the arrest of John O'Neil for the murder of Frederick Hesser, all pretense of decency had disappeared from the region. The Pinkertons could arrest whomever they wanted, wherever they wanted, on whatever pretext they chose. "O'Neill [sic] is rather weak-minded, and seems to be but a few degrees removed from idiocy," the *New York Times* said of O'Neil's case. Of the jury's conviction of O'Neil after three hours' deliberation, the *Times* said: "The scene in court was thrilling. [O'Neil's] two sisters were [frantic] with grief, and they clung about his neck, screaming wildly, until they were forcibly removed by the officers of the court."[12] A last minute intervention saved O'Neil from the gallows, but consigned him to prison for life.

The executed Hibernians left behind at least forty-two children and an unknown number of grandchildren. The press gave minute accounts of the instruments to be used in their deaths. "The Hangman's Rope," the *Shenandoah Herald* reported before the June 1877 executions. The rope, from the Hamilton rope works, was "a little over a half inch in thickness."[13] "THE GHOSTLY GALLOWS," the *Herald* reported two months later. "A Description of the Instrument Which Will be Used on the 21st of June at Mauch Chunk."[14]

Some newsmen treated the hangings as entertainment. "THE GALLOWS," the *Sunbury American* reported of the mass hanging of six AOH men at Pottsville. "THE LAST ACT IN THE DRAMA PERFORMED." Of the day's events, the *American* said:

"Capt. Linden, with his Coal and Iron police, assisted by the Pottsville police, acted as master of ceremonies."[15] The *Miners' Journal* said of Thomas Fisher's execution at Mauch Chunk: "The town was rather pleasantly excited this afternoon."[16]

Some newsmen used coded nativist language. "This month of June has been a most enjoyable one," an editor from Bloomsburg said a week after six men had been hanged on one day at Pottsville, four at Mauch Chunk, and one at Wilkes-Barre. "There have been but few hot days, the nights have been cool and pleasant, the showers have been not infrequent and the moonlight has been glorious. June 1877 deserves a white mark on the calendar of time." In the same edition, the paper carried an article headlined "THE EXECUTIONS. ELEVEN MEN PERISH ON THE SCAFFOLD.—SCENES AND INCIDENTS."[17] Nine months later, Bloomsburg would mount three of the most savage of the "Molly Maguire" executions.

Other newsmen used openly nativist language. In a column titled *"GIRARDVILLE GIBLETS,"* the *Shenandoah Herald* said: "All our peace and order loving citizens were made happy ... that a beginning was to be made at disposing of the 'Mollie' murderers. All were made happy to know that Governor Hartranft had determined to enforce the law, and that in the future, as at the present, 'Mollieism' has got to take a back seat, while white men say what shall be done."[18]

In June 1877, the mass executions at Pottsville and Mauch Chunk convulsed Pennsylvania's coal region. The week before the executions, rumors of escape attempts brought in the state militia. The Eastern Grays patrolled Mauch Chunk's streets. As many as twenty additional companies remained on alert. Two days before the hangings, thirty militia members of the Fourth Regiment of Pennsylvania's Company F arrived at Mauch Chunk at seven in the evening. They quartered at the Market House. A squad of Coal and Iron policemen, led by Pinkerton operative Thomas Alderson, guarded Mauch Chunk Jail inside and out.

Inside the jail at Mauch Chunk, officials situated the scaffold, engineered to drop four men at one time, within view of Alexander Campbell's cell. Several Presbyterian ministers from Hazleton and Slatington escorted a group of young women to Mauch Chunk to view the apparatus. One clergyman stood under the trap while he explained to the group how the drop worked. As he spoke, the trap sprang unexpectedly and the heavy doors fell open. "His high hat alone saved him from a bad hurt," the *New York Herald* reported.[19]

The *Herald* of the jail: "Never was there a darker, more forbidding looking dungeon than the new Carbon County Jail, and never were bolts, bars, iron and stone more grimly associated than in this building, which is the very embodiment of frowning, sullen strength."[20] The night before the executions, authorities again increased the patrol with a special armed force of two hundred men. Inside the jail, men commanded an arsenal of fifty repeating rifles, fifty hand grenades, and a cannon.

Summit Hill, home to numerous alleged "Mollies," was located nine miles southwest of Mauch Chunk. On the day before the mass executions, the *Philadelphia Times* reported a mass meeting at Summit Hill of AOH men. "Fully five hundred Mollies were at the meeting," the *Times* said, "all of whom wore a white cross on the [lapel] of the coat, which seems to be a new feature in the Mollie Maguire ceremonials."[21]

At Pottsville, local military companies held themselves in readiness, as did Harrisburg's Legion Guards. A heavy force of Coal and Iron police, in Franklin Gowen's employ and under Pinkerton operative Robert Linden's authority, guarded Pottsville Jail. Special deputies armed with rifles, revolvers, and hand grenades patrolled the streets and the neighboring hills. The Gowen Guards and the Pottsville Light Infantry stood poised for action.

At Pottsville Sheriff Werner planned to deputize all, including the newsmen, who entered the jail yard to witness the executions. The *New York Herald* reporter said: "I could not help a peculiar sensation over the suggestion that it would be necessary to help to kill a man or six men in order to obtain vantage ground as a news gatherer. Still, the position that has been forced upon me is one that is eagerly sought by many, to the last man in Schuylkill county; by a hundred physicians from different parts of the State, and by representatives of the press all over the country."[22]

The *New York Times* reported that a Philadelphia firm had supplied the ropes, of half-inch Italian hemp, for free. The firm "hoped thereby to secure an advertisement."[23] On Market Street in Pottsville, an undertaker's window exhibited sample coffins marked with the names and heights of the condemned men.

On the day before the executions, a crowd of relatives, mothers and father, wives and children, brothers and sisters, aunts and uncles, nephews and nieces and cousins, crowded the jail's corridors to say their goodbyes. The *Philadelphia Times* said: "Pottsville jail is exactly like all the lock-ups in the Schuylkill Valley—four formidable walls and a turreted tower, like unto a barn-yard edition of a baronial castle." Sheriff Wright of Philadelphia arrived in Pottsville with Benjamin Franklin of the Pinkerton Agency. "They do not want to be seen," the Philadelphia paper said, "but undoubtedly your Jack Ketch [a notorious British executioner] will be on hand to-morrow to teach the Schuylkill county men how to perform his work." The *Times* also described the forthcoming scene at Pottsville Jail on the day of the executions. One hundred and five special deputies, "armed with all the Revolutionary shot-guns the townsfolk can resurrect," would assist the Coal and Iron police.[24]

In the jail yard the next day, fifty newsmen assembled at eight in the morning, joined by one hundred and five special deputies, thirty-six jurors, and "the hundred personal friends of Sheriff Werner, who, despite his boasted parsimony in the matter of passes, found no trouble in gaining admittance," all "clamored at the prison door for entrance."[25] Newsmen promised to publish no names of those in attendance. "The promise was easily made and as easily kept," the *Philadelphia Times* reporter said, "as the cognomens of a couple of hundred Schuylkill county Dutchmen, tickled nigh to death with their weighty honors, would scarcely prove any more interesting reading than an account of a Russian-Turkish squabble."[26]

The gallows at Pottsville, designed to hang six men at once, stood in the jail yard's southeast corner. The *Philadelphia Times* said: "The deputies and the Sheriff's friends examined and chatted over and laughed at the three dread instruments placed side by side. The walked under the traps and they walked over the traps. They critically examined the nooses and fondly patted the supports, and then, tired with their labors, they squatted upon the gallows steps and smoked their pipes and appeared to enjoy themselves hugely."[27]

At seven that morning at Pottsville Jail, priests celebrated Mass for the condemned men. Attendants included sixteen-year-old Kate Boyle, imprisoned for perjury the previous year for offering testimony on behalf of her uncle, James Boyle.

The *New York Times* gave minute details of the Pottsville executions. Sheriff Werner had decided to hang the men in pairs. Priests performed the last rites on the gallows. Hugh McGehan and James Boyle were the first to ascend. McGehan, married shortly before his arrest, wore a dark blue suit with a black necktie. "In his bosom," the *Times* said, "was stuck a bunch of red and white roses." Boyle, also married, wore a black suit "and carried in hand a large red rose, which he smelled occasionally on his way to the gallows."[28]

James Roarity, married with three small children, "was clean shaved, and wore dark striped trousers and waistcoat, black alpaca coat, and white shirt, without collar or tie. A bunch of roses was fastened on his breast." James Carroll, married with four children, "was attired in a brown sack coat, black waistcoat and trousers, a white shirt and turn-down collar, with a black tie, and was without flower or ornament of any kind."[29]

Thomas Duffy, single and in his mid-twenties, lived with his parents. "Duffy had a handsome face," the *New York Times* said, "set off by a heavy dark mustache. He was attired in black clothing, with a velvet collar on his coat, a black, white, and red bow under his collar, a small white rose in his button hole, and a single stud in his shirt bosom." Thomas Munley, hanged with Duffy, was married with three children. Munley wore "a black broadcloth coat with a velvet collar, trousers and waistcoat of black ribbed cloth, white shirt and collar, and black necktie. He wore a jeweled cross in his bosom." Both Duffy and Munley, per the *Times*, were "thick-set, strong looking young men in the flush of health."[30]

The gallows proceedings at Pottsville began at eleven in the morning on Thursday, June 21, 1877, an anniversary date that lodged in the minds of Irishmen. Seventy-nine years before in Ireland's County Wexford, on June 21, 1798, the Battle of Vinegar Hill had marked a turning point for British victory in the battle for Irish independence. At Pottsville, officials sprang the last trap at twenty minutes past one in the afternoon. All but Munley died of strangulation.

The execution of Andrew Lenahan at Wilkes-Barre for the murder of John Reilly took place at ten thirty that morning. A *New York Sun* reporter who spoke with Lenahan the previous day said: "he forgave all who testified against him. He denied that he committed murder, and said that he hoped the day might come when his memory would be vindicated."[31]

That same morning, at twenty-five minutes past ten at Mauch Chunk Jail, Sheriff Raudenbush placed four sets of steel manacles, along with four white cloth caps, at the corners of the gallows that stood inside that jail's first-floor arena. A north window flooded the scene like a spotlight.

One minute later the door to Alexander Campbell's cell opened. All four "Molly" defendants, Campbell, John Donohue, Michael Doyle, and Edward Kelly, carried crucifixes as they ascended the gallows. One hundred and fifty spectators, about a third of them pressmen, watched from the floor where the gallows stood and from the gallery above. As at Pottsville, priests performed last rites from the gallows. Officials manacled the men at their wrists, legs, and feet. They placed the nooses around their necks and drew the white caps over their heads.

At the signal, the trap doors sprang and the four men dropped four and a half feet, their chains crashing and clanging. The *Philadelphia Times* correspondent said: "Strong men turned aside rather than look upon the awful spectacle."[32] Of the executed men at

Mauch Chunk, Campbell left behind two small children, one born while he was imprisoned. John Donohue left behind eight children.

The day after the executions, both the *Philadelphia Times* and the *New York Times* printed Carroll's dying statement. In it Carroll, Tamaqua's former AOH secretary, thanked Pottsville's jail warden and deputy, the keeper, the priest and the nuns, his defense counsel, and the sheriff. He left regards for his father, mother, sisters and brothers, and for his "dear loving wife." He stated: "I do here confess to be innocent of the crime that I am charged with. I never wished for the murder of Yost or any other person ... I hope if I ever wronged any person that they will forgive me as I forgive those who have so falsely belied me. I, as a dying man, have no animosity towards any person. I hope that there will be no reflection thrown on my friends or family for this."[33]

Carroll, along with four co-defendants, was hanged for the murder of Yost on the testimony of James Kerrigan. Defense attorney John Ryon said of the evidence in the Yost case, "there is nothing in this case without Kerrigan." Of Kerrigan's testimony, Ryon said: "There are some powers in this county who can unlock the prison doors at will and carry a witness all around the county, as they have done with Kerrigan, whom they have dressed up in broadcloth and fine linen." He added, "we have proved Kerrigan to have been an unmitigated, infernal liar."[34]

The burial of Campbell, another of Kerrigan's targets, took place at Summit Hill on June 24. The *Philadelphia Times* reported: "His remains were followed from his late home in Lansford, a mile down the mountain, by the largest funeral ever seen in the coal regions, the procession reaching almost from the tavern of the dead man in the valley to the little church on the top of the mountain."[35]

As wakes and funerals continued throughout the region, the *New York Times* vented its disapproval. "IRISH CONTEMPT FOR GOOD ORDER," its headline ran. "MAKING MARTYRS OF THE EXECUTED MOLLIES—THOUSANDS OF PERSONS ASSEMBLED TO DO THEM HONOR." On the morning of the executions, this account read, mourners had transported "two handsome crosses of flowers" up Mauch Chunk's main street to be laid on the coffins of Doyle and Campbell. The *Times* denounced the "ostentatious display of sympathy."[36]

Twenty-nine years later, a reporter for the *Appeal to Reason* interviewed Michael Schoeneman, the jail keeper at Pottsville who had assisted in the executions there. "'They met their death like men,'" Schoeneman told the reporter. "'They were young fellows, full of life and good humor, and they were the best prisoners I ever had in my charge. There was nothing vicious in their conduct. ... They were hanged two at a time, and they died as they lived—whole-souled, manly men. Oh, it was a shame—a burning shame!'"[37]

---

1. *Shenandoah (PA) Herald*, October 2, 1875.
2. Ibid., February 12, 1876.
3. *Mauch Chunk (PA) Democrat*, April 4, 1876.
4. *New York Herald*, May 7, 1876.
5. *New York Sun*, August 25, 1876.
6. *Cambria Freeman* (Ebensburg, PA), August 25, 1876.
7. *Mauch Chunk (PA) Democrat*, October 7, 1876.
8. James Ford Rhodes, *History of the United States of America, From the Compromise of 1850: 1877-1896* (New York: Macmillan, 1919), 71.
9. *Mauch Chunk (PA) Democrat*, July 22, 1876; reprinting *Pottsville Chronicle*.
10. Ibid., October 21, 1876 (this account refers to Donohue as "Yellow Jack").
11. Ibid., December 23, 1876.
12. *New York Times*, October 9, 1879.
13. *Shenandoah (PA) Herald*, March 21, 1877; reprinting *Wilkesbarre Leader*.
14. Ibid., May 19, 1877.
15. *Sunbury (PA) American*, June 29, 1877.
16. *Miners' Journal* (Pottsville, PA), March 29, 1878.
17. *Columbian* (Bloomsburg, PA), June 29, 1877.
18. *Shenandoah (PA) Herald*, May 2, 1877.
19. *New York Herald*, June 21, 1877.
20. Ibid.
21. *Philadelphia Times*, June 21, 1877.
22. *New York Herald*, June 21, 1877.
23. *New York Times*, June 21, 1877.
24. *Philadelphia Times*, June 21, 1877.
25. Ibid., June 22, 1877.
26. Ibid.
27. Ibid.
28. *New York Times*, June 22, 1877.
29. Ibid.
30. Ibid.

31. *New York Sun*, June 21, 1877.
32. *Philadelphia Times*, June 22, 1877.
33. Ibid. See also *New York Times*, same date.
34. *Shenandoah (PA) Herald*, September 21, 1876 (trial of Thomas Duffy).
35. *Philadelphia Times*, June 25, 1877.
36. *New York Times*, June 24, 1877.
37. George H. Shoaf, "The Story of the 'Mollie Maguires,'" *Appeal to Reason*, August 25, 1906.

7

THE AOH CASELOAD: THE OFFICERS

It is an ancient law that a man who conspired to use the courts to destroy his fellow man was guilty of treason to the state. He had laid his hand upon the state itself; he had touched the bulwark of human liberty.

Clarence Darrow

The June 1877 executions at Pottsville and Mauch Chunk in Pennsylvania removed a number of influential AOH men from the political scene, notably Alexander Campbell and James Carroll. Other AOH officers remained in area jail cells awaiting execution.

In February 1877, four months before the mass hangings, the commonwealth had tried Patrick Hester for the 1868 murder of Alexander Rea. Victim of highway robbery, Rea was a mining superintendent for the Locust Mountain Coal and Iron Company. In 1869 Hester, AOH delegate for Northumberland County, had faced charges for Rea's murder. Lack of evidence then had led to an order of nolle prosequi in Hester's case.

Eight years later, at Bloomsburg in Columbia County, two bitterly disappointed Democratic politicians conducted Hester's 1877 trial. In 1872 Charles Buckalew, organizer of the 1865 camp meeting at Nob Mountain, lost the race for Pennsylvania's governorship. In 1875 Francis Hughes, who floated the 1862 resolution for Pennsylvania's secession from the Union, had seen the defeat of Cyrus Pershing for the governor's race. AOH influence helped defeat Buckalew in 1872 and Pershing, Hughes's favored candidate, in 1875.

Hester's trial gave Buckalew and Hughes a public platform against the Irish Catholic benevolent order that had challenged their political aims. As special prosecutors, they relied on testimony from prosecution witnesses Daniel Kelly and James McParlan. In their summations to the jury at Bloomsburg, both Buckalew and Hughes rang the nativist fire bell against the so-called "Molly Maguires."

Buckalew told the jury: "Hester, in speaking to McParlan ... said that he could run matters just as he pleased and that when he wanted a man beaten, or a clean job done, all that was necessary for him to do was to order it done and it was done." Buckalew added that at the time of Rea's murder, "murder and rapine ran wild in Schuylkill county, and no man of average courage dared to tell what he knew ... The Ancient Order of Hibernians was then in its strength." In a four-hour address, Buckalew asserted: "As my distinguished colleague [Francis Hughes] said ... a murder such as this could not be committed unless through a society such as the Ancient Order of Hibernians or 'Mollie Maguires' has been pictured to be."[1]

Hughes painted Pennsylvania's alleged "Mollies" in even darker shades. He instructed the jury on their supposed Irish roots: "They were called Mollie Maguires because they dressed in women's clothes. They used to blacken their faces and put on bonnets and frocks, and go out at nights [sic] and seize a bailiff or an agent of an absentee landlord, and if they did not kill him, they would beat him, or duck him in the bog-pond, and thus they inspired a feeling of terrorism that drove from those counties nearly all owners of soil."[2]

"'Mollie Maguireism,'" Hughes said, "'is of the utmost importance in this case. ... I want you men of Columbia County ... to help exterminate this hellborn organization, and send it back to the Prince of Darkness whence it came. ... if you will stand by the people of Schuylkill, Northumberland and Carbon Counties, you will not establish in that section of Columbia County, that is the fairest portion of all our coal fields, the paradise of Mollie Maguires ... you will not establish there a pest-house worse than ten thousand pest-houses, where these mountaineer robbers may come down upon you farmers in the lowland and burn your houses and destroy the lives of yourselves, your wives and your children.'"[3]

The *Shenandoah Herald* reported Hester's sentencing before Judge William Elwell. Hester said of the prosecution witnesses against him: "'The testimony of Dan. Kelly was false, and he should not have been taken into consideration. Young Harris lied from first to last, and Policeman [Parr] perjured himself.'" Hester declared his innocence "'before heaven, this honorable court, and the court of mankind.'" As he left the courtroom with his two codefendants, all now under sentence of death, Hester "made a low bow to his honor."[4]

Four days before his execution, Hester spoke with a reporter from the *New York Herald*. The reporter said: "Previous to the developments of the murder and the arrest of Hester, he was one of the most influential politicians in this county." Hester told the reporter: "'It has not been a fair trial ... my life has been sworn away to gratify a demand for blood. Had I been tried in 1869 I would have been acquitted; but when I was rearrested and tried last year the excitement against Molly Maguireism prejudiced my case beyond hope, nor can I procure a fair hearing before the Board of Pardons. I well know I can hope for no mercy from the Attorney General, but I had expected better treatment from the balance of the Board.'" Hester concluded the interview: "'Innocence is religion enough for me.'"[5]

The next day, the reporter again spoke with Hester, this time at Hester's request. "On entering the cell," the reporter said, "Hester saluted me with a calm, dignified, reserved air," and responded readily to questions. The former AOH officer spoke of his political career, his service as school director, overseer of the poor, township supervisor, and tax collector, and of his four daughters' careers as township schoolteachers. Hester told the *Herald* reporter: "'I am as innocent of the charge on which I am here as an unborn child. I have been abused like a dog. They have been after my life for a good many years.'" When asked the reason for the charge against him, Hester responded: "'Politics are at the bottom of it.'" Of Daniel Kelly, the chief prosecution witness against Hester at Bloomsburg, Hester said: "'He is all he confessed to be in court—a notorious highway robber and scoundrel. I cannot say why he went against me unless because he was bribed.'"[6] Kelly, like James Kerrigan before him, had admitted to the commission of a murder that brought AOH men to trial.[7] As with Kerrigan, Kelly's testimony secured him immunity from prosecution.

Defense counsel S. P. Wolverton told the jury at Bloomsburg: "'The pages of our history are reddened with the blood of innocent men ... Hester is a man for whom the commonwealth has been gunning for years. Kelly knew this, and he therefore wove his tale in such a manner as to fix the guilt of the murder of Rea upon Hester.'"[8]

Defense counsel John Ryon described Kelly thus: "'A criminal by nature, a knave by practice, a devil at heart. A creature that would barter away the kingdoms of the earth for a drink of whisky, and you are asked to believe this man. ... when the commonwealth of Pennsylvania places such a man upon the stand they corrupt justice.'" Ryon closed his address: "'if men's lives are to be taken away on such evidence as there is against these men the Lord deliver us from trials by jury.'"[9]

Hester told the *New York Herald* reporter of the charge against him: "'I am innocent of the murder of Rea and know nothing of it, and never had it in my mind to injure him. He was a particular friend of mine and was very prompt and punctual in business. Oh, no. I was sorry for his death and am sorry now. I never had any spite against him. It is not probable that I would undertake to kill a man by sending a lot of men that I never knew before.'"[10]

As with prosecution witness James Kerrigan, Daniel Kelly was also a self-confessed killer. "A MAN WHO HELPED TO MURDER RAE [sic] DECLARES HESTER INNOCENT," the *New York Herald* reported the day before Hester's scheduled execution at Bloomsburg. "A STRANGE STATEMENT BY WAY OF CHICAGO."[11]

In March 1878 in Peoria, Illinois, the wife of Dominic Gallagher, a coal miner who had relocated his family to Illinois from Pennsylvania's anthracite region, shared a news report of the Rea case with her husband. Carried in the *Illustrated Police News*, the article included portraits of Hester, Rea, and Kelly. "He knew the parties, and on Monday morning last he went to the law office of Mr. L. Harman and made the following statement under oath," the *Herald* said of Gallagher.[12]

Sometime after Rea's murder, while Gallagher still worked in Schuylkill County's mines, Kelly had confronted Gallagher to tell him of Hester's innocence of the attack against Rea. "'I asked him [Hester] to help do that job,'" Kelly told Gallagher, "'and Hester's reply was that he wanted that thing stopped; that Rae [sic] had been his friend.'"[13]

"'We did it all the same,'" Kelly told Gallagher of Rea's murder. In his affidavit, Gallagher stated further that Kelly "avowed that Hester was innocent; that the plot was carried on and executed without Hester knowing anything about it."[14]

As to Kelly's disclosures, Gallagher's statement read: "I was at a loss to know why he confided this to me; but as soon as I returned home in the evening my wife told me that she had known Kelly before she was married, while she lived in Locust Gap; that he was a desperate and a bad character."[15]

Hester's defense counsel alerted Pennsylvania's Board of Pardons to Gallagher's affidavit. The board refused to consider the new evidence in Hester's case. As with Kerrigan in the Yost case, no charges were ever brought against Kelly.

After Hester's execution the *Boston Pilot*, a Catholic diocesan newspaper, reprinted the *Herald's* interview under the headline

"THREE MEN HANGED. Was Pat Hester an Innocent Man?" The *Pilot* said of Hester's case: "The sentiment had grown to be a conviction in the minds of the people that Patrick Hester, a highly respectable man, was innocent, and would be reprieved." The *Pilot* concluded: "The execution of this man, under the circumstances, is an awful stretch of authority on the part of the Governor of Pennsylvania."[16]

In March 1871 Hester, per an oblique reference by hostile parish priest Father Daniel McDermott, was one of two individuals who had "lobbied the [AOH] charter through the [Pennsylvania] Legislature."[17] The day before Hester's execution, his wife spoke with the *New York Herald*. "'Something that I know nothing about has conspired against him,'" she said. "'It is in the dark; it is for politics, all for politics. They have been seeking his life for ten years.'" The reporter asked Hester's wife of the sentiment of those in her neighborhood regarding Hester's upcoming execution. She replied: "'They don't believe that he will hang. All the working people hope that he will not. They don't believe that the State will hang an innocent man.'"[18]

Via telegraph, news of Hester's suspected innocence reached newspapers all over the country. "Hester clings tenaciously to hope," a Nevada paper said, "and frequently asserts his innocence."[19] Newspapers in South Dakota, Minnesota, Virginia, Ohio, Illinois, Tennessee, and West Virginia repeated the assessment. "He is calm and in good spirits, and still avers his innocence," the *New York Sun* said of Hester the day before his scheduled execution with Peter McHugh and Patrick Tully at Bloomsburg.[20]

On the morning of March 25, 1878, nine months after the mass executions at Pottsville and Mauch Chunk, a frigid wind blew snow mixed with dust through the jail yard at Bloomsburg. Crowds of men and boys jammed the long avenue that led to the jail. The surging crowd overflowed the avenue into the surrounding fields.

Newspaper coverage had helped swell the crowd. Of the gallows itself, the *New York Sun* reported: "Three men can swing together on it—if not with comfort, at least without inconvenient jostling. It is of the old-fashioned drop style, and, if its full fall is given, the expectation of some that Hester's head will be pulled off may be realized."[21]

At the celebration of Mass for the condemned men in Peter McHugh's cell, two Pinkerton operatives joined the congregants. The *New York Sun* reported a crowd of three thousand men, women, and children swarming the jail and perching on tombstones in a neighboring graveyard. "They joked and laughed and bantered each other," the *Sun* said, "as country people do who stand about outside a circus tent while a performance is going on within. There was no sympathy and no solemnity apparent, except momentarily among a few who, standing in a back alley, saw pass them the grief-stricken wives of Tully and Hester, going away from their last interviews with their husbands."[22]

"The day was made a holiday in all the country round," the *New York Times* said. "The morning trains running into Bloomsburg were filled with crowds of laughing, joking countrymen, such as may be seen about Fourth of July times." Wagons and carriages lined Bloomsburg's main street. The *Times* also estimated the crowd at three thousand. The spectators had arrived in town before nine that morning "in steam cars, stages, and every kind of farm vehicle known in Pennsylvania." Of the crowd's tenor, the *Times* said: "They thirsted for gore, and what they couldn't get out of the gallows they drew from brown bottles."[23]

Hundreds, anxious to witness the executions, besieged the office of the county commissioner for admission passes. "Every man," the *New York Times* said, "whose uncle was a second cousin to the Sheriff's step-brother by marriage was on hand early for a pass, and every rural politician in the county was offended if he was refused one."[24]

As with previous coal region executions, proceedings commenced at eleven. The condemned men carried crucifixes. Hester's was fashioned of ivory. As at Pottsville and Mauch Chunk, the sheriff, with his deputies and pass-holders, joined pressmen in the jail yard along with jurymen, counsel for the condemned, and physicians to verify the deaths. As at Pottsville and Mauch Chunk, priests performed the last rites on the gallows.

From McHugh's cell, site of the early morning Mass, a group of women and young girls gathered at the window to gawk at the gallows scene. A Coal and Iron policeman had escorted them to the cell after the Mass there had ended.

"The priests recited the offertory rapidly," the *Columbian* reported, "while from the windows of the cells that McHugh had just left a party of girls admitted by one of the Coal and Iron Police gazed upon the sickening scene. We do not know who they were nor do we wish to. They were probably among those who are a disgrace to their sex."[25]

When the drop fell, the spectators outside the jail yard sent up a howl, and kept it up for several minutes. The clamor intensified when the roof of a coal shed packed with spectators gave way. Several were injured, one boy badly. "The instant that the bodies dropped," the *New York Sun* reported, "there was a rush of the crowd up to the gallows, leaning upon its beams, jostling the doctors, who pursued their medical inquiries, and even elbowing the dangling men, who were fast becoming corpses."[26]

After more than ten minutes' struggle, all three Irishmen died of strangulation. Sheriff Hoffman allowed the bodies to hang for forty minutes before lowering them into the coffins. "This work," the *Sun* said, "was achieved with great difficulty, owing to the crowd's anxious determination to get a view of the dead faces. The deputy sheriffs could hardly move to and fro or even secure the ropes with which the men were hanged, fragments of which were subsequently distributed as mementoes."[27]

After the bodies were cut down, the sheriff opened the jail's front and side doors. The side door opened onto the jail yard. The throng surged into the yard to view the gallows and the bodies of the hanged men.

Outside the jail yard Hester's wife, with her brother-in-law, son-in-law, daughter, and infant grandchild, waited for Hester's body to be brought from under the gallows. Inside the jail yard, the crowd scrambled for souvenirs. Someone stole a gold ring from Hester's hand. So many demanded a piece of rope that deputy sheriffs opened the plaits to distribute single strands. "Many Columbia County homes," the *New York Times* said, "are happy to night over the possession of these precious relics."[28]

A few weeks after the execution, the *Columbian* in Bloomsburg published "HESTER'S LAST LETTER."[29] Addressed to his co-defendants Patrick Tully and Peter McHugh, Hester had written the letter two days before the scheduled execution. Tully and McHugh's membership in Hester's Locust Gap AOH division at the time of Alexander Rea's murder had led to their trial for the killing.

In his letter, Hester advised his co-defendants, "may God prepare us for the next and better world." He parsed the prosecution testimony against him, concluding: "This ... you know ... to be a lie, and in fact every other one that swore against me at the February Court swore false."[30]

"I am not guilty of the murder of A. W. Rea," Hester continued. "I never got up that job or plot that has been sworn against me and that both of you know." He advised Tully and McHugh that they were free to act as they pleased, adding "may God direct every one to do what is right, and may God forgive them that is the cause of my being here." Of his impending death, Hester said: "What I feel most sorry about is my poor family to be left desolate, poor and forlorn ... as for death, I am not afraid, for I am almost tired of this sinful world, for they are after my life these good many years. All that troubles me about dying is, to die of what I am not guilty of, and that both of you know, and may God in His mercy do what is just and right to all."[31]

If Hester hoped by this letter to secure an assertion of his innocence from Tully and McHugh, he hoped in vain. News of Hester's appeal to his co-defendants likely reached the Coal and Iron police at Bloomsburg Jail, and the Pinkertons who helped prosecute the case.

On May 10, 1877, at Tully's sentencing before Judge William Elwell, Tully had told Elwell: "'I never had any justice nor any defense in this case. I was arrested on the eleventh of November and brought to Pottsville jail. I had no friends there, not even one ... I had no counsel, no money to procure counsel. ... therefore I had to take whatever the Court gave me. I had no money and the Court didn't even ask on the stand whether we were provided with a defense or not. That is all I have to say. I am innocent of the crime I am convicted for; I know nothing of it.'"[32]

Ten and a half months later, on the day of Tully's hanging, newspapers published a document titled "Tully's Confession." The *Columbian*, the *New York Times*, and the *New York Sun* gave the document in full. Tully's statement, supposedly given on March 19, 1877, at Bloomsburg Jail to Coal and Iron policeman Thomas Alderson, implicated Hester in Rea's murder. George Elwell, defense counsel for Hester, Tully, and McHugh, and the son of William Elwell, judge of the Bloomsburg court, allegedly transcribed this statement from Tully on March 19, 1878, six days before the scheduled execution.[33]

Tully's supposed confession, in addition to implicating Hester, named additional, unnamed, AOH men in Rea's murder. The *New York Times* said "this part of the confession is to be kept private for some time, in the hope that the guilty men may be arrested."[34] The *New York Sun* said of Tully's published statement: "The stars mark a portion which has been withheld, in order that the ends of justice may not be interfered with. Four of the murderers of A. W. Rae [sic] are still at large."[35]

The *Columbian* reported the wake held for Tully at his home. The newspaper said of Tully's wife: "She was asked if the confession her husband made was true. She said it was not true, and was trumped up by the officials merely to give them an excuse to hang him. She was next asked if her husband had said anything to her about the confession before the execution, and she answered that he had not."[36] The *Philadelphia Times* said: "The wife of Patrick Tully, one of the men hung at Bloomsburg on Monday, says that her husband did not make a confession, but it is absurd to suppose that Judge Elwell would be a party to the imposition of a fraudulent confession on the public."[37]

After the arrest of AOH delegate Thomas Fisher for the murder of Morgan Powell, at least one Carbon County newspaper expressed skepticism. Fisher, a long-time Democratic operative and owner of Summit Hill's Rising Sun Hotel, had served as tax collector for Mauch Chunk Township. In 1872 as a union officer, Fisher had served as accounts auditor for Carbon County's District No. 2 of the Workingmen's Benevolent Association (WBA). In May 1876, the *Mauch Chunk Democrat* said of Fisher's prospects for county tax collector: "The friends of Mr. Thos. Fisher are anxiously looking for his appointment to the tax collectorship. Tom is a good man and deserves reward at the hands of the party he has long and faithfully served."[38]

Four months later, on Wednesday, September 20, 1876, a Coal and Iron policeman arrived at Fisher's Summit Hill hotel with an arrest warrant. Uniformed police accompanied Fisher to Squire Reed's office in Pottsville, where Pinkerton operative Robert Linden informed the Irishman of the charge against him.

The *Mauch Chunk Democrat* reported Fisher's arrest, "ostensibly on a charge of complicity in a Powell murder which happened some years ago." The *Democrat* predicted: "As nothing reliable is known, and Fisher will have a *habeas corpus* hearing soon, we forebear to enlarge upon the subject at present, but rather trust that he'll be able to vindicate himself."[39]

The shooting of Powell, a superintendent for the Lehigh and Wilkes-Barre Coal Company, had taken place five years before, on the evening of December 2, 1871. Powell died two days later. In a dying declaration, Powell named Patrick Breslin and Patrick Gildea as his assailants.

The commonwealth arrested both Gildea and Breslin. A grand jury found insufficient evidence to charge Breslin, but indicted Gildea for Powell's murder. Gildea's trial began on March 5, 1872. A few weeks later, the *Pottsville Standard* reported Gildea's discharge from custody, "the commonwealth abandoning the case."[40]

By the time of Fisher's arrest for the same crime more than four years later, the coal region had been well tutored in the perils of supposed "Molly Maguireism." Prosecution witnesses James Kerrigan and James McParlan had traveled the region telling tales ripped from the pages of Allan Pinkerton's fiction. These included tales of politically influential AOH officers ordering murders, trading murders, and rewarding men for murder. The Pinkertons, along with the prosecution, hoped that where these tales strained credulity, a calculated appeal to ethnic hostility would carry them through.

Both Kerrigan and McParlan had testified in Mauch Chunk at the June 1876 trial of Alexander Campbell for the murder of Lehigh and Wilkes-Barre superintendent John Jones. Jones's murder, both Kerrigan and McParlan claimed, was a trade for the murder of police officer Frank Yost at Tamaqua. Campbell was Fisher's colleague both as AOH officer and as Democratic Party delegate. "This organization of bandits," self-appointed prosecutor Allen Craig told Campbell's jury, "have the power of murdering, plundering, and killing. The organization can be traced back to a foreign shore. It is an unnatural plant in this country, and I HOPE TO GOD it may be uprooted all over the land by courts and jury."[41]

On Fisher's arraignment at Pottsville two and a half months later, the *Shenandoah Herald* reported: "Yesterday as we were sauntering along the street we heard the cry, 'There is another "Mollie" taken in.'" Fisher's arrest came three months after Campbell's conviction for murder and one month after the conviction of Schuylkill County AOH delegate John Kehoe at Pottsville. Charged by Linden with Powell's murder, Fisher "heard the charge, but never blanched," the *Herald* reported.[42]

At the Mauch Chunk trial in December 1876 of Fisher and Patrick McKenna, AOH bodymaster at Storm Hill and yet another Democratic Party delegate, the prosecution brought forward yet another surprise witness to stun and amaze the courtroom. But first, they showcased a few seasoned hands. On Saturday, December 2, John Slattery and Charles Mulhearn arrived at Mauch Chunk. "They were accompanied by several lady friends," the *Carbon Advocate* said, "and two members of the C. & I. Police, and took up quarters at Mrs. Breneiser's boarding-house."[43]

Less than two months before, both Slattery and Mulhearn had testified at the Mauch Chunk trial of AOH bodymaster John Donohue for the murder of Morgan Powell. Both Slattery and Mulhearn had been convicted previously in the alleged AOH conspiracy to murder the Major brothers. Cyrus Pershing's court in Schuylkill County had postponed their sentencing to allow them to testify in Donohue's case. Of the prosecution's routine procedure of arresting AOH men, lodging them in jail, and pressing them to offer the prosecution testimony that secured their release, defense counsel John Ryon said: "'Oh, put him in jail, and you'll always have 'em.'"[44]

Linden escorted Slattery and Mulhearn from Pottsville Jail to Mauch Chunk for the Fisher-McKenna trial. Before testifying in Donohue's case, Slattery had told a *New York Sun* reporter from Pottsville Jail "that he held in his possession a great many political secrets, and that he believed his own position in the future depended solely upon their revelation."[45]

Mulhearn, supervisor for North Schuylkill Township at the time of his arrest, had also testified at Donohue's trial. While awaiting sentencing at Pottsville Jail, Mulhearn had allegedly contacted Linden. "During his confinement," defense counsel John Ryon told the Fisher-McKenna jury, "he [Mulhearn] made a confession to Captain Linden, and he told you that if he had not been arrested he would never have confessed. ... he saw that to become the pet of the Pinkerton agency, and its pure and industrious agents, he must do something ... he saw that he must implicate others."[46]

In Mulhearn's testimony for the Donohue trial, Mulhearn had

claimed "that Powell didn't give the Irish a fair show and that he refused to give a mine breast to Alexander Campbell, now under the death sentence at Mauch Chunk, so it was decided he should die."[47] Mulhearn claimed that AOH assassins from Tuscarora were tapped to carry out Powell's murder. In a spectacular slap at the Roman Catholic beliefs of the AOH men, Mulhearn claimed that Fisher, as with Judas's thirty pieces of silver, had paid Donohue thirty dollars for the murder of Powell.

Mulhearn's testimony at Fisher and McKenna's habeas corpus hearing at Pottsville had secured their imprisonment. In Mulhearn's trial testimony at Mauch Chunk less than three months later, he strayed widely from his previous testimony. In a wrangle over admissibility of evidence John Ryon, in a swipe at Linden, denounced "a gentleman distinguished in obtaining confessions from people like [Mulhearn]." Ryon added: "Never have I seen such a thirst for blood exhibited by the commonwealth as in this case and in this character of cases. I have prosecuted for the commonwealth, but by the living God, I never pressed a question of the correctness of which I entertained a doubt, when the life of a fellow creature was jeopardized by the result."[48]

The same day that Mulhearn closed his testimony, "a horrible surprise awaited the prisoners in the shape of Cornelius T. McHugh."[49] Like Fisher, McHugh had served as a union officer. The two had shared AOH leadership roles, with Fisher as county delegate and McHugh as bodymaster of Summit Hill. As school director for Mauch Chunk Township, McHugh shared Fisher's political influence. As a delegate to 1871 WBA Grand Council proceedings at Mauch Chunk, McHugh had joined the group the *New York Herald* had named an "Immense Politico-Industrial Organization—A New Power Forming in the Land."[50] Arrested on October 22, 1876, for complicity in the murder of Powell, McHugh had been held at Mauch Chunk Jail for more than a month. While incarcerated, the former school director read history, science, and geography.

In the Fisher-McKenna trial, the Pinkertons capitalized on McHugh's erudition to solicit his perjured testimony. McHugh, like

James McParlan before him, claimed that AOH meetings had been used to discuss murder and the trading of murders—in particular, those of Jones and Powell. McHugh named both Fisher and McKenna as attendees at the alleged meeting to discuss these murders, and in the alleged murderous scheme subsequently enacted at Summit Hill. The *Shenandoah Herald* said: "McHugh's testimony was the last straw that broke the camel's back, and Fisher felt it."[51]

Three days later, Slattery entered the courtroom. As with McHugh, the prosecution had a distinct plan to extract perjured testimony from Slattery. With defense counsel's wrangling over its admissibility, it took three days to enact. Finally, on December 14, Slattery gave the intended statement. It indicted the AOH as a criminal organization worldwide. Slattery, former candidate for associate judge, said of the AOH: "'I have talked to men who have been members in England, Ireland, and Scotland, and from them I learned that the order was of the same character everywhere, and the constitution is a mere cloak, that the commission of crime might be concealed, and if a man were arrested for committing crime we, the members, were to prove an alibi by swearing the roof of the court house off if necessary.'" Slattery added: "'I have made up my mind to expose the criminal practices of the order, and I'm not half through yet.'"[52]

"This is encouraging for some people who may not yet have started for Utah," the *Shenandoah Herald* said of regional AOH men terrorized by the ongoing trials. The *Herald* added: "Before Slattery left the stand he caused considerable astonishment by breaking down. The tears trickled down his cheeks and he otherwise demonstrated the fact that he felt his position keenly."[53]

The previous day had brought the testimony of Pinkerton operative James McParlan, who by this time had incarcerated dozens of AOH men. McParlan testified to an alleged conversation held in Fisher's kitchen in July 1875. McParlan said: "I asked [Fisher] if [there] was any prospect of the order being recognized by the church, and he said that it could not possibly be admitted as the clergy knew that as an order it was known to be a cloak for crime."[54]

In his closing statement, defense counsel E. T. Fox warned the Fisher-McKenna jury against "the perjured testimony of men who are willing to swear to anything to save their own lives."[55] Defense attorney Ryon told the jury: "in no case have I seen such a determined effort to gain the admission of evidence unfavorable to the defendant ... these men were arrested by a man calling himself Linden, who comes from Chicago, and he tells you that he is employed by the Pinkerton agency ... who employs Pinkerton is still a mystery. Gentlemen, isn't it time to stop and see if the livery of Heaven is not worn by some men whom we don't understand? Why does this man who represents the Pinkerton agency sit beside counsel and urge on the case?" Ryon added: "I couldn't help thinking during the trial of this case that the employment of some of these gentlemen interested in this case depended upon the number of scalps they brought into this agency."[56]

The jury deliberated for four hours before bringing in two verdicts: murder in the first degree for Fisher, and murder in the second degree for McKenna. When the *Shenandoah Herald* reported the verdict, it described Fisher, along with four other condemned Hibernians, in shackles at Mauch Chunk Jail. The trial of Alexander Campbell for the murder of Powell would be taken up next. Campbell had already received a first-degree murder conviction in the Jones trial. "Whether Campbell will be compelled to wear two pair [of shackles]," the *Herald* mused, "should he be convicted of the murder of Powell, we know not, but as a matter of interest will inquire into it."[57]

"The organization is a banded one," a juror told the *Shenandoah Herald* after the Fisher-McKenna verdict, "and resembles a briar on a farm. If you cut off a branch of that [briar] every now and again you keep it from growing, but if you don't cut it down by the roots it will grow and grow until before you know it will cover your whole farm." The juror concluded: "When I swear I mean business."[58]

A few days later, the *Mauch Chunk Democrat* ran a column titled "Court Gossip." Of Carbon County's jurors, the *Democrat* said: "To be considered a man, 'good and true,' fit to sit in judgment over one of his fellows, the Carbon county test appears to be: First, That a man should know but little of the English language. Second, That he should be a person not passionately fond of reading newspapers, and lastly: That he be endowed with as little general intelligence as possible."[59]

The execution of Thomas Fisher at Mauch Chunk took place on March 28, 1878. Three days before, the triple execution at Bloomsburg of Patrick Hester, Peter McHugh, and Patrick Tully had roused the region's bloodlust.

The *Carbon Advocate* of Lehighton, a half-dozen miles southeast of Mauch Chunk, described the scene on the morning of Fisher's execution. Mauch Chunk Jail stood almost on Broadway's street front, less than a half-mile from the courthouse and the train station at the center of the pretty Victorian town. The jail's proximity to the center of town heightened the day's drama.

Groups gathered on sidewalks and on the doorsteps of businesses. "Others questioned their neighbors as to whether they intended to witness the hanging, in as light a manner as if it were a circus," the *Advocate* said. Incoming trains brought in more spectators who trekked up to the jail. The *Advocate* observed: "A spirit of hilarity, that was altogether out of place, was manifested at different times in the motley crowd which had gathered before the prison."[60]

Some in the crowd had traveled in the evening before to spend the night in town. Officials scheduled the execution for eleven in the morning. Before eight, a crowd began to gather at the jail. Sheriff Raudenbush had ordered the great doors of the jail kept closed until nine thirty. The *Miners' Journal* said: "Long before the hour of opening, the street upon which the jail fronts was filled with an army of pass-bearers. The steps leading to the entrance of the jail were literally packed and the diminutive grass-plots on both sides of the stairway were filled to overflowing with a seething, restless multitude."[61] A reporter for the *Mauch Chunk Democrat*, positioned in front of the jail, feared that the iron railing that ran alongside the front steps would break from the press of the crowd.

At a quarter past nine, the Summit Hill undertaker arrived with a hearse containing an icebox. At a quarter to ten, the official who stood at the jail's entrance began to call the jurors, one by one. Those summoned pushed their way through the crowd and into the jail. By half past ten, the official had not finished summoning deputy jurors. Reporters, waiting in the rain, grew restive. Finally, fearing they would not be admitted, they pushed their way past the official.

Once inside, reporters found access to the first floor, where the gallows was located, restricted by Coal and Iron policemen. The reporters hurried up to the second-floor gallery, where only back seats remained. Soon after they seated themselves, Sheriff Raudenbush rapped on Fisher's cell door. The condemned man entered the arena. He mounted the scaffold with two priests and two Coal and Iron policemen bearing candles. The priests performed the last rites from the scaffold.

The gallows had previously hanged four Hibernians at Mauch Chunk and three at Bloomsburg. When Fisher ascended the gallows, the *New York Herald* reported: "The rabble at the foot of the gallows shouted, 'Here goes the eighth.'"[62]

Fisher prepared to speak. The *New York Sun* reported: "In its eagerness to hear what the culprit would say, the crowd surged up to the gallows with such violence that a number of men were shoved under the fatal platform, an exceedingly dangerous position, not only for themselves, but for the priests and officials above, since those men, in their struggles down there in the darkness, were liable at any moment to spring the triggers of the trap and let it fall." Coal and Iron police shoved the crowd back. Fisher gave his statement, "a final emphatic and detailed averment of his innocence."[63]

At ten minutes before eleven, officials handcuffed and manacled Fisher. They placed heavy chains upon his lower limbs. Like the Hibernians hanged before him at Mauch Chunk Jail, Fisher would hear the rattle of chains during his final struggles. The *New York*

Herald said: "Chains, being a mark of special odium, called forth another burst of barbarous epithets."[64]

The executioner positioned the rope and drew the white bag over Fisher's head. The condemned man, the *Herald* said, "remained alone on the fatal trap in comparative darkness. He could be heard saying in clear, ringing tones, 'Jesus, Mary, Joseph, save me; have mercy on me, Jesus, Mary, Joseph, Jesus, Mary, Joseph.' His voice was clear as a bell, but a shudder was noticeable in his frame."[65]

Raudenbush sprang the trap. The *New York Sun* said: "The crowd was thrilled with excitement. Men clambered upon each other's shoulders and knocked off the hats of those in front of them to catch a glimpse of the dying culprit. They pushed their way again even inside the frame work of the scaffold and once more the oaths, complaints, and threats echoed through the corridor."[66]

It took Fisher more than twelve minutes to die. Finally, the physicians pronounced his death. The *New York Herald* said: "The crowd rushed up, and one brute removed the covering off the head of the dead body. The Sheriff protested, but he might as well have talked to the ravenous wolves of the plains scenting the blood of a wounded deer. The scene was indescribable and sickening."[67]

Raudenbush allowed Fisher's body to hang for more than thirty minutes. Once the corpse was removed, the corridor was cleared "so as to give ingress to such of the general public as desired to see the gallows."[68] About one thousand thrill seekers availed themselves of the opportunity.

Fisher left behind a dying statement. Published by the *Irish World* in New York, it included these assertions: "I am innocent of the murder of Morgan Powell as the child unborn. ... My life has been taken away by a combination of men and not for crime. The only thing they could prove against me, in justice, was that I was a County Delegate of the Ancient Order of Hibernians, and that I never denied." Fisher added: "I forgive all who have had a hand in my death."[69]

The ongoing cycle of so-called "Molly Maguire" hangings in Pennsylvania lasted from June 1877 to October 1879. Three took place on one day in Bloomsburg, Columbia County; a total of seven on three separate days in Mauch Chunk, Carbon County; a total of nine on four separate days in Pottsville, Schuylkill County; one in Sunbury, Northumberland County; and one in Wilkes-Barre, Luzerne County. The regularly scheduled executions had a corrosive effect on the region's populace.

At the executions of Patrick Hester, Peter McHugh, and Patrick Tully at Bloomsburg on March 25, 1878, and of Thomas Fisher at Mauch Chunk three days later, local sheriffs with armies of hand-picked special deputies staged carnivals of depravity that were eagerly attended by thousands of men, women, and children. Against the ongoing hideous spectacle of public hanging as entertainment, the condemned Irishmen had only their good suits, their roses, their crucifixes, and their prayers.

As the trials and executions rolled on, AOH men in Pennsylvania's coal region knew that none among them was safe. Pinkertons in the pay of coal and railroad interests were issuing arrest warrants. Pinkertons were guarding the jails. Pinkertons were guarding the courthouses. Pinkertons were scripting prosecution testimony culled from bogus confessions. Defense witnesses who challenged the scripted testimony were being arrested and jailed for perjury. Self-confessed murderers who served as prosecution witnesses were securing immunity from prosecution. Ongoing arrests, along with threats of future arrests, were arising from bogus confessions.

Irish Catholic defendants faced treachery from other sources: from Archbishop James Frederick Wood, from the local and national press, from their state and national AOH officers, from their parish priests, from judges, and, in some instances, from their own defense counsel. Those who turned for relief to Pennsylvania's Supreme Court faced similar obstacles. The commonwealth's highest court consistently upheld the lower courts' decisions, while instating financial obstacles against defendants already impoverished by defense costs and imprisonment.

Defendants who turned to Pennsylvania's Board of Pardons, a board created in 1873 through the instrumentality of Franklin Gowen, faced another roadblock. Pinkerton operative Robert Linden, in Gowen's employ, was personally advising that board against relief to Hibernian supplicants.

Coal region communities coped as best they could. A few months after Thomas Fisher's arrest, Father Joseph Brehony of St. Joseph's Church at Summit Hill, home to numerous alleged "Molly Maguires," began a series of weekly meetings. In 1875, Fisher and Brehony had worked together to negotiate the mineworkers' wage with coal operator Charles Parrish. Now, the *Mauch Chunk Democrat* reported the priest's gathering of parishioners "for the purpose of organizing a colony for the West or South-West." The *Democrat* advised: "Parties desirous of joining the movement should not defer it too long as the required number (100) will, very probably, be easily obtained."[70]

From Philadelphia, the *Catholic Standard* said of Brehony's effort: "Removal or starvation are the alternatives that now stare thousands of the coal region broadly in the face." The *Standard* added, "every *legitimate* movement to get people away who are now laboring in and about the mines and breakers of our anthracite coal regions for wages which simply place them in a condition of slow starvation, has our warmest sympathy and our strongest wishes for its success."[71]

Less than four months before the "Molly Maguire" hangings at Bloomsburg and Mauch Chunk, the *Tamaqua Courier* printed an editorial comment. "We have the first man yet to meet who is not dissatisfied with Mr. Gowen's new mode of adjusting the wages of his miners," it said. "His present plan is not only a blow at the wages of the miners but also at the individual operators. Mr. Gowen has not quite absorbed all of the latter individuals, and hence he must make new restrictions in order to embarrass them still more, and then seize one after the other, as they become helpless ... until he can look all over the Anthracite coal region and say, 'I am monarch of all I survey,' and he is nearly that now."[72]

Some months later, the *Miners' Journal* ran a brief notice for "Mr. Gowen's Lecture."[73] The Pottsville paper had at its offices a number of rooms designated "the Atheneum rooms," reserved for a gentleman's club called the Pottsville Atheneum. Located within the club's rooms, this notice advised, was a sign-up chart that would give members and "stockholders"—presumably, stockholders of the Philadelphia and Reading Railroad and its Coal and Iron Company—preferred seating for Franklin Gowen's upcoming appearance.

The *Miners' Journal* also reported Gowen's evening lecture given on April Fools Day in 1878 at Pottsville's Academy of Music. Gowen spoke just days after the executions of AOH leaders Patrick Hester at Bloomsburg and Thomas Fisher at Mauch Chunk.

Throughout his oversight of the "Molly Maguire" caseload, Gowen had made use of anniversary dates. Authorities in his sway named June 21, 1877, as the date for the largest mass hangings in Pottsville and Mauch Chunk. Seventy-nine years before, on June 21, 1798, on County Wexford's Vinegar Hill in Ireland, England had claimed a victory there that helped end the Irish Rebellion.

On March 17, 1877, three months before the first "Molly Maguire" hangings, Gowen had signed into being his "Miners' Beneficial Fund," a fraudulent insurance scheme designed to replace the benefits previously offered to workingmen and their families through both the defunct miners' union and the AOH. In previous years, St. Patrick's Day had been a day of celebration and honor for the coal region's AOH men. As their 1871 constitution directed, they attended Mass in a body and paraded in regalia. Newspaper coverage of Gowen's beneficial fund formed on St. Patrick's Day in 1877 named Cyrus Pershing as a trustee.[74] Pershing's court sentenced more Hibernians to death than any other court.

Gowen's speech on April 1, 1878, the *Miners' Journal* noted, marked the first anniversary of the Pottsville Atheneum. The *Journal* headlined its coverage "TRADES UNIONS. MR. GOWEN'S SPEECH. The Atheneum Anniversary last Evening—Mr. Gowen on Trades Unions and Labor Reform—The Workingman in America."[75]

Gowen's speech received far less press coverage than the ongoing "Molly Maguire" trials and executions. The April Fools event at Pottsville appears to have been a somewhat private celebration.

D. B. Green, a judge in a number of "Molly" trials, opened the evening's program. Green had served in the trial of Thomas Munley, where Gowen had given his much-publicized and oft-quoted speech. Green introduced Gowen to a packed room, with even standing room taken. Prominent Pottsville residents, along with "some visitors from abroad,"[76] had seated themselves on the stage. "'Mr. Gowen,'" Green said, "'needs no introduction to a Pottsville audience. Pottsville has always claimed him as a citizen, and has followed his career with interest and felt a personal pride in his achievements.'"[77]

The *Reading Eagle* also chronicled Gowen's speech. He spoke impromptu, the *Eagle* said, to his "large and glittering" audience. In the many conflicts he had had, Gowen told listeners, "with the Mollie Maguires, secret societies and investigating committees he had formed a very low opinion of his opponents, who had played the part of labor reformers." Gowen himself, the *Eagle's* account continued, "thought he would come and make a speech in favor of the working-men, such as the labor reformers ought to make; he would be a labor reformer himself and show the laborers where, in his opinion, their true interest lay."[78]

Gowen denounced the evils of trade unions. He denounced their leaders as demagogues. To ridicule the many resolutions union leaders had passed against his company in the preceding half-decade, Gowen gave his own, singular resolution. It resolved: "'That the laboring man of this country can better pursue his own individual happiness by following it out individually instead of collectively.'"[79]

In support of this stance, Gowen challenged the tenets of the country's Declaration of Independence. That Declaration had, Gowen said, "affirmed that all men are created equal and endowed with certain inalienable rights, among which are life, liberty and the pursuit of happiness."[80] But Gowen disagreed with the country's founders.

The Reading paper described Gowen's beliefs: "There were two great classes of people in this world—men of genius, or intellectual men, and those who were not so, the men of labor. ... Men were not created equal; all were equal in death, but in mind there were distinctions which would live when time was forgotten."[81]

With specifics, Gowen denounced the tyranny of the unions that had organized against his commercial interests. He claimed that the influence of similar unions in England had led to England's downfall. He repeated his love of individual, rather than collective, effort.

In conclusion, Gowen asserted, "the extravagance of the rich was the benefit of the poor." He claimed, "the burdens of the Government must be borne by the laboring classes." And he insisted, "there could be no greater blow to labor than the overtaxing of its employers." The *Eagle* concluded: "The speaker was rapturously applauded."[82] On the motion of Judge Cyrus Pershing, chief judge for the "Molly Maguire" trials, the audience tendered Gowen its thanks for his address.

The major New York papers ignored Gowen's speech. Somehow, Patrick Ford's *Irish World* got wind of it. "Stand aside Tom Jefferson!" Ford said. "Hide your head George Washington—all ye, the galaxy of heroes and statesmen that adopted the immortal and unchangeable truth on which this Republic is founded! Hide yourselves away out of the sight and the light of the great Gowen, who has actually discovered the secret of how to screw men down into a coalhole and starve them while digging out for himself the luxuries ... 'Intellect!' 'Genius!' We don't know how a selfish wretch like this dares to pronounce sublime words—the sublime meaning of which he does not even comprehend."[83]

In his speech, Gowen asserted that he recognized that challenging trade unions was death to political hopes, and stated he would never be a candidate for political office. Nonetheless, Ford's paper asked: "What does this indolent and stupid man think of the working citizens of Pennsylvania when he supposes that even a single man of them will cast a vote for him or the atrocious politicians associated with him?"[84]

Gowen kept his promise. He did not pursue political office, but contented himself with railroad administration and the ongoing "Molly Maguire" caseload. John Kehoe's hanging at Pottsville would be the seventeenth of twenty-one such executions in Pennsylvania's coal region. In Gowen's long and bitter personal contest against Kehoe, the railroad mogul would manifest his loathing of Irish Catholics in general, and of political reformers in particular.

---

1. *Shenandoah (PA) Herald*, February 23, 1877.
2. *Argument of Hon. F. W Hughes, Commonwealth versus Patrick Hester, Patrick Tully, and Peter McHugh* (Philadelphia: G. V. Town & Son, 1877), 19.
3. Ibid., 31-32.
4. *Shenandoah (PA) Herald*, May 15, 1877.
5. *New York Herald*, March 22, 1878.
6. Interview conducted March 22, 1878, published in ibid., March 23, 1878.
7. Kelly was initiated as an AOH member in 1868 at Big Mine Run.
8. *Shenandoah (PA) Herald*, February 17, 1877.
9. Ibid., February 24, 1877.
10. *New York Herald*, March 23, 1878.
11. Ibid., March 24, 1878.
12. Ibid.
13. Ibid.
14. Ibid.
15. Ibid.
16. *Boston Pilot*, March 30, 1878.
17. "The Church and Secret Societies. A Discourse Delivered by Rev. Daniel I. McDermott, at New Philadelphia, Pa.," *Catholic Standard* (Philadelphia), October 17, 1874. McDermott did not identify the second individual. See chapter 3, 89, n. 125.
18. *New York Herald*, March 24, 1878.
19. *Silver State* (Unionville, NV), March 26, 1878.
20. *New York Sun*, March 24, 1878.
21. Ibid.
22. Ibid., March 26, 1878.
23. *New York Times*, March 26, 1878.
24. Ibid.
25. *Columbian* (Bloomsburg, PA), March 29, 1878.
26. *New York Sun*, March 26, 1878.
27. Ibid.
28. *New York Times*, March, 26, 1878.
29. *Columbian* (Bloomsburg, PA), April 12, 1878 (Hester's letter was dated March 23, 1878).

30. Ibid.
31. Ibid.
32. Ibid, May 18, 1877.
33. George Elwell and Charles Brockway both served as defense counsel for Hester, Tully, and McHugh. At the time of the trial, Elwell and Brockway also shared ownership of Bloomsburg's *Columbian* newspaper.
34. *New York Times*, March 26, 1878.
35. *New York Sun*, March 26, 1878.
36. *Columbian* (Bloomsburg, PA), April 5, 1878.
37. *Philadelphia Times*, March 30, 1878.
38. "Summit Hill and Vicinity," *Mauch Chunk (PA) Democrat*, May 27, 1876.
39. Ibid., September 23, 1876; italics in original.
40. *Pottsville (PA) Standard*, March 23, 1872.
41. *Shenandoah (PA) Herald*, July 1, 1876.
42. Ibid., September 22, 1876.
43. *Carbon Advocate* (Lehighton, PA), December 16, 1876.
44. *Shenandoah (PA) Herald*, December 11, 1876.
45. *New York Sun*, October 29, 1876.
46. *Shenandoah (PA) Herald*, December 14, 1876.
47. *New York Herald*, October 23, 1876.
48. *Shenandoah (PA) Herald*, December 9, 1876.
49. Ibid.
50. *New York Herald*, April 12, 1871.
51. *Shenandoah (PA) Herald*, December 11, 1876.
52. Ibid., December 15, 1876.
53. Ibid.
54. Ibid., December 14, 1876.
55. Ibid., December 18, 1876.
56. Ibid., December 16, 1876.
57. Ibid., December 19, 1876.
58. Ibid.
59. *Mauch Chunk (PA) Democrat*, December 23, 1876.
60. *Carbon Advocate* (Lehighton, PA), March 30, 1878.
61. *Miners' Journal* (Pottsville, PA), March 29, 1878.
62. *New York Herald*, March 29, 1878.
63. *New York Sun*, March 29, 1878.
64. *New York Herald*, March 29, 1878.
65. Ibid.
66. *New York Sun*, March 29, 1878.
67. *New York Herald*, March 29, 1878.
68. *New York Sun*, March 29, 1878.
69. *Irish World* (New York), April 13, 1878 (Fisher's statement is dated February 28, 1878).
70. *Mauch Chunk (PA) Democrat*, November 4, 1876.
71. *Catholic Standard* (Philadelphia), February 3, 1877; italics in original.
72. *Tamaqua (PA) Courier*, January 5, 1878
73. *Miners' Journal* (Pottsville, PA), March 29, 1878.
74. *Shenandoah (PA) Herald*, March 23, 1877.
75. Ibid., April 5, 1878.
76. Ibid.

77. Ibid.
78. *Reading (PA) Eagle*, April 2, 1878.
79. Ibid.
80. Ibid.
81. Ibid.
82. Ibid.
83. "Gowen versus Jefferson," *Irish World* (New York), April 20, 1878.
84. Ibid.

8
JUG-HANDLED JUSTICE

As to the trial of this cause, we have only to say that the proceedings, to our minds, were extraordinary. The rules of evidence were strained to a tension never before heard of in the history of criminal jurisprudence; principles of law established that are dangerous in the extreme; and precedents set which, if followed, will make it impossible for innocent persons to obtain justice in a Court of law.

> Defense counsel for John Kehoe
> Harrisburg, Pennsylvania, April 1878

I would sooner die than swear a wilful [sic] lie on my fellow man.

> John Kehoe to W. R. Potts
> Pottsville Jail, ca. March 1878

By 1878, Franklin Gowen's animus against John Kehoe had grown into a vendetta. In September, after Kehoe lost yet another battle before Pennsylvania's Board of Pardons, Kehoe's attorney Samuel Garrett wrote to the *Chicago Tribune*. Garrett exposed Gowen's malice. Kehoe, Garrett said, had refused Gowen's overtures to broker a pardon for him if Kehoe would agree to swear a lie against Pennsylvania's sitting Republican governor, John Hartranft: specifically, that Hartranft had traded cash for votes. "Kehoe refused point blank," Garrett said of Gowen's attempt to solicit the perjured testimony. "This made Gowen mad, and he has pursued Jack vindictively, has made every effort to convict him, and now has the rope around his neck."[1]

Garrett also described an incident that had taken place in Gowen's office at Philadelphia, when a priest called on the railroad president to discuss the case against alleged "Molly Maguire" Dennis Donnelly. In passing, the priest told Gowen "he did not think the Board of Pardons or Gov. Hartranft would allow Kehoe to be executed on the testimony against him." Gowen "jumped up excitedly, and, striking his fist on the table, shouted: 'D—n the Governor! If he don't hang Kehoe, we will hang him!'"[2]

Despite Gowen's yearning for Kehoe's execution, the railroad president stayed well away from the capital trial that secured the Irishman's death sentence. Gowen's Pinkerton operatives also kept their distance. Gowen's appearance of disinterest in Kehoe's capital trial allowed the *New York Sun* to say at the close of the trial: "Kehoe's conviction was accomplished without the testimony of any accomplices or detectives, and is a righteous one."[3]

A web of white supremacist leanings, decades of press manipulation, frustrated political ambition, fraudulent political and business dealings, and professional and familial relations connected the team that prosecuted the January 1877 case of the Commonwealth vs. John Kehoe. George Kaercher, Schuylkill County's district attorney in charge of the case, had worked in Gowen's law office during the late 1860s. Two years after Kehoe's trial, Kaercher intersected with Gowen in Paris during a European tour. Eight years after the trial,

Kaercher married Annette Hughes, daughter of Francis Hughes, another prosecutor in Kehoe's case.

Guy Farquhar, married in 1864 to Francis Hughes's daughter Frances Elizabeth, also served as a prosecutor in Kehoe's case. In the late 1860s, Farquhar had joined Hughes to form the law firm of Hughes and Farquhar.

On his death in 1913, the *Trinity Church Monthly* eulogized Farquhar, a former Sunday school teacher who helped found the Episcopal Club of Central Pennsylvania. "'For thirty-three years,'" it said, "'he served as vestryman and for twenty-one years of that time as one of the wardens of the parish. ... he was at all times the wise counselor and adviser of the vestry and rector ... in the truest sense of the word a *Churchman*.'"[4] The *Pottsville Republican* spoke of Farquhar's "'manliness, fearlessness and sympathy.'" His character, the paper added, "'will live with those who knew him and make better men and citizens and more honorable lawyers of all men who were blessed with his personal acquaintance.'"[5]

In the late 1880s, Farquhar served as an officer to the National Bar Association. In 1908, at the funeral of former U.S. President Grover Cleveland, he rode twelfth in a line of twenty-six carriages hired to ferry dignitaries to Cleveland's service.

In spring 1878, in a letter written from Pottsville Jail, Kehoe described the activities of Farquhar's younger brother Fergus, also a Pottsville attorney. "But iff [sic] I had sworn that Lie on Gov hartranft," Kehoe told Quaker attorney Ramsay Potts, "I would Be Pardoned long ago they ofered [sic] one [Kehoe's wife, Mary Ann] Both Money & Pardon if I would do it. Firgus [sic] Farquhar was Appointed By Gowen to Pay the money. but I would not take it. [T]hey all know that I am innocent [sic]."[6]

In 1875 Fergus Farquhar, like his brother Guy a Schuylkill County Democratic operative, had shown his anti-Irish bias through the pages of the *Pottsville Chronicle*. In October 1875, the *Pottsville Standard* said: "Mr. Fergus Farquhar ... according to the testimony adduced, is responsible for much of the brilliancy which adorns the columns of our sprightly evening contemporary, the *Chronicle*."[7] If

Farquhar authored the *Chronicle's* election coverage, he used it to spread political venom.

In October 1875, Cyrus Pershing served as president judge of Schuylkill County's Court of Oyer and Terminer. Pershing also captured the Democratic nomination for the governorship that year. Three of the four prosecutors in Kehoe's capital trial strongly backed Pershing's challenge to Hartranft's re-election.

During the Hartranft-Pershing campaign, the *Pottsville Chronicle*, possibly under Fergus Farquhar's pen, accused the *Miners' Journal* in Pottsville of arousing "the banded murderers of this region to opposition 'gainst Pershing, the bugle call for them to fall in for Hartranft." A correspondent to the *Pottsville Standard* who signed himself "Macarius Vigilante" said of the *Chronicle's* calls for vigilantism that fall: "Did [it] ever think for a moment honestly, there was such a bug-bear as 'Molly Maguires!' ... The *Chronicle* wants to catch and hang every Irishman, whose name is *Pat*, because if he ain't a Mollie Maguire, he may become one."[8]

Three years before, Guy and Fergus Farquhar had backed the election of Pershing for Schuylkill County's president judge against the Democratic incumbent, James Ryon. Anthony McCormick, a former treasurer for Butler Township, testified to his own role in corrupt electioneering in that contest. McCormick's statement gave credence to Kehoe's allegation of Fergus Farquhar as a bagman for corrupt Democratic dealings.

In court proceedings, McCormick said that Fergus Farquhar, along with a second Democratic operative, had told McCormick "that if I could get some votes for Judge Pershing, I would get some money for it; I said ... I wanted it before I left town; Mr. Farquhar said, Hold up till I come back and I will see if I can get the money for you." Farquhar met again with McCormick, "and said he hadn't the money then, but they were making up the money and he would have [it] ... in a few days; he asked me how much I could do for Pershing; I told him there was one man in Big Mine Run who could get him some votes. Will you assist him? he says, I said, Yes, if I get the money."[9]

Fergus Farquhar denied McCormick's allegations. The *Pottsville Standard* said of McCormick's testimony: "the gist of the whole matter is developed and the cat exhumed from the Pershing meal tub."[10]

In June 1874, Thomas Foster, publisher of the *Shenandoah Herald*, served with Fergus Farquhar as secretary to Schuylkill County's Democratic convention. Over the years, both men had watched uneasily as local Democratic Irishmen had strengthened their political potency through AOH agency. Foster's *Herald* peddled some of the era's worst yellow journalism. In May 1877, with numerous "Molly Maguire" executions pending, he let slip his view of Irishmen as non-whites.

Francis Hughes also served as a prosecutor in Kehoe's trial. On Hughes's death in 1885, Gowen eulogized him in a letter to Hughes's son-in-law, Guy Farquhar. "'It seems to be but yesterday,'" Gowen reminisced, "'that I sat in the court at Pottsville when a law student, admiring Mr. Hughes splendid mental and physical proportions, as he towered above every one else, in the trial of some great case.'"[11]

When Hughes closed for the prosecution in Patrick Hester's trial at Bloomsburg, the *New York Herald* said that his "fine presence, sonorous voice and white hairs heightened the dramatic effect of his powerful speech."[12] Seventeen years before, in reporting a Democratic meeting at Pottsville, the *Memphis Daily Appeal* had described Hughes as "one of the ablest men in the Pennsylvania delegation. ... said to be a man of high honor."[13]

Others disputed those views. In 1858, when Hughes unexpectedly sprang a series of pro-slavery resolutions on Schuylkill County's Democrats, the *Miners' Journal* described him as the "great thunderer of the Democracy," the "bell weather whose incentive is office, and whose motto is subserviency."[14] In 1866, Hughes joined with southern sympathizers to form a "National Union Party." The *Bedford Inquirer* accused that group of "'stealing the livery of Heaven to serve the Devil.'"[15]

In 1872, Hughes backed Pershing's candidacy for Schuylkill County's judgeship. At Erie three years later, Hughes backed

Pershing for governor, despite opposition from many Democrats. The *New York Herald* described the Erie convention as one "'of political tramps and vagabonds,'" adding: "'the old Bourbon Copperhead politicians ... who flourished during the war, have taken possession of the party.'" These included "'that noted tramp Francis W. Hughes, of Schuylkill.'"[16] In 1875, when Hughes changed his views on the currency overnight to support Pershing's grab for workingmen's votes, the *Pittsburg* [sic] *Commercial* said: "The persistency of this Pottsville demagogue reminds us forcibly of what Solomon says about a fool—'as a dog returneth to his vomit, so a fool returneth to his folly.'"[17]

In 1862 Hughes and his nephew Francis Dewees, the first chronicler of the "Molly Maguire" history, served as delegates to Pennsylvania's Democratic convention at Harrisburg. Convention delegates elected both men as officers, with Hughes as permanent president. The convention's ninth resolution described the negro race "as an inferior and dependent race."[18]

In Kehoe's 1877 capital trial, numerous nativist prosecutors stood on the Democratic side of the political divide: Hughes; his son-in-law and law partner Guy Farquhar; and Hughes's future son-in-law, sitting district attorney, George Kaercher. Prosecutor Charles Albright, who again appeared in court in his Civil War uniform complete with general's sword, represented Republican nativists. In 1860, Albright had served as a delegate to the Republican convention at Chicago that nominated Abraham Lincoln. Allegations of corrupt dealings preceded Albright's participation in that event.

"By his demise," the *New York Tribune* said during Albright's final illness, "Northeastern Pennsylvania loses one of its best and most influential citizens. His name was prominently brought before the public some four or five years ago in connection with the prosecution of the Mollie Maguire trials ... He was prominent as a lawyer ... and is generally honored and respected."[19] Brigadier General Elisha Marshall said of Albright's efforts during the Battle of Fredericksburg: "'no braver, more intelligent and gallant officer ever drew a sword in defense of the Union.'"[20]

Albright's early business dealings had proven less illustrious. In August 1854, an Ebensburg newspaper carried a small notice advertising Albright's sale at his law office of "a large lot of household and kitchen furniture" in advance of the attorney's relocation to Kansas.[21] Albright set up his new law office in Wakarusa in Kansas Territory next door to the office of the *Kansas Herald of Freedom*.

One year later, the *Herald of Freedom* published an editorial. There was, it said, "'something wrong somewhere.'" The paper reprinted the following notice: "'All persons indebted to the American Settlement Company, are hereby *Cautioned* against making payment to Charles Albright, as he is no longer authorized to receive moneys in behalf of the Company.'"[22]

"Where has He Gone?" the *Herald* asked the following year. "The Pittsburgh *Gazette* advertises for *Charles Albright*, Esq., who emigrated to Kansas from Cambria county, Penn., in the fall of 1854. We trust the inquiry is set on foot with the view of bringing him to justice for his frauds upon the people in connection with the Council City imposition, and that our readers will aid in finding him."[23]

A decade and a half later, when Albright ran for Pennsylvania's congressman-at-large, the allegations of corruption surfaced again. From Ebensburg, the *Cambria Freeman* published a notice from Albright's outraged former townsmen "to expose and hold up before the honest voters of the State the ways that are dark and the tricks that were *not* vain of this political demagogue and shyster." Ebensburg's residents charged that Albright, before leaving for Kansas, had solicited funds from local men for "the purchase of town lots in what was then known as Council City, in Kansas." Albright never returned to Ebensburg. In 1856, he relocated from Kansas to Mauch Chunk, Pennsylvania. "Albright played the same game with several citizens of Johnstown," the *Freeman* said, "as was recently ventilated by the *Mountain Echo*."[24]

The *Centre Reporter* said of Albright in October 1872: "His fortunes have vastly improved since his swindling sale of paper town lots in Council city, Kansas, to confiding people in Cambria county. Since that there has been a war, and in it there have been shoddy contracts, besides such small pickings as his bounty for lending his name to fill the quota of Banks township, Carbon county."[25]

Other papers accused Albright as a bounty jumper. A half decade later, when he again ran for state legislature, the *Harrisburg Patriot* resurrected the accusation. The *Patriot* charged that as a Civil War colonel Albright had "raised a regiment of nine months' men during the war, with an appointment as Colonel. When he had brought his regiment to Harrisburg he had himself mustered in one night as a private, thus filling the quota of his township and pocketing $500 bounty. Next day he was mustered out as a private and in as a Colonel. In this ingenious manner he got the bounty, his town saved a man, and the country was short one private solder."[26]

Albright's position as a leading Republican and corporate counsel for Charles Parrish's Lehigh and Wilkes-Barre Coal Company, Carbon County's largest employer, made him an odd choice for lead counsel in Kehoe's capital case in Schuylkill County. But as a prosecutor in Carbon County's "Molly Maguire" trials, Albright had already garnered numerous verdicts of guilt. And he retained personal ties to Kehoe's trial judge.

"Judge Cyrus L. Pershing, wife and daughter, of Pottsville, spent Wednesday night in this borough, the guests of General and Mrs. Albright," the *Mauch Chunk Democrat* reported the year after Kehoe's trial. "Judge Pershing and General Albright were boys together in Cambria county."[27]

Albright and Pershing shared more than boyhood memories. As attorneys, both represented Pennsylvania's railroad and coal interests. Both advised clients in both English and German. Both were skilled in press manipulation. Both embraced nativist views.

"He resided in this place in 1854," the *Cambria Freeman* said of Albright in 1872, "the year in which the bill organizing Kansas into a territorial government passed Congress and was approved by President Pierce. At that time he (Albright) was engaged in the practice of the law here, and was also one of the editors of the *Alleghanian*, a Republican and Know-Nothing sheet published in this place."[28]

Pershing shared Albright's newspaper experience, along with his anti-Irish, anti-Catholic animus. From early January through May 1, 1856, Pershing served as interim editor for Johnstown's *Allegheny Mountain Echo*. The future judge of Schuylkill County's "Molly Maguire" trials aired his views in a March 1856 editorial titled "A Picture of Know-Nothingism." There was no necessity, Pershing advised readers, "for the existence of the Know Nothing party as an independent organization. Its spirit—and we admit that there is a good deal that is peculiar and laudable too, in its spirit—would have been better spent if infused into other parties to correct their motives and their action."[29]

In 1875, when Pershing ran unsuccessfully for Pennsylvania's governorship, the *National Republican* characterized him as "a bribe-taker, an active and earnest rebel sympathizer, the flexible tool of vast corporations, to whose bidding he bended, often shielding them in the Legislature."[30] Less than two years later Kehoe, who had helped defeat Pershing in 1875 through the state apparatus of the AOH, stood before the bitterly disappointed office-seeker as a defendant in a capital case.

Along with his boyhood friendship with Pershing, Albright brought to the "Molly Maguire" prosecutions zealotry and a knack for invention. In mid-September 1864, Union authorities had sent Albright, then colonel of the 202nd Regiment of Pennsylvania's Volunteer Infantry, to Pennsylvania's Columbia County to gather information against suspected Confederate activists. Albright's investigation of the so-called "Fishing Creek Confederacy" ended in debacle. An aide to Major General Darius Couch characterized the affidavits and statements gathered by Albright as "'trash.'"[31] Major General George Cadwalader characterized the entire proceedings as "'a grand farce.'"[32] Twelve years later, Albright's prosecution of Pennsylvania's so-called "Molly Maguires" gained him national acclaim.

In spring 1878, in a letter written from Pottsville Jail, John Kehoe told his friend Ramsay Potts that there was "no evidence in my Case that should Convict me there was Good evidence that Proved my inocence [sic] But it was All Jug handled Justice."[33] The term had surfaced before in August 1877, when Schuylkill County's Democrats held their county convention less than two months after the mass hangings of AOH men at Pottsville and Mauch Chunk. The *Miners' Journal* said: "The ticket nominated by the Democratic Convention yesterday is decidedly of the jug-handle type—all on one side. The three principle candidates are all of the German persuasion, all live in the same town, in the same ward, on the same street, and the same side of the street."[34]

The *Journal* added: "The whole performance simply shows that in the wiping out of the Mollie Maguires the whole Irish nationality got a worse name than they deserve and their political brethren have consequently abandoned them." It concluded: "The platform is well framed to catch the votes of the workingmen."[35]

Among the *Journal's* unnamed "candidates of German persuasion" was Adolph Schalck, future district attorney for Schuylkill County. Schalck would shepherd Kehoe's case to its conclusion. Born in Wiesbaden, Germany, Schalck emigrated with his family to Pottsville when he was a schoolboy. While in his late teens, he worked as a reporter for the *Schuylkill Demokrat*, the local German organ of the Democratic Party. He clerked in the law office of Franklin Gowen and joined the Schuylkill bar in 1866 at age twenty-one. When Gowen moved his law office to Philadelphia, Schalck remained at Pottsville and worked under George De B. Keim, a second future president of the Philadelphia and Reading Railroad.

At Pottsville, Schalck promoted the efforts of the German order of "Harugari," which conducted its business exclusively in German. The order sought, per the *Pottsville Standard*, "to cultivate and spread the German language and ideas in this country."[36] Schalck served as secretary to Pottsville's Standard Publishing Company. Shortly before Schalck's election as district attorney, the company purchased the *Pottsville Chronicle*, run by Solomon Foster, brother to Thomas Foster, editor of the *Shenandoah Herald*. From their twin perches, the Foster brothers broadcast local editorials for two of the region's most virulent nativist sheets.

Schalck's boosterism of German influence intertwined with the white supremacist leanings of numerous "Molly Maguire" prosecutors. A number of men involved in the prosecutions, through lineage and practice, showed German sympathies. Their carefully stacked juries counted many Germans, or "Pennsylvania Dutchmen," among them.

"Germans can consult and receive advice in their own language," prosecutor Charles Albright advised early clients to his law practice.[37] A Bloomsburg paper said of Cyrus Pershing, who sentenced Kehoe to death, "Judge Pershing not only talks fluently our Pennsylvania Dutch, but is an excellent German scholar."[38] On the news that Governor John Hartranft, who signed twenty death warrants for Irishmen convicted as "Mollies," was at the close of his second term in office a candidate for the U.S. government's Berlin mission, a Pittsburgh paper said: "Hartranft ... has one very strong point in his favor—that he can talk German fluently and is well posted in German affairs."[39] A biographer of Franklin Gowen noted that Gowen's mother's ancestors had emigrated from Germany in 1683 with Francis Pastorius, leader of the first German settlement in Pennsylvania.[40]

British influence also generated enthusiasm for ongoing trials. Louis Jennings of the *New York Times*, responsible for that paper's coverage when the trials first began, was born in London. During Jennings's tenure at the *Times*, the *National Republican* said: "The Republican party and the Administration should not be held responsible for the utterances of the *Times*. It ... is, as we have said, the mere organ of a lot of Englishmen, who are ignorant of our history, the traditions of the country, its politics, and even its geography."[41] The *National Republican* said of Jennings, along with his fellow Englishman, historian James Anthony Froude: "they believe that a portion of the human race was intended by Providence to labor for the benefit of others, to remain stagnant as regards intellectual progress, and that to enlighten them would be not only to disturb their contented conditions, but to overthrow government itself."[42]

To a Philadelphia reporter, Kehoe stressed the influence of "British gold" over Gowen's business enterprises. Of Gowen's influence over the press, Kehoe told the reporter: "his money easily subsidized the great dailies of Philadelphia and through the country by the big advertising bills he paid them. It is known that he spent the whole profits of the mines for a year or two in this miserable way of airing his lawyer's logic in the public press."[43]

Charles Dana of the *New York Sun* and Alexander McClure of the *Philadelphia Times* served as megaphones for Gowen throughout the "Molly Maguire" trials. "Charles A. Dana is the apostle of slanderous journalism, and Aleck McClure is his disciple," the *National Republican* said of these two. It deplored their "untruthfulness, blackguardism and disregard of the character of others."[44] The *Republican* deplored, as well, the "horde of pigmies who crouch at the feet of Charles A. Dana, and learn from that veteran calumniator how to demoralize the public by decrying everything that is good in the world."[45]

Of McClure's eventual sink into the day's yellow journalism, the *Republican* said: "He ... was the trusted friend of Mr. Lincoln ... since he has joined the corps of scandal mongers ... his better nature has disappeared ... when his friend Gowen, of the Reading road ... prepares an argument to show why the coal monopolies should be allowed to continue their cruel exactions, he finds room for it in his columns ... In short, he has become so inoculated with the views of the Detective press that the very foundations of his existence are poisoned, and, like Dana, he has sold himself body and soul to the most disreputable influences."[46]

McClure, in particular, would press Kehoe's case to its tragic conclusion. Coal region editors matched McClure's fervor. Of the public's ravenous appetite for sensational press, the *Republican* concluded of McClure and Dana: "So long as human nature remains as weak as it is, and prone to the gratification of morbid appetites for sensational lampoons and disgraceful vilification, we may expect them to flourish with their ill-gotten gains.'"[47]

In January 1877, prosecutors in John Kehoe's capital trial at Pottsville, Pennsylvania, adhered to the former strategy used in so-called "Molly Maguire" cases. For their primary prosecution witnesses, they used two self-confessed killers. Neither would serve jail time.

The charge brought against Kehoe, the beating that led to the death of mine supervisor Frank Langdon at Audenried, was a crime of fifteen years' standing. Langdon, badly beaten outside of Charles Williams's Carbon County hotel on June 14, 1862, had subsequently spent that night in one of the hotel's back rooms. Suffering from a severe head wound, he had received no medical attention. The next morning, Langdon walked home to Honeybrook, in Schuylkill County, a distance of about a mile. Two days later, at one in the afternoon, Langdon died at his home.

Within six weeks of the opening of Kehoe's trial two additional AOH men, Neil Dougherty and John Campbell, had been convicted of second-degree murder in Langdon's beating and subsequent death. The *Shenandoah Herald* reported their sentencing hearing. It described Dougherty's address to the court: "'your honors ... I never beat or tried to beat Langdon ... I thank your honors for appointing to defend me three such gentlemen as conducted my case. ... It grieves my heart to stand convicted of a crime I never committed, and (here he almost broke down) to leave my poor father and mother and wife and four small children alone in the world, but I suppose that it cannot be helped.'"[48]

Campbell told the court: "'Your honors, there were no stones or clubs used in killing Langdon. It was only a billy in the hands of Donohue.'" Of his own involvement in the attack, Campbell said: "'I never threw a stone at the man; I never threw a club at him; I never even threw a chew of tobacco at the man and never had anything to do with the murder. I thought of "coming out" before, but I concluded to wait and let the public know how innocent men are convicted.'" He added: "'The man who is guilty of that murder ... is Jack Donohue. He is the man who struck the blow that killed Langdon and I will prove it.'" To make his case, Campbell pulled out "a couple of rough-looking attempts at map-making and laid them upon the table."[49]

By May 1876, at the time of Kehoe's arrest for various alleged "Molly Maguire" conspiracies, Kehoe had moved well beyond the mines of Schuylkill County. As AOH county delegate, he had traveled to the order's state convention at Pittsburgh and its national convention at New York. He had cemented relationships with national officers Patrick Campbell and Terrence Reilly, a relationship that led to their thwarted effort, in 1876, to raise a thirty-thousand-dollar national defense fund for Schuylkill County's AOH men charged as "Mollies."[50]

Regionally, Kehoe had seen AOH men attain elected office as township supervisors, tax collectors and assessors, overseer of the poor, and, in five instances, township school director. Kehoe had twice been elected high constable. Christopher Donnelly, elected in 1876 as school director for New Castle Township, served with Kehoe from 1874 to 1876 as Schuylkill County's AOH treasurer. In 1874, Donnelly helped secure the Democratic nomination that sent James Reilly from Pottsville to U.S. Congress.

Kehoe's ambition toward state office surfaced in 1872, when he placed his name in consideration for Democratic candidate to Pennsylvania's state assembly. Kehoe's ties to Pennsylvania's most powerful Republicans surfaced during his efforts toward commutation of his death sentence. In late November 1878 the *Miners' Journal*, avid for Kehoe's execution, asked: "Who raised the cry that Kehoe had been convicted on general principles and because he was Jack Kehoe? None other than Kehoe's friends." The paper added: "Kehoe was a county delegate, and, in the opinion of his associates, a power in the State. ... heaven and earth are being moved by friends and so-called friends of Kehoe to defeat justice by having his sentence reversed."[51]

Alexander McClure wrote decades later: "Exhaustive efforts were made on the part of [Republican operative Robert] Mackey and others to save the life of Kehoe, but Hartranft yielded to these importunities only to the extent of delaying the execution for an unusual period."[52] Mackey's influence carried weight. On his death in January 1879, the *New York Times* eulogized the Republican operative as "PENNSYLVANIA'S NOTED POLITICAL CHIEFTAIN ... one of the most prominent leaders of the Republican Party."[53]

Kehoe's ties to Pennsylvania's labor leaders surfaced in his spring 1878 letter to Quaker attorney Ramsay Potts. Kehoe told Potts that he would contact "John W. Morgan & Dr. McKibben ... of Cours [sic] I Need not tell you who to see you Know them all your self. I will write a long letter to John W. Killinger him & me used to Be Good old friends."[54]

At the time of Kehoe's writing, Potts, Morgan, McKibben, and Killinger, four men Kehoe hoped could help save his life, served in elected office.[55] In 1874 Morgan, a Labor Reformer from Shenandoah, advocated on behalf of a Miners' Hospital Association. The same year, Labor Reformers in convention at Mahanoy City declared Morgan "a *bona fide* representative of labor" and commended him to workingmen "irrespective of party."[56] In spring 1876, Pittsburgh's *National Labor Tribune* advised miners in favor of the passage of House Bituminous Ventilation Bill No. 66 to send their signatures to "Jonathan C. Fincher or John W. Morgan, who are our warm friends." The *Tribune* added: "Mr. Morgan is a practical miner from Schuylkill county, a member of the house."[57]

At the time of Kehoe's writing to Potts, John W. Killinger served as Republican representative from Pennsylvania's Fourteenth District to the U.S. House of Representatives. "Go and hear the champion of labor," the *Shenandoah Herald* said during Killinger's run for Congress in 1876.[58]

"I Need not tell you who to see you Know them all yourself,"

Kehoe told Potts.[59] All the men named in Kehoe's letter were warm friends of labor.

On Kehoe's arrest in May 1876 along with ten other AOH men, the *Philadelphia Times* described the Irish prisoners thus: "some of whom had enjoyed both social and political influence."[60] It would take an effort to erase Kehoe's accomplishments from the public mind. To turn sentiment against him during his capital trial, prosecution witnesses used a classic nativist trope. They accused Kehoe of desecrating the American flag.

A band had performed at Williams's hotel on the night Langdon was beaten. During an intermission, Langdon had given a short speech from the hotel porch to promote an upcoming 4th of July celebration that would include a Sunday school parade and a picnic.

"At the meeting at Williams's Hotel," Pennsylvania Supreme Court Justice James Sterrett wrote in the opinion that denied Kehoe's appeal, "... Kehoe came to the hotel seemingly desirous of making trouble. During the procession, preceding the meeting, he took a flag from Langdon's hands and, making a wrap of it, struck the latter in the face. Afterwards he spit upon the flag hanging from the porch of the hotel, and, being remonstrated with, replied he would do worse than that before he went home."[61]

Two witnesses in particular testified to Kehoe's desecration of the flag: William Canvin and Patrick Brady, an outside watchman for J. B. McCreary & Co. at the time Langdon was beaten. Brady had subsequently served, for many years, as a watchman for Charles Parrish's Lehigh and Wilkes-Barre Coal and Iron Company. To defense counsel John Ryon, Brady admitted having shot and killed a miner named Patrick Ferry. Brady told prosecution counsel that on his trial at Pottsville for Ferry's killing, his claim of self-defense had led to an acquittal.

To convict Kehoe of a hanging offense, the prosecution had to prove premeditation. On January 10, 1877, Brady took the stand. Charles Albright, self-appointed lead prosecutor, advised him: "If you knew of any altercation that took place between Kehoe and Langdon, before the death of Langdon, tell us what was said?" Brady responded: "About three weeks before Langdon was killed Jack Kehoe met him near his own door; they had some words." The *Shenandoah Herald* gave Kehoe's quote, allegedly overheard by Brady, in a headline: "The Chief of the 'Mollies,' On Trial for the Murder of Langdon. The 'Buck' Brady Testifies Against Kehoe. He Swears He Heard Kehoe Tell Langdon 'You Son of a B—h, I'll Kill You Before Long, for You're Only Robbing the People Here by Your Docking.'"[62]

Though Brady had testified against other Langdon defendants in previous trials, this was his first mention of Kehoe's alleged threat against Langdon. To defense counsel Ryon, Brady stated that fifteen years before, he had told two men of Kehoe's alleged threat. Both men were now dead. Officer Charles Grim, of Charles Parrish's Lehigh and Wilkes-Barre Coal and Iron police, had subpoenaed Brady for Kehoe's trial. At Pottsville, Albright had taken Brady's statement about Kehoe's alleged threat against Langdon about a week before Kehoe's trial began.

Ryon drew forth the information that "docking" referred to Langdon's refusal to credit mineworkers who worked by the cart for "dirty coal." Kehoe had worked not by the cart, but by the "breast," or section in the mine. Coal worked by the breast was brought up unmixed and impure, with no threat of its miner being docked for impure coal. Hence, Kehoe had no motive to confront Langdon about docking.

Nonetheless, Pennsylvania's supreme court justice, Sterrett, used Brady's testimony as evidence of premeditation. Sterrett's opinion stated: "This evidence showed that three weeks before the murder, Kehoe had used threats against Langdon, saying: 'You son of a bitch, I will kill you before long, because you are robbing me and robbing the men by your docking.'"[63]

Prosecution witness William Canvin also testified to Kehoe's alleged actions the night that Langdon was beaten. At the time of the incident, Canvin had charge of the outside machinery at J. B. McCreary's. "I took the flag upon the [hotel] porch," Canvin told the prosecution, "and went down again when Kehoe went up and spit upon the flag; I told Kehoe that he ought not to do that, and while we were talking, Kehoe's father came up and said, 'John, you ought not to do that,' and Kehoe answered, 'I will do worse before I go home tonight.'"[64]

John Kehoe's father Joseph described his son's working conditions at J. B. McCreary's colliery. "'John worked in the north pitch of the slope where Langdon was employed,'" Joseph Kehoe told defense counsel, "'he worked by the yard; his coal didn't come under the inspection of the ticket boss; I have no memory whatever of being at the meeting at the hotel on the evening of the 14th of June, 1862; I'm not sure that I ever saw John and Langdon speak together; I never heard John speak ill of Langdon.'"[65]

At the time of the attack on Langdon, John Kehoe, aged twenty-four, had lived with his parents and siblings at Honeybrook, a few hundred yards from Langdon's house. To defense counsel, prosecution witness Canvin denied having been "at Langdon's house with Kehoe about a week before Langdon was beaten, and ... Langdon bringing out a jug or can of liquor" out of which the three men had drunk. Canvin denied that Langdon asked him "to be on hand as he was going to get the band and have a little spree." Canvin denied that Kehoe himself had carried the American flag part of the way from Honeybrook to Williams's hotel in Audenried on the evening that Langdon was beaten.[66]

To defense counsel Ryon, during John Campbell's trial, Canvin hinted at having killed a man in Hazleton. He denied that the killing had taken place at a house of prostitution. Defense counsel Samuel Garrett asked Canvin if he was ever charged with complicity in the killing of Kehoe's brother Joseph. Joseph Kehoe, Kehoe's junior by five years, had died from injuries sustained at the bottom of a mineshaft; injuries sustained while Canvin stood above him.

The *Shenandoah Herald* recorded Canvin's response. "'I'll tell you all about that,' answered William, rubbing his hands. 'You see the rope had given way in several strands, and I had informed the bosses of it, and when [Joseph] Kehoe wanted to go down I told him not to, but he would, and it broke. Now could you expect me to hold the two ends of that rope together, with a cage hanging on one end of it?'" The *Herald* added: "Everybody laughed, of course, and Mr. Garrett appeared satisfied with the explanation."[67]

Other prosecution witnesses in the Langdon trials provided comic relief. George Graeff, eager to prove himself compliant, testified in John Campbell's trial that he had seen Campbell, along with two others, on the night in question. Graeff testified that after seeing Campbell, he had seen "about twenty men of the same kind and they all had billies in their hands." Defense counsel Garrett asked Graeff where he had seen this. "I don't remember," Graeff said, "but it wasn't hell." Garrett persisted: "Mr. Graeff, were these men armed with cannons or muskets or pistols?" Graeff responded: "I did not see any, sir."[68]

In Kehoe's trial, prosecution witness Thomas Horn told defense counsel Ryon that Officer Grim had told him "to meet Canvin at Hazleton." Ryon asked: "Didn't you say that one of these men sent for you to fix up your evidence?" Horn responded: "I may have said one of them sent for me, but not to fix up my testimony and Officer Grim told me to see Canvin that he might refresh my memory on points that I may have forgotten."[69]

Horn, partially blind, had been brought in to offer eyewitness testimony of the night that Langdon was beaten. Ryon, catching Grim signaling Horn in the courtroom, objected: "'May it please the court I object to any one prompting this witness.'" The argument that followed "was closed by the witness remarking that he was blind in one eye, and did not see Officer Grim shake his head."[70]

The month before Kehoe's execution, Kehoe spoke with a *Philadelphia Times* reporter. Kehoe told the reporter: "'Bill Canvin, the man who swore I spit on the flag that night, killed my brother Joe and I saved him [Canvin] from being killed. They wanted to kill Canvin for that, but I prevented it. Yet he swore my life away.'"[71]

The *Shenandoah Herald* reported defense counsel Ryon's closing address in Kehoe's trial for the murder of Langdon. Per the *Herald's* account, Ryon first:

picked up, metaphorically speaking, General Albright handled him rather roughly for some five or ten minutes and then dropped him so suddenly that his hearers almost imagined that the general was killed by the fall, but he wasn't. Mr. Hughes then came in for his share of attention, after which the press of the county, notably the Herald, was canvassed in anything but a gentle manner for manufacturing public sentiment unfavorable to the prisoner. Grim and the coal and iron police were torn to pieces ... but all of those already mentioned escaped lightly in comparison with William Canvin. Raising his voice until he must have been heard in the jail, Mr. Ryon exclaimed, "What reliance can be placed upon the tissue of lies uttered by that man Canvin—a man with the mark of Cain upon his brow, the man who was fixed up by Grim, the coal and iron policeman, and ... a man who for years has gone unwhipped of justice."[72]

The *Miners' Journal* reported Ryon's speech thus:

First, he spoke of the Coal and Iron police, and particularly the one who brought this prosecution viz: Charles Grim. He hurled bitter anathemas at the corporations who employed them, made a short Labor vs. Capital speech, spoke of the "old shaggy wolf standing at the door," and said the jury wanted bread and couldn't get it. ... . He then turned around to the press of the county, who he said had spoken more about Kehoe and said more hard things against him than all the press in the country had said about and against Hayes and Tilden, by the thousand fold. He could not say that the press was bought, but he intimated as though there was a possibility of it.

Mr. Ryon then turned his attention to "Bill Canvin." He said Canvin lied right along ...[73]

Kehoe said of the prosecution witnesses against him: "I never thought that men would Be so wicked they swore every way they wanted them ... I would sooner die than swear a wilful [sic] lie on my fellow man."[74]

On Kehoe's conviction for first-degree murder, the *New York Sun's* front-page coverage said: "It is proved that Kehoe told Langdon prior to the murder that he would kill him, and it was further proved that Kehoe was one of the six men who followed Langdon ... who beat him with billies and stones until he was dead. Kehoe then was the leader among the Mollies, and began the disturbance ... by taking the American flag from Langdon's hands and striking him in the face with it after having spit upon it."[75]

On April 16, 1877, Judge Cyrus Pershing sentenced Kehoe to death. By this time, eleven AOH men had been convicted of first-degree murder, and dozens of lesser crimes. Pershing summoned Kehoe to stand before the court. The Irishman, the *Miners' Journal* reported, "walked over to the little black desk, where so many Mollies have stood before him and heard their fates. He was very nervous, and took a Bible in his hands."[76]

Kehoe held the Bible in his hands for the duration of his statement. He told the court:

> All I have to say is of course that I never beat Langdon in my life, and never saw anyone else beat him. Of course I was in the saloon at the time he was beat, and when I came out I was told that he was beat. Of course George Beck swore there were several men there, but I cannot remember who they were. I had nothing to do with it of course. From the evidence against me I don't think it would be capable to convict me, but it was prejudice. I never had anything to do with Langdon. We lived opposite one another for about two years in Honeybrook and we lived peaceably, and I met him every day pretty near. I worked with him and he had no quarrel with me nor me with him. We lived good friends there, of course.
>
> They say that I threatened him, but I wish to tell you from the time I went there to the time I left, I never knew a breast of coal to be worked by the wagon—every bit was by the yard ... It was only manufactured evidence.
>
> ... Langdon ... was never struck by a flag by any person. Of course, I was there along with him [to Williams's hotel]; I went to

Honeybrook and Jeanesville and I carried the flag myself, and when we came in front of the hotel I wound the flag upon the pole and gave it to him and he stood it upon the porch. ... he told me to come into the saloon and take a drink, and I went into the saloon and we had a drink. ... He went out and told me to stop until [he] got back; he told me to wait until he came, and he would fetch Jake Myers, a coal operator, and when I went out I was told that Langdon was after being beaten. ... If I had beat Langdon he would have been apt to know it, for I was as well acquainted with him as with my own brother. I don't know as there is any use of saying any more.[77]

Two days before Pershing sentenced Kehoe to death, the *Mauch Chunk Democrat* published an editorial headlined "An Extraordinary Verdict."[78] The *Democrat's* editors wrote in protest of the latest verdict of first-degree murder in the "Molly Maguire" cases, against Patrick O'Donnell in Carbon County. As in Kehoe's case, Albright and Hughes led the prosecution team against O'Donnell.

While opposing "anything savoring of 'Molly Maguireism,'" the Mauch Chunk editors ascribed the verdict in O'Donnell's trial to the ignorance of the jurymen:

> And while we pity them for this, we own that we are getting daily more disgusted with a system which in order to accomplish certain ends, holds ignorance at a premium. Guilty of murder in the first degree, when the individual on trial was clearly and unequivocally entitled to an acquittal! No intelligent juror's judgment would have been guided by the testimony of three such witnesses ... Guilty of murder in the first degree! And who is it that says so? Why the twelve wise men (?) from the pineries of Carbon county, a majority of whom had been suffered to enter the jury-box just because they were considered sufficiently ignorant to be easily cajoled into a nonsensical verdict!"[79]

On the evening of January 13, 1877, three days before the jury in

Langdon found Kehoe guilty of first-degree murder, three hundred workingmen, most of them German, gathered in New York's Masonic Hall on East Thirteenth Street. They met to commemorate events that had taken place at Tompkins Square on January 13, 1874, when a mass daytime rally of unemployed workers had devolved into violence. Samuel Gompers had witnessed the rally. He later described mounted policemen armed with clubs "attacking men, women, and children without discrimination. It was an orgy of brutality."[80]

Three years later, the German workingmen gathered at Masonic Hall mounted their protest "against the inhuman treatment of miners in the Pennsylvania collieries, and the prosecutions of the Molly Maguires." One of their number told the crowd: "the coal owners and the railroad corporations had bribed and bought all the newspapers in Pennsylvania and New York ... to make public opinion for the monopolists, and to force the world to believe that the miners are violent, infamous and murderous. ... McPartland [sic] was a spy among the workingmen in the interest of the mine owners ... he treacherously urged them to desperate and unlawful acts, at the instigation of their employers ... there is no testimony to show that such an organization as the Molly Maguires exists."[81]

The New York gathering resolved: "That this mass meeting of workingmen, in the name of the workingmen of this city, protest against the infamous treatment to which the miners of Pennsylvania are subjected, and the proposed wholesale execution of men against whom the only testimony was that of hired witnesses. This meeting further considers it the duty of all workingmen, but more especially those in Pennsylvania, to raise their voices against the proposed hideous human butchery."[82]

In January 1878, the Pennsylvania Supreme Court issued its ruling in Kehoe's case. The ruling affirmed the judgment of Schuylkill County's Court of Oyer and Terminer. From April through December 1878, Pennsylvania's Board of Pardons at Harrisburg would hold numerous meetings, official and unofficial, to consider Kehoe's request for commutation of his death sentence. A storm of sensational press would raise accusations of political interference. While numerous unseen hands played musical chairs with the pardon board's membership, Kehoe's wife Mary Ann and his defense counsel would make strenuous efforts on his behalf.

---

1. "Pennsylvania. Politicians Pulling at the Hangman's Rope," *Chicago Tribune*, September 7, 1878.
2. Ibid.
3. *New York Sun*, January 17, 1877.
4. *Trinity Church Monthly* quoted in *Schuylkill County, Pennsylvania: Genealogy—Family History—Biography*, vol. 1 (Chicago: J. H. Beers, 1916), 7; italics in original.
5. *Pottsville Republican* quoted in Beers, *Schuylkill County*, 6-7.
6. John Kehoe to W. R. Potts, ca. March 1878, John Kehoe File, M 170.18 MI, Schuylkill County Historical Society, Pottsville, PA.
7. *Pottsville (PA) Standard*, October 23, 1875.
8. Ibid., October 16, 1875.
9. Reported in ibid., September 28, 1872.
10. Ibid.
11. Marvin W. Schlegel, *Ruler of the Reading: The Life of Franklin B. Gowen* (Harrisburg: Archives Publishing Company of Pennsylvania, 1947), 275.
12. *New York Herald*, February 24, 1877.
13. *Memphis Daily Appeal*, June 13, 1860.
14. *Jeffersonian* (Stroudsburg, PA), January 7, 1858; reprinting *Miners' Journal*.
15. *Bedford (PA) Inquirer*, August 3, 1866.
16. *Sunbury (PA) American*, September 17, 1875.
17. *Pittsburg [sic] Commercial*, November 18, 1875.
18. *Columbia Democrat and Bloomsburg (PA) General Advertiser*, July 12, 1862.
19. *New York Tribune*, September 28, 1880.
20. *Alleghanian* (Ebensburg, PA), January 22, 1863.
21. *Democrat and Sentinel* (Ebensburg, PA), August 17, 1854.
22. *Kansas Herald of Freedom* (Wakarusa, Kansas Territory), October 6, 1855.
23. Ibid., November 29, 1856.
24. *Cambria Freeman* (Ebensburg, PA), September 13, 1872.
25. *Centre Reporter* (Centre Hall, PA), October 4, 1872.
26. *Ottumwa (IA) Weekly Courier*, November 13, 1878; commenting on *Harrisburg Patriot* account.
27. *Mauch Chunk (PA) Democrat*, June 29, 1878.
28. *Cambria Freeman* (Ebensburg, PA), September 13, 1872.
29. *Allegheny Mountain Echo, and Johnstown (PA) Commercial Advertiser and Intelligencer*, March 5, 1856.
30. *National Republican* (Washington, DC), September 25, 1875.
31. Richard A. Sauers and Peter Tomasak, *The Fishing Creek Confederacy: A Story of Civil War Draft Resistance* (Columbia: University of Missouri Press, 2012), 146.
32. Ibid., 56.

33. Kehoe to Potts, ca. March 1878.
34. *Miners' Journal* (Pottsville, PA), August 10, 1877.
35. Ibid.
36. *Pottsville (PA) Standard*, March 9, 1872.
37. *Democrat and Sentinel* (Ebensburg, PA), August 24, 1854.
38. *Columbian* (Bloomsburg, PA), October 22, 1875.
39. *Pittsburg [sic] Commercial*, December 24, 1878.
40. Schlegel, *Ruler*, 3.
41. *National Republican* (Washington, DC), December 6, 1873.
42. *New York Times*, January 31, 1874.
43. *Philadelphia Times*, June 27, 1877.
44. *National Republican* (Washington, DC), August 14, 1875.
45. Ibid., August 10, 1875.
46. Ibid., August 13, 1875.
47. Ibid., August 14, 1875. Despite its criticism of the *New York Sun* and the *Philadelphia Times*, the *National Republican* made no reference to the "Molly Maguire" coverage of these two papers.
48. *Shenandoah (PA) Herald*, April 3, 1877.
49. Ibid.
50. See "A Hibernians' Row," *Philadelphia Times*, August 30, 1876.
51. *Miners' Journal* (Pottsville, PA), November 29, 1878.
52. Alexander K. McClure, *Old Time Notes of Pennsylvania*, vol. 2 (Philadelphia: John C. Winston, 1905), 396.
53. *New York Times*, January 2, 1879.
54. Kehoe to Potts, ca. March 1878.
55. Ramsay Potts served as Republican representative to Pennsylvania's state assembly; Dr. David McKibben and John W. Morgan as Democratic representatives to the same body.
56. *Shenandoah (PA) Herald*, August 29, 1874; italics in original.
57. *National Labor Tribune* (Pittsburgh, PA), March 4, 1876.
58. *Shenandoah (PA) Herald*, October 16, 1876.
59. Kehoe to Potts, ca. March 1878.
60. *Philadelphia Times*, May 10, 1876.
61. *Weekly Notes of Cases Argued and Determined in the Supreme Court of Pennsylvania, the County Courts of Philadelphia, and the United States District and Circuit Courts for the Eastern District of Pennsylvania*, vol. 5 (Philadelphia: Kay & Brother, 1878), 82.
62. *Shenandoah (PA) Herald*, January 11, 1877.
63. *Weekly Notes of Cases*, 82.
64. *Shenandoah (PA) Herald*, January 11, 1877.
65. Ibid., January 13, 1877.
66. Ibid., January 11, 1877.
67. Ibid., January 6, 1877.
68. Ibid., January 8, 1877.
69. Ibid., January 12, 1877.
70. Ibid.
71. *Philadelphia Times*, November 19, 1878.
72. *Shenandoah (PA) Herald*, January 16, 1877.

73. *Miners' Journal* (Pottsville, PA), January 16, 1877. Ryon's address to the jury in the Langdon trial lasted three hours and ten minutes. Though an official stenographer recorded the trial's proceedings, no copy of the address has yet come to light.
74. Kehoe to Potts, ca. March 1878.
75. *New York Sun*, January 17, 1877.
76. *Miners' Journal* (Pottsville, PA), April 20, 1877.
77. Ibid.
78. *Mauch Chunk (PA) Democrat*, April 14, 1877.
79. Ibid.
80. Samuel Gompers, *Seventy Years of Life and Labor* (New York: E. P. Dutton, 1957), 87.
81. *New York Sun*, January 14, 1877 (see also *New York Herald*, same date).
82. *New York Sun*, January 14, 1877.

9

MARY ANN

I can't do anything ... I have no money; my wife, who is the noblest woman in the world, has done everything she could, and my counsel, too.

John Kehoe to *Philadelphia Times* reporter
Pottsville Jail, November 1878

WITH THE ONGOING arrests of dozens of Irish Catholic men in Pennsylvania as alleged "Molly Maguires," newspapers launched an orgy of coverage that made the prosecution's argument for them. Personal ambition drove much of this coverage. Personal vendettas drove some of it. In this, two newsmen stood out from the pack.

Thomas Fielders, a reporter for Thomas Foster's *Shenandoah Herald*, rode his coverage of the "Molly Maguire" trials on a journalistic career that took him from Pennsylvania's hard coal region to New York, and from New York to London. For their particular target, Fielders and Foster chose John Kehoe, Schuylkill County delegate for the Ancient Order of Hibernians (AOH), along with Kehoe's family. In exchanges that escalated dramatically in 1875, Kehoe engaged with Foster, Fielders, and an unnamed Girardville correspondent who called himself "Americus."

In early September 1875, in the midst of the Hartranft-Pershing duel for Pennsylvania's governorship, five murders in less than three weeks ignited the coal region. The *Shenandoah Herald* ran a column from Girardville, where Kehoe served as high constable. "GIRARDVILLE. ... DRUNKEN OFFICIALS," the *Herald's* headline ran. "Is it not a disgrace to our borough that those whom we have elected to protect us and preserve the peace should get drunk and fire off a revolver at such a time of intense excitement? This matter should be traced out, and if the party is guilty should be kicked out of the office he now disgraces." The unnamed Girardville correspondent added: "Your editorial last evening has echoed the feelings of every heart in our place—that is of respectable citizens—and our people are determined to wait no longer on the actions of tardy officials."[1] With this column, the *Herald* issued a cry for violence against Irish Catholics in general, and Kehoe in particular.

One week later, the *Herald* published an editorial comment headlined "OUR NOTICE." It included the first in a series of "coffin notices," the alleged work of mysterious "Molly Maguires." The scrawled coarseness of the *Herald's* first coffin notice belied the literacy of the five AOH men charged as "Mollies" who served as township school directors and their fellows who served as tax collectors and assessors. Complete with curiously professional drawings of skull and crossbones, and of a shotgun, the notice signed "P molley" gave the *Herald's* editor "24 hurse to go to the divil ... ye son of A Bitch." It concluded "we aint done Shooting yet." In the same column, the *Herald* advised: "The incarnate fiends, who plan the murders are the parties that must be wiped out."[2]

Two weeks later the *Herald* ran an editorial headlined "THE SITUATION." It advised: "The organization of Mollies is composed of bad and cunning men ... the law is utterly powerless to reach them ... for the next few months the law of the courts should be set aside and that of Judge Lynch be substituted for it." It concluded: "The silent, swift and sure action of the 'vigilantes,' with a single example of their power would strike terror into the hearts of every evil doer in the region and make Schuylkill county the quietest and most orderly section of the State for the next decade."[3]

A few days later, a column appeared headlined "LYNCH LAW." It reminded readers of San Francisco's vigilance campaign from 1849, when its committee's "famous fire bell" had summoned men to action. The *Herald* said: "The rope employed was a thousand yards in length and oftentimes a thousand members of the committee stood on it at a time, so there could be no possible question but that the whole people were directly interested in the work of purgation." The *Herald* advised: "there is every reason to suppose it will work equally as well here ... all the circumstances are favorable, the condition of society requires that it be done and the people are here who are willing to do the work."[4]

The next day, the *Herald* published more hate speech from Girardville, home to Kehoe, his wife Mary Ann, and their five children. One month before this column ran, the couple had suffered the death of their youngest child, three-month-old Elizabeth. "GIRARDVILLE. ... THE MOLLIES," the column anonymously authored by "Americus" announced. "Our people have long enough calmly submitted to indignities heaped upon them by these imps of satan, or Mollie Maguires, and they have at last determined that at once and forever the outrages of this association have got to be suspended or the leaders, who are well known, will themselves be *suspended.*"[5]

A few days later came the headline "THE REIGN OF TERROR," telling of yet another supposed coffin notice sent to yet another mine supervisor. The *Herald* exhorted: "Are you, free born citizens, going to allow yourselves to be cowed down and murdered by ... cutthroats, whom it would be an act of justice to shoot down at sight? Will you allow your wives and children to be terrified, when you are at home, lest some miscreants enter and murder you in cold blood ... and find themselves thrown, without a protector, upon the cold charity of the world? No, you are men and will act like men."[6]

The following day Kehoe wrote to the *Herald's* editor. Foster held Kehoe's letter, dated October 10, 1875, until the following June, when he published it as a taunt after Kehoe's arrest and incarceration. From his position as Girardville's high constable, Kehoe told Foster: "I am surprised at the zest displayed by you through the medium of the daily (Herald) on the situation of affairs in the county, and believe that the stand taken by you is unwarrantable. We are thoroughly aware that lawless acts have been committed during the past few months, but does the 'REIGN OF TERROR' facilitate a return to quietness and good feeling?"[7]

Kehoe defended the AOH, saying: "nothing can be more unjust than to charge the order with any acts of lawlessness, and nothing can be more inconsistent with the wishes of the people than the agitation of this matter by the leading papers of this county. The articles which have appeared on this matter have done an incalculable amount of harm, and, as a friend to law and order, I *would* advise their cessation."[8]

A week after Kehoe wrote to Foster, Girardville's "Americus" said through the *Herald*: "if we are adding fuel to the flames we are proud to know it and hope the flames will burn so fierce and so high that it will make it *too hot* for a Mollie Maguire to exist in this region. They began this warfare and law-abiding, peaceable citizens have got to end it now and forever, and there is only one way, that is, the utter extermination of the murderers."[9]

When Foster's *Herald* refused to publish Kehoe's letter in October 1875, Kehoe turned to the *Miners' Journal*. "Charged with Sowing the Seeds of Hatred and Dissension," the *Journal* headlined Kehoe's letter. Kehoe had confronted E. S. Steltz, suspected author of the "Americus" articles, at the Girardville depot. There, Kehoe told Steltz "that if he was the author of the articles which appeared in the Herald, as many supposed him to be, it would be more charitable for him or any other correspondent to encourage brotherly love instead of sowing seeds of antagonism which sooner or later may lead to bloodshed."[10]

Kehoe also addressed the *Herald's* venom:

As for that gentle hint of the advocate of lynch law, who on making comments on the letter of "Americus" warns me and all other men not to lay profane hands on any idea connected with that able sheet, the Molly Maguire Herald. All I have to say is do not fear brave Tom, the Mars of Shenandoah, or his noble band of Vigilantes. He, the editor, has known me many years, and I defy him or any other man to say that I ever encouraged unlawful proceedings. I am sorry to state that since the advent of the Daily Herald, it has done more to create a spirit of antagonism among the citizens of Mahanoy Valley than ever the lifetime of the editor can undo. Now, Mr. Editor, I am loth to say anything detrimental about any citizen of the county; but, can the editor of the Herald justly deny that many of the "coffin notices" which have appeared in the Herald, were manufactured in the sanctum of the Herald? Make capital of certain subjects, eh? Did he not take advantage of affairs in Schuylkill to gain notoriety and circulation for his Molly Maguire sheet?[11]

The public calls of the *Shenandoah Herald* for vigilantism echoed the private views of Allan Pinkerton and his operative, Robert Linden. Linden led the Pinkertons' January 1875 post-midnight raid on the Samuels's Missouri farmhouse, where the hurling of a fireball through a kitchen window had led to the death of Jesse James's eight-year-old brother Archie Samuels.

Seven months later, Pinkerton wrote to his Philadelphia superintendent, George Bangs. "'If Linden can get up [a] vigilence [sic] committee that can be relied upon, do so,'" Pinkerton told Bangs in late August 1875. "'When M.M.'s meet, then surround and deal summarily with them. Get off quietly. All should be securely masked.'" Pinkerton added: "'Let Linden get up a vigilence [sic] committee. It will not do to get many men, but let him get those who are prepared to take fearful revenge on the M.M.'s. I think it would open the eyes of all the people and then the M.M.'s would meet with their just deserts [sic].'" Pinkerton advised: "'Place all confidence in Mr. Linden, he is a good man, and he understands what to do.'"[12]

A Pinkerton operative report filed by Linden six weeks later detailed Linden's failed attempts to generate enthusiasm for coal region lynching parties against AOH men: "THE OPERATIVE HAS VISITED DIFFERENT PLACES IN THE COAL REGIONS WITH THE VIEW OF GIVING NECESSARY INFORMATION TO SOME OF THE LEADING CITIZENS, ADVISING THEM AS TO WHO THE PARTIES ARE WHO HAVE COMMITTED THE RECENT ASSASSINATIONS ... BUT AS YET THERE SEEMS TO BE SO MUCH APATHY AMONG THE BETTER CLASS OF CITIZENS, AS WELL AS THE AUTHORITIES, THAT NO DEFINITE STEPS HAVE BEEN TAKEN TO MAKE EXAMPLES OF THE WELL KNOWN ASSASSINS."[13]

Less than two months later, the *Philadelphia Times* reported: "A LOUD CALL TO JUDGE LYNCH. A Schuylkill County Miner and His Sister Assassinated by a Mob of Masked Men."[14] The *Herald's* calls for vigilantism had yielded murderous results at Wiggan's Patch.

The reporter Fielders, probable author of the *Herald's* inflammatory columns, appeared at Wiggan's Patch on the morning of the murders of Mary Ann Kehoe's pregnant sister, Ellen McAllister, and her nineteen-year-old brother, Charles O'Donnell. From the downstairs bedroom in Margaret O'Donnell's house, Fielders recorded post mortem proceedings.

That morning Kehoe, Girardville's high constable, traveled to his mother-in-law's house to investigate the killings. "'We want the Shenandoah Herald man out here,'" Kehoe told the coroner. "'We're not going to have him in the house. Send him out ... he has no right here.'" The coroner ignored Kehoe's request and used Fielders to record post-mortem testimony. "The Herald man," Fielders later wrote of himself, "however, was not of such pliable stuff as to comply with the insulting demands of that character and didn't go out, but remained where he was until his business was finished."[15]

Fielders and Foster's malevolence toward Kehoe and Kehoe's family appeared bottomless. Ten days after the raid at Wiggan's

Patch, the Columbia Hose and Steam Fire Engine Company at Shenandoah cast a bell for their tower. Foster served as company director and Fielders as one of three men appointed to purchase the new bell. Cast less than two weeks after the murderous post-midnight raid on Kehoe's in-laws, the bell bore this inscription: "'Vigilance. / I am Always Ready. / I was cast December 20th, 1875.'"[16]

After Kehoe's arrest, Foster unleashed his star reporter. On May 26, 1876, less than three weeks after Kehoe's arrest, a *Herald* headline ran: "'MURDER WILL OUT.' *FIVE MORE MURDERERS ARRESTED AND LODGED IN JAIL.* ... The Kehoe Family in Bad Odor." Lehigh and Wilkes-Barre Coal and Iron police, working in concert in three counties, had arrested five men for the 1862 murder of Frank Langdon, an unsolved crime of fourteen years' standing. Kehoe's brother Michael, a Mahanoy City miner described in one report as lame, was among those arrested. "Michael Kehoe," the *Herald* described him, "a brother of THE NOTORIOUS JACK KEHOE, county delegate of the 'Mollies' in this section."[17]

The *Herald* concluded the article: "DEATH TO ALL 'MOLLIES' is the cry that resounds from one end of the coal region to the other, and never let it be silent until the devilish order is irretrievably dismembered ... then and not till then will the people be satisfied with the vengeance wreaked upon those to whom murder was but child's play, arson but a pleasure, and wickedness of all kinds but the natural outpourings of vile and devilish hearts."[18] In a second article published that day, the *Herald* said: "The weather here is hot enough to give some of the 'Mollie Maguires' an idea of what is preparing for them; but, warm as it is in the open air, what must it be in the jail? and how a hot-tempered, corpulent youth like JACK KEHOE must swelter!"[19]

Three weeks after Michael Kehoe's arrest, the court at Carbon County finally granted him, along with two codefendants, a habeas corpus hearing. One day after hearing the evidence, Judge Samuel Dreher dismissed all charges against the three Irishmen. But Michael Kehoe's bogus arrest, and its subsequent press coverage, connected the Kehoe name with the Langdon murder.

Whether motivated by ambition, ethnic hatred, malice, or sadism, Fielders wielded a lethal pen in a region, and a country, avid for ethnic scapegoats. Fielders became the primary recorder of both the "Molly Maguire" trials and the hearings conducted on their behalf. His reporting added greatly to the cloud of distortion that attends this historical canon.

After Fielders traveled to Columbia County to chronicle Patrick Hester's trial at Bloomsburg for the murder of Alexander Rea, the *Columbian* said: "the *Herald* could not exist without sensational wind, and the young man who has been doing its correspondence during and since the murder trial is peculiarly fitted to furnish it with the kind of material its existence requires." In a second article that day the *Columbian* said of Fielders: "like most reporters he draws altogether too much on a vivid imagination, and consequently he comes to Bloomsburg and writes letters to the *Herald* about all sorts of things that never occurred here." It added: "Fielders is sent forth to gather the news, and grind out sensational letters to keep that journal in material."[20]

Fielders's unsavory reputation extended over the coal region. A week later, the *Carbon Advocate* reported from Mauch Chunk Jail, in Carbon County: "Sheriff Raudenbush appears to have a not very exalted idea of reporters, and some of the craft find it a hard job to gain admittance. The Shenandoah Herald man, for instance, would hardly be admitted though he should have every member of the bar to intercede for him."[21]

On December 10, 1877, the *Miners' Journal* at Pottsville changed hands. The new publisher hired Fielders as the *Journal's* local editor. The following March, a Tamaqua paper reported under the headline "That Cowhiding Affair": "We cannot help condemning the action of Thos. B. Fielders, of the *Miners' Journal*, for assaulting Sol. Foster, Jr., with a whip last Saturday."[22] Solomon Foster, the alleged target of Fielders's attack, was Thomas Foster's brother and the publisher of the *Pottsville Chronicle*, a rival of the *Miners' Journal*.

On November 18, 1878, Pennsylvania's governor, John

Hartranft, signed Kehoe's death warrant. The *Shenandoah Herald*, which had appeared on newsstands every day since August 21, 1875, when it began its daily editions, published no newspaper that day. A Delaware paper commented: "To the surprise of many the paper was not issued to-day but allowed to drop out of existence without a parting word from its editor. The daily will be substituted by a weekly publication, to be edited by T. J. Foster."[23] With Kehoe's execution assured, the *Herald's* work appeared to be done.

On November 21, 1878, from his office at Pottsville Jail, Sheriff Matz read Kehoe his death warrant. By that date, Hartranft had issued and withdrawn the document twice. "'Well, Sheriff, have you got another one of them?'" Kehoe asked Matz as he entered Matz's office. At the close of the reading, Kehoe said: "'That's the end of it. I accept the death warrant cheerfully. It comes from an honest man. I am satisfied to die.'"[24]

Then Kehoe turned to the reporters gathered to hear the reading of the warrant. Fielders sat among them. Kehoe said: "'I hope the reporters will have nothing more to say about me.'" Singling out Fielders, Kehoe said: "'You, in particular ... have told more lies than enough now, God knows. You don't know what time you will be called yourself.'"[25]

On the afternoon before Kehoe's execution, a reporter from the *Philadelphia Times* visited the condemned man. "I saw Jack Kehoe in the afternoon," the reporter said. "The one request that he made of the Sheriff to-day was that no representative of the ... *Journal*, bitter in its opposition to the Mollies, should be permitted to witness his execution."[26]

From the time of the Civil War to her husband's incarceration in May 1876, Mary Ann Kehoe knew the tragedy of violent death and the power of nativism. Her brother John O'Donnell had died in the Civil War while serving as a private in Pennsylvania's 81st Volunteer Regiment. Her sister Margaret McAllister and her brother Charles

O'Donnell had died in the murderous raid at Wiggan's Patch. Four months before that, her baby girl Elizabeth, aged three months, had died in Girardville while newspapers hounded her husband, John Kehoe, and called repeatedly for his lynching. Kehoe's brother Joseph, in what may have been a targeted killing, had died from injuries sustained at the bottom of a mineshaft.

Mary Ann was the first of her parent's family of eight children to be born in the United States. Records of the O'Donnell family's emigration from Ireland's County Donegal have not been found. From information gleaned from U.S. census records, the family emigrated sometime between 1845 and 1848. Whether they experienced the horrors of Ireland's famine is not known.

Mary Ann was born in Pennsylvania circa 1849. A census report from 1860 describes her, aged eleven, attending school and living at Tamaqua, in Pennsylvania's Schuylkill County, with her parents Manus, a coal miner, her mother Margaret, and seven siblings. At age seventeen or eighteen, Mary Ann married John Kehoe at Mahanoy City. A census report from 1870 lists her keeping house there with her husband, a hotelkeeper, while caring for three children under the age of three.

By the time of her husband's first sentencing hearing in April 1877, Mary Ann had seen decent men in the Yost trial, including her cousin by marriage, James Carroll, condemned to death on testimony that would become the basis for Allan Pinkerton's dime novel. She had seen that testimony severely cripple an international benevolent order whose members, in her husband's words, "are law-abiding, and seek the elevation of their members."[27]

During the Yost trial, Mary Ann had withstood cross-examination by Franklin Gowen, a man determined to destroy her husband and everything he believed in. After the raid on her mother's house and the murder of her two siblings, she had withstood her parish priest's condemnation not of the murderers, but of Ancient Order men. "Beware of the Mollie Maguires," Father Daniel O'Connor had said. "If you have a brother among them pray for his repentance, but have nothing further to do with him, and remember that he is cut off from the Church. ... These men ... are the scum of their kind; they are not American citizens, but Irishmen, and a disgrace to the name and to their country."[28]

Still, she believed in the efficacy of the law. In early April 1877, Kehoe's wife brought two of their children to his sentencing hearing at Pottsville. In this one instance, the law worked in Kehoe's behalf. John Ryon, Kehoe's counsel, had likely advised Mary Ann that her husband's sentencing would be deferred. "Mrs. Kehoe was plainly but becomingly dressed," the *Shenandoah Herald* said, "a heavy black shawl contrasting well" with her complexion.[29]

At the Pottsville hearing, Ryon asked the Schuylkill court to postpone Kehoe's sentencing for a few weeks. Kehoe's attorney needed the time to file an appeal with Pennsylvania's supreme court. Ryon had just discovered the passage of a bill by Pennsylvania's legislature, signed by Governor John Hartranft, that required that the "writ of error" required for appeals to the state supreme court in homicide cases must now be filed twenty days from the date of sentencing, or it would not supersede a warrant of execution. "Under the rules of the Supreme Court," the *Boston Pilot* explained, "the writ would then be returnable in so short a time, that the prisoner could not get his 'paper book' written and printed. The result would be that his case would be *non-prossed*, and not decided on its merits."[30]

The new rule adopted by the Pennsylvania Supreme Court in the midst of the "Molly Maguire" cases created a greatly expedited legal process in capital cases. It heavily burdened defense attorneys and swept cases through the higher court at an alarming rate. The new rule also burdened defendants required to pay for the publication of the new "paper books," along with the costs of counsel, to appeal their cases.

"'Should Kehoe be sentenced this morning,'" Ryon told Schuylkill's Court of Oyer and Terminer, "'I would not undertake to get up a paper book because I could not possibly have it finished in time, and should this be the case I know exactly what my friends on the other side would say at the supreme court. They would repeat exactly what they said in the Carroll case when the supreme court offered me two or three days of an extension. I did not take it of course, because it would have been of no benefit to me, and as Mr. Gowen was present, cocked and primed and waiting to explode, I gave him his opportunity.'"[31] As Ryon had likely predicted, the Schuylkill court granted his request for a postponement of Kehoe's sentencing.

The delay availed little. Two weeks later, Cyrus Pershing sentenced Kehoe to death. One year after that, Pennsylvania's supreme court refused to grant Kehoe relief. One last avenue remained open to him.

On April 9, 1878, Mary Ann traveled to Harrisburg to attend the first of Kehoe's hearings before the Board of Pardons. Kehoe's execution was scheduled for May 18. "Among the cases to be heard then," the *Miners' Journal* said, "is that of Jack Kehoe, whose faithful wife has not yet abandoned hope. Mrs. Kehoe's dream by night and the object of her labor by day, is to save her husband from being executed on the 18th prox. She will go to Harrisburg with by far the best prepared case of any presented by the long list of Mollies. She has a very numerously signed petition in Kehoe's behalf and moreover is said to have the affidavits of Neil Dougherty and John Campbell to the effect that Kehoe is innocent of the Langdon murder."[32]

The *Philadelphia Times* reported of the hearing: "Mrs. Kehoe, who has been unremitting in her efforts to save her husband from the gallows, was the most eager listener and observant spectator, occasionally weeping as the condemned was feelingly referred to."[33] Governor Hartranft appeared and seated himself near the room's side door, "almost hidden by the expansive form of his private secretary."[34] Pennsylvania congressman John Morgan, promoter of the mine safety ventilation bill, attended, as did Bernard Dolan, who preceded Kehoe as AOH county delegate. Next to Morgan sat Samuel Losch, Pennsylvania's Republican congressman from Schuylkill Haven who in 1875 had helped initiate a legislative investigation into the company charter of Franklin Gowen's railroad.

The meeting commenced at two thirty in the afternoon and lasted more than four hours. Defense attorneys John Ryon and

Anthony Campbell spoke passionately on Kehoe's behalf. "We claim he was convicted wrongfully and illegally," their printed statement to the board said. "That the evidence is not only consistent with, but clearly proves his innocence."[35]

The attorneys addressed the prosecution testimony of Patrick Brady, brought forward at Kehoe's trial to show premeditation on Kehoe's part. Kehoe's counsel said of Brady: "it is well known the character of this man. He deliberately killed Patrick Ferry. ... Evidence has come to light since [Brady's] acquittal [of the murder of Ferry], showing cool deliberation and premeditation."[36]

Of prosecution witness William Canvin, Kehoe's defense counsel said: "It came out incidentally during the trial that he had killed a person in a drunken brawl, and it is said in a house of prostitution. He also caused the death of a brother of John Kehoe, and was afraid his friends would retaliate. ... His character is sufficient to cast discredit on any statement he makes, while his malice against this defendant should cause a person to severely reflect on his testimony."[37]

Defense counsel presented affidavits from convicted "Molly" codefendants John Campbell and Neil Dougherty, along with a letter from attorney Martin L'Velle. Dougherty maintained that despite prosecution testimony, Kehoe was not present when Frank Langdon was beaten outside Williams's hotel at Audenried. Dougherty's affidavit said further: "it is his firm belief that the said John Kehoe is innocent of the murder of the said Frank W. S. Langdon."[38]

Like Dougherty, Campbell swore to being present at Audenried on the night that Langdon was beaten. Campbell stated he had seen "John Donohue strike and beat the said Langdon with a large club or piece of wood, and that the said John Kehoe was not present at the time, nor did he know of Donahue's [sic] intention to beat and abuse the said Langdon." Campbell restated that Kehoe "was not present when he [Langdon] was beaten and had no knowledge of the beating until it took place, and had no previous knowledge from any of the parties engaged in the beating of any intention to beat Langdon." When told that swearing to this statement would destroy all hope for Campbell's own pardon, Campbell said: "'Kehoe is an innocent man, and I know it, and I care not what they do to me.—I am willing to swear to it; Kehoe is innocent.'"[39]

Martin L'Velle served as defense counsel for John "Yellow Jack" Donohue in Donohue's trial for the murder of Morgan Powell. The commonwealth executed Donohue at Mauch Chunk on June 21, 1877. In early April 1878, before Kehoe's pardon hearing, L'Velle corresponded with Kehoe's defense attorneys. L'Velle said of his last interaction with Donohue: "In my last interview with him in Mauch Chunk prison a brief period before his execution and when all his earthly hopes favorable to his case had fled, I requested of him to inform me of one thing and he cheerfully said he would if he knew, and I then asked him the question: 'Is Jack Kehoe guilty of the Langdon murder?' and he answered, emphasizing by slapping me on the knee, 'He is as innocent, my son, as you are.'" Donohue's response, L'Velle said, gave him "much anxiety."[40] L'Velle repeated it to Kehoe's prosecutor, Charles Albright.

"As to the trial of this cause," Kehoe's defense counsel advised the board, "we have only to say that the proceedings, to our minds, were extraordinary. The rules of evidence were strained to a tension never before heard of in the history of criminal jurisprudence; principles of law established that are dangerous in the extreme; and precedents set which, if followed, will make it impossible for innocent persons to obtain justice in a Court of law."[41]

Ryon told the board "he was asking less than justice." Campbell, in an address that lasted an hour and a half, told the board that Kehoe "was the victim of a grasping corporation ... which sought his blood, and [reminded] the board that in the hanging of Thomas P. Fisher at Mauch Chunk on the 28th of March a judicial murder had been committed." The *Philadelphia Times* parenthetically reported the name of the "grasping corporation" as Gowen's Philadelphia and Reading Railroad Company.[42]

The pardon board closed Kehoe's hearing without ruling. The following day, on Wednesday, they met again. After a brief session, they again adjourned without ruling. On Friday, April 12, 1878, the board met again. It postponed its decision in Kehoe's case until May.

The *New York Herald* reported: "as Kehoe's execution had been fixed for the 18th inst. the action of the Board will necessitate the granting of a reprieve in the case by the Governor."[43]

Governor Hartranft subsequently withdrew Kehoe's death warrant. An eight-month wrangle over a man's life had begun.

As late spring moved toward early summer, the workings of the pardon board remained hidden from public view. Of the May hearing at Harrisburg, the *Miners' Journal* said: "It was fully expected that the case of John Kehoe … would have been disposed of at the present meeting of the Board of Pardons, but for some reason the case was not referred to at all by the meeting of the present week."[44] Of the June hearing, the *Mauch Chunk Democrat* said: "The Board of Pardons, at perhaps the last sitting it will have before the November election, took no action in the case of John Kehoe."[45]

Kehoe's case had become a hot potato. No one wanted to touch it. In an interview reported on June 11, 1878, an unnamed member of the Board of Pardons told the *Philadelphia Times*: "Kehoe's case is altogether out of our hands and in those of the Governor, who cannot pardon him or commute his sentence without a recommendation from the board."[46] A week later, Kehoe's defense counsel told the *Miners' Journal*: "The case is now before the proper tribunal for final decision and we ask no more than simple justice when we request that it be left there for final adjudication, and that the Board be allowed all the time they desire for consideration, without being interfered with by newspaper controversy."[47]

In a letter dated June 18, 1878, Pennsylvania's lieutenant governor John Latta, one member of the four-man pardon board, told the *Pottsville Chronicle*: "'The Kehoe case is yet in the hands of the board of pardons. It was held under advisement at the time of meeting, hoping some light would be thrown on the case from trial of certain parties then pending in Mauch Chunk. It was not brought up at the last meeting of the board. Presume it will be at next meeting.'"[48]

In November 1878, the *Philadelphia Times* reported the breakdown of votes for Kehoe's April 1878 hearing.[49] Per this report,

Attorney General George Lear and Secretary of Internal Affairs William McCandless had voted against Kehoe's request for commutation. Lieutenant Governor Latta and Matthew Quay, secretary of the commonwealth, had voted in Kehoe's behalf. The split vote had led to the case being continued.

Less than a week after the board voted in Kehoe's April hearing, Governor Hartranft sent a recommendation to Pennsylvania's state senate on behalf of Secretary Quay, one of Kehoe's supporters, for the office of Recorder for Philadelphia. On May 2, 1878, Quay took up the new appointment. "He has not resigned as Secretary of the Commonwealth," the *Pittsburg* [sic] *Commercial* said, "but John B. Linn, his deputy, will discharge the duties of the office for the time being."[50] Linn, a Bellefonte attorney who had served as Quay's deputy secretary, now held the swing vote on Pennsylvania's Board of Pardons.

The petition Mary Ann Kehoe presented to the pardon board in April included one thousand signatures. Father Daniel O'Connor led the petitioners requesting Kehoe's commutation of sentence. After the murders at Wiggan's Patch, O'Connor had condemned the so-called "Mollies," including Mary Ann's brothers, as the "scum of the earth." The petition he now advocated asserted that Kehoe "was tried at a time when there existed a very great excitement in the public mind growing out of the commission of a number of serious crimes in the coal region, which excitement was greatly intensified by newspaper articles printed from day to day, greatly circulated among all classes of the people in said county, whereby undue prejudice was excited in the public mind against the said John Kehoe, and he was not able to secure a fair and impartial jury before which to be tried."[51]

The re-shuffling of Pennsylvania's pardon board did not stop Mary Ann's efforts on behalf of her husband. Nor did a false story circulated by prosecutor Albright of the supposed death of a witness crucial to Kehoe's case. But the Kehoes faced formidable challenges in the authority of two pardon board members. The nativism of both Secretary McCandless and newly appointed Secretary Linn would hold final sway in Kehoe's case.

On the nomination in September 1878 of former Civil War general William McCandless to Pennsylvania's state senate, a Delaware paper applauded McCandless's tenure as the commonwealth's secretary of internal affairs, an office "which he filled with marked and manifest ability, and with more than Roman purity and integrity."[52]

McCandless, who suffered injury twice during the Civil War, shared markers with fellow "Molly Maguire" prosecutors. These included allegiance to the Democratic Party, disappointed political ambition, evidence of white supremacist leanings, and allegations of illegal activity. In 1869 and again in 1878, McCandless failed to secure the Democratic nomination in Pennsylvania's gubernatorial contest. The *New York Sun*, in describing Democrats gathered for the 1869 Harrisburg convention, said: "the most ignorant was Gen. McCandless."[53] In 1874, with McCandless a candidate for Pennsylvania's secretary of internal affairs, the *Harrisburg Telegraph* reported that on leaving the Union army, the general had rushed headlong into the whiskey business in Philadelphia. Government officials subsequently shut him down, charging "illicit distillation."[54]

McCandless's career also generated accusations of white supremacist leanings. In 1867, in an article headlined "Bad Taste," Philadelphia's *Evening Telegraph* denounced a resolution from McCandless that commended a Republican senator in Washington as "the representative of the white men of Pennsylvania."[55] The following year, McCandless presided in Philadelphia at a state convention to select delegates to attend the national convention, on July 4th in New York City, of the "White Boys in Blue." McCandless's band of conservative soldiers and sailors passed a number of resolutions, including one stating: "That every principle of justice to the tax-burthened [sic] white citizens of the Union, demands the immediate abolition of the 'Freedmen's Bureau.'"[56]

In 1876, McCandless showed his political sympathies with "Molly" prosecutors Franklin Gowen, Charles Buckalew, and Francis Hughes. In October 1876, on behalf of Democratic presidential nominee Samuel Tilden, McCandless traveled to Indianapolis, where he installed himself at the Occidental Hotel. McCandless, the *New York Times* said, "sticks close to his room in the Occidental, and has many visitors, with each of whom he has confidential interviews. What ... the Democrats expect him to do, is a Democratic secret; but ... it is evident that Tilden's 'still hunt' in Indiana means enormous frauds upon the ballot-box."[57] From Columbus, Ohio, the *State Journal* said of Pennsylvania's Democratic leaders, including McCandless: "'Republicans beware! Our State is being invaded by a lot of political tramps from Pennsylvania ... sowing the seed of Copperheadism among our people.'"[58]

Two years later, while John Kehoe's fate lay at the mercy of Pennsylvania's Board of Pardons and McCandless held one of four votes, McCandless ran as a losing candidate to Pennsylvania's state assembly. The *Cambria Freeman* listed a group of such candidates who contested their losses in "frivolous and groundless cases," including "last, and least worthy of all, *Buck* McCandless."[59] Before McCandless's defeat, the *Somerset Herald* described his political friends as "so frightened at his evident weakness ... they have about concluded to haul him off the track."[60]

During the same election cycle John Gallagher, AOH state delegate for Pennsylvania, published a card to Irish voters. Gallagher said of candidates for upcoming elections: "Men ... who proscribed my nationality and religion are not entitled to my vote; men who assembled in their midnight conclaves to carry out their dark designs, which would not bear the light of day, and who are now seeking the suffrages of the Democratic party, should not be tolerated; they should be denounced from every hillside, mountain top and valley in the land." Gallagher censured a number of Democratic candidates as bad, but "not quite as bad as the Democratic 'Buck,' commonly called McCandless. I know the antecedents of these fellows, and the Democratic party can issue no patent of nobility that can elevate them in my estimation."[61]

In Pennsylvania's Northumberland County the *Sunbury American*, one of the coal region's most virulently anti-Catholic publications, showed its affection for McCandless's pardon board colleague, John Linn. The *American* published occasional historical articles by Linn. On his appointment in 1873 as deputy secretary of the commonwealth, that paper said: "Mr. Linn possesses all the necessary qualifications for this position, and his numerous friends here will be pleased to hear of his appointment."[62]

Less than two years before that, the *Sunbury American* had warned area residents of "the Irish Catholic element, which is fast ruining the Democratic party." An article in the same edition chastised Patrick Hester for his efforts toward naturalization of Irish American voters. Before his death Hester, hanged as an alleged "Molly" in March 1878, was a repeated target of the *American*. "Are they not going to rule the country as soon as they get strong enough," the *American* asked of Irish Catholic voters naturalized under Hester's guidance, "and then wont [sic] they show us who are to be our masters?"[63]

The *New York Herald* reported the outcome of John Kehoe's second hearing before Pennsylvania's Board of Pardons, decided on September 4, 1878: "One democrat and one republican voted for commutation, and one democrat and one republican against Kehoe's life, now in the hands of Governor Hartranft, whose action is looked forward to with much interest." The board having deadlocked two to two, it rested with Hartranft to sign Kehoe's death warrant. The *Herald* concluded: "The decision by the Board of Pardons is a surprise, a different result having been expected."[64]

Kehoe's counsel Anthony Campbell, convinced that Kehoe was innocent, described Kehoe's conviction of first-degree murder as "a judicial outrage." Campbell denounced prosecution evidence given at Kehoe's trial by John Tyrell Jr., "a mere lad" at the time Langdon was beaten, and that given by Patrick Brady, "who had himself been guilty of murder." Campbell denounced rumors of political brokering for pardon as "base insinuations," without foundation. Kehoe, he added, "might to-day be a free man had he given his consent to fully implicate men high in authority in negotiating for the purchase of the Mollie Maguire vote in the year 1875." In addition, John Donohue had "solemnly declared Kehoe's innocence." John Campbell "had also fully exculpated him from complicity in the crime."[65]

Kehoe's defense counsel John Ryon argued that Kehoe's jury in Schuylkill County had convicted him on insufficient evidence. Ryon severely criticized the opinion of Justice Sterrett of Pennsylvania's supreme court in affirming the judgment of the lower court. "Nothing new was developed in the case," the *New York Times* said, "the reargument having been considered necessary for the intelligent action of the new Secretary of the Commonwealth, Mr. Linn."[66]

Mary Ann Kehoe had again traveled from Girardville to Harrisburg to attend her husband's hearing in early September 1878. "Mrs. Jack Kehoe was an attentive listener to the arguments," the *Philadelphia Times* said. "She appeared like one who expected a favorable verdict."[67]

The board held its deliberations on Tuesday evening, September 3. Mary Ann left Harrisburg for home the next morning, before the board rendered its verdict. She would wait for news of the board's decision at the telegraph office in Pottsville.

The *New York Times* described Kehoe's wife as "a tall woman of good appearance and considerable intelligence." The *Times* added: "On her the blow will fall with crushing weight. ... One of the counsel for Kehoe said to-day, after the decision of the board had been announced, 'Mrs. Kehoe is even now sitting in the telegraph office waiting for the first news from the board. It will be a sad blow for her. She has worked night and day to save her husband from dying on the scaffold, and has left nothing undone.'"[68]

An unnamed correspondent to the *Harrisburg Telegraph* attended Kehoe's hearing. He said: "I have been present at hundreds of trials ... I have never heard before of a man being convicted of murder in the first degree upon such slim testimony as that brought against Jack Kehoe. ... That men should testify—and be believed—as to the exact words uttered by others *fifteen years* before, seems incomprehensible." The correspondent, who did not know Kehoe personally but had heard his counsel's arguments, added: "I was astonished to hear that the Board of Pardons has refused to recommend a commutation. On the argument ... they could have safely recommended a pardon. ... If a man is a murderer, before the rope is adjusted let him be proven such, and not be hung through hot blooded clamor, or because of charges that may be as false as the sentiment that cries out for innocent blood."[69]

A few weeks later, the *Sunbury American* reported: "President Gowen, of the Reading railroad company, denies emphatically the story that he had been instrumental in preventing the board of pardons from recommending a pardon for Jack Kehoe."[70]

After the board rendered its decision on September 4, board member Lieutenant Governor John Latta, who had voted consistently in Kehoe's behalf, returned home by train to Westmoreland County via the Fast Line. The *Pittsburg [sic] Commercial* reported that as Latta stepped off the train on its arrival at Greenburg, as the train moved off, he "was thrown down with such violence as to fracture his right arm above the elbow."[71] The *Columbian* described Latta's injuries as dislocation of the shoulder and concussion. It added: "Considerable anxiety is felt at his recovery."[72]

In part due to Latta's injuries, the Board of Pardons cancelled its October meeting, frustrating any further attempts to be made on Kehoe's behalf. Alex McClure's *Philadelphia Times*, in the midst of another hotly contested gubernatorial contest, would spend the next two months clamoring for Kehoe's execution. Mary Ann Kehoe would persist in her efforts to secure relief for her husband.

To further complicate the signing of John Kehoe's death warrant, its issuance twined through Pennsylvania's 1878 gubernatorial contest between Democrat Andrew Dill and Republican Henry Hoyt. With the controversy over the signing of the warrant, Kehoe's life became political fodder for nativists. The timing gave newspapers hostile to

Kehoe free rein to rebroadcast Franklin Gowen's accusations of AOH cash-for-votes brokering, and to launch fresh accusations against the Irish Catholic benevolent order.

Alexander McClure of the *Philadelphia Times* proved the most rapacious of this journalistic pack. In mid-October 1878, McClure sent a correspondent who signed his columns "J. H. L." to interview Charles Albright, counsel for the Lehigh and Wilkes-Barre Coal Company and self-appointed prosecutor in Kehoe's capital case. "'Should the Governor [Hartranft] withhold the death warrant in the case of Kehoe,'" Albright told the reporter, "'it would surround the Executive with the gravest suspicion.'"[73]

Along with "J. H. L.'s" coverage, McClure ran an editorial telling readers that the agencies that swayed the Irish vote in Schuylkill County to Republicans in 1875 were again at work in Allegheny County and elsewhere, and "though Jack Kehoe is in prison under sentence of death his influence in party politics is scarcely less than that which for so long gained him immunity from his crimes."[74]

Some editors pushed back. The *Harrisburg Telegraph* said: "Mr. 'J. H. L.' of the Philadelphia *Times* is a fair man ordinarily, but the atmosphere of the *Times* office and the orders of his superiors have united to crush out his veracity." The *Telegraph* added: "Now, 'J. H. L.' has sallied forth again. And this time it is to get up a sensation on Jack Kehoe, the Molly Maguire." The *Telegraph* described the reporter's coverage on Kehoe as "well written fiction."[75]

The *Juniata Sentinel and Republican* said: "McClure's *Times* on Monday contained a long communication ... that charges that the Republicans bought the Mollie Maguire vote for Hartranft in 1875, through Jack Kehoe, and the reason that Kehoe is not hung is because of said service to the Governor. It is an ugly article; an ugly charge, and to the untrained reader is calculated to do harm."[76] From Bloomsburg, the *Columbian* said: "The death warrant of Jack Kehoe has not yet been signed by Governor Hartranft and it is said will not be until after the election. ... The conduct of the Executive in this matter is a disgrace to the state, and thus trifling with a man's life for political purposes is an outrage on humanity."[77]

On November 6, 1878, Hoyt defeated Dill. The next day, a Centre County newspaper reprinted an interview of Hartranft from the *Cincinnati Enquirer*. If authentic, in this interview Pennsylvania's sitting governor revealed his ignorance of the details of Kehoe's case, his ignorance of the biographies of many AOH men charged as "Mollies," his ignorance of the Pinkertons' treachery, and his ignorance of the treachery of the Democratic politicians who prosecuted the "Molly Maguire" caseload. In this interview, Hartranft also revealed his own casual anti-Irish bias and his ineptitude in dealing with the intricacies of the commonwealth's "Molly Maguire" cases.

"'There is no doubt of Kehoe's guilt, is there?'" the reporter asked Hartranft. "'Perhaps no doubt of his general guiltiness,'" Hartranft said, "'but a great deal of uncertainty about his guilt on the specific case in which he is convicted. You see he was convicted for participation in a conspiracy by which a police officer was killed. There is no doubt of such a conspiracy having existed, and on that very ground most of these men have been convicted and hung; but it is a question in my mind whether the testimony shows conclusively that Jack was in it at the time the killing took place.'"[78]

Kehoe was never charged with the killing of police officer Frank Yost, the conspiracy to which Hartranft alluded. Hartranft continued his explanation: "'For instance, one of those who were hung was proved to have simply coughed as a signal ... . He didn't strike a blow or help kill the man, but only gave the signal to others: but still they held him as guilty of the murder, and he was hanged for it. That way of construing the law was something new to these ignorant people, and they appealed to me to interfere on the ground that the condemned man had really done nothing in the murder; but I decided that I had no right to interfere, and so let the law take its course.'" Hartranft added that the pardon board was really only an advisory board, and that he would take no action in Kehoe's case until after the election.[79]

Six days after Hoyt defeated Dill, Hartranft wrote to Attorney General Lear. Hartranft advised Lear that under the provisions of Pennsylvania's new constitution, provisions that Gowen had helped draft, no pardon or commutation of sentence could be granted without a recommendation from a majority of the members of Pennsylvania's newly established Board of Pardons. The discretionary power of the governor in such cases, Hartranft told Lear, "seemed to be abolished."[80]

In 1873, Gowen had served as a delegate to Pennsylvania's 1873 Constitutional Convention, called to oversee revisions to that document. On the issue of the governor's power to pardon, Gowen had advised his fellow delegates: "The question of the pardoning power in this Commonwealth has attracted a great deal of public attention during the last two or three years. It may be very well in theory, and probably in practice, to admit the fact that mercy is one of the most graceful attributes that can deck the Executive office of this Commonwealth, but at the same time we cannot help admitting that the stream of mercy has flown in such copious volumes during the last two or three years, that if the public can reach this question they will be very apt to take the pardoning power out of the hands of the Executive altogether."[81]

Gowen added: "I think it is well to follow the suggestions of the committee for some advisory board, and I think three or four are enough."[82] The revised constitution established the new Board of Pardons on exactly the lines Gowen recommended. The new board held the power of life and death for the duration of the "Molly Maguire" caseload and beyond. Historic records held by the board at the state archives show that Pinkerton operative Robert Linden corresponded routinely with board members, in most cases recommending against relief for so-called "Molly Maguire" defendants.

After receiving Hartranft's musings on limits to the executive pardoning power in Kehoe's case, Lear advised Hartranft: "After the refusal of the Board of Pardons to recommend a pardon or commutation the Governor has no more responsibility in the matter of issuing the warrant than the Sheriff has in executing it when it comes into his hands. The acts of both follow as the legal consequences of the sentence of the courts."[83] Thus assured, Hartranft reissued Kehoe's death warrant for the third time.

It devolved to a *Philadelphia Times* reporter to deliver the news to Kehoe. The reporter visited the condemned man at half past seven on the evening Hartranft signed Kehoe's third death warrant. The warden at Pottsville Jail notified Kehoe of his visitor. "'Hello! Hello!'" Kehoe called out. "'I was just saying a few prayers, before going to bed.'"[84]

The warden gave the reporter a candle for the duration of his visit. "'What brought you here?'" Kehoe asked the reporter. "'To inform you that Governor Hartranft has ordered your execution,'" the reporter answered. Kehoe repeated what his defense counsel, Samuel Garrett, had told the *Chicago Tribune* a few months before: "'Gowen told Father Gallagher he would hang Hartranft if he [Hartranft] didn't hang Kehoe, and I don't blame the Governor.'" Kehoe paused. "'Yet how is this? The Governor said he never would hang me, and here he issues a warrant after withdrawing one. I never believed he would to it. What would you do if you were me?'"[85]

"'I would prepare for the worst,'" the reporter said. "'What can you do?'" Kehoe replied: "'I can't do anything ... I have no money; my wife, who is the noblest woman in the world, has done everything she could, and my counsel, too. If I had money and liberty for a short time I could find men who stood with me in the bar-room when Langdon went out and who know I was there all the time Langdon was being beaten. God knows I never touched a hair of Langdon's head. He and I were butties [sic]. We paraded together to meeting and drank together, and he left me to go for a friend to bring him down, and when he was beaten I was in the tavern yet.'"[86]

Kehoe told the reporter: "'I am resigned to my fate. I know I'm not going to be hung for beating Langdon, but because the howl is, "Jack Kehoe is responsible for all the murders committed in the coal regions." Governor Hartranft is the victim of the newspapers. They gave him no rest until he signed my death warrant. Oh, it's hard; but let them crack their whip.'"[87]

Kehoe asked the reporter to contact his defense counsel and advise them to call on Kehoe at the jail. The two men discussed additional defense witnesses who might strengthen Kehoe's last appeal to the Board of Pardons.

The reporter described Kehoe's cell, "bare of all furniture but a bed and two stools. A prayer book and a few other religious publications are his only companions, in the perusal of which he takes much comfort." The reporter described the jail's guard of Coal and Iron police, strategically placed to prevent any escape attempts by any "condemned Mollie." Of Kehoe's pending execution, the reporter said: "The same gallows will be used for him which sent the Yost and Sanger murderers into eternity, and the execution will be private."[88]

But Samuel Garrett, Kehoe's defense attorney, refused to give up the fight. The *Philadelphia Times* reported: "Mr. Garrett says he is convinced from what he has learned as one of Kehoe's attorneys that his client is innocent of the crime for the commission of which he was convicted, and that his execution would be a judicial murder."[89]

By the time Hartranft signed Kehoe's third death warrant, sixteen AOH men convicted of "Molly Maguire" capital crimes had been publicly tortured to death in four counties. Large crowds had witnessed the executions, with some among them likened to "ravenous wolves of the plains scenting the blood of a wounded deer."[90] Like Garrett, Kehoe's wife Mary Ann would continue her efforts on her husband's behalf.

In the third week of November 1878, John Kehoe's attorney Samuel Garrett publicly declared that he was entirely convinced of Kehoe's innocence of the murder of Langdon.[91] On December 4, 1878, Garrett appeared again before the Board of Pardons at Harrisburg. He hoped, he told them, to locate a witness who could prove Kehoe's innocence of Langdon's murder.

Garrett supplied the board with a sworn affidavit. Within the past few days, the attorney had received information that a witness named McHugh, thought to be dead, was still living, and that McHugh's testimony would establish Kehoe's innocence of the murder of Langdon. The affidavit stated that both Kehoe and his counsel had been "led to believe by the Commonwealth in the trial of this case, that the said McHugh was dead." Charles Albright, lead prosecutor in Kehoe's case, had circulated the false rumor that Patrick McHugh, the witness who could prove Kehoe's innocence, was dead.

William Foyle, an attorney from Towanda, also addressed the false rumor. "The report of his [Patrick McHugh's] being dead I think arose in this way," Foyle told Governor Hartranft on Kehoe's behalf, "his [McHugh's] brother died in 1874 & Genl Albright supposing it to be the witness conveyed a wrong impression to the friends of Kehoe."[92]

The same month these Board of Pardons proceedings took place, Albright was embroiled in a contested election for state representative. From Ebensburg, the *Cambria Freeman* reminded voters of Albright's sale in the mid-1850s of bogus deeds to the town's unsuspecting residents in aid of his Kansas "Council City" scam. Twenty-four years after Albright floated the fraudulent property scheme, the *Freeman* warned Carbon County's residents against "the slippery Charles Albright, who at one time resided in this place, and of whom some of our citizens do not entertain very pleasant recollections."[93]

Patrick McHugh, the new witness in Kehoe's case, had been at Williams's hotel at Audenried on June 14, 1862, the night that Frank Langdon was beaten. Nine months after Kehoe's conviction for first-degree murder in January 1877, McHugh had visited Carbon County. He had met with friends of Kehoe and assured them of Kehoe's innocence.

Kehoe's death warrant set the date for his execution for December 18, 1878, just two weeks from the pardon board's early December hearing. On December 4, Garrett requested a special sitting of the board to be held on December 13. The board agreed to the request. If Garrett could find and depose McHugh, and McHugh's testimony warranted a new hearing, the board would grant the additional hearing.

Garrett's actions before the board set events in motion. "KEHOE'S NEW WITNESS," the *Philadelphia Times* reported a week later. "WHAT PATRICK M'HUGH WILL SWEAR. The Wife of the Condemned Mollie Maguire Hunts Up the Man Supposed to be Dead and Has His Deposition Taken for the Board of Pardons' Consideration."[94]

At eight in the morning on Saturday, December 7, 1878, Kehoe's wife Mary Ann left her home in Girardville and traveled ninety miles north to Pennsylvania's Bradford County, the rumored home county of McHugh. Mary Ann left behind a son and four daughters, all under the age of twelve. Traveling by train, she arrived at Towanda at five in the afternoon. On Sunday morning, she traveled twenty miles south to Dunshore. There, she learned that McHugh lived out in the country, on his farm in Wilmot Township.

Mary Ann hired a carriage for the six-mile drive. On reaching McHugh's farm, she learned that he had gone to town mail a letter to Garrett. McHugh had read in the *Philadelphia Times* that his testimony could help Kehoe's case. His letter informed Garrett that he was willing to offer testimony. Mary Ann left McHugh's farm without seeing McHugh. On her way back to Dunshore, the two met on the road. They returned to McHugh's farm and discussed Kehoe's case. "He told me all he knew about the Langdon affair," Mary Ann told a *Philadelphia Times* reporter a few days later.[95]

The next morning, on Monday, December 9, McHugh met Mary Ann at a railway station south of Dunshore. They traveled to Foyle's law office at Towanda, where Foyle deposed the farmer. The next day, Mary Ann returned to Pottsville with McHugh's affidavit. Kehoe's attorneys made copies and circulated them to the Board of Pardons. Foyle wrote to Hartranft to urge Kehoe's case.

"McHugh is shure [sic]," Foyle told Hartranft, "Jack Kehoe was not present at the murder of Langdon. McHugh is a man of good character and I believe truthful in every respect. His affidavit is not trumped up to meet the emergency but in my judgment is entitled to great weight in the final disposition of the case." Foyle added: "To hang Jack Kehoe in the light of this newly discovered evidence would be a piece of judicial murder. I think the death warrant ought to be revoked, and further action in the case postponed by the board of pardons till this newly discovered testimony is fully presented to the board, which should in my judgment procure a commutation of the death penalty if not a full pardon."[96]

Foyle assured Hartranft: "I drew the affidavit at the request of Mrs. Kehoe who came into my office yesterday and have no further connection with the case and no interest in it except to see that justice is done. I know this new evidence will withstand the utmost scrutiny and will vindicate your action in the premises, and must satisfy even the Philadelphia Times which is craving for Jack Kehoe's blood innocent or guilty. It makes ... a difference to all of us and especially to you Governor as chief executive of the State whether an innocent man shall be hanged in the face of the discovered evidence establishing his innocence."[97]

On Wednesday, December 11, Mary Ann spent two hours with her husband at Pottsville Jail. The *Philadelphia Times* said: "The meeting was private, the keeper leaving the two alone in the cell." The reporter added: "Mrs. Kehoe presents a tired appearance from worriment and travel. She entertains great hope from this affidavit. Kehoe has been much cast down of late, but feels more hopeful since his wife's return."[98]

All now depended on the commonwealth's four pardon board members. In April 1878, Pennsylvania's attorney general George Lear had voted against Kehoe's request for commutation of sentence. In September, evidently swayed by counsels' arguments, Lear had voted in Kehoe's favor. On Thursday, December 12, two days after Mary Ann Kehoe returned from Towanda with McHugh's deposition, Lear wrote to Garrett. Lear advised Kehoe's attorney that he would be in Harrisburg on Tuesday, December 17, the day before Kehoe's scheduled execution, to attend the pardon board meeting to consider McHugh's new evidence. Lear doubted Kehoe's chances. Lear told Garrett: "'Gen. McCandless writes that he has read the affidavit and finds no reason to alter his opinion as to the guilt of John Kehoe, and therefore declines to vote for any other bearing [sic] of the case.'"[99] Lear added: "'My hands are washed of Kehoe's blood, and if others want to do the same, I will aid them.'"[100]

The *Philadelphia Times* launched an attack on McHugh's affidavit. Attorney Foyle wrote again to Hartranft from Towanda. Foyle told Hartranft: "I shall not doubt the integrity of witness McHugh until some reasonable proof is given that he has sworn falsely produced in some other form than newspaper 'squibs' for which no one claims responsibility." Foyle added: "as I understand it from pamphlets sent me some time since with the compliments of Franklin B Gowen containing the trial of [Thomas Munley] ... It took the Commonwealth aided by that astute lawyer and with all the machinery of Pinkertons Detective agency about fourteen years to obtain the evidence to establish the guilt of Kehoe meager as it was ... is it too much to ask that Kehoe should have at least two years to look up evidence to prove his innocence?"[101]

Foyle closed his letter: "Asking your pardon for having trespassed so much upon you and with no other apology than a desire to advance the cause of justice and truth in behalf of a condemned man whose life is now trembling in the balance."[102]

With Lear and McCandless opposed to commutation, and Hartranft refusing to withdraw the death warrant, Kehoe's life rested with Secretary of the Commonwealth Linn. Garrett refused to give up. On Saturday, December 14, he arrived again in Harrisburg and told the *Philadelphia Times*: "'Kehoe is worth half a dozen dead men yet.'" The *Times* added: "Mr. Garrett said he thought that the Commonwealth was beaten long ago, and all that was necessary now was to beat the newspapers."[103]

Three days later, the day before Kehoe's scheduled execution, Garrett faced the full Board of Pardons at Harrisburg. He had hoped to bring with him a map and accompanying documents to clarify Langdon's beating at Audenried, but found them missing from the court records. Garrett told the board "that from 1876 to 1877 there was not a fair trial in Schuylkill County; that the jury wheel did not contain the names of four Irishmen."[104] He laid out McHugh's new evidence and begged the board to reconsider.

To Garrett's plea, McCandless responded: "'If this man Kehoe is not guilty of murder in the first degree, he is guilty of nothing, and I have not changed my opinion as to his guilt.'" After the hearing adjourned, McCandless told a *New York Times* reporter: "'We have refused to reopen the case. That's how the matter stands. Kehoe will swing.'"[105]

Shortly after noon, news of the board's decision reached Pottsville from Harrisburg. "The Board of Pardons have refused to hear McHugh," a dispatch from Garrett said. "This is final. Kehoe must hang. S. A. Garrett."[106]

Mary Ann Kehoe, waiting at the telegraph office with her children, asked for a copy of Garrett's message. "With this in her hands," the *Philadelphia Times* said, "and her ... children treading on the hem of her skirts and her husband's father by her side she walked to the jail and to Jack Kehoe's cell. In the masculine voice that betokens her strength of will and her perseverance she read to her husband the message that tolled his death knell." Kehoe, the reporter observed, "scarcely trembled. His brave little wife, who is as comely as she is undaunted, cried not once, but placed her hand upon one of his arms and bade him to bear it nobly."[107]

Two months after voting against Kehoe's request for commutation, Linn retired from the office of secretary of the commonwealth. He returned to private practice at Bellefonte, and to the writing of history. "Mr. Linn is a courteous and honorable gentleman," the *Centre Democrat* said, "who makes a fair record in whatever he undertakes, and as a lawyer will be an acquisition to the bar of this county."[108]

---

1. *Shenandoah (PA) Herald*, September 4, 1875.
2. Ibid., September 11, 1875.
3. Ibid., September 25, 1875.
4. Ibid., September 29, 1875.
5. Ibid., September 30, 1875; italics in original.
6. Ibid., October 9, 1875.
7. Ibid., June 8, 1876 (letter dated October 10, 1875).
8. Ibid.; italics in original.
9. Ibid., October 18, 1875; italics in original.
10. *Miners' Journal* (Pottsville, PA), October 22, 1875.
11. Ibid.

12. Pinkerton's letter quoted in Wayne G. Broehl Jr., *The Molly Maguires* (1964; repr., New York: Chelsea House/Vintage, 1983), 247-48.
13. Robert Linden, operative report, 20 October 1875, Reading Railroad Molly Maguire Papers, Hagley Museum and Library, Wilmington, DE.
14. *Philadelphia Times*, December 11, 1875.
15. *Shenandoah (PA) Herald*, December 18, 1875.
16. Reported in *Evening Herald* (Shenandoah, PA) on July 15, 1891.
17. *Shenandoah (PA) Herald*, May 26, 1876.
18. Ibid.
19. Ibid.
20. *Columbian* (Bloomsburg, PA), March 16, 1877.
21. *Carbon Advocate* (Lehighton, PA), March 24, 1877.
22. *Tamaqua (PA) Courier*, March 9, 1878.
23. *Morning Herald* (Wilmington, DE), November 19, 1878 (datelined Shenandoah, PA, November 18, 1878).
24. *Philadelphia Times*, November 22, 1878.
25. Ibid.
26. Ibid., December 18, 1878 (this account incorrectly identified the *Miners' Journal* at Pottsville as the "*Shenandoah Journal*").
27. *Shenandoah (PA) Herald*, June 8, 1876.
28. *New York Times* and *Philadelphia Times*, December 23, 1875, along with Archbishop Wood's pastoral letter of excommunication. See also *Shenandoah Herald*, December 25, 1875.
29. *Shenandoah (PA) Herald*, April 3, 1877.
30. *Boston Pilot*, April 14, 1877.
31. *Shenandoah (PA) Herald*, April 3, 1877.
32. *Miners' Journal* (Pottsville, PA), March 29, 1878.
33. *Philadelphia Times*, April 10, 1878.
34. *Miners' Journal* (Pottsville, PA), April 12, 1878. See this account for pardon board attendees; for Losch's support of the investigation of the Philadelphia and Reading charter, see *Harrisburg Telegraph*, February 16, 1875.
35. A. Campbell, S. A. Garrett, John W. Ryon, *A Brief Statement of the Facts to be presented to the Board of Pardons at Harrisburg*, 9 April 1878, John Kehoe Case Folder. Clemency File, 1874-1900 (Series 15.17); RG-15, Department of Justice (Board of Pardons). Pennsylvania State Archives, Harrisburg.
36. Ibid.
37. Ibid.
38. *Miners' Journal*, April 12, 1878.
39. Ibid.
40. Ibid. If Donohue beat Langdon, his motive remains inexplicable. During Neil Dougherty's trial, prosecution witness Isaac McCallum testified: "John Donohue worked at the Honeybrook colliery during the month of June 1862, though Donohue worked but for a single day." See *Shenandoah Herald*, November 29, 1876, for McCallum's testimony.
41. Campbell, Garrett, and Ryon, *Brief Statement of Facts*.
42. Ryon and Campbell's statements given in *Philadelphia Times*, April 10, 1878.
43. *New York Herald*, April 13, 1878.
44. *Miners' Journal* (Pottsville, PA), May 10, 1878.
45. *Mauch Chunk (PA) Democrat*, June 8, 1878.
46. *Philadelphia Times*, June 11, 1878.

47. Reported in *Miners' Journal* (Pottsville, PA), June 21, 1878.
48. *Harrisburg Patriot*, June 22, 1878; quoting *Pottsville Chronicle* dated June 21, 1878.
49. See *Philadelphia Times*, November 20, 1878.
50. *Pittsburg* [sic] *Commercial*, May 2, 1878.
51. Reported in *Philadelphia Times*, August 5, 1878.
52. *Morning Herald* (Wilmington, DE), September 11, 1878.
53. *New York Sun*, July 15, 1869.
54. *Harrisburg Telegraph*, September 28, 1874.
55. *Evening Telegraph* (Philadelphia), January 25, 1867 (McCandless referred to Senator Edgar Cowan).
56. Ibid., July 2, 1868.
57. *Clearfield (PA) Republican*, October 4, 1876; quoting Indianapolis correspondent of *New York Times*.
58. Ibid.; quoting *State Journal* (Columbus, OH).
59. *Cambria Freeman* (Ebensburg, PA), December 13, 1878; italics in original.
60. *Somerset (PA) Herald*, October 2, 1878.
61. *Pittsburg* [sic] *Commercial*, October 29, 1878.
62. *Sunbury (PA) American*, February 15, 1873.
63. Ibid., October 7, 1871.
64. *New York Herald*, September 5, 1878 (dateline Harrisburg, September 4, 1878).
65. Campbell's argument given in *Harrisburg Patriot*, September 4, 1878.
66. *New York Times*, September 4, 1878.
67. *Philadelphia Times*, September 4, 1878.
68. *New York Times*, September 5, 1878.
69. *Harrisburg Telegraph*, September 6, 1878; italics in original.
70. *Sunbury (PA) American*, September 27, 1878.
71. *Pittsburg* [sic] *Commercial*, September 6, 1878.
72. *Columbian* (Bloomsburg, PA), September 13, 1878.
73. *Philadelphia Times*, October 14, 1878.
74. Ibid., October 11, 1878.
75. *Harrisburg Telegraph*, October 15, 1878.
76. *Juniata Sentinel and Republican* (Mifflintown, PA), October 16, 1878.
77. *Columbian* (Bloomsburg, PA), October 18, 1878.
78. "Hartranft and Kehoe. ... Cincinnati Enquirer's Pennsylvania Letter," *Milheim (PA) Journal*, November 7, 1878.
79. Ibid.
80. Hartranft-Lear correspondence published in *Miners' Journal* (Pottsville, PA), November 15, 1878.
81. *Debates of the Convention to Amend the Constitution of Pennsylvania*, vol. 2 (Harrisburg: Benjamin Singerly, 1873), 361.
82. Ibid.
83. *Miners' Journal* (Pottsville, PA), November 15, 1878.
84. *Philadelphia Times*, November 19, 1878.
85. Ibid.
86. Ibid.
87. Ibid.
88. Ibid.
89. Ibid., November 21, 1878.
90. *New York Herald*, March 29, 1878 (execution of Thomas Fisher).

91. Ibid., November 22, 1878.
92. W. M. Foyle to Governor John F. Hartranft, 10 December 1878, John Kehoe Case Folder. Clemency File, 1874-1900 (Series 15.17); RG-15, Department of Justice (Board of Pardons). Pennsylvania State Archives, Harrisburg.
93. *Cambria Freeman* (Ebensburg, PA), December 13, 1878.
94. *Philadelphia Times*, December 11, 1878.
95. Ibid., December 12, 1878.
96. Foyle to Hartranft, 10 December 1878.
97. Ibid.
98. *Philadelphia Times*, December 12, 1878.
99. *Irish World* (New York), January 11, 1879; quoting *Miners' Journal*.
100. Ibid. See also *New York Times*, December 16, 1878.
101. W. M. Foyle to Governor John F. Hartranft, 14 December 1878, John Kehoe Case Folder. Clemency File, 1874-1900 (Series 15.17); RG-15, Department of Justice (Board of Pardons). Pennsylvania State Archives, Harrisburg.
102. Ibid.
103. *Philadelphia Times*, December 15, 1878. See also *New York Times*, same date.
104. Pennsylvania Board of Pardons hearing reported in *New York Times*, December 18, 1878.
105. Ibid.
106. *Philadelphia Times*, December 18, 1878.
107. Ibid.
108. *Centre Democrat* (Bellefonte, PA), February 20, 1879.

10

THE LAST SERVICE

Kehoe expressed his satisfaction that the day was one of the Virgin Mary's feast days, for, he said, he had great confidence in her intercessory power.

Philadelphia Times reporter
Pottsville Jail, December 18, 1878

After John Kehoe's arrest for alleged "Molly Maguire" crimes in May 1876, he was held in dungeon conditions at Pottsville Jail for two years and seven months. Those conditions included leg irons bolted to the wooden floor. Jailers pushed meals through a small opening in the cell's steel door. Contraband candles supplied by visitors helped alleviate the gloom.

On the morning of Kehoe's execution, a reporter for the *Philadelphia Times* described the cell's contents. "In one corner was his small iron bedstead," the reporter said. "On a couple of small shelves were his pipe and tobacco and a handful of cigars. Tin cup, hat, clothing, and a dozen other things were all hung on nails driven in the walls. Over a table was a picture of the Blessed Virgin and the child Jesus, and on the table were three well-thumbed prayer-books and a number of religious works, including 'Devout Life,' 'Daily Steps to Heaven,' 'Life of St. Alphonsus,' 'Elevation of the Soul,' 'The Sinner's Guide' and 'Poor Man's Catechism.' All these bore evidence of usage."[1]

Five years before, the *Morning Star and Catholic Messenger* had advertised a new biography of St. Alphonsus Liguori, the founder of the Redemptorists, as "a very suitable and appropriate book for a Christmas or New Year's present."[2] The book's author, Mother Austin Carroll, served as superioress of the St. Alphonsus Convent of Mercy in New Orleans. Born in County Tipperary, Carroll had lived through Ireland's famine. "She ... learned to be generous to the poor during the famine years," a biographer said.[3]

Carroll's biography of St. Alphonsus, the book likely found in Kehoe's cell, described the saint's ordeals. These included clashes with clergy and abandonment by his followers. "The very pulpits resounded with anathemas," Carroll's account said. "Even his friends were silenced by the mockery and contempt which everywhere greeted them. Not one was to be found in the city of his birth to say a word in his defence."[4]

Of an attack coordinated to vilify Alphonsus, Carroll said: "A wretched creature was suborned to defame Alphonsus ... But he took these slanders quite calmly, knowing that persecution is the inseparable accompaniment of works undertaken for God."[5] His enemies "had determined to crush his Congregation root and branches."[6] In addition: "The devil, unable to annihilate the Congregation by persecutions from without, endeavored to stir up treasons within, the surest means of destroying a work that had evidently come from God."[7]

Of Alphonsus's devotion to the Blessed Mother, Carroll said: "He treated of the humility of Mary as contrasted with the pride of men, the ardent love of Mary and the coldness of men, the union of Mary's will with the Divine will, and the opposition of the will of men to the will of God. He depicted the precious death of Mary, and the help she affords her cherished servants in their last hour."[8]

Carroll's biography repeated Alphonsus's words to his followers: "'My brothers, let us place ourselves in God's hands, and distrust human means; for the Congregation is a divine work, not the work of man, nor is man capable of upholding it.'"[9] Carroll described Alphonsus's attitude toward suffering: "'Persecutions,' said he, 'are to the work of God what frosts are to plants in winter; far from being hurtful, they make them take deeper root, and become more fruitful. ... Let us kiss the very walls of our cells, and the more we are persecuted the more closely let us be united to Jesus Christ.'"[10]

"When a picture of Our Lady was put in his hands, he began to invoke her, and recommend himself to her protection," Carroll said of Alphonsus's approaching death. "Our lady herself consoled him in his last moments."[11]

The same news account that described the contents of Kehoe's cell described his execution. "KEHOE HANGS," the *Philadelphia Times* said. "THE DEATH OF THE MOLLIES' EX-KING. Proclaiming to the Last His Innocence of Frank Langdon's Murder, He Meets a Terrible Death Upon the Scaffold in Pottsville's Jail-Yard —Details of the Execution."[12]

The previous afternoon, after relating the news of his pending execution to her husband, Mary Ann Kehoe had located a photographer and accompanied him to Pottsville Jail. Wrapped in a heavy cloak against a light snowfall, she had stood in the jail yard while Kehoe was photographed. After standing for his photo, Kehoe said goodbye to his defense counsel. His parting from his parents and five children, a son aged eleven and four daughters under the age of ten, had taken place earlier that afternoon.

By six the next morning, Kehoe was fully awake. His signed card for publication thanked his spiritual advisors, including the nuns who had visited his cell, his counsel, the prison keepers, and the warden.

Shortly after seven that morning, Father Gallagher celebrated the first of two Masses. The Philadelphia reporter described the setting:

> In one corner of the corridor, in a large, double cell used as a sort of storehouse for the shoes made by the convict laborers, the Sisters had erected a small altar. As I entered this in the dark hours of the morning the chill look of the prison was left behind and there in a convict cell was a perfect fac-simile of a convent chapel. ... The shoe-shelves had been concealed and the dingy room brightened up by plentiful drapery of white muslin, covering every wall. This the Sisters, who had made all these arrangements, had festooned and ornamented with evergreens. On the altar were lighted candles.

The small congregation included Kehoe and his wife Mary Ann; Martin Bergin, a fellow "Molly Maguire" prisoner; two Sisters of Saint Joseph from St. Patrick's Church, and two Sisters of St. Francis from neighboring St. Clair. "There was not a chair in the cell," the reporter said, "and each one present kneeled upon the hard floor, rising only during the services that followed, when the priest read the gospel."[13]

Father Gallagher entered the room with two acolytes. The reporter said: "The priest wore vestments of gold cloth, and this fact bore, at least to Jack Kehoe, a special significance. Gold, in the Church's parlance, is pure spotless white, and white is the color of the Blessed Virgin, and the fact that the vestments of the priest were of gold, showed that the day was one of the feasts of the Blessed Virgin."[14]

At the end of the Mass, "Kehoe expressed his satisfaction that the day was one of the Virgin Mary's feast days, for, he said, he had great confidence in her intercessory power. The Mass celebrated in that prison cell was a 'low' one in the church category, but, it was, indeed, solemn. It was specially offered up for the grace of a happy death for Kehoe, and all present received Holy Communion."[15]

At eight o'clock, a second Mass began. Then Kehoe and his wife shared breakfast. The *Philadelphia Times* reported: "At about half-past 9 o'clock, Father Gallagher actually forced Mrs. Kehoe from her husband's arms, and the brave but now sobbing woman was conducted, together with Kehoe's sister, to another part of the prison, where she remained until the execution was over. In Kehoe's cell the priests and the Sisters prayed fervently by the side of the man who soon was to die."[16] Then the priests administered the last rites of the Catholic faith to the condemned man.

At twenty minutes past ten, accompanied by Fathers Gallagher and Brennan, Kehoe entered the yard of Pottsville Jail. Sheriff Matz and Warden King preceded the trio. Deputy sheriffs and jurors followed behind. The reporter observed: "Down in a far corner of the yard stood the dull-grey framework of the scaffold. Against the prison wall and behind the scaffold stood a low frame structure, unpainted and hastily erected, and with a covering of rough bagging. This concealed the executioner, whose name was kept a secret and who was hid lest Mollie Maguire vengeance should make a target of his body."[17]

The reporter counted almost three hundred spectators crowding the jail yard. Others stood outside the prison walls.[18] These, he wrote, "strained their ears in the vain hope of being able to boast that they had heard the dull thud that spoke of the drop of the trap and of Jack Kehoe's death."[19] A squad of Coal and Iron policemen guarded the prison door.

Heavy clouds threatened overhead on the cold December morning. As Kehoe walked toward the scaffold, a rush of wind brought a fall of snow. Kehoe wore a black suit. A nosegay of flowers, a parting gift from his wife, adorned his lapel. He carried a lighted candle and wore a rosary around his neck.

As the group neared the gallows, Father Gallagher recited the "Kyrie Eleison." As Kehoe reached the scaffold's steps, a gust of wind extinguished his candle. The reporter said: "At the foot of the hangman's instrument, both priests knelt upon the ground and as the snow fell about them and on their uncovered heads they prayed aloud."[20]

The priests mounted the scaffold. Father Gallagher, who had

attended Kehoe at Pottsville Jail, "drew Kehoe to his breast as he would a child, embraced him, kissed him upon the lips, whispered a word in one ear, turned instantly about and walked down the gallows' steps."[21] Father Brennan shook Kehoe's hand warmly.

Alone on the gallows with the sheriff and warden, Kehoe looked out over the assemblage. He took a step forward. "'I am not guilty of the murder of Langdon,'" he said. "'I never saw the murder committed.'"[22] He bid the crowd goodbye and stepped back underneath the noose. The sheriff manacled his hands behind his back, and strapped his feet and arms.

Sheriff Matz positioned the noose around Kehoe's neck and drew the knot behind his left ear. Father Gallagher, stationed underneath, recited the "Pater Noster." Kehoe, hearing the prayer, became "firm and apparently-self composed." Matz dropped the white bag over Kehoe's head. "He had seen his last of earth," the reporter said. Matz again tightened the noose. The executioner sprang the trap, "and Jack Kehoe was struggling betwixt heaven and earth, in the throes of death."[23]

Kehoe died of strangulation. The rope cut so deeply into his neck, it drew blood. The Philadelphia reporter said: "Kehoe, despite his bandaged arms and feet, struggled hard. A description of the contortions he underwent would scarcely be pleasant food for reading."[24]

As the dying man struggled above the two priests, Father Gallagher granted Kehoe a plenary indulgence. Father Brennan recited the "Confiteor." Their service ended, the priests left the yard. Father Gallagher took the news of her husband's death to Mary Ann.

Kehoe's body remained dangling. The reporter observed: "The moment it fell, a half-dozen of the county's doctors ran toward it and it became a race between them to see who should first pounce upon the wrist of the dying man to feel his pulse and to announce to a few newspaper men who, standing almost beneath the struggling form, were anxious less they should lose the exact record of the heart's pulsations at each successive moment. The doctors struggled around the body for several minutes and then one of them, in hasty tones, called out in a loud voice: 'Sheriff, he is dead.'"[25] Matz cut the rope.

Policemen stationed underneath caught the body as it fell and delivered it to the undertaker for transport to Kehoe's Hibernian House in Girardville.

The *Chicago Tribune* reported the execution under "CRIMINAL NEWS." "Jack Keogh [sic]," it said, "the Mollie Maguire, Hanged at Pottsville, Pa. The Penalty of the Law Administered with Shocking Awkwardness."[26]

"THE TWO JACKS," the *Daily Globe* reported from St. Paul. "Jack Ketch Finally Conquers Jack Kehoe, the King of the Mollie Maguires."[27] "JUSTICE TRIUMPHANT," the *Daily Republican* reported from Wilmington, Delaware. "'Jack' Kehoe the King of the Mollie Maguires Executed.'"[28] "THE LAST OF JACK KEHOE," the *Patriot* said from Harrisburg. "THE MOLLIE KING LAYS DOWN HIS SCEPTRE ON THE GALLOWS AT POTTSVILLE."[29]

"His career is now at an end," the *Harrisburg Telegraph* said. "But what, we ask, will the scorpions and vultures of the press do for excuses to malign those in authority."[30]

In a *Philadelphia Times* editorial, Alexander McClure said of Kehoe's legal case: "justice was shuffled about from post to pillar by the jugglery of the Board of Pardons until her skirts were draggled with reproach and her locks grasped to be shorn by those who assumed that faith with crime was a higher duty than fidelity to law or the protection of society."[31] The *New York Sun* described Kehoe as a "murder master and politician."[32] The *New York Times* described him as "chief of the Molly Maguires in Schuylkill County, and probably the most powerful leader of the order in the State." Kehoe had, the *Times* said, "conducted a bold, aggressive campaign of violence and murder."[33] The *New York Tribune* said: "It would be ... harsh to say, 'The grave is the best place for Kehoe,' but such is the opinion of the community."[34]

Months before his execution, Kehoe had spoken with a reporter for the *New York Sun*. "'I've never had justice,'" he told the reporter. "'The newspapers and the people are down on me, because they say I'm a Molly; and to say that in Schuylkill County of a man is about as good as signing his death warrant. ... with my last breath I shall say I'm an innocent man, unjustly condemned. As for being a Molly Maguire, that I am not, and never was, and I know nothing about any such society. I was a member of the Ancient Order of Hibernians, but that was all.'"[35]

In the *Irish World*, Patrick Ford said: "Mr. Kehoe was a man of intelligence and influence, elected to be High Constable of the borough of Girardville. Also Bodymaster of the Ancient Order of Hibernians. He had used his position, and influence, and intelligence to procure bail and legal advice for miners accused of crimes."[36]

A few weeks after Kehoe's execution, Ford published an editorial headlined "Judicial Murder of John Kehoe." From Illinois, the *Cairo Bulletin* said of Ford's January 11th edition: "he struck off and published, one million, three hundred thousand copies—a number large enough to supply every fifth voter of the United States with a copy."[37]

From Pittsburgh, the *Telegraph* said of the editor of the *Pittsburgh Leader* who, like McClure of the *Philadelphia Times*, had lobbied strenuously for Kehoe's death: "the editor of the *Leader* last evening acknowledged himself to be the mysterious executioner, and confessed to have pulled the rope which ended Jack Kehoe's existence." The *Leader's* editor, the *Telegraph* said, "seems to have hold of a long mystic cord which runs through the State, and which the Philadelphia *Times* pulls at the other end. In some unexplained way the Governor, who must be attached to this mystic cord, is thus controlled, and when the *Leader* and the *Times* in unison pulled him to the signing of the Kehoe death warrant, the influence was too powerful to be resisted." The *Telegraph* concluded: "But will not these powerful editors lose their grip on the mystic chord, when the ghost of Jack Kehoe comes to haunt their editorial sanctums?"[38]

Kehoe's card, published in the *Miners' Journal*, thanked all who had offered him aid and sympathy. He added: "'I hope they may be rewarded in another and better world.'" He thanked his many friends, "'who in various ways assisted me, and gave evidence of their friendship in my darkest hours.'" He concluded: "'That God may bless and reward them is the prayer of Yours, John Kehoe.'"[39]

As faith suffused John Kehoe's last days, it marked the ordeals of his fellow Hibernians executed as "Molly Maguires." Shortly before James Roarity's hanging in June 1877, Roarity received a letter from Meencorvick, in Ireland's County Donegal. "'Dear Loving Son,'" Roarity's father Columbus told him, "'I sit to write to you the last letter that I'll ever write, again, and don't be afraid to meet your doom or your Judge. If you are going to suffer innocent I am sure God will spare your soul, and its [sic] far better to suffer in this world than in the world to come. No matter how long we suffer in this cursed world, its [sic] nothing beside eternity.'"[40]

Columbus continued: "Dear James, we are praying night and day for you; but it seems all in vain. But don't be afraid, God is merciful and good. And before you die, declare to your Judge and to the world whether you are guilty or innocent, and we are not sorry, for well I believe your letter saying you are innocent." He added: "I hope, through the intercession of the Blessed Virgin, that you are going to meet with a happy death." Of Roarity's family in Ireland, Columbus said: "we never stop praying night and day, in hopes still that God will spare you. And so He will and have that place prepared for you that will cause you joy and consolation during eternity ... so keep yourself stout in heart. I wish I was going to eternity along with you. I would be content; for, dear son, I don't know what to say or do, but really I'll be ever praying for you; and may the Lord of Heaven protect you in your last agony, and will. Don't be afraid." He concluded: "We all join in prayer and with the help of God you will be all right."[41]

In a letter written to his codefendants shortly before their joint execution at Bloomsburg, Patrick Hester advised Peter McHugh and Patrick Tully: "I believe our time in this world is short, and may God prepare us for the next and better world." Hester added: "And as for death, I am not afraid, for I am almost tired of this sinful world, for they are after my life these good many years. All that troubles me about dying is to die of what I am not guilty of, and that both of you know, and may God in His mercy do what is just and right to all."[42]

Susan McManus, wife of Peter McManus, hanged as the last alleged "Molly Maguire," wrote to a local editor while her husband remained incarcerated. McManus signed with an "X" above the designation "Her Mark," indicating that she had someone transcribe her letter for her. She said: "I was not married, nor was I in this country at the time of the murder. I still firmly believe in my husband's innocence, and hope that while man proposes for him a shameful doom, He who sees the sparrow's fall may otherwise dispose his fate."[43]

Of his own fate, condemned "Molly Maguire" Alexander Campbell told a New York reporter, while laying his right hand over his heart: "'here's a man who has been convicted by the most godless perjury, but who will go to his doom, if it be God's will, without faltering, knowing that the Great Judge will overrule the rulings of the Court that sentenced me to a double death.'"[44]

Hugh McGehan, who had led a peaceful parade of miners through the town of Tamaqua during the Long Strike of 1875, expressed himself in a poem. McGehan could not read or write. A reporter transcribed his words. They included a message to McGehan's wife, married to him one month before his arrest for an alleged "Molly Maguire" crime.

> My name is Hugh McGeghan,
> My age just twenty-four;
> I was born in County Donegal,
> On Erin's pleasant shore.
>
> I left my aged parents,
> Like many of my race,
> And now I'm held in durance vile,
> Bowed down with sore disgrace.

I was but eighteen years of age,
When to this land I came;
No crime upon my conscience,
And on my head no shame.

The first place that I worked a shift
Was in the Jeddo mines;
There too the men can testify
How well I served my time.

The day I left my native land,
I took a solemn oath,
That liquor vile of any kind
Should never go down my throat.

My vow I still am keeping,
And will until I die,
Be it on a bed of flowers
Or on the gallows high.

I'm now accused of murder,
The same I do deny;
And when my trial will come on,
Those traitors I'll defy.

But perjury has got [its] way
Throughout our happy land;
And like O'Connell, I must hear
Them swear on every hand.

May God have mercy on those men;
Their deeds they can't secrete
When called to face an angry God
Before the judgment seat.

But such is life to Irishmen,
And evermore will be;
For it always were since that bright day
When Paddy's land was free.

By the Holy Virgin Mary,
What I say here it's true,
I never knew Jim Kerrigan
Or any of his crew.

I never kept his company,
Which he must know right [well];
But still to save his guilty neck
He would swear us into [hell].

They have another man on hand
To swear our lives away;
His name I cannot mention,
For he has two or three.

McKenna and McParlan,
And the other I don't know;
But he's prov'd himself a traitor
To his own dear country.

Here's to my kind friends one and all,
My enemies also;
Unto my foster parents,
That I have brought so low;

And to my true and patient wife,
To me she is most dear;
I know that she will grieve for me
While I am lying here.

But bear up bravely little one,
And soon you'll see me free,
To face those tyrants one and all
That try to bury me.

To walk among my fellow men,
With head erect and strong,
And to show these vile accusers
That they are in the wrong.

Now if I don't get clear of this,
And those men do ga'n the day,
There's one request I humbly ask
Of those that mourn for me.

To offer up a [prayer] for me
Both morning, night and noon,
To hope in heaven my soul will shine
Upon the judgment day.[45]

In early February 1878, with ongoing "Molly Maguire" executions scheduled at Bloomsburg and Mauch Chunk, the *Irish World* published a notice. Seventy-five years after the Dublin execution of Irish rebel leader Robert Emmet, the *Irish World* announced the establishment at Mauch Chunk of the Robert Emmet Monument Association.[46]

Six years before, in late February 1872, alleged "Molly Maguire" James Carroll had hosted Labor Reformers in convention at his Carbon County home in Nesquehoning. All of the candidates nominated at Nesquehoning, the local paper reported, "pledged themselves to support the principals of the Labor Reform Party."[47]

On March 25, 1878, on the same day that souvenir hunters scrabbled for pieces of rope under the gallows at Bloomsburg, Mauch

Chunk's new Robert Emmet Monument Association hosted a parade, with an evening ball to be held at Oak Hall in Nesquehoning.

St. Patrick's Cornet Band would lead the parade. An orchestra was hired for the ball. The *Mauch Chunk Democrat* advised: "They invite all the friends of Irish Nationality to participate, with or without regalia. They are requested to wear an emblem of Erin at least. ... Robert Emmet's dying speech will be read by P. J. Meehan, Esq."[48] A few weeks later, Meehan would serve as defense counsel at Mauch Chunk for AOH defendants James McDonnell and Charles Sharpe.

On September 20, 1803, British officials had hanged Irish rebel leader Emmet for treason at Thomas Street in Dublin. Officials had denied Emmet's request to wear his green uniform, that of a rebel general, for his execution. British legislation had changed the penalty for treason from hanging, drawing, and quartering, to hanging and removal of the prisoner's head. Emmet's executioner performed this duty in view of the crowd gathered on Thomas Street. Holding the severed head aloft, the executioner proclaimed: "'This is the head of a traitor, Robert Emmet.'"[49]

On the day before his execution, Emmet had addressed the court at the close of his trial in Dublin's Green Street courthouse. At Oak Hall in Nesquehoning seventy-five years later Meehan, defense counsel in Mauch Chunk's "Molly Maguire" trials, read Emmet's "Speech From the Dock." Meehan read Emmet's speech on the same day that three grotesque executions of Irishmen, including that of Patrick Hester, had taken place at Bloomsburg.

Meehan gave Emmet's speech to the court: "When my spirit shall have joined those bands of martyred heroes who have shed their blood on the scaffold and in the field in defence of their country, this is my hope, that my memory and name may serve to animate those who survive me." Emmet spoke of "that government which upholds its dominion by impiety against the most high, which displays its power over man as over the beasts of the field, which sets man upon his brother, and lifts his hands in religion's name against the throat of his fellow." Emmet spoke for his countrymen. He said: "If there be a true Irishman present, let my last words cheer him in the hour of his affliction."[50]

Of the court's administration of justice, Emmet said: "sentence was already pronounced at the Castle before your jury was impanelled. Your lordships are but the priests of the oracle."[51]

"My lords," Emmet told his judges, "you are impatient for the sacrifice. The blood which you seek is not congealed by the artificial terrors which surround your victim. It circulates warmly and unruffled through its channels, and in a short time it will cry to heaven."[52]

Emmet told the British court in 1803: "Let no man write my epitaph, for as no man knows my motives dares now vindicate them, let not prejudice or ignorance asperse them. Let them rest in obscurity and peace: my memory be left in oblivion and my tomb remain uninscribed, until other times and other men can do justice to my character. When my country takes her place among the nations of the earth, then, and not till then, let my epitaph be written. I have done."[53]

---

1. *Philadelphia Times*, December 19, 1878.
2. *Morning Star and Catholic Messenger* (New Orleans, LA), December 14, 1873.
3. Paula Diann Marlin, "Mother Mary Teresa Austin Carroll," https://www.mercyworld.org/catherine/mercy-foundresses/mother-mary-teresa-austin-carroll/.
4. Austin Carroll, *The Life of St. Alphonsus Liguori* (New York: New York Catholic Protectory, 1874), 121.
5. Ibid., 140.
6. Ibid., 175.
7. Ibid., 536.
8. Ibid., 200.
9. Ibid., 423.
10. Ibid., 495.
11. Ibid., 624-25.
12. *Philadelphia Times*, December 19, 1878.
13. Ibid.
14. Ibid.
15. Ibid.
16. Ibid.
17. Ibid.
18. *New York Times*, December 19, 1878. This account reported one hundred and fifty spectators within the jail yard and two to three hundred standing outside the prison walls.

19. *Philadelphia Times*, December 19, 1878.
20. Ibid.
21. Ibid.
22. Ibid.
23. Ibid.
24. Ibid.
25. Ibid.
26. *Chicago Daily Tribune*, December 19, 1878.
27. *Daily Globe* (St. Paul, MN), December 19, 1878.
28. *Daily Republican* (Wilmington, DE), December 19, 1878.
29. *Harrisburg Patriot*, December 19, 1878.
30. *Harrisburg Telegraph*, December 19, 1878.
31. *Philadelphia Times*, December 19, 1878.
32. *New York Sun*, December 19, 1878.
33. *New York Times*, December 19, 1878.
34. *New York Tribune*, December 19, 1878.
35. Reported in *New York Sun*, December 19, 1878.
36. *Daily Cairo (IL) Bulletin*, January 14, 1879.
37. *Irish World* (New York), January 11, 1879.
38. *Pittsburgh Telegraph*, December 19, 1878; italics in original.
39. *Miners' Journal* (Pottsville, PA), December 20, 1878.
40. Wayne G. Broehl Jr., *The Molly Maguires* (Cambridge: Harvard University Press, 1964), 338. See also Kevin Kenny, *Making Sense of the Molly Maguires* (New York: Oxford University Press, 1998), 249-50.
41. Broehl, *Molly Maguires*, 338-39.
42. *Columbian* (Bloomsburg, PA), April 12, 1878.
43. Letter of Susan McManus, *Northumberland Democrat* (Sunbury, PA), September 6, 1878.
44. *Catholic Standard* (Philadelphia), March 17, 1877; reprinting *New York World*.
45. *Shenandoah (PA) Herald*, September 12, 1876.
46. *Irish World* (New York), February 2, 1878.
47. *Mauch Chunk (PA) Coal Gazette*, February 23, 1872.
48. *Mauch Chunk (PA) Democrat*, March 16, 1878.
49. Patrick M. Geoghegan, *Robert Emmet: A Life* (Dublin: Gill & Macmillan, 2002), 22.
50. Ibid., 250.
51. Ibid., 252.
52. Ibid., 253.
53. Ibid., 253-54.

11

END OF THE ROAD

Having sown the wind, you are going to reap the whirlwind?

> Bondholder to Philadelphia and Reading shareholders
> Philadelphia, 1884

By 1880, Franklin Gowen's reckless management had driven the Philadelphia and Reading Coal and Iron Company into receivership. His bombast helped him secure appointments both as a receiver in that year's bankruptcy proceedings and as president of company subsidiaries. But his bluster did not impress his London financiers, the McCalmont brothers Robert and Hugh. In February 1881, the brothers told Gowen via letter: "'you treat every one who opposes you personally as having sinister motives, and being an enemy of the Company. The truth is, that you have so long held unlimited sway that you confound the Company with yourself, and are unable to understand how anyone can honestly differ from you. This is one reason, and not the least, why we think no effectual reform possible while the Company is under your control.'"[1]

In March 1881 the McCalmonts' preferred candidate, Frank Bond, secured the company's presidency. In April, Gowen rented the Academy of Music at Philadelphia to rally shareholders to his side. Blond and imperious, he mesmerized opera hall listeners as he had mesmerized coal region juries. Participants at the overflow meeting included John Hartranft, former Pennsylvania governor during the "Molly Maguire" trials. Hartranft looked on from a private box as Gowen ridiculed former Reading president Charles Smith, along with the McCalmonts and their favored candidate, Bond.

In June 1881, Gowen again rented Philadelphia's opera hall, this time to strong-arm coal and iron men and state representatives. Former Civil War general Robert Patterson introduced Gowen to the rapt assembly as "'a man who is known in every city and State in the Union ... whose courage redeemed the Schuylkill region from a set of robbers, and pirates, and murderers; the only man in this State who had the nerve, the ability, and the perseverance to do it.'"[2] Gowen's opera hall speech gained him the support of influential Philadelphians. A trip to New York secured him the backing of New York Central owner William Vanderbilt.

In October 1881 the McCalmonts, fearing Gowen's re-election as company president, appealed directly to the Reading's investors. In a written address to company stockholders, they condemned Gowen's rash policy of buying up coal land in Pennsylvania. They declared his "'incapacity to learn'" a "'radical defect in business intellect.'" They cautioned: "'Whoever differs from him must be wrong; he will tolerate no contradiction or resistance; and when he meets serious opposition, no matter from whom, no matter after what previous forbearance or favor to himself, it is met with furious charges of corrupt or malicious motives, and with insults which are nothing short of public outrages.'"[3]

Despite the McCalmonts' warning, in January 1882 shareholders who gathered at Philadelphia's Association Hall for the annual meeting of the Philadelphia and Reading elected Gowen president. A block of shares from Vanderbilt cemented Gowen's victory. Years later, the *New York Sun* declared Gowen's win of the presidency that year "the most brilliant battle of his belligerent career."[4]

After Gowen's election and Bond's defeat, the McCalmonts liquidated their company holdings. They sold every bond and share they owned. Some dated from the year Gowen was born.

One month after Gowen's election as company president in January 1882, Reading Vice-President George De B. Keim, with publisher J. B. Lippincott and others, threw Gowen a victory banquet at Philadelphia's Hotel Bellevue. A floral display on one wall of the banquet room spelled out Gowen's name in carnations and tea roses. Dinner included freshly caught shad, game birds on toast, breasts of capon, and out-of-season strawberries and tomatoes.

Banquet guests included Vanderbilt. At each place setting stood an eighteen-inch steel replica of a Reading locomotive. Black wool rose from its chimney, and white cotton from its valve. Its "cowcatcher" held a drawer filled with iced punch. Its tender held imported cigarettes.

The following year, in February 1883, the Reading emerged from receivership. Gowen had often assured shareholders that he would resign the presidency when that event transpired. In May, shareholders circulated a petition asking him to remain in office. In November, Gowen informed the Reading's investors he would not seek the company's presidency. He recommended a successor: Keim, the Reading's vice president and former solicitor general.

In January 1884, though business leaders in New York and Philadelphia and seventy-eight members of Pennsylvania's state legislature asked Gowen to remain in office, he handed the reins to Keim. As incoming president, Keim inherited twelve million dollars in floating debt. In May 1884, the Reading went into receivership again.

In 1885 Charles Smith, who preceded Gowen as president of the Philadelphia and Reading Railroad, self-published a pamphlet titled "The Gowen Coal Policy." Smith authored the pamphlet with J. W. Jones, a former Reading official. A compilation of published articles critiquing Gowen's management, it reads as one long declaration of outrage.

In November 1884, after studying the just-issued report of the Reading receivers, a bondholder who signed himself "Anglo-American" authored one of the pamphlet's articles. Though Gowen's policies had driven the company into bankruptcy and receivership for the second time, Gowen was again asking shareholders to reinstate him as company president. This bondholder told fellow investors: "You, year after year, have, at your meetings, sanctioned the reckless, if not criminal, financing of your managers, at whose head was Mr. Gowen. You disregarded the warnings which were given you, that this blind faith in your chief was carrying the Company into that condition, when it would have either to file a fiat in bankruptcy or repudiate its debts. You turned a deaf ear to the appeals made to you, by ruined men and women, to stay his hand."[5]

"Having sown the wind," the bondholder asked, "you are going to reap the whirlwind?"[6] Gowen's plan for rehabilitation of the company "depends upon his borrowing more money, and raising the price of coal—two utopian, and therefore Gowenian, ideas."[7]

Smith's pamphlet also included a letter drafted by the McCalmont brothers. Dated November 1881, after shareholders had removed Gowen from the presidency for the first time, this letter said of Gowen's tenure: "The causes of the dismal downfall just related are: bad administration; latterly, very bad and extravagant finance; frequently, quarrelsome and domineering conduct toward neighboring and competing companies; and, above all, a wild attempt to buy up a monopoly of the coal trade of Pennsylvania, a policy now seen to be unsound in itself, on account of the unmanageable size and nature of the operation, and carried out in detail with a reckless disregard of economy and prudence."[8]

And the pamphlet contained a letter from an unnamed Philadelphia correspondent. This writer laid out the company's debt burden dating from 1869, when Gowen had taken charge, to his tenure in 1883: a result in bonded debt of ninety-eight million dollars. Gowen's apologists, this writer said, pleaded with naysayers to overlook "his falsified predictions, his foibles of temper, his illogical finance." The correspondent added: "His failure has been conspicuous, and, it is to be hoped, his vocation as a borrower of English money correspondingly discredited."[9]

The unnamed Philadelphia correspondent deplored Gowen's "insane desire to obtain a monopoly of the coal traffic [by arraying] himself against all other coal owners and transporters."[10] The writer added: "The proneness of the man to 'see visions and dream dreams' was astonishing. The 'future success of the Company,' was dependent, as all must have seen who were not dazzled by his specious but glowing representations, upon his ability to raise the wind in London and elsewhere."[11] But the money Gowen raised from London financiers "could not shake off the incubus of the coal land purchases." His resulting ruin was "foretold by thoughtful men."[12]

From 1880 to 1881, Gowen's conjuring of support from English investors included three conclaves at London's Cannon Street Hotel. A second unnamed Philadelphia correspondent said: "The Londoners had swallowed his 'airy nothings' at a gulp ... But time wears threadbare the most ample cloak of humbug, however artfully it may be disguised."[13] Gowen's desire for monopolistic control through purchase of coal land was "the canker worm which has been eating up the vital part of the property."[14] This correspondent quoted Lady Macbeth: "No man, it may be affirmed, could more 'look like the innocent flower,' and at the same time, 'be the serpent under it,' than Mr. Gowen."[15]

The writer continued: "It may be well asked, how is it that Mr. Gowen has not been pulled up in his mad career? But it is difficult to give any explanation, other than that of the usual apathy of stockholders, so long as they receive dividends, or the promise of them, and do not trouble to ascertain whence they come."[16]

In November 1885, Gowen issued a letter to Reading shareholders blasting Keim's leadership. On December 11, 1885, Gowen again rented Philadelphia's opera hall to woo company shareholders. So persuasive was his effort that Keim resigned his presidency in advance of the upcoming annual meeting. "There are few speakers in the world," the *Philadelphia Times* said of this speech, "who can electrify an audience as can Mr. Gowen."[17] A short time before, an unnamed financier had given his view of Gowen to the paper's reporter: "'He carries sublime courage with him and can talk a setting hen off from her nest with his wonderful gift of speech ... His imagination is grand, and his tongue is as smooth as burnished gold.'"[18]

Gowen's 1885 performance at Philadelphia's Academy of Music was his last public song and dance. On February 11, 1886, a syndicate headed by J. P. Morgan offered a reorganization plan to Reading trustees. The trustees accepted.

In the *Philadelphia Times*, an anonymous member of Morgan's syndicate told of Morgan's plan to bring peace and prosperity to the Reading: "'In order to do this, it has been found necessary to get rid of Mr. Gowen. We have all combined to get him out of railroad management, just as all the powers of Europe combined to crush Napoleon, and there will be no peace until Mr. Gowen is in St. Helena. He is an able and brilliant man and in some respects a veritable Napoleon, but he is no railroad manager. ... The trouble with Mr. Gowen is that he wants to be fighting all the time. When he was after the Molly Maguires, he was in his element, but as a railroad manager he is a failure.'"[19]

In 1887, Franklin Gowen made his last sojourn to Europe. That fall, he returned home to his wife and daughter at his Mount Airy mansion, named "Cresheim" after his mother's ancestral German village. He returned to private law practice.

In the succeeding years Gowen, or other family members, evidently donated the Gowen family homestead to the Lutheran Church. In October 1889 the new Theological Seminary of the Lutheran Church at Mount Airy, a six-acre pastoral retreat, was formally dedicated at the site of the old homestead of Gowen's late father.

Two months after that, on Monday, December 9, 1889, Gowen wrote to his insurance agent to exchange his ninety thousand dollars in life insurance for paid up policies. Then he traveled to Washington and checked into Wormley's Hotel, just blocks from the White House. Gowen was scheduled to argue a case before the Interstate Commerce Commission (ICC) on behalf of Ohio oil refiner George Rice. At the nadir of his career after his ouster from the Philadelphia and Reading, Gowen had turned to advocating on behalf of individuals against powerful corporations.

On Thursday evening, December 12, someone matching Gowen's description entered the hardware store of D. N. Walford on Pennsylvania Avenue, a little more than a mile from Wormley's Hotel. The well-dressed customer told the clerk he wanted a good revolver. He purchased a nickel-plated, pearl-handled Smith and Wesson .38, along with a partial box of shells.

The next afternoon Rice, Gowen's client, met with Gowen at one o'clock in Gowen's room at Wormley's Hotel. Rice later observed that Gowen's spirits "had never seemed brighter."[20] Around two o'clock, Gowen entered the hotel's dining room. ICC judge Thomas Cooley, also a guest at Wormley's, joined Gowen at his table for lunch. Earlier in the day, the two men had chatted together.

As did Rice, the dining room staff would later say that Gowen had seemed in excellent spirits. Later that afternoon, a hotel chambermaid stopped by Gowen's room. She found the room key on the inside, with Gowen in the room behind the locked door.

The next morning, the maid returned to the room and found the door still locked, with the key still on the inside. She returned at noon to find the same. Alarmed, she informed the hotel's proprietor, James Wormley.

Wormley went to Gowen's room. The hotel owner stood on a chair in the hallway and looked through the room's transom. He saw the dead body of Gowen, fully clothed, lying on the floor. "The pistol itself," the *New York Times* reported, "lay on the hearth several feet from the body and its ivory handle was crimsoned with blood, which had also soaked through Mr. Gowen's coat and underwear."[21]

Wormley summoned a policeman. They removed the transom and sent for a youth small enough to wedge through the opening. The boy wriggled through and dropped to the floor. He went to the door, unlocked it, and admitted those in the corridor. The policeman had Gowen's body removed to the morgue without a coroner's examination.

Friends of Gowen in Washington, notified of the event, hurried to the police station to protest the body's hasty removal. They contacted Coroner Patterson. After viewing the body, an apparent suicide, Patterson decided no inquest was needed. He allowed an undertaker to remove the body for burial preparation.

At nine that night Gowen's nephew Francis Gowen, an attorney who shared Gowen's law practice, arrived in Washington with Pinkerton superintendent Robert Linden and J. E. Hood, another Gowen relative. Francis Gowen directed the undertaker to place his uncle's body in a plain oak coffin. Then he, with Hood, oversaw its transfer to the Baltimore and Ohio Railroad Station. At ten thirty their private train, including the palace car Delaware, left Washington to transport Gowen's body to Philadelphia.

Francis Gowen dismissed the theory of suicide. He retained Linden to investigate his uncle's death. In Washington, Linden met with the superintendent of police and the police officer who first viewed Gowen's body.

On December 18 Linden and a detective of the Washington police force visited Walford's hardware store, taking with them the revolver found at the scene of Gowen's death. Both Walford and his clerk identified the weapon as that purchased on Thursday evening by the man fitting Gowen's description. Walford removed the pearl stock from the revolver and identified his store's price mark. The store's cash book showed the purchase, dating from Thursday evening.[22]

Walford gave an *Evening Star* reporter the details of Linden's visit. "From the description of the man who purchased the revolver there is no doubt left but that the man was Mr. Gowen," the reporter said. "Capt. Linden and Detective Horne were both fully satisfied that Mr. Gowen purchased the pistol and took his own life."[23]

The *Star* reporter also interviewed Coroner Patterson. He found the physician just leaving home, driving his own buggy. While trying to calm a spirited horse, Patterson proclaimed the murder theory "an utter absurdity."[24]

Linden, the *Star* reporter concluded, "has about given up the quest and will return home today. ... He is said to be a deep man, however, whose plans lie far beneath the surface and who is in the habit of doing exactly what he is unexpected to do."[25]

"WAS GOWEN MURDERED?" the *New York Sun* asked six days later. "A Startling Story by a Former Molly Maguire Lodge Master."[26] A former officer of the "Molly Maguires" had allegedly contacted a coal region paper with a theory of Gowen's supposed murder that rivaled Allan Pinkerton's fantasias. The *Sun* added: "it is known that [Robert Linden], at the request of Francis I. Gowen, employed a number of special detectives to trace all the Molly Maguires who had recently been released from the penitentiary. The Superintendent of the Pinkertons had a complete list of these ex-convicts, and he placed his men upon their tracks with instructions to report to him every move they had made since their release."[27]

Apart from securing Linden a new caseload investigating AOH men newly released from prison, the murder theory gained little traction. The *New York Times* gave Gowen's death front-page coverage. It said: "His prosecution of the Molly Maguires illustrated both his ability and his courage. ... His arguments in some of those cases were forensic models." The *Times* added: "In the burst of popular approval which followed ... his name was proposed for Governor of Pennsylvania."[28]

A reporter for the *Times* interviewed George De B. Keim shortly after news of Gowen's death reached him. Keim, sitting president of the Reading Coal and Iron Company, said: "'I was never more shocked in my life than at the melancholy news which reached me from Washington a few moments ago. The last man whose death I expected was Mr. Gowen. It is inexplicable, and I am momentarily expecting some explanation of this sad ending of one of the most brilliant men this country has ever produced.'"[29]

The *New York Sun* speculated that Gowen, disappointed at the forthcoming failure of George Rice's case against the railroads and

Standard Oil Company, had taken his life in a fit of depression. "Mr. Gowen found it impossible to prove the claims made by his client," the *Sun* said. "While there was a moral certainty of the facts, they could not be established. The evidence, being almost entirely under the control of the railroads, was not easily reached. Mr. Gowen felt that he had a good case, a case worthy [of] his talents and energies, but he could not develop it. This was provoking, humiliating. A theory held among the lawyers who have been before the Inter-State Commission during the week is that the disappointment attending his failure to make out his case caused temporary insanity, that resulted in suicide."[30]

Gowen's death so shocked ICC Judge Thomas, already failing in health, that he left Wormley's Hotel and returned home to Ann Arbor, Michigan. From Maine, a newspaper reported of Thomas: "The suicide of Gowen, with whom he was intimate and with whom he lunched the last time the latter was in the dining room of the hotel where the suicide occurred, greatly affected him."[31]

A few years later, a Wilkes-Barre reporter interviewed Gowen's private secretary, W. R. Taylor. When asked if he knew why Gowen had taken his life, Taylor responded: "'No, it will always be a mystery to me. I felt that if any human being could stand up and face adverse circumstances it was Mr. Gowen. ... I never suspected he was breaking down and I was wholly unprepared for his tragic death.'"[32]

The *Pittsburg* [sic] *Dispatch* lauded Gowen's "fierce opposition to political dishonesty and his active work against discrimination and trusts."[33] "He was an intellectual giant," the *Baltimore Sun* said, "so honest that he would not avail himself of legitimate opportunities to acquire wealth as a railroad president, brave, even to recklessness, and withal a gentle, cultured Christian."[34]

"'There can be little doubt of the motive for Mr. Gowen's suicide,'" said Charles Smith, who preceded Gowen as president of the Philadelphia and Reading Railroad. "'I believe it was caused purely by mortification over his failure in the management of the road ... for twelve months he has had absolutely no connection whatever with the company in which he took such a keen interest for a long time. Mr. Gowen was virtually dismissed as counsel for the Reading about a year ago, and since then he has not drawn a penny from the company.'"[35]

Albert O'Brien, assistant manager for the Reading Railroad, said: "'He was an aggressive man, strong in his convictions. Possessed of much warmth of feeling, he loved his friends. Like all aggressive or affirmative natures, he made enemies; but he had troops of friends, who were bound to him with hooks of steel.'"[36]

The Brotherhood of Locomotive Engineers noted that by Gowen's death, one of the age's "arch tyrants" had been removed. Gowen's "inhumanity to man," the union men noted, "made thousands mourn."[37]

From Mahanoy City, at the heart of Schuylkill County's coal region, the *Tri-Weekly Record* reported the news. The miners, it said, would give Gowen credit where due and feel sympathy for his bereaved family, but "they never can forget that he used all the means in his power, both fair and foul, to crush out their spirit of independence as men and citizens of America. The gall and bitterness of the six months struggle of 1875 ... The cry of famishing babes and weeping wives ... the threats that he would make them succumb to his demand if he had to turn Schuylkill county into a 'howling wilderness,' is still remembered and will be long after all that is mortal of him has been consigned to the cold ground."[38]

---

1. Quoted in Marvin W. Schlegel, *Ruler of the Reading: The Life of Franklin B. Gowen* (Harrisburg: Archives Publishing Company of Pennsylvania, 1947), 219-20.
2. Ibid., 225.
3. Ibid., 228.
4. *New York Sun*, July 26, 1885.
5. Jones and Smith, *Gowen Coal Policy*, 4-5.
6. Ibid., 5.
7. Ibid., 6.
8. Ibid., 7.
9. Ibid., 8.
10. Ibid., 11.
11. Ibid., 15.
12. Ibid., 16.

13. Ibid., 22.
14. Ibid., 27.
15. Ibid., 18.
16. Ibid., 28.
17. Quoted in Schlegel, *Ruler*, 266.
18. Ibid., 264.
19. Ibid., 269.
20. Ibid., 286.
21. *New York Times*, December 15, 1889.
22. *Evening Star* (Washington, DC), December 18, 1889.
23. Ibid.
24. Ibid.
25. Ibid.
26. *New York Sun*, December 24, 1889.
27. Ibid.
28. *New York Times*, December 15, 1889.
29. Ibid.
30. *New York Sun*, December 16, 1889.
31. *Portland (ME) Daily Press*, December 20, 1889.
32. Account from *Wilkes-Barre (PA) Record* reported in *Evening Herald* (Shenandoah, PA), May 4, 1892.
33. *Pittsburg [sic] Dispatch*, December 15, 1889.
34. *Baltimore Sun*, December 16, 1889.
35. Ibid.
36. *New York Times*, December 15, 1889.
37. Brotherhood of Locomotive Firemen and Enginemen, *Journal of Proceedings of the Second Biennial Convention* (Terre Haute: Moore & Langen, 1890), 38.
38. Reprint of *Tri-Weekly Record* column from unnamed source dated December 17, 1889; private collection of Ellen Engelhardt.

12

THE SECOND GREAT CONTEST

How can any one who abhors the oppression of negroes, be in favor of degrading classes of white people? Our progress in degeneracy appears to me to be pretty rapid. As a nation, we begin by declaring that "all men are created equal." We now practically read it "all men are created equal, except negroes." When the Know-Nothings get control, it will read "all men are created equals, except negroes and foreigners and catholics."

Abraham Lincoln to Joshua Speed, 1855

Every advantage that the human race has won has been at fearful cost, at great contest, at suffering endured. ... It has come to these poor miners to bear this cross, not for themselves ... but that the human race may be lifted up to a higher and broader plane than it has ever known.

Clarence Darrow to Anthracite Mine Strike Commission
Philadelphia, 1903

On January 28, 1903, renowned Chicago defense attorney Clarence Darrow drafted a letter to his wife, Ruby. Darrow's nickname for his wife was "Ruben." He headed the letter, written in pencil on mustard-colored notepaper, "In Court-Room / Philadelphia, Jan 28th."[1]

"Dearest Ruben," Darrow's letter began, "I am writing you a line in the court room surrounded by lawyers & miners & xx maggots of all sorts. I have been cross-questioning witnesses all day & am tired & I wish you were here & I could crawl into your arms & rest & sleep & feel better in the morning." Darrow added: "Every day I get some telegram about running for mayor ... I think ... I will tell them that I will not — for all the time there comes before me a vision of six months at some quiet lake in the north of England or in Italy with only you – & with it a chance to write a play – a long story – about you & me and every body."[2]

Among those Darrow cross-examined that day in Philadelphia were representatives of independent coal operators in Pennsylvania's anthracite region. Twenty-eight years after the region's Long Strike had ended, the four hundred eighty-four square miles that supplied the coal that heated the country's homes, schools, and offices and fired its industry remained a battlefield.

In the twenty-five years between the mass hangings of Pennsylvania's alleged "Molly Maguires" and its Great Strike of 1902, the English, Irish, German, and Welsh mineworkers of its anthracite region had given way to men of Italian, Polish, Ukrainian, Hungarian, Lithuanian, Turkish, and Armenian descent. A handful of men still controlled the mineworkers' destinies and those of their families. These included financier J. Pierpont Morgan, whose patrician New England roots traced back to 1636; railroad president George Baer, whose ancestor from Zweibrücken, Germany, had settled in Pennsylvania circa 1740; and union leader John Mitchell.

An elite fraternity of financial and industrial interests now shaped the leadership of the Philadelphia and Reading Railroad. Baer's involvement dated to 1870, when as an attorney in Reading, Pennsylvania, he had brought suit against the company. Impressed with his talent, the railroad had hired Baer as corporate counsel. Baer had moved from that position to director, and eventually to company president. By the time of his death, Baer's influence extended over a number of Pennsylvania industries where he served in presidencies and directorships. Those business interests included railroads, coal, iron, steel, paper, and insurance.

As co-owner of the *Somerset Democrat* in the early 1860s, Baer had learned the art of press manipulation. As an autocratic lawyer of German descent, he was heir apparent to Franklin Gowen's Philadelphia and Reading Railroad. After Baer's Civil War service at Antietam, Bull Run, Chancellorsville, and Fredericksburg as captain of the One Hundred and Thirty-third Regiment of Pennsylvania Volunteers, a regiment he had formed, Baer moved to Reading to practice law.

In 1877, the Railroad Strike tore through the country. Baer and Gowen's shared animus against labor led them both to a Berks County courtroom, where they helped the district attorney mount marginally successful prosecutions against strikers accused of violence.

The influence of J. P. Morgan, "'The Uncrowned King'" of finance,[3] would eventually take one of these railroad magnates to the zenith of his career and the other to his nadir. In 1886 Morgan, by that time a financial and industrial powerhouse whose holdings included a controlling interest in the Philadelphia and Reading Railroad, formed the syndicate that successfully, and finally, maneuvered Gowen out of the railroad's presidency. "MR. GOWEN RETIRES AT LAST," the *New York Sun* had reported of Morgan's coup. "*HIS OPPOSITION TO THE REORGANIZATION OF READING FUTILE.*"[4] Three years later, Gowen committed suicide.

Four years after that, Baer and Morgan formed a lasting alliance. Among other efforts, Baer helped Morgan open a railway line to Pittsburgh. After helping Morgan consolidate competing anthracite-carrying railroad lines into a cohesive unit, Baer continued to serve Morgan as a legal and financial advisor.

By 1901, Morgan controlled about a third of the country's railways. That year, he installed Baer as president of three entities: the Philadelphia and Reading Railroad, the Philadelphia and Reading Coal and Iron Company, and the Central Railroad of New Jersey. The following year, both men figured prominently in the industrial drama known as the Great Strike of 1902.

In background and demeanor, union president John Mitchell could scarcely have differed more from Morgan and Baer. A second-generation Irish immigrant, Mitchell was born in 1870 in Braidwood, Illinois. Orphaned at age six and raised by a pitiless stepmother, Mitchell had left school at age ten to do farm labor. At age twelve, he had entered the mines of the Chicago, Wilmington, and Vermillion Coal Company. As "trapper boy," Mitchell opened and closed the doors that controlled mine ventilation. Then he moved on to mule driver. At age fifteen, Mitchell joined the Knights of Labor. In 1898, at age twenty-eight, he ascended to the presidency of the United Mineworkers of America (UMWA), having helped found the union at Columbus, Ohio, in 1890. During his tenure as UMWA president, Mitchell increased its membership from forty thousand to three hundred and fifty thousand mineworkers.

On Mitchell's death in 1919, the *Evening Herald* in Albuquerque said that his early experience had moved him "not to bitterness ... but to a broad and eager sympathy for thousands of his fellow workers in the mines." The paper noted Mitchell's death as "a loss to the country and particularly to labor, for Mitchell had the vision that labor most needs in its leadership."[5]

"He was born in the pit's mouth," the *New York Times* said, "going to school from 4 to 10. ... self-educated, an authority on economics, and something of a lawyer, all his learning acquired under the lamp after the day's labor." The *Times* described Mitchell as "one of the most remarkable Americans of our time." It said of Mitchell's tenure as UMWA president: "for nine years he fought its battles without losing the respect of any man. His commonsense, his fairness in controversy, his courage, and his public spirit made him a national figure."[6]

In Cleveland at the UMWA convention held within a week of

Mitchell's death, two thousand delegates representing five hundred thousand coal miners marched in a body from their convention hall to St. John's Cathedral to honor the fallen leader. From Indian Territory in Oklahoma, a news account praised Mitchell's "dynamic type of Americanism, who led in a cause he knew to be right but who furthered his cause only by methods that were fair to his opposition."[7]

In early 1900, two years into Mitchell's UMWA presidency, the union numbered fewer than nine thousand members. Most were bituminous mineworkers, with only about six percent of anthracite mineworkers engaged. But Mitchell's background and his extraordinary gifts helped him merge miners of many ethnicities, cultures, and religious faiths into one gigantic unit. His air of quiet dignity, augmented by austere black suits worn with high linen collars, helped him gain the mineworkers' trust.

From 1900 to 1902, Mitchell and his union officers held meetings in kitchens, taverns, and parish halls throughout Pennsylvania's hard coalfields. They secured the backing of priests, notably Rev. John Curran, a future friend of Theodore Roosevelt. Mitchell and his men convinced the mineworkers that their only hope of wages sufficient to give their families a decent life lay in unity.

As Mitchell and his men traveled the region, UMWA recruitments soared. With union membership came the courage for collective action in the form of strikes. On September 17, 1900, between eighty and one hundred thousand anthracite miners walked out in protest. Six weeks later operators, impelled by political pressure, posted a ten percent wage increase on the doors of their collieries. But the coal operators steadfastly refused to meet with Mitchell, or to recognize the mineworkers' union.

Mitchell continued to organize. In March 1902, he drew up the miners' demands. These included recognition of the UMWA, a minimum wage scale, an eight-hour day, a twenty percent wage increase, and use of the legal ton for the weighing of coal. The operators held their line. They refused to meet with Mitchell. On May 12, 1902, one hundred and forty-seven thousand anthracite miners, men and boys together, walked off.

Of the slate-pickers he had met throughout his travels in mining country, Mitchell said: "'They have the bodies and faces of boys but they came to meetings where I spoke and stood as still as the men and listened for every word. I was shocked and amazed ... as I saw those eager eyes peering at me from eager little faces; the fight had a new meaning for me; I felt that I was fighting for the boys, fighting a battle for innocent childhood.'"[8]

Throughout the summer of 1902, the strike wore on. Despite Mitchell's earnest and repeated calls for calm, sporadic violence erupted, some of it extreme. Some miners broke the strike and returned to work, eliciting taunts of "scab," or worse, against them and their families. On July 30, a mob at Shenandoah attacked the brother of a deputy sheriff and beat him to death. The beaten man had been protecting non-union workers.

After the fatality, Governor William Stone sent in the National Guard. By mid-October, the number of troops in the region approached nine thousand. Mine operators brought in gangs of newly recruited Coal and Iron police. Their actions in some instances accelerated the violence, and included the accidental shooting, and killing, of a thirteen-year-old boy.

On June 7, 1902, came widespread new reports of the hanging and burning in effigy of J. P. Morgan at Wilkes-Barre. In mid-July William Clark, a Wilkes-Barre photographer, wrote to Baer, now the head of the region's coal cartel, and asked him to settle the strike for the good of the region. On July 17, Baer responded.

"I beg of you not to be discouraged," Baer told Clark. "The rights and interests of the laboring man will be protected and cared for – not by the labor agitators, but by the Christian men to whom God in His infinite wisdom has given the control of the property interests of the country, and upon the successful Management of which so much depends."[9]

Baer had cribbed his "divine right" letter from one written by King George III in reference to the American colonies. Within seven months, Clarence Darrow would dub the railroad president "King George the last."[10]

"Mr. Baer has been denounced for his sacrilegious statement everywhere," a Kansas paper said after Baer's letter became known.[11] From Boston came this assessment: "'The doctrine of the divine right of kings was bad enough, but not so intolerable as the divine right of plutocrats.'"[12] Throughout the country, public sympathy favored the striking mineworkers. Contributions poured into union headquarters in recognition of the mineworkers' plight.

As the strike wore on through the fall, consumers turned from anthracite to bituminous coal. In New York, soot from soft coal usage clogged city dwellers' lungs and obscured the skyline. A miasma shrouded even the Brooklyn Bridge. Schools closed for lack of fuel. Some city residents chopped up telegraph poles to use for firewood.

Winter approached. Many, including President Theodore Roosevelt, feared civil unrest if the strike continued. The poor of the eastern cities heated their homes with anthracite coal burned in kitchen stoves. Without an assured supply, whole families could freeze to death.

On October 1, 1902, Roosevelt acted. He invited the coal operators and the union representatives to Washington to discuss "'the failure of the coal supply, which has become a matter of vital concern to the whole nation.'"[13]

Two days later, five railroad presidents led by Baer and four UMWA representatives led by Mitchell converged on the temporary White House at Lafayette Square. The railroad presidents had spent the previous night in the luxury of private train cars. Carriages staffed with footmen in plum-colored livery conveyed them to the historic meeting. The union men had spent the night in the smoking car of a night train. For their meeting with the president, they took a streetcar from their hotel.

Roosevelt, confined to a wheelchair after an accident, urged all assembled to consider the needs of the public. Mitchell expressed the union's willingness to arbitrate with any commission the president would appoint. The coal men balked. "'We cannot agree to it,'" Baer said. "'We cannot agree to any proposition advanced by Mr. Mitchell.'"[14] Refusing all negotiation, the railroad and coal magnates claimed widespread regional violence and pressed Roosevelt to send in federal troops.

Roosevelt, recognizing the stalemate, adjourned the meeting. He advised all to return at three o'clock with written statements on their respective positions.

At three, the group reconvened. The coal men read from a number of typewritten statements. These accused the strikers as criminals and as "'fomenters of ... anarchy.'" The coal operators, in Roosevelt's words, "'did everything in their power to goad and irritate Mitchell,'" using language that was "'insulting to the miners and offensive to me.'" On hearing Baer refer to the union men as outlaws, Roosevelt repressed the urge to take him "'by the seat of the breeches and nape of the neck and chuck him out of that window.'" Mitchell, in Roosevelt's estimation, "'towered above'" the meeting's other participants.[15]

Roosevelt's stenographer recorded proceedings. The next day, the reports hit the press. "COAL OPERATORS REFUSE TO DEAL WITH MITCHELL OR RECOGNIZE THE UNION," an Alabama paper said.[16] "*FIRM STAND OF OPERATORS AGAINST MITCHELL*," a Connecticut paper related. "Baer Plainly Criticizes Roosevelt for Inviting Such a Man to Meet Him—Operators Unanimous in Calling on the President for Federal Troops."[17]

"STRIKE WILL CONTINUE," a headline from Iowa read. "Coal Operators Insolently Refuse to Arbitrate and Demand Troops."[18] "FAILS TO END STRIKE," came from Nebraska. "Conference at White House Comes to Naught After Much Talk. OPERATORS REMAIN OBDURATE AS EVER. ... MITCHELL'S CONCESSIONS SCOFFED AT."[19]

Winter was coming. A Delaware paper asked: "WILL ROOSEVELT TAKE STEPS TO OPEN MINES? Whole Country Waits With Bated Breath for Next Move of President."[20]

A week later Elihu Root, Roosevelt's secretary of war, traveled to New York. Dodging reporters, Root denied that he had gone to the city as Roosevelt's envoy. He told the press his business in New York was personal—he had come to register to vote in the upcoming election.

Reporters followed Root's movements. From his home on Sixty-ninth Street, the secretary of war went to the voters' registration station. Reporters verified that his name appeared third on the books. Root breakfasted alone at the Union League club. He went from there to the foot of West Thirty-fifth Street, along the Hudson River. There, J. P. Morgan's yacht the *Corsair*, christened under the word meaning "pirate," lay at anchor. Morgan's sailors recognized Root immediately, and escorted Roosevelt's secretary of state on board the yacht.

Root and Morgan's meeting aboard the *Corsair* lasted five hours. Together, they drafted an arbitration proposal along the lines of Mitchell's suggestions. Morgan carried the proposal to the Union Club, where a group of mine owners waited. From the club, Morgan contacted Baer by phone. Spared the taint of dealing with the union leaders directly, the coal men agreed to Morgan's proposal.

"TO ARBITRATE," the *New York Sun* announced three days later. "Coal Operators Propose Commission."[21] At the time of Baer's death, an Omaha newspaper gave this point of view of proceedings: "The late George F. Baer, the noted anthracite coal baron, was one of the few modern monopolists who defied the politicians and scoffed at Teddy Roosevelt's big stick. When Roosevelt found that his stick fell short, he induced J. Pierp [sic] Morgan to tell Baer where he headed in and Baer took the hint. Where vinegar fails, sugar wins."[22]

On October 23, from Bloomsburg, Pennsylvania, the *Columbian* announced: "COAL STRIKE ENDED. Miners Ordered to Return to Work." The strike had lasted one hundred and sixty-three days.

With Roosevelt's actions, the federal government had turned from its previous role of strikebreaker to that of arbitrator. At Wilkes-Barre, Mitchell told union delegates: "when the arbitration proposition was accepted labor all over the land breathed a sigh of relief. That this strike has given labor new dignity no one can deny. Labor occupies a position now that it never occupied before."[23]

The proceedings of the Anthracite Mine Strike Commission recommended by President Roosevelt took place in Scranton and Philadelphia from November 14, 1902, to February 14, 1903. The commission, an eclectic seven-man board, included representatives from business, the military, and the clergy, as well from trades unions. Carroll Wright, federal commissioner of labor, served as recorder. Federal judge George Gray served as chairman. All parties to the dispute—coal operators, including presidents of coal roads and independent mine owners; non-union mineworkers and union mineworkers—agreed to abide by the board's decision.

Roosevelt instructed the commission "to inquire into, consider, and pass upon the questions in controversy in connection with the strike in the anthracite region, and the causes out of which the controversy arose." The president advised: "By the action you recommend ... you will endeavor to establish the relations between the employers and the wage workers in the anthracite fields on a just and permanent basis, and, as far as possible, to do away with any causes for the recurrence of such difficulties as those which you have been called in to settle."[24]

More than five hundred and fifty witnesses testified in commission hearings. Records of proceedings include fifty-six volumes of testimony. As Franklin Gowen had corralled previous legislative proceedings, George Baer served as lead counsel for the railroad and coal concerns. Clarence Darrow represented the United Mine Workers of America (UMWA). Darrow told the commission: "This contest is one of the important contests that has marked the progress of human liberty since the world began—one force pointing one way, another force the other."[25] Darrow and Baer, embracing wildly divergent ideologies, represented the opposing forces.

Progressive journalist Henry Demarest Lloyd, called as an expert witness, characterized the Great Strike of 1902 as "the Waterloo of capitalistic absolutism in this country."[26] Of the commission's efforts, brought about in part by public pressure, Demarest said: "We acknowledge the superb sense of justice in the American people which gave us this arbitration."[27] He added: "we are grateful that we live in an age where justice is not denied to those strong enough to get it."[28]

Charles Brumm of Schuylkill County also spoke on behalf of the mineworkers. Brumm told the commission: "Ever since the coal companies destroyed the Workmen's Beneficial association [sic], twenty-five years ago, they have been denying their workmen the right to be represented by men of their own choosing." Brumm added: "They say peace reigned for twenty-five years in the coal region, prior to the coming of the union. Yes, peace reigned as it does with slaves under the lash of the master. ... Thank God, Mitchell came out of the West."[29]

UMWA president John Mitchell opened proceedings with a harrowing account of the dangers attending the lives of underground workers. Committee members, who within the previous weeks had visited both the mineworkers' homes and the anthracite coal mines, listened in silence. Mitchell told the commission: "Our little boys should not be forced into the mines and breakers so early in life; our little girls should not be compelled to work in the mills and factories at an age when they should be in school. These children are future citizens of our nation; their parents should be enabled to give them at least a common school education, so as to equip them to bear the grave responsibilities which will ultimately devolve upon them."[30]

Darrow questioned Rev. J. V. Hussie, rector of St. Gabriel's Roman Catholic Church in Hazleton. Hussie described conditions in the Hazleton region as "truly deplorable," with the miners' homes not really homes, but "habitations." He described the miners as "frugal, conservative men, reasonable in their demands." They were also devout. In sickness, Hussie said, "the miner is scarcely able to pay for attendance and medicine and a death means a long-standing debt."[31]

Because the mineworkers received such poor wages, their children left home for work as soon as they were able. The girls left for the silk mills and similar industries. The boys, Hussie testified, "go into the breaker as soon as they are able to toddle out of the house."

Hussie concluded "that lack of intelligence and want of charity on the part of the mine bosses ... are responsible mainly for the ills of which the miners complain."[32]

Conditions in the breaker rooms had changed little since the 1870s. In May 1877, the *Mauch Chunk Coal Gazette* had published mining accidents for the month of April. The paper's notice appeared just under an announcement of death warrants signed in the "Molly" cases. At Cross Creek Colliery, in Drifton, twelve-year-old Daniel Gallagher had been crushed to death by a breaker roller. "During an interval of a few minutes," the account said, "caused by a car being off the track at the foot of the plane, the boys got playing, and the deceased wended his way up to the platform, and in crossing the chute his foot slipped, and he was precipitated into the rollers, and was not observed till he was half-way through the screw."[33]

Twenty-five years later, Darrow questioned Andrew Chippie, a twelve-year-old slate picker in the Jeddo colliery of Markle & Co. Four years before, Andrew's father had died in a mine accident. His mother kept boarders, but needed her son's salary to feed the family.

Andrew made forty cents a day for ten hours' work in the slate picking rooms. He began working six weeks before the Great Strike began. Because of debts owed by his father for rent at company housing and supplies from the company store, Andrew's first pay check left him owing Markle & Co. more than sixty dollars.

The boy told the commission that he worked, often in the cold, in a bent position all day, separating coal from slate. When his pace slackened, the breaker boss pulled on his ears. Mike Baker, an eighteen-year-old breaker boy, testified to being clubbed frequently by the boss.

Sixty-year-old miner James Gallagher, also of Markle & Co., also forced to trade at the company store, remained always in debt. When the debt got too large, the company moved him to "a good chamber" in the mine.[34] When nearly out of debt, Gallagher was returned to a chamber where yields were meager. His pay averaged less than a dollar and a quarter a day. Because his son was the secretary of a UMWA local, when the strike ended Markle & Co. refused

Gallagher re-employment and evicted him from company housing. The company did the same to twelve other men involved in union relief activities.

When the miners' attorneys called eight-year-old Stanley Gustick to the stand, Judge Gray intervened. "'The commissioners see how small he is,'" Gray said, "'and will agree that he is too small to be working in the breaker.'"[35] Allen Row, aged fifteen, testified: "he had his leg wrenched off by the machinery at one of the Pennsylvania company's breakers and never received anything from the company."[36]

Briefly, levity broke through the proceedings with the testimony of ten-year-old Paul Hemhand. "'Do you understand what an oath is?'" Gray asked the boy kindly. "'Yes, sir,'" the boy said. "'What happens to boys who don't tell the truth?'" Gray asked. "'Go to hell,'" the boy replied.[37] But no one laughed when the slate picker showed the commission his hands, his fingernails worn below the quick from sorting coal from slate.

Henry Coll told of his experience with G. B. Markle & Co. "BRUTAL TREATMENT BY COAL COMPANY," an Illinois paper said. "Miner Tells of Corporation's Inhumanity in Time of Suffering and Misery."[38] Coal company president John Markle had attended the White House meeting with President Roosevelt. Markle had joined Baer in demanding federal troops. During Coll's testimony, neither Markle nor any of his company's attorneys appeared in court. Coll's testimony went into the record unchallenged.

The testimony of Coll, one of thirteen union committee men evicted from Markle & Co. housing after the strike ended, visibly moved commission members. The *Scranton Tribune*, which reported proceedings, said of Coll: "One of his eyes is gone, his left leg is stiffened, his right arm crooked, and a number of his ribs bent and twisted from fractures." Darrow asked Coll if he had been hurt in the mines. "'There isn't a whole bone in my body except my neck,'" the miner replied.[39]

When Coll suffered a fractured skull, he spent two years in the hospital. A company official, supposedly safeguarding the relief fund donated to Coll by his fellow mineworkers, seized the fund and applied it to the back rent and coal bill that Coll's family had accrued during his hospital stay.

Toward the strike's end, Markle & Co. had advised Coll to quit the company house. Though Coll owed back rent for the strike period, the company had made no demand for payment. Six days after Coll received the notice to quit, a sheriff came with deputies and ordered the family, including Coll's ill wife and her blind mother, aged one hundred, out of the house.

Coll asked for one day to find alternative housing. The sheriff agreed to take the request to Markle. Soon after, the sheriff returned to the house and told Coll: "'You will have to get out in five minutes or we will be forced to put you out.'"[40] Coll's only offense against Markle & Co., he told Darrow, was his service on the union's relief committee.

Two deputies carried Coll's aged mother-in-law to another house. Coll's wife, ill with bronchitis, dressed and went into the street. She spent a few hours there in a cold rain, packing household goods into boxes and barrels.

Late in the day Coll secured a new house at Hazleton, about seven miles away. The next day, Mrs. Coll had such severe congestion, she could not talk. Coll took her to the doctor, who treated her. When he heard the couple's story, the doctor refused payment. Despite his ministrations, Coll's wife had died in the middle of the night, choking to death in her husband's arms. "'And you buried her yesterday?'" Darrow asked Coll. "'Yesterday,'" Coll replied, sobbing.[41]

Judge Gray, the *Scranton Tribune* said, "looked compassionately at the weeping man on the stand."[42] Roman Catholic bishop John Spalding of Peoria, Illinois, a member of the commission, wheeled his chair around and trained his gaze on the rear wall of the courtroom. Other commission members lowered their gazes.

When Coll recovered himself, Darrow asked after his mother-in-law's health. The shock of her daughter's death, Coll related, had devastated the aged woman to such an extent that the priest had administered the last sacraments. "'That's all, Mr. Coll,'" Darrow concluded. "'That's enough,'" Gray said.[43]

The plight of the silk mill workers also stirred the commission. The *Scranton Tribune*, operating just a few miles from the Dunmore mill, told of the "SAD LOT OF LITTLE SILK MILL GIRLS."[44] From Birmingham, Alabama, a headline reported "Little Girls Tell Heartrending Stories of Overwork."[45] "LITTLE GIRLS WHO WORK NIGHTS," a headline from Minneapolis said.[46] The entire country was ruminating on Pennsylvania's feudal employment practices.

Darrow called four girls to the stand. All were daughters of mineworkers. Eleven-year-old Theresa McDermott testified to working at the Dunmore silk mill, on her feet at all times, from seven in the morning until six in the evening, for two dollars a week. Anna Denko, aged fourteen, worked from six thirty in the evening till six thirty in the morning, with a half-hour break for lunch. She walked to work in all weathers, a journey of an hour each way, and received five-and-a-half cents an hour. Rosie Huser, aged eleven, who also worked nights, earned the same. Helen Sisach, aged eleven, testified through an interpreter. She had been working nights at Dunmore for more than a year. She received three cents an hour.

Efforts by counsel before the Anthracite Mine Strike Commission to paint union men as terrorists reached back even to the "Molly Maguire" conflict. On February 11, 1903, Ira Burns spoke on behalf of the independent coal operators. Burns resurrected the address that Franklin Gowen had made to a jury in July 1877 in the trial of alleged "Molly" Thomas Munley.

"Many years ago," Burns said, "our commonwealth grappled with a hydra-headed monster of crime in the anthracite regions, and finally wiped the assassins off the face of the earth. But then there was a man of fertile brain and nerve behind the machinery of the law. Unfortunately, Franklin B. Gowen is dead, and has left no successor."[47]

Burns quoted directly from Gowen's address in Munley, with the coalfields as "'the theater of the commission of crimes such as our very nature revolts at,'" conducted by an organization that had "'hung like a pall'" over the country. "'Behind it,'" Burns quoted, "'stalked darkness and despair, brooding like grim shadows over the desolated hearth and the ruined home,'" with "'hundreds of unknown victims whose bones now lie mouldering over the face of this county.'"[48]

The next day, George Baer gave his closing on behalf of the railroad presidents. "BAER SAYS UNITED MINE WORKERS FORM A MONSTER MONOPOLY, THREATENING INDUSTRY," a paper from Butte, Montana, reported. "President of the Reading Company Denounces Labor Leaders, Who, He Says, Looked on While Their Men Committed Violence."[49]

In recalling the struggles of his predecessors at the Reading, men who included Gowen, Baer compared their labors to "those of Sisyphus."[50] The foreigners in his employ, Baer told the commission, "have come to this country with confused ideas of what free government means."[51] In keeping with his theory of divine rights, Baer speculated on why the Lord "should have stored the fuel deep down in the bosom of the earth and compelled men to bore through solid adamant to reach the hidden treasure, and dig it in darkness and danger."[52] In keeping with his elitist and nativist views, Baer speculated on why the Lord "should have made men of different races, different strength and different capacity."[53]

Baer mused on the teachings of Roman philosopher Seneca. He told the commission: "The perplexing question why one man should be strong, happy and prosperous, and another weak, afflicted and distressed may be answered by Seneca's suggestion that the purpose was to teach the power of human endurance and the nobility of a life of struggle."[54] In closing, Baer suggested that "socialistic experimenters" could be sent to the Philippines, where they could implement "a social scheme of their own." It would, he said to laughter, "be such a grand missionary enterprise and would relieve this country of a congested population that would certainly be a relief to us."[55]

Clarence Darrow, speaking for the union men, followed Baer in his address to the commission. In opening, Darrow deplored the excesses of the strike in which "men on both sides were turned into wild beasts and forgot that common sympathy and common humanity which, after all, is common to all men."[56] But if civilization, Darrow believed, rested upon "the labor of these poor little boys, who from 12 to 14 years of age, are picking their way through the dirt, clouds and dust of the anthracite coal, then the sooner we are done with this civilization and start over anew, the better."[57]

Of Baer's statement that in his denial of the union, he had the breaker boys' interests at heart, because union membership radicalized the boys, Darrow said: "I have no doubt the railroad president loves children. Neither have I any doubt that the wolf loves mutton."[58] Of the conflict in general, Darrow said: "Gentlemen, this was an industrial war. ... you on your side were fighting 147,000 men, with their wives and their children, and the weapons you used were hunger and want. You thought to bring them to terms by the most cruel, deadly weapon that any oppressor has ever used to bring men to his terms—hunger and want."[59] He said of the railroad and coal men: "this strike, from first to last, was due to the blind, autocratic, stupid spirit of these operators, that their men should not organize—nothing else."[60]

Darrow continued: "These gentlemen precipitated this greatest conflict between capital and labor which the world has ever seen, this most gigantic strike in history, because, in their minds, it was a question of mastery—nothing else; because they felt and they believed that upon this contest depended the question of whether they should be the masters or whether the men should be the masters."[61] The railroad and coal men, with their "feudal ideas," believed they had been "placed in the ownership and the possession of industry" absolutely.[62]

"I believe," Darrow said, "the operators were induced and urged by the railroad companies to believe that here in the coal region was the final struggle to determine who were the masters in this country, whether the men were chattels, or whether they were men, endowed with the same right to look the other contracting party squarely in the face."[63] The strike, Darrow said, "came on because these men refused to recognize their workmen as human beings."[64] All the evils that flowed from the six-month conflict "grew from the blind determination of these men that there should be no organization of labor."[65]

Darrow defended the miners' reputations, those men "who toil while other men grow rich, men who go down into the earth and face greater dangers than men who go out upon the sea, or out upon the land in battle, men who have little to hope for, little to think of excepting work." He protested the coal operators' smearing of his clients "as assassins, as brutes, as criminals, as outlaws, as unworthy of the respect of men and fit only for the condemnation of courts."[66]

Darrow reminded the commission of "the cripples, of the orphans, of the widows, of the maimed, who are dragging their lives out on account of this business, who, if they were mules or horses would be cared for, but who are left and neglected."[67] He reminded the commission of the previous year's wage for laborers, a sum averaging three hundred and thirty-three dollars. These laborers, Darrow said, possessed the same instincts of love and hope, and charity and kindness, that distinguished all who lived.

Darrow spoke of UMWA leader Mitchell, "that cool, calm, considerate, humane leader who, from the beginning to the end, has come out of every contest victorious, has faced every situation and won—not because he is wiser ... greater ... better than the rest, but because his face is turned toward the morning and the future, and he is moving with the progress of the world."[68] Darrow spoke, too, of Baer's skilled workmen, "that class who do not mine coal, but who mine men ... who get their profits, not from digging so many tons of coal, but from exploiting so many hours of labor of some one more unfortunate than themselves."[69]

What could impel the labor of a twelve-year-old boy working in a cloud of coal dust for ten hours a day, Darrow asked of the coal men. "That you may get gold. That is all." Darrow continued: "Where are your sons and your daughters? ... until you, Mr. Railroad President, or you, Mr. Lawyer, will take your child by the hand and lead him up the breaker stairs and sit him down to pick at that trough of moving coal, until you will take your pale girl to the silk mills, let me speak for the children of the poor."[70]

Coal region industries, Darrow inferred, had colluded in their exploitation of children. He asked why owners had located their silk mills in Scranton and the surrounding region. He answered: "They went there because the miners were there. They went there just as naturally as a wild beast goes to find its prey. They went there as the hunter goes where he can find game. Every mill in that region is a testimony to the fact that the wages that you pay are so low that you sell your boys to be slaves of the breaker and your girls to be slaves in the mills."[71]

Darrow said: "The evidence in this case shows that every single one of these industries is run by the labor of these children."[72] He traced the miners' woes to the coal operators' "old stubbornness, their old willfulness." They would rather, he said, "see their property destroyed than to concede that the men in their employ were human beings, with a human mind, with a human soul."[73]

Of the evictions conducted by Markle & Co., Darrow said: "They took out their stoves and their chair and their beds and their sour kraut and they left them in the street. And they got through with this glorious job at 6 o'clock at night of a November day, when the rain was coming down and it was dark ... And then the superintendent turned his back upon them and drove away and went home and got his supper and reported to John Markle!" Darrow added, to applause: "the fiendish cruelty of John Markle ... turned these helpless people into the street simply to satisfy his hellish hate."[74]

Of the army of accountants Baer had paraded before the commission, Darrow said that the coal operators had been deceived by their "doctors of figures," by "doctors who have doctored up figures."[75] He derided the testimony "of so-called expert accountants, who have manipulated and twisted and used figures for the sake of defrauding 147,000 men, that a few might grow still richer and still greater by the iniquities practiced upon the many."[76]

"Every request, every demand, every prayer of these men had been contemptuously refused," Darrow said of the union men.[77] Of the operators: "no doubt, they want to do the right." Instead, "they have been misled ... they are blindly placing their faces against progress ... they are standing in the way of the natural, peaceful, laudable evolution of the human race."[78]

Trade unionism, Darrow told the commission, was "not all good." It was in an evolutionary stage. But "where else in the history of the world has any general, either in industrial life or on the field of battle, in two short years moulded together such a heterogeneous mass into such ... grand and valiant and brave and noble veterans as these who faced starvation for their fellow-men?"[79]

In contrast, the coal operatives had turned the region into "a howling wilderness."[80] Darrow said of them: "The blunders are theirs, and the victories have been ours. The blunders are theirs because, in this old, old strife they are fighting for slavery, while we are fighting for freedom. They are fighting for the rule of man over man, for despotism, for darkness, for the past. We are striving to build up man. We are working for democracy, for humanity, for the future, for the day that will come ... and which will remember our struggles, our triumphs, our defeats, and the words which we speak."[81]

Darrow concluded: "I did not come into the state of Pennsylvania to stir up dissension and hatred and bitterness." He hoped that his efforts had "done something to bring peace and harmony and quiet and prosperity to this valley which should be blessed, but which has been cursed."[82] Darrow's address met with sustained applause.

News of Baer, conspicuously absent during Darrow's summation, came a few days after the commission closed its proceedings. After finishing his own statement before the commission, Baer had left the courtroom at noon and decamped for Atlantic City, where he stayed for three days. Decades before, Franklin Gowen had used the seaside resort to entertain clients, including state legislators, with lavish hotel stays that included visits to brothels. A news report said that Baer had gone to Atlantic City "in a state of physical collapse." Baer's three days' rest had enabled him "to throw off the ill effects of both grippe and nervous strain." He had returned home "much improved."[83]

Bishop John Spalding, one member of the seven-man commission, traveled to New York after its proceedings closed. The day after Baer and Darrow finished their summations, Spalding spoke at Carnegie Hall. He titled his address, in aid of the St. Vincent de Paul Society, "'How to Make the Most of Life.'" Spaulding's address included these musings: "'The course of human history has not been directed by justice, it has not been directed by reason.'" The bishop told listeners: "'Men work for money, thinking it is the most serviceable thing in life. ... It is a mighty means of power—it is almost the real form of power in our day.'"[84]

Spalding believed differently: "'I have come to the conclusion that great wealth degrades, that only the noblest of men can possess wealth and remain undegraded.'" The bishop added: "'Life does not consist in having an abundance of the material things in life. ... It is not what you have, it is what you are. What a man thinketh in his heart, so is he.'" He concluded: "'Character is the very essence of human life. Character is based on eternal principles; mind is based on eternal truth. Build up your character; become true, sincere, loving, patient, honest. Nothing else can give such deep satisfaction as the consciousness of striving earnestly, day by day, to conform life to the principles of Jesus Christ.'"[85]

On March 18, 1903, the Anthracite Mine Strike Commission completed its report. A few days later, news of its decision reached the public. "COAL MINERS WIN AND LOSE," the *New York Tribune* said.[86] The commission had granted the mineworkers a retroactive ten percent wage increase and a nine-hour workday. It had approved the use of local arbitration boards for settlement of disputes. The report condemned both the lawlessness in the region and the use of Coal and Iron police. But, like the coal operators, the commission refused to recognize the union.

Mitchell, en route to an ongoing strike in Huntington, West Virginia, called the commission's decision "a decided victory for the miners." Of the commission's refusal to recognize the union, Mitchell said: "the decision of the commission and its awards were in themselves recognition of the power and influence of the United Mine Workers."[87]

From Chicago, Darrow expressed gratification at the commission's decision. "'For the miners it was a practical recognition of the union,'" Darrow said. "'They won a victory unparalleled in the history of strike settlements.'"[88] From AFL headquarters in Washington, Samuel Gompers judged the decision "a complete victory for the men who earn their daily bread by toiling hundreds of feet below the surface of the earth."[89]

A regard for learning as a vehicle for moving forward in life pervaded the benevolent and labor organizations of the "Molly Maguire" saga and its aftermath. This respect for scholarship flowed through the five Irish Catholic school directors charged as alleged "Mollies," through the libraries of the Western Federation of Miners, through the aims of the United Mine Workers of America, and through the ideology of the American Federation of Labor.

AFL president Samuel Gompers told the Anthracite Mine Strike Commission in 1902: "'Just now the miners' union should take in and educate the unlettered thousands from southern Europe whom the coal companies have brought over here to work in their mines.'"[90]

During the same hearings, the coal operators ridiculed the notion of workingmen, especially non-English-speakers, striving for literacy. In goading Mitchell over the proposed eight-hour workday, corporate attorney Wayne MacVeagh had said of Abraham Lincoln: "Mr. Lincoln had a right to work in the coal mines of Illinois, if he had had the chance, fourteen hours a day, if he wished to do so, to buy another spelling book and another reader in order to enfranchise the laboring men of the world." MacVeagh asked Mitchell: "there are Abraham Lincolns in your coal mines today?" Mitchell responded: "If Abraham Lincoln was digging coal now, he would be a stronger advocate of the eight-hour day than I am."[91] A burst of laughter from courtroom spectators met this ridicule of the mineworkers by Philadelphia and Reading Railroad president George Baer: "the eight-hour system, it is proposed, shall bring about

—that leisure to enable them to learn to read good novels and sound religious books."[92]

William Haywood, secretary-treasurer of the WFM, described just such an enlightened environment among workingmen. The decade before Baer gave his cynical assessment, Haywood at age fifteen had joined his stepfather at the Ohio Mine and Milling Company in Humboldt County, Nevada. Haywood said of his camp experience: "we were all great readers." He added: "I did not have many books of my own, but the miners all had some. One had a volume of Darwin; others had Voltaire, Shakespeare, Byron, Burns and Milton. These poets were great favorites of my stepfather. We all exchanged books, and quite a valuable library could have been collected among these few men."[93]

In 1875, from the heart of the anthracite coal region, John Kehoe had described the aims of the Ancient Order of Hibernians: "a chartered organization, recognized by the commonwealth, and composed of men who are law-abiding and seek the elevation of their members."[94] Bernard Dolan, Kehoe's predecessor as AOH county delegate, had described the electoral aims of AOH men: to vote into office "men who will devote their time to secure the welfare of the Commonwealth, and assuage the sufferings of the poor laboring class, who they consider their brothers in toil."[95]

A belief in non-violence, and especially in arbitration for industrial disputes, also united WBA leadership and the alleged "Mollies" from the 1870s with UMWA leadership from the early 1900s. "'Our position is too well known to repeat,'" UMWA president John Mitchell told a reporter in August 1902. "'We favor arbitration.'"[96] In April 1871, the *New York Herald* had reported the proceedings of WBA proceedings at Mauch Chunk. "Important Session of the General Council of the Miners' Union," the *Herald* said. "The Wages Question to be Settled by Arbitration."[97] Alleged "Molly Maguire" Michael Lawler had served as one of four WBA signatories to the eventual arbitration agreement secured through that council.

Strands of nonviolent advocacy also bound WBA and AOH leadership from 1875 with Mitchell's UMWA leadership from 1902. In an address to union men at Wilkes-Barre in October 1902, Mitchell said on behalf of union leadership: "'We ... advise that acts of lawlessness by the coal and iron police and by strikers be denounced, and the services of members of the union tendered to local authorities to preserve law and order.'"[98] In April 1875, WBA divisional president John Welsh had advised fellow unionists during the Long Strike: "'I want to appeal to you ... not to transgress the law. Your enemies are praying that you may do so; almost their every act since the commencement of the suspension has been deliberately designed to incite you to outbreak. Mr. Gowen and those who support him are only too well assured that the public will not sympathize with them if you are peaceful.'"[99] In October 1875, AOH county delegate Kehoe had said of a local Girardville resident who advocated vigilantism: "'it would be more charitable for him or any other correspondent to encourage brotherly love instead of sowing seeds of antagonism which sooner or later may lead to bloodshed.'"[100]

The hope for a decent life that flowed through these progressive movements was rooted in patriotism and the belief that the United States, conceived in democracy, could provide such lives for its workers. In 1902, Mitchell told the strike commission: "as to the matter of lawlessness ... before being president of a union, before being a member of a union, I am an American, over and above everything else. I believe that every man should first be an American."[101]

"You sons of liberty awake," Jack O'Brien had written twenty-eight years before from Tamaqua, in the midst of Pennsylvania's Long Strike. "Your hearths and altars are at stake; / Arise, arise for freedom's sake, / And strike against monopoly."[102]

"Your American eagle is [not] dead," O'Brien's second stanza advised. "Again his giant wings are spread / To sweep upon the tyrant's head, / And down with usurping monopoly."[103]

The year after Baer's appearance at the Anthracite Mine Strike Commission on behalf of railroad and coal interests, he attended a dinner at Philadelphia's newly opened Bellevue Stratford hotel. "MILLIONAIRE FARMERS HAVE A RUSTIC BANQUET," a headline from Birmingham, Alabama read.[104]

The nineteen other millionaires who attended Philadelphia's "annual country dinner" included numerous financial leaders, along with railroad executives.[105] Joseph Wharton, co-founder of Bethlehem Steel and founder of the Wharton School at the University of Pennsylvania, joined the diners who made their way to the banquet room through a faux cornfield where live roosters strutted. A faux farm stall, decorated with fantastically carved and lighted vegetables, housed a large stuffed bull. A rail fence penned in a pig and a calf, both presumably live, along with three stuffed rams.

The menu included terrapin, mushrooms, and canvasback duck. Diners pressed their own cider from a press set up for the occasion. Waiters offered consommé cups brought in on toy hay wagons, and conveyed to guests via red toy wheelbarrows. Yet more exotically carved vegetables, some topped with moss wigs, decorated the banquet table.

"For the oysters," the news account said, "the banqueters were supplied with miniature pitchforks, while they dissected their salad with toy rakes. Terrapin was conveyed to their mouths with small hoes."[106]

Ten years later, while walking to his office on a Saturday morning, Baer, aged seventy-one, collapsed on a street in Reading, Pennsylvania. A passerby helped the railroad president to a nearby tailoring shop, where an auto was summoned to convey him home. Baer died at home the next day. His wife, his five daughters and his sons-in-law, his four physicians, and his coachman attended him at his bedside.

Baer left an estate estimated at between five and ten million dollars. His claim to "divine right" lingered even in reports of his death.

Two decades later, in 1935, W. E. B. Du Bois said of the ideology that distorted the recording of Reconstruction-era history: "It ... has ... led the world to embrace and worship the color bar as social salvation and it is helping to range mankind in ranks of mutual hatred and contempt, at the summons of a cheap and false myth."[107] Of this dangerously skewed system, Du Bois said: "I cannot for a moment subscribe to that bizarre doctrine of race that makes most men inferior to the few."[108]

---

1. Clarence Darrow to Ruby Darrow, 28 January 1903, University of Minnesota Law Library, Clarence Darrow Digital Collection, The Anthracite Coal Strike, The Letters,
   http://moses.law.umn.edu/darrow/letters.php?pid=641&skey=1903.
2. Ibid.
3. *New York Tribune*, April 1, 1913.
4. *New York Sun*, September 18, 1886.
5. *Evening Herald* (Albuquerque, NM), September 15, 1919.
6. *Harrisburg Telegraph*, September 15, 1919; reprinting *New York Times*.
7. *Chickasha Daily Express* (Indian Territory, OK), September 17, 1919.
8. Robert L. Reynolds, "The Coal Kings Come to Judgment," *American Heritage* 11 (1960), https://www.americanheritage.com/content/coal-kings-come-judgment.
9. Geo. F. Baer to Mr. Clark, 17 July 1902, UMN Law, Darrow Digital, Anthracite Coal Strike, Miscellaneous, George Baer's "Divine Right" Letter, http://moses.law.umn.edu/darrow/documents/Baer_letter_cropped.pdf. Baer later claimed that this letter was forged.
10. UMN Law, Darrow Digital, Proceedings of The Anthracite Coal Strike Commission, reprinted from the *Scranton Tribune* 1902-03, http://moses.law.umn.edu/darrow/documents/
    Proceedings_Anthracite_Strike_Cropped_OPT_Fina_OCR.pdf, 252 (pdf 253 of 297).
11. *Topeka (KS) State Journal*, September 17, 1902.
12. Quoted in Doris Kearns Goodwin, *The Bully Pulpit: Theodore Roosevelt, William Howard Taft, and the Golden Age of Journalism* (New York: Simon and Schuster, 2013), 313.
13. Ibid., 314.
14. Ibid., 315.
15. Ibid., 315.
16. *Birmingham (AL) Age-Herald*, October 4, 1902.
17. *Daily Morning Journal and Courier* (New Haven, CT), October 4, 1902.
18. *Evening Times-Republican* (Marshalltown, IA), October 4, 1902.
19. *Omaha Daily Bee*, October 4, 1902.
20. *Evening Journal* (Wilmington, DE), October 4, 1902.
21. *New York Sun*, October 14, 1902.
22. *Omaha Daily Bee*, May 3, 1914.
23. *Columbian* (Bloomsburg, PA), October 23, 1902.
24. UMN Law, Darrow Digital, Proceedings of Anthracite Strike Commission, 271 (pdf 272 of 297).
25. Ibid., 269 (pdf 270 of 297).
26. Ibid., 208 (pdf 209 of 297).

27. Ibid.
28. Ibid., 209 (pdf 210 of 297).
29. Ibid..
30. Ibid., 5.
31. Ibid., 66 (pdf 67 of 297).
32. Ibid.
33. *Mauch Chunk (PA) Coal Gazette*, May 4, 1877.
34. UMN Law, Darrow Digital, Proceedings of Anthracite Strike Commission, 72 (pdf 73 of 297).
35. Ibid., 87 (pdf 88 of 297).
36. Ibid., 89 (pdf 90 of 297).
37. Ibid., 88 (pdf 89 of 297).
38. *Rock Island (IL) Argus*, December 9, 1902.
39. UMN Law, Darrow Digital, Proceedings of Anthracite Strike Commission, 77 (pdf 78 of 297).
40. Ibid.
41. Ibid., 78 (pdf 79 of 297).
42. Ibid.
43. Ibid.
44. *Scranton (PA) Tribune*, December 16, 1902.
45. *Birmingham (AL) Age-Herald*, December 16, 1902.
46. *Minneapolis Journal*, December 16, 1902.
47. UMN Law, Darrow Digital, Proceedings of Anthracite Strike Commission, 225 (pdf 226 of 297).
48. Ibid.
49. *Butte (MT) Inter Mountain*, February 12, 1903.
50. UMN Law, Darrow Digital, Proceedings of Anthracite Strike Commission, 237 (pdf 238 of 297).
51. Ibid., 232 (pdf 233 of 297).
52. Ibid., 233 (pdf 234 of 297).
53. Ibid.
54. Ibid.
55. Ibid., 239 (pdf 240 of 297).
56. Ibid., 240 (pdf 241 of 297).
57. Ibid., 245 (pdf 246 of 297).
58. Ibid., 246 (pdf 247 of 297).
59. Ibid., 248 (pdf 249 of 297).
60. Ibid., 249 (pdf 250 of 297).
61. Ibid.
62. Ibid.
63. Ibid.
64. Ibid., 255 (pdf 256 of 297).
65. Ibid., 257 (pdf 258 of 297).
66. Ibid., 240 (pdf 241 of 297).
67. Ibid., 245 (pdf 246 of 297).
68. Ibid., 268 (pdf 269 of 297).
69. Ibid., 243 (pdf 244 of 297).
70. Ibid., 246 (pdf 247 of 297).
71. Ibid.
72. Ibid.

73. Ibid., 248 (pdf 249 of 297).
74. Ibid., 263 (pdf 264 of 297).
75. Ibid., 242 (pdf 243 of 297).
76. Ibid., 244 (pdf 245 of 297).
77. Ibid., 253 (pdf 254 of 297).
78. Ibid., 269 (pdf 270 of 297).
79. Ibid., 268 (pdf 269 of 297).
80. Ibid., 247 (pdf 248 of 297).
81. Ibid., 268-69 (pdf 269-70 of 297).
82. Ibid., 269 (pdf 270 of 297).
83. *Morning Astorian* (Astoria, OR), February 17, 1903.
84. *New York Tribune*, February 16, 1903 (Spalding noted only Andrew Carnegie as rising above his great wealth).
85. Ibid.
86. Ibid., March 22, 1903.
87. Ibid.
88. *Washington Times*, March 22, 1903.
89. Ibid.
90. UMN Law, Darrow Digital, Proceedings of Anthracite Strike Commission, 96 (pdf 97 of 297).
91. Ibid., 24 (pdf 25 of 297).
92. Ibid., 238 (pdf 239 of 297).
93. William D. Haywood, *Bill Haywood's Book: The Autobiography of William D. Haywood* (New York: International Publishers, 1929), 23.
94. The *Shenandoah (PA) Herald* published Kehoe's remarks, dated October 22, 1875, on June 8, 1876.
95. *Miners' Journal* (Pottsville, PA), October 13, 1875.
96. *Scranton (PA) Tribune*, August 21, 1902.
97. *New York Herald*, April 12, 1871.
98. *Richmond Dispatch*, October 7, 1902.
99. *New York Herald*, April 3, 1875.
100. *Miners' Journal* (Pottsville, PA), October 22, 1875.
101. UMN Law, Darrow Digital, Proceedings of Anthracite Strike Commission, 151 (pdf 152 of 297).
102. *Harrisburg Patriot*, March 4, 1875.
103. Ibid.
104. *Birmingham (AL) Age-Herald*, November 21, 1904 (from Philadelphia dispatch to *New York Herald*).
105. Ibid.
106. Ibid.
107. W. E. B. Du Bois, *Black Reconstruction in America, 1860-1880* (1935; repr., New York: The Free Press, 1998), 723.
108. Ibid., 725.

13

THE WESTERN CASELOAD: THE WFM

I want to hold up to your gaze the work of the Pinkerton Detective Agency. Don't you know perjury and false witness always follows in its trail?

> Orrin Hilton
> Defense counsel, trial of Stephen Adams
> Grand Junction, Colorado, July 1908

FOR MORE THAN THREE DECADES, Pinkerton operative James McParlan, aka McParland, left fingerprints on criminal cases that spanned the continental United States. McParlan learned his trade in the 1870s from Allan Pinkerton and Robert Linden, the engineers of Pennsylvania's "Molly Maguire" caseload.

The success of Pinkerton's "Molly" caseload in Pennsylvania's northeastern coal region depended heavily on jurors' acceptance of McParlan's testimony. In June 1876, after McParlan helped convict five defendants in the Yost trial, a former Pinkerton operative who had worked with McParlan wrote in protest to the *Irish World*. "Mac-

Parlan [sic] used to be a uniformed watchman," D. J. Browne said, "and on account of his dexterity in opening doors and making out imaginary reports, was picked out for the 'Molly Maguire' business. Don't you see, those innocent men down there confessed all to him after a *ten days' acquaintance?* Pinkerton has now received a hundred thousand dollars from the coal owners, and after all his strategy it is a bad point for him that he cannot swing a couple of Irishmen. *He has had men down there running saloons and in every capacity, yet not one has found out anything except* MacParlan [sic]."[1]

Nothing about McParlan, including his name, could be trusted. Pinkerton reports and correspondence from 1874 to 1875 refer to the operative variously as "J. McF," "James McFarlan," "Jas. McFarlain," and "Jas McFarland."[2] McParlan traveled Pennsylvania's coal region undercover as "James McKenna." During the Pennsylvania trials, he identified himself as "James McParlan." Given the copious use in Pinkerton reports of the identifier "J McF," McParlan, touted during the "Molly Maguire" trials as an Irish Catholic from Ulster, may well have been a Presbyterian from the Ulster-based Scottish clan of MacFarlane. Glasgow-born Allan Pinkerton may have handpicked a fellow Scotsman to conduct Pennsylvania's "Molly Maguire" caseload.

Details of McParlan's personal bio also shifted with the wind. "You were a sailor during the younger period of your life?" Clarence Darrow asked the detective during the Idaho trial of Stephen Adams. "Yes, sir," McParlan responded. "How many years?" Darrow asked. "Probably thirteen."[3]

Allan Pinkerton's dime novel, *The Mollie Maguires and the Detectives*, gave a far more prosaic account of McParlan's younger years. Per Pinkerton, McParlan's bio included stints in a chemical factory at Durham, England, and in a Belfast linen warehouse. After emigrating to New York, McParlan worked in dry goods before moving on to Chicago. There, after clerking for a liquor wholesaler, he opened his own store on Canal Street. In October 1871, the Chicago Fire claimed that establishment. The following year, McParlan signed on with the Pinkerton agency.

In 1877 author Francis Dewees expanded McParlan's bio. "He worked as a teamster for a road-contractor, drove a meat-wagon, was a deck hand on a lake steamer, and chopped wood in the wilds of Michigan," Dewees said.[4] McParlan's work as a deckhand blossomed decades later, under Darrow's questioning, into a fantasia of thirteen years before the mast. Dewees also gave Pinkerton's probable rationale for hiring McParlan. "His brain is logical," Dewees said of the operative's testimony during the "Molly Maguire" trials, "his memory wonderful, his expressions accurate. ... he has defied cross-examination. ... for many hours at a time has he answered the questions of able counsel, but, ever cool, calm, and deliberate ... he has not lost his head nor has his testimony been in the least degree shaken."[5]

Thirty years later, in Idaho, McParlan identified those precise traits in his choice of Harry Orchard as main prosecution witness against the Western Federation of Miners (WFM). Thirty years after McParlan testified in Pennsylvania, Orchard became the new McParlan.

But by then, the country had moved forward in sophistication and awareness. Pinkerton fantasias, spouted this time by Orchard, no longer gripped the national imagination as they had in the 1870s.

In their pursuit of political and labor activists, the drafting of false testimony backed by perjured corroboration was Pinkerton stock-in-trade. In the mid-1870s, throughout Pennsylvania's coalfields, Pinkerton operative Robert Linden helped draft such testimony to accuse more than one hundred members of the Ancient Order of Hibernians (AOH), an Irish Catholic benevolent order, of conspiracy to commit murder. Linden helped bring these charges against AOH men in Pennsylvania's northeastern and its western coalfields. For the most part, the cases in western Pennsylvania failed to secure convictions.

But under the adage "if it ain't broke, don't fix it," Pinkerton operatives used the same boilerplate for at least three decades to draft courtroom testimony against labor activists. A decade and a half after Linden drafted charges of conspiracy against AOH officers in Pennsylvania's "Molly Maguire" cases, Pinkerton agent J. H. Ford accused Knights of Labor officers at Homestead, Pennsylvania, of poisoning non-union men. Thirteen years after that, Pinkerton superintendent James McParlan accused Western Federation of Miners (WFM) officers of assassinating, by bombing, former Idaho governor Frank Steunenberg.

Over a thirty-year span, the Pinkertons manufactured perjured testimony to accuse dozens and dozens of benevolent and trade union officers of conspiracies to commit murder. Where ethnic hatred energized juries in northeastern Pennsylvania, the false accusations of supposed "Molly Maguire" terrorism secured twenty-one executions and dozens more convictions leading to terms of imprisonment. In most other instances, the accusations failed. The false accusations of poisoning at Homestead in 1892 produced mixed results.

On June 30, 1892, at Andrew Carnegie's steel works in Homestead, Pennsylvania, Knights of Labor mechanics and transportation workers walked out in protest after the collapse of their collective bargaining agreement. Henry Frick, Carnegie's manager, subsequently closed the plant. Carnegie and Frick's preparations in anticipation of labor strife had begun the previous January. These included a high fence topped with barbed wire, sniper towers equipped with searchlights, and high-pressure water cannons equipped to spray boiling liquid.

Two months before the walkout, Frick had secured the services of the Pinkerton National Detective Agency. On the night of July 5, 1892, three hundred Pinkertons armed with Winchesters boarded two barges bound for Carnegie's mill. They reached the plant at four in the morning. Armed strikers, along with their families, waited for them on the hill at Homestead.

From St. Paul, the *Daily Globe* reported: "DOGS OF WAR

UNLEASHED And Redden Their Fangs in the Heart's Blood of Locked-Out Workmen and Hired Thugs. ... A FEARFUL DAY'S WORK ON SATAN'S MODEL."[6] More than two dozen died, with fatalities on both sides.

The prospect of industrial war waged by a private detective agency on one side and striking workingmen on the other energized the country. Less than two weeks after the battle at Homestead, Joseph Pulitzer's *Evening World* in New York reported the proceedings of a congressional committee at Washington. The committee adopted an amendment to the Sundry Civil bill "making it unlawful for any Government official to contract with a person or firm which employs Pinkerton detectives or any other association of men as armed guards."[7]

Pulitzer's *World*, heartened by the action of Congress, predicted "THE DOOM OF PINKERTONISM." "The clouds are gathering over the Pinkerton system," it said. "The press all over the country, with a few discreditable exceptions, is outspoken in denunciation of the practice of sending armed bands of men ... to suppress labor strikes ... Their presence where labor troubles exist provokes rioting, and is perhaps in many instances intended to do so. If a single shot is fired by an excited individual in a mob the Winchesters do their work, and volley after volley tells the true mission of the Pinkerton butchers."[8]

In early August, Charles Dana's *New York Sun* gave details of the Senate's discussion at Washington, where a special committee of seven had met to investigate "the origin of the Pinkerton force and the uses to which they have been put." Illinois Senator John Palmer, a Democrat, deplored the floating armies of Pinkertons furnished for corporate use nationwide. "'These forces,'" Palmer said, "'are responsible neither to God nor man, only to those who hire them. ... They ought to be hounded down by such means as are employed against enemies of mankind.'"[9]

Senator Joseph Hawley, a Republican from Connecticut, described the hiring by the Carnegie Company of Pinkerton forces at Homestead "either a blunder or a crime." Wilkinson Call, a Democrat from Florida, defined the "invasion of a State by the Pinkerton forces ... 'treason' within the Constitutional definition of the term." Senator Jacob Gallinger, a Republican from New Hampshire, believed "that Congress should, by bill or otherwise, protect the people of the country from the invasion of an illegal, unauthorized, and murderous mob of men."[10]

According to Pulitzer's *World*, Pinkerton recruiters targeted the most disenfranchised, the most marginalized, and the most vulnerable before hiring them and arming them with Winchesters. Pinkerton agents trolled military recruitment offices to hire young men deemed unfit for government service. They searched the docks of the country's seaports to recruit those "found going to sea as a last resort of employment."[11] The *Critic* described Pinkerton agents as "'criminals of the lowest order—men who were not allowed to live in civilized society ... and only come out of their holes when they are employed by him [William Pinkerton] to commit murders.'"[12]

"The system must go," the *Pittsburg* [sic] *Dispatch* said, deploring its "evil tendencies."[13] In Seattle, an editor described Pinkerton men as "thugs."[14] From Rock Island, Illinois, an editor called for Pennsylvania's citizens to "aid their other brethren in the other states in rooting out an infamous system that is destroying the liberty and prosperity of our people."[15] From Topeka came the denouncement of "a lawless band of mercenaries subject to hire of millionaire corporations, to murder troublesome [employees] who conceive the idea that they are entitled to the common rights of American freemen."[16]

A correspondent to a St. Paul newspaper deplored the Pinkertons' "armed band of murderous ruffians ... a menace to our institutions, a curse to society, and an insult to a free and independent people."[17] A detective from a rival Chicago detective firm told the congressional committee "that Pinkerton men were usually the scum of the earth, and that one of Pinkerton's present superintendents is an ex-convict." He added: "in strikes detectives were often induced to manufacture evidence, as their employers would imagine that they were doing nothing if they failed to report progress of some sort."[18]

The storm of outrage continued. National labor leaders deplored the Pinkertons as a "'band of organized pirates.'"[19] Meanwhile, the federal bill threatened to stall in committee, with some arguing that states, not the federal government, held purview over the issue of the hiring of corporate armed guards.

Nonetheless, in March 1893, with very little fanfare, the federal Anti-Pinkerton Act was made permanent. The act provided: "'An individual employed by the Pinkerton Detective Agency, or similar organization, may not be employed by the Government of the United States or the government of the District of Columbia.'"[20] By 1899, more than half of U.S. states or territories had enacted similar legislation.

Pennsylvania secured her legislation less than a year after the battle at Homestead. "The employment of the Pinkerton hirelings at Homestead has had one good result," a Mifflintown newspaper observed. "It has secured from the House of Representatives of the Pennsylvania Legislature the passage of a bill prohibiting the employment of other than citizens of the State in the preservation of the peace."[21]

Pinkerton intervention at Homestead yielded another result. Their ongoing battle against the Knights of Labor, based on perjured testimony, revealed the methods of intimidation they used to secure false witness. One such perjurer, a cook at Carnegie's mill at Homestead, gave minute details on how the Pinkertons concocted their plots.

Accusations of corruption pockmarked the Pinkertons' long career. At Homestead in the early 1890s, a cook at the steel plant gave credence to such accusations. Patrick Gallagher, gulled by the Pinkertons into giving false testimony against two officers of the Knights of Labor, later recanted his testimony.

In December 1892, Gallagher testified that Robert Beatty and Hugh Dempsey, former master workman of the Knights of Labor District Assembly No. 3, had paid him fifty dollars to poison the coffee of nonunion workers at the Homestead steel plant. Dempsey and Beatty served prison sentences based on Gallagher's testimony.

Seven months later Gallagher recanted verbally, in the presence of witnesses. The secret, he said, "was killing him."[22] L. K. Porter, a Knights of Labor defense attorney who represented both Dempsey and Beatty, witnessed Gallagher's recantation. Porter subsequently read Gallagher's statement to a *New York Sun* reporter.

"Dempsey and Beatty are entirely innocent," Gallagher's statement said. "I never got any powders or poison from them, and I never administered any in the mill. I was told by Pinkerton detectives who arrested me that if I did not do as they wanted me to do, they would indict me for murder and have me hanged. They got me drunk and prepared a confession for me. I was kept supplied with money and whiskey for forty-two days, while a detective shadowed me all the time. I was told that if I attempted to get away I would be shot."[23]

The Pinkertons told Gallagher "they were after Dempsey because he was at the head of the Knights of Labor, and that organization was no good and ought to be broken up." Gallagher stated further that the Pinkertons had assured him that if he agreed to testify against the union men, "they would not push a murder charge against me, and that I would go free. At the most I would get only sixty days to satisfy the public."[24]

Gallagher said: "They continually cautioned me not to get mixed in my story, but to swear to what they said and stick to it. They made me rehearse the story frequently. There were other witnesses who were to take their cue from me and make their stories corroborate mine."[25]

Gallagher, convicted of the poisoning allegation, served jail time. During his incarceration, Pinkerton agents kept the cook supplied "with money, provisions, and clothes" to encourage his testimony against the Knights of Labor men. Gallagher reiterated: "They kept continually telling me to swear this case through and stick to it ... I was told they had twenty-five witnesses to bolster up my story. They had me so badly frightened and kept me drunk so long that I did not know whether I was living or dead half the time."[26]

On witnessing Gallagher's recantation, Dempsey's attorney, Porter, said: "From the first I have been entirely satisfied of Dempsey's innocence, and, more than that, there was never any poison administered in the Homestead mill. This is the unfortunate result of reputable people of Allegheny county importing thieves and convicts from Chicago and other places and using them as detectives."[27]

J. M. Davidson, who had corroborated Gallagher's initial trial testimony, recanted along with Gallagher. After both prosecution witnesses recanted, Pennsylvania's Board of Pardons received several hundred letters, along with petitions signed by thousands, requesting Dempsey's pardon. In late January 1896, Dempsey received his freedom. Members of Pennsylvania's four-man pardon board noted as one reason for granting Dempsey's commutation of sentence "'that the principal witnesses, P. J. Gallagher and J. M. Davidson, who testified against the petitioner at the time of the trial, have filed an affidavit taken upon notice to the Commonwealth, retracting the testimony given at the trial.'"[28]

Dempsey, a husband and father, served almost three years' time for Gallagher's perjured allegation of poisoning. The pardon board advised Pennsylvania's governor, Daniel Hastings, that before Dempsey's arrest, he "had borne an excellent character in the community ... had never before been charged with any crime; he held a high position in the labor organizations of Pennsylvania and was noted for his peaceable character and gentle disposition ... was a good husband and attentive to all the duties assigned to him."[29]

At Homestead, Pinkerton agent J. H. Ford had worked up the allegations of poisoning against the Knights of Labor men. Ford based his accusations on conversations he claimed to have overheard. He alleged, the *Pittsburg* [sic] *Dispatch* reported, "that poison had been systematically used. He had seen it and the attorneys now have some of it in their possession. It was a dark brown powder." At the Homestead mill at the time of the alleged poisonings, Ford told the *Dispatch* reporter, "'doctors examined the food and said it was pure. Then they examined the water and that was bad. ... The doctors, most of them, said it was typhoid fever. It shows how much they know.'"[30]

"WHAT HOMESTEADERS SAY," the *Dispatch* said of Ford's allegations. "Physicians There Do Not Give Much Credence to the Sensation." The *Dispatch* account reported: "Dr. Barten, a prominent physician, said that he attributed the sickness to typhoid fever, and that the idea that the men were poisoned was absurd. All they physicians and druggists seen expressed themselves in a like manner."[31]

Of such materials were Pinkerton trial cases crafted.

After Pinkerton operative James McParlan helped send twenty-one Irish Catholic men to the gallows in Pennsylvania, he took his stock-in-trade to the West. There, McParlan's animus against Irish Catholics mutated into a vendetta against organized labor.

McParlan's service in Pennsylvania gained him the position of superintendent of Pinkerton's western division, headquartered in Denver. In the West, the Pinkerton called himself "McParland." From 1899 to 1905, despite the enactment of a federal law against his agency, McParland helped foment the climate of corruption, unrest, and terror that led to the Colorado Labor Wars between the state's mine owners and the Western Federation of Miners (WFM). In Colorado's gold and silver region, McParland infiltrated the WFM with dozens of Pinkerton agents. As in Pennsylvania, McParland's unholy passage through Colorado churned up a chaotic wake.

McParland transferred his signature experience as an undercover Pinkerton agent, his infiltration of Pennsylvania's coal region AOH lodges, to the Pinkertons' business plan against organized labor in the West. In 1907, five years after his defense of the United Mine Workers before the Anthracite Mine Strike Commission, Clarence Darrow faced a jury in Idaho. As soon as the WFM formed, Darrow told Idaho jurors, "the mine owners set to work to destroy it ... as one of their chief means of destroying it they hired the Pinkerton detective agency, with one McParland at the head in the West."[32] Darrow added: "We will show that amongst other things they repeatedly hired detectives and placed these detectives in positions of responsibility as secretaries and presidents of local unions, and they sent those detectives out amongst the union men at their meetings to advise strikes, and whenever there was a strike to advise violence and bloodshed and dynamite and [murder]. ... from one end to the other of this mining region ... most of the talk and most of the inciting to violence and crimes has come from their hired men through the Pinkerton detective agency."[33] The mine owners, Darrow said, had also indulged in a campaign of vilification, abuse, and slander against the WFM.

According to Charles Siringo, a twenty-year Pinkerton operative, corrupt political engineering also marked McParland's career, including vote-buying through use of "'repeaters.'" In a self-published exposé, Siringo noted: "The truth of such matters was kept hidden in the breast of the operatives and superintendents and disclosed to the clients by word of mouth."[34]

By 1905, McParland's influence in Colorado and Idaho extended to both states' governors. *Miners Magazine* gave McParland's personal assessment of Colorado's governor, James Peabody: "'a good friend of the [Pinkerton] agency,'" with "'few ... willing to admit that all he did was in accordance with the Constitution of the United States.'"[35] Idaho's governor, Frank Gooding, another confrere of McParland, figured directly in the events that flowed from the bombing death of former Idaho governor Frank Steunenberg.

Around dinnertime on the evening of December 30, 1905, Steunenberg walked home through newly fallen snow to his turreted two-story clapboard house on Sixteenth Avenue in Caldwell, Idaho. Moments before he reached his side gate, Steunenberg's wife and his two youngest children had risen from their knees in the living room, their evening prayers completed.

Steunenberg reached the wooden gate that led to his side door. He maneuvered the wooden slide, opened the gate, and stepped through. When he turned to close the gate behind him, a bomb exploded. Its force lifted the former governor off his feet and pitched him more than ten feet into his yard. The blast shredded his legs and removed his clothing from the waist down. It blew out windows in neighboring houses. Parma's townspeople, sixteen miles west of Caldwell, heard the explosion. Investigators later found metal shards and wadding, and a fragment of Steunenberg's hat brim, hundreds of yards from the blast site.

From inside the house, Steunenberg's thirteen-year-old daughter saw the flash. With her mother, she ran with to her father's side. Neighbors rushed to the site. So fierce was the bomb's destructive force, rescuers had difficulty maneuvering the governor's mangled body onto a blanket and transporting it into his house. Inside the house, windows had shattered, strewing shards of glass. A mantle clock dislodged by the force had struck Steunenberg's five-year-old son while he lay on a leather couch, waiting for his father to come home.

Three Caldwell doctors came to Steunenberg's bedside. On seeing the extent of his injuries, they said they could do nothing. That evening, a little after seven o'clock, Steunenberg died in his brother Will's arms.

On hearing the news, Idaho's Governor Gooding, along with a car full of influential politicians and state officials, hired a special train for the thirty-mile trip northwest to Caldwell from Boise. The politicians crammed into cars alongside volunteers brandishing "squirrel rifles, broom handles and baseball bats."[36] Someone tied down the locomotive's whistle. Listeners for miles heard the train make its nighttime passage to Caldwell.

On December 31, 1905, the following day, the chief justice of Idaho's supreme court telephoned Pinkerton superintendent James McParland at Denver. In this call and in a follow-up telegram, Chief Justice Charles Stockslager requested McParland's assistance in the investigation of Frank Steunenberg's assassination. The same day, newspapers countrywide reported the horror. From Los Angeles to New York, accounts blamed the "Coeur d'Alene Dynamiters."[37]

After midnight on the night of the bombing, Harry Orchard, later described by attorney Edmund Richardson as "'this vile, this loathsome, this damned creature,'"[38] joined the late-night crowd that gawked in the cold, cadging souvenirs at the Steunenberg bomb site. Orchard had arrived in Caldwell a few months before. A few weeks before Steunenberg's murder, Orchard had booked himself into the Saratoga Hotel under the alias "Thomas Hogan." He had introduced himself variously to hotel guests as a real estate developer and as a sheep rancher.

Clarence Darrow described Orchard as "a cheap soldier of fortune, a shoe-string gambler, who never degraded himself by work for any great length of time."[39] Orchard was, Darrow added, "the most monumental liar that ever lived on the face of the earth."[40] The birth-name of Orchard, a bigamist who had abandoned wives in Canada and Colorado, was Albert Horsley.

Orchard's biography surfaced during the trials. Among other enterprises, he had burned his cheese factory to collect the insurance money. He had conned farmers into buying hail insurance. An inveterate gambler, he had stolen both money and sheep. He had schemed to kidnap a child to cover a debt owed. He also had worked as a miner in Colorado, where had he joined the Western Federation of Miners (WFM). Sometime during his multifarious career, Orchard had told G. L. Brokaw, a companion, "that he had been a Pinkerton employee for some time."[41] One-time miner and union member Albert Horsley, aka Thomas Hogan, aka Harry Orchard, was also a self-admitted Pinkerton operative.

In Caldwell, Orchard did all he could to provoke his own arrest after Steunenberg's murder. Before the attack took place, Orchard had made himself well known to Caldwell's locals, playing cards and lounging in the barroom of the Saratoga Hotel. Before the bombing, Orchard had openly canvassed the former governor's house on Sixteenth Avenue, examining it from a distance with field glasses.

On the Saturday evening of the murder Steunenberg, as was his habit, had visited the Saratoga Hotel, Orchard's home base, to pick up the town's weekly newspaper. Following his usual routine, Steunenberg had read the paper in the hotel barroom before walking home.

After the bombing, Orchard's behavior attracted notice. With one hundred newly deputized sheriffs surging through town, Orchard conspicuously refused to discuss the murder. Instead, he buttonholed one of Caldwell's outraged locals to ask about the purchase of sheep. Orchard's dodgy behavior stirred the memory of townsmen. They recalled that while at the Saratoga, he had shown a particular interest in their former governor.

On the night of the murder Sheriff Harvey Brown, of Oregon's Baker County, traveled by train from Boise to Caldwell with the powerful Idaho contingent. The following day, alerted to Orchard's behavior, Brown viewed him through the hotel window. Brown identified Orchard as a miner who had worked in eastern Oregon.

On New Year's Eve, the day after Steunenberg's murder, a search of Orchard's hotel room revealed traces of plaster of Paris, thought used to construct the bomb, and the fishing line thought to have triggered it. The carpet held traces of white powder. On New Year's Day Caldwell's sheriff, along with a deputy, arrested Orchard at the Saratoga Hotel bar. They led him to the courthouse for arraignment, and from the courthouse to the Canyon County jail.

The week after Steunenberg's assassination, accusations against the Western Federation of Miners (WFM) seeped into the news coverage. Newspapers reported the finding in Harry Orchard's luggage of "a leather postal card ... addressed to Charles Moyer, president of the Western Federation of Miners."[42] An unidentified private detective retained possession of this evidence. Defense attorney Edmund Richardson later argued that Orchard "had bought this card and addressed it and put it in his pocket so it would be found when he was arrested."[43]

On January 4, the *Denver Times* reported that Orchard, a union member, had lived in Idaho's Coeur d'Alene mining region "until the time of the trouble there in 1899." Other accounts linked Orchard to Colorado's 1904 Independence Depot explosion at Cripple Creek, a blast that had killed thirteen nonunion men.

"Orchard was a prominent member of the Western Federation of Miners during the great Cripple Creek strike of 1904," the *Spokane Press* reported on January 23. "The general belief is that Gov. Steunenberg was assassinated for sending the state militia to Coeur d'Alene and quelling the riots, at which time many miners were confined in the 'bull pen' established at his direction." The *Coeur d'Alene Press* said: "Governor Steunenberg took a very active part in the suppression of the riots in the mining districts in 1899 ... On this account he made many enemies among the miners, and since that affair he has received many threatening letters."[44]

After Orchard's arrest, detectives from the Pinkertons' northwestern offices and from the Thiel Detective Service, a Pinkerton rival headquartered in Chicago under the supervision of Wilson Swain, swarmed into Caldwell. The Pinkerton office sent an operative from Spokane to oversee activities. The two rival detective agencies raced each other to uncover evidence to help them win the case from Idaho's officials.

Two Idaho politicians with their sights on the looming gubernatorial election—Democratic candidate Charles Stockslager, chief justice of Idaho's Supreme Court; and incumbent Republican governor Frank Gooding, a prominent sheep rancher—stage-managed the hiring of private detectives in the Steunenberg case. Stockslager, whose dealings with McParland dated to Stockslager's tenure in Kansas as prosecutor for Cherokee County, favored the Pinkerton men. Two decades before, in 1886, McParland had secured a confession in an arson and fraud case in Columbus, Kansas, that had helped cement Stockslager's reputation. Gooding, hoping the mine owners would cover the costs, initially favored the services of the Thiel agency. Stockslager persuaded Gooding to place his trust in the Pinkertons.

Gooding's personal, and very public, involvement in the murder case that election year aroused indignation in Idaho and countrywide. "'Why should the Governor assume the role of prosecutor?'" asked William McConnell, Steunenberg's predecessor as governor.[45] The *Salt Lake Herald* thought Gooding "a hasty, impetuous, hotheaded, ill-tempered and undignified executive" whose constant need to engage the press had "made both himself and his state ridiculous."[46] An Idaho newsman said of Gooding's re-election chances: "The Republicans have little hope of electing Gooding, for his administration has been so rotten that they are not supporting him with any warmth."[47]

An Oklahoma newsman said: "The statement attributed to him [Gooding] that the accused labor leaders 'will never leave the state alive,' is hardly the proper thing for an executive bent only on exact justice."[48] From Boise, the *Capital News* said: "'Somebody ought to muzzle the big chief. ... His constant fear that the public will lose sight of him ... has made a laughing stock of the prosecution.'" The Boise paper added that Idaho could no longer afford Gooding's "'opera bouffe habit of individual vanity.'"[49]

Socialist journals joined the clamor. *Wilshire's Magazine* in New York considered Gooding a "dull, blundering creature that sits in the governor's chair."[50] From Kansas, a reporter for *Appeal to Reason* thought Gooding "a close, calculating, energetic, unscrupulous commercial proposition, ready to turn a dollar at any time, regardless of the means employed."[51]

But a second Oklahoma newsman described Gooding's "strenuous 'law and order' campaign ... supported by the mining, commercial and railroad interests of the state."[52] And in Washington, President Theodore Roosevelt felt so supportive of his fellow Republican's law and order offensive against organized labor, he sent Secretary of War William Howard Taft to Idaho to speak on Gooding's behalf. Taft's championing of Gooding at Boise three days before the election sounded on similar rhetorical lines. Afterward, Taft told Idaho's Senator Weldon Heyburn of Gooding: "'It would be a national calamity if he were defeated.'"[53] Roosevelt celebrated Gooding's re-election in a letter to his daughter Alice: "'Yes, we have elected Gooding Governor in Idaho; it is a big victory for civilization.'"[54]

Gooding's re-election, along with his supposed stance on law and order, rested on the credibility of McParland's case against the WFM officers. McParland's credibility would soon crumble when challenged by three of the era's most effective defense attorneys. But the detective's successful seduction of state officials in both Colorado and Idaho, and through them, of Theodore Roosevelt in the White House, remains a classic chapter in the Pinkertons' long campaign against labor.

On January 7, 1906, having received Governor Gooding's formal request to send James McParland to Idaho to investigate the Steunenberg murder, William Pinkerton gave his assent. McParland arrived in Boise on the evening of January 10. Justice Stockslager, accompanied by the Pinkerton superintendent from Spokane, met McParland at the depot. McParland subsequently installed himself in Suite 35 of Boise's Idanha Hotel.

After dinner that evening, McParland invited Stockslager and Gooding to his suite, where he made his pitch. He would accept the case only if he could work independently of the Thiel agency. Stockslager and Gooding agreed. McParland gave Gooding his second demand: he wanted Orchard removed from the jail at Caldwell and taken to the penitentiary at Boise. Again, Gooding agreed.

The next day, Gooding sent a letter to the sheriff at Canyon County jail advising him that the Pinkertons had been employed in the case and would work under McParland's supervision. Gooding advised further that all assistance "'should be cheerfully rendered and will be fully appreciated by me.'"[55]

The commissioners at Caldwell removed the Thiel agency from the case. McParland wrote to the Pinkerton brothers: "'I have done what I could to overthrow Swain, never letting an opportunity pass.'"⁵⁶ The Pinkertons' command of the western mining region now embraced not just Colorado, but the entire Northwest. The assassination of Steunenberg and the Pinkertons' snatch of the case had opened sizable business opportunities for them.

But McParland still faced opposition at Caldwell. Both Sheriff Nichols and Judge Frank Smith, of Caldwell's district court, refused to approve Orchard's removal to Boise.

On January 12 Gooding escorted Judge Smith to McParland's suite at the Idanha. Smith remained closeted with McParland until almost one in the morning. At the meeting's end, the Caldwell judge promised to use his influence with the sheriff to have Orchard transferred to Boise. He also agreed not to issue a writ of habeas corpus unless directed to do so by Idaho's supreme court.

Gooding then sent McParland to Idaho's supreme court. Two of the court's three justices, including Stockslager, assured McParland that it was "'perfectly legal'" to have Orchard removed to Boise.⁵⁷ They promised to sustain Judge Smith in his denial of Orchard's writ of habeas corpus.

But in Caldwell, Sheriff Nichols remained dug in. On January 11, Nichols had told the *Idaho Daily Statesman*: "'You may state in your paper that Orchard stays right here until the case against him is decided, and state it strong enough that it will be understood by everybody.'"⁵⁸ Six days later, the state hired criminal prosecutor James Hawley to take on the Steunenberg case.

That day, Hawley wrote to Sheriff Nichols: "'I don't believe your jail or the jail of any county is at present a secure place.'" He encouraged Nichols to release Orchard for temporary placement at the penitentiary at Boise. He assured him: "'I don't believe any responsibility would rest on you for any bad results.'"⁵⁹

McParland's hotel suite would have benefitted from a revolving door. Late that day, Gooding escorted Sheriff Nichols to Suite 35. McParland and Nichols met for an hour. McParland reported of that meeting: "'I think that we'll succeed in getting the prisoner transferred in a very short time.'"⁶⁰

The next day, Sheriff Nichols petitioned Governor Gooding for

Orchard's removal to Boise. In his request, Nichols cited "'grave, serious, unusual and extraordinary circumstances.'"[61] The day after that, Nichols and his deputy escorted Orchard to Boise. To avoid notice, they embarked and debarked several hundred yards from the train stations at Caldwell and Boise. At Boise, they delivered Orchard to Eugene Whitney, the penitentiary's warden.

Whitney housed Orchard on death row next to two convicted murderers. Relays of guards watched him day and night. Per McParland's instructions, the guards did not speak to the prisoner at all.

Orchard remained in his cell for three days. On Monday afternoon, January 22, 1906, McParland caught the streetcar in front of the Idanha hotel and rode to the penitentiary. Whitney, in a rig, met the detective and drove him to the prison. There, Whitney escorted McParland to his office, where Orchard waited. Whitney introduced the two men and left them to speak privately.

In Harry Orchard, James McParland met a version of his former self: the young Pinkerton operative who had stood up, thirty years before, to grilling by defense attorneys in Pennsylvania's "Molly Maguire" cases.

McParland opened proceedings with Orchard by telling him that the guards had Orchard's fellow prisoner, Fred Bond, on a deathwatch. They were "'fattening him up for the occasion'"[62] of his execution.

The two men remained closeted for three hours. After McParland left the penitentiary, he met with Governor Gooding at the Idanha. Their meeting lasted until after midnight.

The next day, McParland met with Orchard again. He informed Orchard that if Orchard testified against the Western Federation men, "'we would get the leaders and that was all that the State of Colorado or the State of Idaho wished.'"[63] If Orchard agreed to testify that the "inner circle" of WFM officers had ordered multiple murders, including that of Frank Steunenberg, McParland could guarantee Orchard immunity from prosecution in Colorado. McParland also advised Orchard that with such testimony, the state of Idaho would "'no doubt take care of him.'"[64]

Over the next few days, McParland met repeatedly with Orchard in the warden's office. On Sunday, January 28, 1906, the two met again. This time McParland's personal stenographer joined them to notate Orchard's statement. Orchard's dissertation of alleged WFM crimes took three days to complete.

By February 1, McParland had Orchard's transcribed confession, sixty-four pages in all, in hand. In it, Orchard confessed to setting the bomb that had killed Steunenberg. He took responsibility for the deaths of seventeen other men: two Colorado mine supervisors killed by explosion; thirteen nonunion men bombed at Colorado's Independence railroad depot; Denver detective Lyte Gregory, shot down in the street; and a passerby killed by a bomb. Orchard also detailed alleged assassination plots against numerous high officials in Colorado: the governor, two state supreme court justices, an adjutant general, and the president of a mining company. The inner circle of the WFM, per Orchard's confession, had ordered this criminal spree.

One man stood out in Orchard's rigmarole. In Pennsylvania's "Molly Maguire" trial testimony, McParland and his prosecution cohorts had spoken repeatedly of men willing to do "a clean job" of murder. Thirty years later, Orchard's confession replaced "clean job" with "any old thing." Orchard said it repeatedly of WFM member Steve Adams, a Cripple Creek miner, and of Steve's supposed gang: "they were ready for any old thing, from running men out of the district to killing them, as long as they got the money."[65]

Orchard's statement included this testimonial: "'I awoke,'" it said, "'as it were, from a dream, and realized that I'd been made a tool of, aided and assisted by members of the Executive Board of the Western Federation of Miners, and once they had led me to commit the first crime I had to continue to do their bidding or otherwise be assassinated myself ... I resolved, as far as in my power, to break up this murderous organization and to protect the community from further assassinations and outrages from this gang.'"[66]

Testimony given during the Haywood trial linked Orchard to A. W. Gratias, aka Pinkerton operative "No. 42." As McParland had infiltrated Pennsylvania's AOH lodges undercover, Gratias had infiltrated the WFM undercover.

In early 1905, Gratias had introduced Orchard to WFM men outside Denver. The same year that a bomb killed Steunenberg, Orchard and his Pinkerton gang, not the WFM gang, had tried unsuccessfully to induce union men to plant a bomb in a hotel basement in Globeville, Colorado. Orchard, a self-admitted Pinkerton operative, had laid this abortive terrorist plot with the help of Gratias, Pinkerton agent "No. 42," who took his instructions from McParland. Orchard's intersection with Gratias in Globeville, Colorado, proved Clarence Darrow's assertion that Pinkerton men exhorted union men to "'violence and bloodshed and dynamite and [murder].'" [67]

Hotel owner Max Malich and miner Joe Mahalich, defense witnesses in the trial of William Haywood, testified to Harry Orchard's attempts to recruit fellow terrorists through the agency of undercover Pinkerton operative A. W. Gratias. Malich, former WFM president of a smeltermen's local, kept a hotel, bar, and grocery in Globeville, a neighborhood north of Denver. In early 1905 Gratias, an undercover Pinkerton operative described by defense counsel Edmund Richardson as "this grinning hyena,"[68] introduced Orchard to both Malich and Mahalich at Malich's hotel bar.

Soon after Gratias introduced Orchard to Malich, Orchard came to the bar alone and invited the hotelkeeper outside for a private conversation. "'What is the matter with you fellows out here?'" Orchard asked Malich. "'It seems to me the scabs are getting the best of it.'" To deal with the nonunion workers brought in during the smeltermen's strike, Orchard told the hotelkeeper, they should "'blow that damned hotel off of the earth.'"[69] The American Smelting and Refining Company owned the Globeville hotel that housed more than one hundred nonunion workers.

Mahalich, who frequented Malich's bar, gave similar testimony. Clarence Darrow asked Mahalich of Orchard: "Did you ever have any talk with him about blowing up the boarding house at Globeville?" Mahalich responded: "Yes sir. ... He asked me if I knew that hotel, that Globe hotel, and I told him yes ... I told him that I boarded there once for two months, and he asked me if I knew that they had got a concrete basement and I told him that I ain't positive sure that they have, and I never took particular notice, but I think there is ... and he says if I wanted to go with him to blow that hotel up, and he says, if we don't do it you can't never get rid of the scabs."[70]

Both Malich and Mahalich refused Orchard's bait. Mahalich said: "I told him I would not go, that I did not intend to kill anybody that I never intended to fight a thousand men myself and I would not stick my fingers in it."[71] Malich testified that he told Orchard: "'I would not stand for that [under no] circumstances, and if you do anything I am going to denounce you.'"[72]

A few months after Malich refused Orchard's overtures and threatened to expose his plan, someone tossed a bottle of acid through Malich's bedroom window one evening while he was undressing. Malich's three-year-old son lay asleep on the bed. Splatters of acid hit Malich's wrist and burned through the flesh to the bone. The child escaped unharmed. Malich said of the attack: "the doctor called it ... acid; I didn't know what it was."[73]

During his stint as an operative in Pennsylvania's "Molly Maguire" trials, James McParland learned the dark art of press manipulation. Along with the manufacture of bogus confessions in murder trials, the Pinkerton business plan included the widespread publication of these false statements in newspaper columns and book form.

In their cases against both the Ancient Order of Hibernians (AOH) in 1876 and the Western Federation of Miners (WFM) three decades later, the Pinkertons relied on a carefully crafted chain of spurious evidence. McParland's testimony against AOH men in 1876 found its bookend in Harry Orchard's testimony against WFM men in 1907. Both McParland and Orchard charged officers of labor and benevolent organizations with numerous, hideous, crimes. Both McParland and Orchard gave testimony too startling to be believed. Both McParland and Orchard relished the notoriety their headlines generated.

To bolster the lurid and widespread sensational press coverage of the "Molly Maguire" cases, in 1877 Allan Pinkerton released his dime novel *The Mollie Maguires and the Detectives*. Published while trials remained ongoing, it gave, in full, the opening argument of the trials' self-appointed lead prosecutor, Franklin Gowen.[74] Another published account of a "Molly" trial included McParland's sensational trial testimony. It ran to almost three hundred pages and quickly sold out its first printing. Thirty years later McParland used the same scheme, but to far lesser effect.

By 1907, the public outrage that had fueled the passage of the 1893 Anti-Pinkerton Act had subsided. During the Idaho trial of William Haywood, McParland used the services of the Associated Press (AP) to help press his case against the labor leaders. In April 1907, with Haywood's trial looming, AP general manager Melville Stone wrote to his boyhood friend Robert Pinkerton. Stone, seemingly unfazed by the uproar against the Pinkerton agency a decade and a half before, informed Pinkerton that he was sending his best reporters to Boise to cover Haywood's trial. Stone asked Pinkerton to arrange for his reporters to meet with McParland.

Robert Pinkerton forwarded Stone's letter to McParland, and instructed McParland to give Stone's reporters John Kennedy and Martin Egan "'all proper consideration.'"[75] On April 30, Kennedy and Egan arrived in Boise. Two days later, they met with the prosecution's lead players: McParland, Idaho's governor Frank Gooding, and prosecutor James Hawley.

Kennedy advised McParland that he and Egan were preparing a two-thousand-word piece for Stone. It would introduce readers to the Western Federation caseload. McParland asked Kennedy to read the article aloud to him. Kennedy complied. Kennedy then sent the copy to Stone. It included McParland's corrections. Under Robert Pinkerton's supervision, the prosecution in Haywood had seized control of the national press.

Newspapers ran the AP article the following Sunday. Based on the lethal vaudeville of Orchard's confession recorded under McParland's direction, it broadcast the prosecution's allegations countrywide. "WEIRD STORY OF THIRTY MURDERS IN MINERS' TRIAL," a headline from Birmingham, Alabama, said. "History of Moyer-Haywood and Pettibone Case Most Remarkable in American Courts. ... At Trial of Haywood on Thursday Harry Orchard Will Tell of Crimes Which Have Terrorized Idaho for Fifteen Years."[76] From Washington, the *Evening Star* reported the "GHASTLY STORY OF THE COEUR D'ALENE." It added: "CONFESSION OF HARRY ORCHARD. Question Whether It is a Fabrication of the Pinkertons or an Amazing Record of Crime."[77]

Through the AP, Orchard's confession had the potential to reach eight hundred newspapers countrywide. The *Evening Star* said of McParland's role: "Whether the Mine Owners' Association has made any effort to aid in the prosecution ... the miners are convinced that it has. What lends color to their conviction is it was a Pinkerton detective who secured the confession from Harry Orchard, and it is a well-known fact that the Pinkerton detective service has played an active part in the miner troubles in the Rocky mountains."[78]

At least twice, the Pinkertons used the term "inner circle" to aid their conspiracy theories. In 1877, Allan Pinkerton's "Molly Maguire" fiction stated that his undercover operative must "secure admission to the inner circle of this labyrinth of iniquity."[79] In 1907, McParland resuscitated the term. The *Salt Lake Tribune* reported prosecutor Hawley's assertion, based on Orchard's confession: "the inner circle of the Western Federation of Miners is responsible for some of the most fiendish crimes ever committed anywhere—all to carry out the purpose of the circle."[80] Innumerable newspapers printed similar copy.

Part and parcel of Orchard's confession was McParland's

supposed religious conversion of this serial murderer who had supposedly admitted his crimes to atone for the error of his ways. With McParland's blessing, S. S. McClure's reporter, George Kibbe Turner, spent two weeks interviewing Orchard in his cell at Boise Penitentiary. Turner shaped the confession/biography crafted by McParland and Orchard into manuscript form for magazine and book publication. In July 1907, with the Haywood trial ongoing, *McClure's Magazine* published its first of five monthly installments of Orchard's autobiography, replete with Orchard's fervid descriptions of his spiritual awakening under McParland's tutelage.

Other echoes from the AOH trials reverberated through the WFM trials. As Kerrigan had corroborated McParland's testimony in 1876, McParland hoped to use Stephen Adams in 1907 to corroborate Orchard's tale.

In this instance, McParland would prove a poor case manager in the peddling of false testimony backed by perjured corroboration. But despite the paucity of his western caseload, with his agents, his influence, and his political bedfellows, McParland would manage to engage a sitting U.S. president in his efforts against the WFM officers.

---

1. *Irish World* (New York), June 3, 1876; italics in original.
2. For "J. McF," see, for example: James McParlan, operative reports, 23 January 1875, 24 January 1875, 28 January 1875, Box 1001, Reading Railroad Molly Maguire Papers, Hagley Museum and Library, Wilmington, DE; for "James McFarlan," see letter, Benj. Franklin (for Allan Pinkerton) to F. B. Gowen, 23 February 1875, ibid.; for "Jas. McFarlain," see operative report, James McParlan, 4 May 1875, ibid.; for "Jas McFarland," see ibid.
3. University of Minnesota Law Library, Clarence Darrow Digital Collection, Cases, Bill Haywood Trial – 1907, Steve Adams trial transcript, vol. 2, http://moses.law.umn.edu/darrow/documents/Idaho_v_Adams_transcript_vol_2_pp_506_1061.pdf, 866 (pdf 361 of 556).
4. F. P. Dewees, *The Molly Maguires: The Origin, Growth, and Character of the Organization* (1877; repr. New York: B. Franklin, 1969), 81.
5. Ibid., 79-80.
6. *Daily Globe* (St. Paul, MN), July 7, 1892.
7. Reported in *Evening World* (New York), July 19, 1892.
8. Ibid., July 21, 1892.
9. *New York Sun*, August 3, 1892.
10. Ibid.

11. J. Bernard Hogg, "Public Reaction to Pinkertonism and the Labor Question," *Pennsylvania History* 11, no. 3 (1944): 178; referencing *New York World* quoted in *Journal of the Knights of Labor*, July 21, 1892.
12. Ibid.
13. *Pittsburg [sic] Dispatch*, October 7, 1892.
14. *Seattle Post-Intelligencer*, October 16, 1892.
15. *Rock Island (IL) Daily Argus*, October 24, 1892.
16. *Advocate and Topeka (KS) Tribune*, October 26, 1892.
17. *Daily Globe* (St. Paul, MN), November 6, 1892.
18. *Pittsburg [sic] Dispatch*, November 19, 1892.
19. *Daily Globe* (St. Paul, MN), November 16, 1892 (from address of officers of the American Federation of Labor, the Amalgamated Association of Iron and Steel Workers of America, and the Homestead advisory board).
20. Cornell Law School, Legal Information Institute, 5 U.S. Code § 3108. Employment of detective agencies; restrictions, https://www.law.cornell.edu/uscode/text/5/3108.
21. *Juniata Sentinel and Republican* (Mifflintown, PA), May 17, 1893.
22. Gallagher's statement printed in full, *New York Sun*, July 15, 1893.
23. Ibid.
24. Ibid.
25. Ibid.
26. Ibid.
27. Ibid.
28. *Journal of the House of Representatives of the Commonwealth of Pennsylvania* (Harrisburg: Wm. Stanley Ray, 1897), 262.
29. Ibid., 264.
30. *Pittsburg [sic] Dispatch*, December 13, 1892.
31. Ibid.
32. UMN Law, Darrow Digital, Haywood trial transcripts, Haywood trial, vol. 4, http://moses.law.umn.edu/darrow/documents/Vol_4_Haywood_Transcript_p_1583_2123.pdf, 2065 (pdf 486 of 544).
33. Ibid., 2065-66 (pdf 486-87 of 544).
34. Charles A. Siringo, *Two Evil Isms: Pinkertonism and Anarchism* (Chicago: Charles A. Siringo, 1915), 23.
35. J. Anthony Lukas, *Big Trouble: A Murder in a Small Western Town Sets Off a Struggle for the Soul of America* (New York: Simon & Schuster, 1997), 246.
36. Ibid., 56.
37. See *Los Angeles Herald, New York Tribune, San Francisco Call*, December 31, 1905.
38. Lukas, *Big Trouble*, 706.
39. UMN Law, Darrow Digital, Haywood trial transcripts, Haywood trial, vol. 4, 2068-69 (pdf 489-90 of 544).
40. Ibid., 2070 (pdf 491 of 544).
41. Elizabeth Jameson, *All That Glitters: Class, Conflict, and Community in Cripple Creek* (Chicago: University of Illinois Press, 1998), 228.
42. *Omaha Daily Bee*, January 4, 1906; *Salt Lake Tribune*, same date.
43. UMN Law, Darrow Digital, Haywood trial transcripts, Haywood trial, vol. 11, http://moses.law.umn.edu/darrow/documents/Vol_11_Haywood_Transcript.pdf (pdf 474 of 714).
44. *Coeur d'Alene (ID) Press*, January 6, 1906.

45. Quoted in Lukas, *Big Trouble*, 348.
46. *Salt Lake Herald*, August 12, 1906.
47. *Silver Messenger* (Challis, ID), August 28, 1906.
48. *Daily Ardmoreite* (Ardmore, OK), November 2, 1906.
49. *Evening Capital News* quoted in Lukas, *Big Trouble*, 359.
50. Lukas, *Big Trouble*, 359.
51. Ibid.
52. *Daily Ardmoreite* (Ardmore, OK), November 2, 1906.
53. Quoted in Lukas, *Big Trouble*, 405.
54. Ibid., 406.
55. Ibid., 165.
56. Ibid., 166.
57. Ibid., 173.
58. Ibid.
59. Ibid., 174.
60. Ibid., 173.
61. Ibid.
62. Ibid., 196.
63. Ibid., 198.
64. Ibid., 199.
65. Harry Orchard, *The Confessions and Autobiography of Harry Orchard* (New York: McClure, 1907), 57.
66. Ibid., 200.
67. UMN Law, Darrow Digital, Haywood trial transcripts, Haywood trial, vol. 4, 2065-66 (pdf 486-87 of 544).
68. UMN Law, Darrow Digital, Haywood trial transcripts, Haywood trial, vol. 11 (pdf 508 of 714).
69. UMN Law, Darrow Digital, Haywood trial transcripts, Haywood trial, vol. 6, http://moses.law.umn.edu/darrow/documents/Vol_6_Haywood_Transcript_p_2840_3380.pdf, 2991 (pdf 154 of 545).
70. Ibid., 3046-47 (pdf 209-10 of 545).
71. Ibid., 3047 (pdf 210 of 545).
72. Ibid., 2992 (pdf 155 of 545).
73. Ibid., 3000 (pdf 163 of 545).
74. Allan Pinkerton, *The Mollie Maguires and the Detectives* (1877; repr., New York: Dover Publications, Inc., 1973). For Kerrigan's statement, see pp. 464-68; for Kelly's statement, 546-48; for Gowen's address, 509-41.
75. Quoted in Lukas, *Big Trouble*, 636.
76. *Birmingham (AL) Age-Herald* May 5, 1907.
77. *Evening Star* (Washington, DC), May 5, 1907.
78. Ibid.
79. Pinkerton, *Mollie Maguires*, 21.
80. *Salt Lake Tribune*, June 5, 1907.

14

THE SEDUCTION OF THEODORE ROOSEVELT

That we warn the courts and law officers of Idaho to be watchful of every move by James McParland, as we unhesitatingly declare that where there is a money consideration he will do anything no matter how low or evil, to accomplish his purpose. ... there is not to-day, in the United States outside prison walls, a more conscienceless and desperate criminal than McParland.

> Resolution, citizens of Parsons, Kansas
> May 1906

NINE DAYS after securing Harry Orchard's confession at the penitentiary at Boise, James McParland caught the night train to Denver. A fire onboard delayed his journey. In Denver, McParland put Orchard's confession to use.

At nine a.m. on February 13, 1906, McParland and his clerk met with Colorado supreme court justice Luther Goddard at the Pinkerton office. McParland's clerk read Orchard's statement aloud to the justice. It included the description of a bomb buried at

Goddard's own front gate. After lunching with McParland, Goddard went home and examined his gate. As Orchard's statement predicted, at the bottom of his gate the judge found a screw, the supposed vehicle for Orchard's trip wire. The next day at Goddard's property, McParland had Colorado's adjutant general Bulkeley Wells dig up an unexploded bomb.

"Then Detective McParland began to dig," Joseph Wanhope reported in *Wilshire's Magazine* that spring. "He discovered bombs placed here and there and everywhere by the 'inner circle,' and began to dig them up. Some years before he had dug up a suit of clothes on the banks of a Kansas river, in order to acquit a notorious criminal of a charge of murder, the finding of the clothes being evidence that the deceased had committed suicide. Two witnesses employed by him, who swore to the digging, went to the penitentiary for perjury, though the murderer was acquitted. This incident occurred in Parsons, Kansas, between 1881 and 1885, and is a matter of court record."[1]

Two days after McParland's men dug up the unexploded bomb at Goddard's gate, two men arrived in Denver via separate trains: criminal prosecutor James Hawley, Idaho's choice for the Steunenberg case; and James Mills, deputy warden of the state penitentiary at Boise. Mills had traveled to Denver on behalf of Idaho's governor, Frank Gooding. In his briefcase Mills carried requisition papers addressed to Colorado governor Jesse McDonald for the extradition of three officers of the Western Federation of Miners (WFM): president Charles Moyer, secretary-treasurer William Haywood, and former board officer George Pettibone.

Frank Cary, from McParland's Denver office, met Hawley at the train depot. Cary placed Hawley in a closed carriage and installed him at the Savoy Hotel, where the hotel manager waived registration. Cary advised the attorney to take his meals in his room and to stay off Denver's streets.

At ten the next morning, on Friday, February 16, McParland's group met at the governor's office. The gathering included Governor McDonald and Chief Justice William Gabbert, two additional alleged targets of Orchard's alleged bombs; Justice Goddard, whose front yard had yielded the unexploded bomb; James Miller, an attorney for the mining interests; and two state Republican Party leaders—David Moffat, a Cripple Creek mine owner and president of Denver's First National Bank; and William Evans, head of the Denver Tramway Company.

McParland summarized Orchard's statement for the group and asked for the extradition of the three WFM men. It would be, he advised, "'death to the case'"[2] to involve Colorado's attorney general. After hearing McParland's presentation, Governor McDonald agreed to sign Governor Gooding's request for extraditions. The papers would not, Colorado's governor said, make their way into the office of the secretary of state until the following week. By then, McParland would have secured secret passage to Idaho for his prisoners. In Idaho, Governor Gooding had moved forward with arrangements: the donation of a special train, with its passage given special priority.

The meeting at Governor McDonald's office lasted five hours. At its end, McParland had secured every tool he needed for the illegal transport of the WFM men. The group denied McParland only one request. They refused to grant the Pinkerton superintendent permission to drive the train himself.

After the group dispersed, Sheriff Alexander Nisbet of Denver, along with corporate attorney Williams, rendezvoused at the Pinkerton office. For the abduction of each of their three targets, Sheriff Nisbet assigned one Pinkerton operative and four deputy sheriffs. While this special force waited, McParland's aide-de-camp, Cary, supplied them with cigars, drinks, and a meal.

Moyer's abductors struck first. They grabbed the WFM president from a train bound for South Dakota's Black Hills, where miners were fighting for the eight-hour workday. A second group surprised Haywood at a Denver rooming house, in bed with a woman not his wife. A third seized Pettibone as he returned home after midnight.

The abductors installed all three WFM men in a secluded wing of the county jail on West Fourteenth Avenue. Word had leaked to the press, and reporters gathered outside. At 3:00 a.m., the jailers transferred their charges to the warden's office. From there, they hustled them out a back door and onto carriages, en route to the Oxford Hotel. At the hotel, they installed the prisoners in separate rooms.

At 5:40 a.m., the prisoners were roused and taken into the hallway, where special deputies waited with handcuffs and shackles. Ten minutes later, the WFM officers boarded Governor Gooding's special train. Boarding with them were Colorado's Adjutant General Wells, chosen as the train's engineer; Mills of Idaho's state penitentiary; and three Pinkerton operatives.

The train departed Denver. It hurtled through station depots, securing water from water tanks and changing engines only at isolated sidings. Though McParland remained behind in Denver, he had provided a lavish lunch for the captors and prisoners on board the train, including a hundred cigars, three dozen quarts of beer, and a quart of Old Crow bourbon. The prisoners ate while handcuffed. After lunch Adjutant General Wells, who held the keys to the cuffs in his pocket, gave each captive a tin cup full of bourbon.

The trip broke all records for speed for the Denver-Boise run. In less than twenty-eight hours, at 9:15 a.m. on Sunday, February 18, 1906, Governor Gooding's special train reached Boise. On reaching Idaho's state capital, Haywood mused: "'I am in the enemy's country.'"[3]

By Monday, news of the abduction had reached the newspapers. A report from Denver said: "public sentiment here favors Moyer and Haywood, because they were given no opportunity to combat the allegations. Legal authorities declare that the Idaho and Colorado authorities acted illegally and can be prosecuted for kidnapping Moyer and Haywood."[4]

In Denver WFM general counsel John Murphy, ill with tuberculosis, issued a statement from his sickbed. "'The case is clearly kidnapping,'" Murphy said, "'and the local officers, detectives and some others whom I will not mention conspired together to kidnap them. They were not even allowed a chance to test the validity of the extradition papers, nor were they allowed in any manner to notify their attorneys. Why, they could not even tell their wives of their arrest before they were hustled out of the city to a place where it is extremely doubtful whether they will get a fair trial.'"[5]

After signing the requisition papers, Governor McDonald decamped from Denver to Colorado Springs. When told of the night's events, McDonald feigned surprise. He had, he told the *Portland Oregonian*, "'no knowledge of a plan to spirit the men out of town.'"[6]

In some instances, McParland got the headlines he craved. "WESTERN DYNAMITERS RIVAL MOLLY MAGUIRES OF THE EAST," the *Minneapolis Journal* said. "COLORADO JUDGES MARKED FOR DEATH ... Man Who Broke Up Molly Maguires Says Labor Leaders Will Die."[7]

With the WFM officers safely behind bars at Boise, McParland's count of alleged WFM murder victims continued to rise. On February 20 McParland claimed knowledge of thirty murders committed under the federation's auspices. Among these, he described the June 1901 murder in a Telluride livery stable of nonunion shift boss J. W. Barney. This supposed murder victim was still alive. Ten months after his alleged demise, Will Barney had appeared in divorce proceedings in San Miguel County, Colorado.[8]

On February 22, McParland again expanded his list of alleged victims. "MILLIONAIRES ON DYNAMITERS' LIST," the *Minneapolis Journal* reported. "Denver Bankers Slated to Die, Is Latest Charge Against Western Miners' Leaders."[9] This list of supposed victims included Moffatt, the president of Denver's First National Bank who had attended McParland's conclave in Governor McDonald's office.

On February 20, at the penitentiary in Boise, WFM attorney Edmund Richardson met with Moyer, Haywood, and Pettibone. Richardson gave the prisoners their first knowledge of Orchard's confession. "They were very much amused," Richardson told the press, "saying it was a cock and bull story."[10]

Five weeks before McParland's midnight abduction of the WFM

officers in Denver, Murphy, the federation's general counsel, had sent a letter to fellow attorney John Nugent in Idaho. Murphy wrote, he told Nugent, owing "to the newspaper reports indicating that there was a determination to connect the Western Federation of Miners with the murder of Ex-Gov. Steunberg [sic] of Idaho, and also with the blowing up of a railroad depot in the Cripple Creek district a couple of years ago." Murphy told Nugent he had advised federation lawyers in Denver to secure "a reputable lawyer in Idaho to look after the defense of these men, so that they might not be the victims of a conspiracy, which I have reason to believe exists."[11]

Murphy told Nugent: "I wish to state that I do not believe there is any association of men in the world that is freer from criminal designs than the Western Federation of Miners."[12] Murphy's letter continued:

> Its officers understand that no organization can or should live, that commit unlawful acts; or to accomplish lawful things by unlawful means. Every day the organization is aiding widows and orphans. It is burying the dead who are killed in the discharge of their duties in the mines, and other dangerous places in which it is necessary for men to work for a livelihood. It is taking care of the sick, building hospitals and the like; and in all of its councils I have never heard any of its officers advocating crime; but, on the contrary, they have expressed themselves in a vigorous manner against its perpetration, and anywhere that it was known that the members of the organization might be likely to violate the law, a warning for them to desist from doing so, and staying within the law, has been sent. In Colorado large numbers of their members were arrested and thrown into prison and charged with heinous crimes. For the time being I was stunned and shocked at the terrible charges, and they came from such a high source that I thought there must be some foundation for them. And yet knowing the attitude of the organization against crime, I was compelled to believe that at least the organization itself would be found wholly disconnected with any evil doings of individual members. The

result has been that out of all of those horrible and terrible charges, not a single conviction occurred; but, on the contrary, some of the accusers of the members of the organization have found their way to the penitentiary on account of their own evil doings. ... In dismissing a large number of cases the district attorney admitted to me that he had no evidence but took the word of the attorney for the mine owners, that he had criminal evidence against the men so charged.[13]

Murphy continued: "Whoever murdered Gov. Stuenberg [sic] was a cold, cowardly rascal, and he deserves the full penalty of the law, and the Western Federation of Miners will have nothing to do with his defense. But when it is attempted to fasten black crime on this organization, that helps the widows and orphans of deceased miners, aids their sick member, builds hospitals, and endeavors to raise the moral and intellectual place of their members,-then it is the duty of the organization to step in and prevent any man being convicted by reason of the conspiracy existing."[14] He added: "the most stringent inquiry always showed the organization absolutely disconnected with any offense charged, and also showed that the members were victims of a conspiracy, and that the charges were made only for the purpose of inciting hatred and the ill-will of the public against the organization, and its members, for the purpose of accomplishing the evil designs of the accusers."[15]

Somewhere in Boise in early 1906, in James McParland's desk or valise or in the hotel vault of the Idanha, lay the document McParland hoped would execute the officers of the Western Federation of Miners (WFM). But bogus or authentic, fact or fiction, perjury or truth, Harry Orchard's statement alone would not hang the union men. McParland needed corroboration.

At age thirty-nine Steve Adams, a laborer with a "common school education"[16] from a Missouri country school, had worked most of his life. From age ten or eleven, Adams worked on his parents' farm. In his late twenties, he traveled throughout the Northwest doing farm, ranch, and railroad work. He dressed beef in Kansas City. In Spokane, he worked in a sawmill.

In Colorado's mining section, Adams hauled rocks. He eventually bought his own wagon and joined the Teamsters' Union. As a miner in Colorado, in a region aflame with anti-union fervor, he joined the WFM. "I was elected President once of the Miners' Union," Adams told Clarence Darrow, "but never served. I left there."[17]

In late 1903, Adams married. His new wife Annie, a widow, brought one son to the marriage. Six days after their wedding, an explosion at Cripple Creek's Vindicator mine in Colorado killed two supervisors. Adams, swept up in arrests of union men, remained locked up without charge or trial for ninety-three days. On June 6, 1904, when the explosion at Victor's Independence depot killed thirteen nonunion men, Adams fled the Cripple Creek district. "I was told there was a mob looking for me," he told Darrow.[18]

The explosion at the depot, fueled by more than one hundred and fifty pounds of dynamite fastened beneath the train station's platform, convulsed the region. It gave the mine owners license to declare open war on the union men. The Cripple Creek Citizens' Alliance, in concert with the Mine Owners' Association, threatened the local sheriff with lynching, installed their own man, and brought in one hundred deputies. After dragooning local law enforcement, the Alliance rampaged through union halls and stores, dumping coal over food stocks. They left a message signed "'Citizens' Alliance'" on a blackboard at Victor hall: "'For being a union man, deportation or death will be your fate.'"[19]

The Alliance deposed political office holders who belonged to the union or sympathized with it. They made mass arrests and crowded prisoners into wooden bullpens, rife with vermin. They prosecuted more than fifteen hundred men in kangaroo trials and deported more than two hundred of those they convicted, including a former judge and a former state attorney general. Six months after Adams left the region, Adjutant General Sherman Bell summed up the white heat that fueled Colorado's opposition to trade unions: "'Kill 'em—when one of 'em pokes his head up, slug it—shoot 'em down—exterminate 'em.'"[20]

In the chaos that followed the violence, numerous WFM men fled the region. Floods of men decamped to Denver. Adams left Colorado for Idaho and a possible homestead for his new family. He met up WFM executive board member Jack Simpkins, and helped Simpkins cut trails and sow grass on Simpkins's homestead. The two men also helped clear land and build houses for Simpkins's neighboring homesteaders. Eventually, Adams made his way to Denver, where he and his wife rented a small house. In Denver, Adams invited Harry Orchard, a fellow WFM member from Cripple Creek, to board in his household. As Ancient Order of Hibernian (AOH) men in Pennsylvania had done with McParland three decades before, Adams had unknowingly invited a cuckoo into his nest.

In February 1905 Adams left Denver for Park City, Utah, and a job in the silver mines. The following August Adams's uncle, James Lillard, telegraphed Adams to join him at his ranch north of Baker City, Oregon. Adams took up an adjoining homestead, and sent for his wife to join him.

Adams spent that late summer and fall "hauling a good deal of stuff from Baker City; improving my place."[21] He laid almost three-quarters' mile of thirteen-inch pipe, and installed a pumping plant for irrigation. He sowed two hundred and twenty-five acres of wheat.

On the evening of February 19, 1906, Adams returned from his granary and entered his barn lot. His uncle was away in Texas. As Adams walked toward the tool-house, three men confronted him: Chris Thiele,[22] of Pinkerton's Seattle branch; Colonel James Panting, a special deputy sheriff; and Sheriff Harvey Brown of nearby Baker City, the same man who had identified Harry Orchard after Steunenberg's murder.

Thiele asked Adams's name and the whereabouts of his family. Adams directed him to the house. "So he told those fellows to watch me," Adams told Clarence Darrow, "while he went in the house, and he went in the house and came back and he [hollered] he says, 'That is the man; take him in.'"[23]

Adams asked under what authority he was detained. "Sheriff Brown then handed me a fugitive warrant ... it had Steunenberg's name on it; something in connection with Steunenberg. ... We went in the kitchen and I changed my clothes, and I was put in a hack and taken to Baker City, Oregon."[24]

Adams's wife and two sons, one a newborn, remained behind at the homestead. Denied legal counsel, Adams spent the night locked in a jail cell at Baker City. The next morning, he demanded to see an attorney. Sheriff Brown complied, but denied Adams a private conference with attorney C. A. Moore.

Thiele and Brown then placed Adams in a closed carriage and took him to the train depot for transportation to Boise. Attorney Moore accompanied the three men. At the depot, Governor Frank Gooding's aide met them, holding Gooding's requisition papers securing the fugitive warrant for Adams's arrest. To Darrow, Adams described Moore's legal advice to him: "He said, 'I can hold you on these papers, but,' he says, 'I advise you to go on down with those fellows.'"[25]

Sheriff Brown told Adams he was being taken to Boise. "'If you go down there and do what those people want you to, you will come out all right,'" Brown told Adams. "'I am on the inside, and know what I am talking about.'"[26] Adams agreed to make the trip to Boise.

Late that evening Thiele delivered Adams to the penitentiary. "I was stripped and taken into the warden's office there," Adams told Darrow, "and then into a little room; stripped and searched and then throwed into the cell [with] that Harry Orchard."[27]

Adams gave the dimensions of the death row cell as about four feet by five or six. He described it as "a 'blind cell', what we call a 'sweat-box', or something like that; close, solitary confinement cell next to us." Adams stayed in that cell "six or seven days."[28] Orchard, a self-admitted Pinkerton operative, remained in the cell with Adams almost the entire time, leaving each day for an hour or two.

On the fifth or sixth day, at nine in the morning, the warden took

Adams from his cell to the clerk's office. There, for the first time, Adams met McParland. "'Steve,'" McParland told him, "'I am a friend of yours ... Harry Orchard has made a confession and he has implicated you in some crimes in this state ... you want to think of your family and your children.'" McParland added: "'you ... have got good people, and you have been well-raised.'"[29] Orchard's confession implicated Adams in numerous crimes, including the explosion at Victor that had killed thirteen non-union men and instigated the Mine Owner's Association offensive against labor. Orchard stated further that WFM officers had ordered that crime, along with numerous, heinous, others.

McParland advised Adams: "'what we want you to do is to corroborate Harry Orchard's testimony and help convict the officers of the Federation of Miners, Haywood, Moyer, Pettibone, St. John and Simpkins ... you do that and you will never be prosecuted, and I will see that you will come out all right; we will all stand by you.'"[30]

During the "Molly Maguire" trials, the prosecution had bribed infamous prosecution witness James Kerrigan with a beaver coat. At Homestead, the Pinkertons had plied their prospective star witness with whiskey, clothes, and cash. In the office at Boise's penitentiary, McParland handed Adams cigar after expensive cigar.

Darrow asked Adams of McParland's offer: "Did he say what would be done if you did not do it?" Adams replied: "He said if I did not do it, I would be prosecuted in North Idaho or taken back to Colorado and mobbed or hung there."[31]

As prosecution witnesses had done in Pennsylvania, McParland wanted Adams "to connect the formal chain of evidence ... to make a corroborative story with Harry Orchard's confession."[32] Adams told Darrow of McParland: "He said he prosecuted the Molly Maguires and hung twenty-three of them, by using them as witnesses that had actually done the killing themselves. He said that he paid them well after he secured these confessions, and they was never prosecuted."[33]

That first day, Adams spent eight or nine hours with McParland. When the warden came back, Adams was again "throwed in the cell with Harry Orchard."[34] Orchard kept Adams up most of that night, talking.

The next morning, the warden took Adams to see McParland again. This time the Pinkerton told Adams: "'This is the last time I will ever see you, the last chance you will ever get to save yourself.'" Adams asked what would become of his family if he corroborated Orchard's statement in court. McParland told him: "'I will stand by you, and I will see that you never are prosecuted on anything that you implicate yourself in in this state, and you will soon be back on your place on the little ranch in Oregon.'" Adams agreed to sign McParland's statement. He told Darrow he signed it to save his life. As to the statement's credibility, Adams told Darrow: "I have no personal knowledge of any truth in it."[35]

Adams described the taking of his statement in the clerk's office. "I would answer the best I could by what I had been told to say." If Adams's answers did not suit McParland, McParland corrected them. Darrow asked Adams "whether those answers had been talked over beforehand?" Adams responded: "They had."[36]

Prosecutor James Hawley unwittingly drew forth Adams's most damning testimony. "Well, I told him what I was to tell; I acted my part in the little tragedy," Adams told Hawley on cross-examination.[37] "If I failed to get this little story that I was to tell [just] right, he [McParland] would help me out."[38] Adams added: "he [McParland] simply got me by the nose and led me through; that is how it occurred."[39] Adams persisted through Hawley's questioning. Hawley asked: "And you answered these questions the way he [McParland] told you to answer them?" Adams responded: "The way I had been instructed to, yes."[40]

Adams continued: "If I got tangled up and got the story mixed a little, he would correct me." Additionally: "He told me that Harry Orchard had said in his confession, he had mixed me up in this affair, and he wanted to make evidence through this and use me as a tool."[41] Adams stated plainly: "He wanted to connect the Federation officials with all of these crimes."[42] As to the specifics of his performance, Adams said: "McParland took me through the whole thing." He added: "Harry Orchard was coaching me at night in the cell; all of the time in the cell."[43]

McParland and his stenographer spent an entire day taking down Adams's corroboration of Orchard's statement. A week later, the penitentiary clerk brought a typewritten statement to Adams. Drafted in narrative form by Hawley, the document needed only Adams's signature. The clerk, a notary, had also stripped and searched Adams on the night he entered the prison. Adams told the clerk that this written statement "was not anything like the statement I had given to McParland; that I supposed I would have to sign it in order to save my life."[44]

The penitentiary clerk, along with Warden Whitney and McParland, witnessed Adams's signature. Then he was "put in a nice little room"[45] on the penitentiary's hospital ward. Orchard joined him there. Pinkerton agent Thiele traveled again to the Oregon homestead and transported Adams's wife Annie and the couple's two sons to the penitentiary at Boise. This time, Thiele had no warrant. Prison officials housed Adams's family on the female ward, where Adams joined them every day for dinner. A few weeks later, officials moved the family, including Adams, to a small cottage previously used by the warden. "Harry Orchard came over and eat his meals there too," Adams told Darrow.[46]

Adams also met a few times with Governor Gooding. Gooding told Adams "that me and Orchard ought to stick together and go through with these confessions, was the only way we would ever save ourselves."[47] Gooding also sent Adams a message through Fred Bond, the convict awaiting execution. When Bond met with Gooding to discuss his own clemency plea, Gooding told the condemned man "'that if [Adams] did not tell what he knew, and what they knew he ought to know, they had evidence that would hang him so damned high salt peter would not save him.'"[48]

Through the spring and summer of 1906, prison officials held Adams and his family on penitentiary grounds without charges. Officials denied them visitors, including attorneys, except in the presence of guards. They opened Annie Adams's correspondence. They denied her "the right to come down to the city to do shopping, or for any purpose."[49]

In early September 1906 Steve Adams's uncle James Lillard, in Boise to attend the National Irrigation Congress, arranged to have dinner with his nephew at the penitentiary. When they met, Adams told his uncle he was being held against his will. He asked Lillard to engage legal counsel.

Clarence Darrow, in Lillard's confidence, secured the services of Idaho's former governor John Morrison, a friend of the murdered former governor, Frank Steunenberg. On September 7 Annie Adams, on the ruse of an emergency errand to buy diaper rash ointment, left the penitentiary and delivered an envelope to Morrison's law office. It contained this communication from Stephen Adams:

"'This is to certify that the statement that I signed was made up by James McParland, detective, and Harry Orchard, alias Tom Hogan. I signed it because I was threatened by Governor Gooding, saying I would be hung if I did not corroborate Orchard's story against the officers of the Federation Union of Miners [sic]. Witness Annie Adams.'"[50]

On the same day Darrow, along with attorney John Nugent, filed a petition at district court in Boise for a writ of habeas corpus. The judge granted the writ and set the hearing for the next day.

When Adams drafted his recantation, he was living with his family in the prison's female ward. Darrow asked Adams what happened to him after he asked for his liberty. "I was taken and throwed in the cell from which Bond had been hung," Adams said. As before, Warden Whitney escorted Adams to McParland in the clerk's office. "Mr. McParland tried to get me to go on through with that statement," Adams said, "walked up and down the floor, and lectured me all of the afternoon, for about two hours; to go on; was trying to make me change my mind, trying to scare me into it."[51]

Adams resisted McParland's threats. At some point during his ordeal, Adams told Warden Whitney: "'This case smells of hell.'"[52]

Adams held firmly to his recantation. On September 8, the judge granted his release. "STEVE ADAMS FREE A FEW MINUTES," the *San Francisco Call* reported. "Suspected Colorado Murderer Jailed Immediately After His Release on Writ."[53] Officials took Adams, now charged with the murder of Denver detective Lyte Gregory, to Ada County jail. "What became of that charge?" Darrow asked. "I was discharged on it," Adams said.[54]

Though the charge of Gregory's murder was eventually dismissed, the news of Adams's arrest took over the previous news coverage. Adams's charge, that McParland and Orchard had manufactured Adams's corroboration of Orchard's so-called confession, dropped from public view.

Adams's official arrest initiated a string of legal events. Charged, on the basis of Orchard's confession, with the murders of two Idaho claim jumpers and a Colorado mine superintendent, Adams would sit for two trials in Idaho and one in Colorado. Orchard's confession also fueled the eventual trials at Boise of WFM officers William Haywood and George Pettibone.

In October 1907, a Maryland paper said of Orchard's tale, as told by *McClure's Magazine*: "This man might almost have stepped out of the pages of some old, awful story or play, were it not for the fact that high explosives ... were almost entirely his agent."[55] A Vermont reviewer said that if not "for the tragic significance of this record, the reader might suppose he had blundered on a comic opera war plot."[56] From Detroit, a reviewer observed: "The story of Orchard is remarkable; that it failed to impress the jury in the Haywood case was due mainly to the bad character of Orchard for truth and veracity. He had lied and cheated and failed to keep his promises for years, hence little credence could be placed in his narrative."[57]

By 1907, the trials that flowed from Orchard's confession had made him a national celebrity. In 1908, the McClure Company published *The Confessions and Autobiography of Harry Orchard*. In 1914, Harvard Law Library placed Orchard's book in its collection.

On July 24, 1907, defense counsel Clarence Darrow addressed a Boise jury in the trial of Western Federation of Miners (WFM) secretary-treasurer William Haywood. "Gentlemen, I sometimes think I am dreaming in this case," Darrow said. "[A] man can be placed on trial and lawyers seriously ask to take away the life of a human being upon the testimony of Harry Orchard. Lawyers come here and ask you, upon the word of that sort of a man, to send this man to the gallows; to make his wife a widow, and his children orphans—on [Orchard's] word. For God's sake what sort of a community exists up here in the State of Idaho that sane men should ask it?"[58]

But by the first decade of the twentieth century, Pinkerton superintendent James McParland, in the pay of mining and financial interests, had become a one-man band. By riding the reputation he gained during Pennsylvania's "Molly Maguire" trials, McParland could seduce and cajole state officials throughout the West and Northwest. He could strong-arm, bribe, or threaten local sheriffs and judges. He could engineer state-sanctioned kidnappings across state lines. He could have men held in jails and prisons, even on death row, without habeas corpus proceedings. He could solicit, on threat of death, perjured confessions and perjured corroborations.

But McParland's manufactured evidence could not survive the scrutiny of three of the era's most effective defense attorneys: Darrow, Orrin Hilton, and Edmund Richardson. These attorneys knew the Pinkertons' reputation for treachery and violence. They knew that with their defense of WFM officers they put themselves, and their families, at risk. They moved forward nonetheless.

In May 1906, while Haywood, Charles Moyer, and George Pettibone remained incarcerated at Boise, the citizens of Parsons, Kansas, published a resolution. It stated: "While said McParland lived among us, he was of infamously bad character ... He, to the knowledge of our people, was engaged in the commission of almost all the crimes known to the criminal law." McParland's stay in Parsons, per this document, had taken place in 1886. Ten years later its citizens, including merchants, lawyers, and judges, said in published resolutions: "That we warn the courts and law officers of Idaho to be watchful of every move by James McParland, as we unhesitatingly declare that where there is a money consideration he will do anything no matter how low or evil, to accomplish his purpose. We caution all persons that have any connection with the trial of these men, that there is not to-day, in the United States outside prison walls, a more conscienceless and desperate criminal than McParland."[59]

Nine months later, at Wallace, Idaho, defense attorney Richardson tried to raise the Parsons matter in his cross-examination of McParland. The court refused to allow the testimony. As the detective left the witness stand, Richardson said to him: "'I have the affidavits relative to the Parsons affair.'" When McParland, challenged the lawyer, Richardson told him: "'I am not afraid of you.'"[60]

"The spectators cheered Richardson and hissed McPartland [sic]," the press reported of this exchange. "It was some time before order could be restored, and Judge Woods [sic] threatened to have the court cleared and fine the spectators for contempt."[61]

Two defense witnesses who agreed to testify on behalf of the Western Federation of Miners (WFM) met violent ends. "What has become of Mr. Smelzer?" Clarence Darrow asked Charles Moyer in the Haywood trial. Frank Smelzer, a WFM executive board member, lived in Silverton, Colorado. "He was killed a few evenings ago by an accident in Denver," Moyer replied. "On his way up to this trial?" Darrow asked. "He was leaving for Boise to appear as a witness in this case," Moyer said. "And he was killed on the railroad trestle, was he?" Darrow persisted. "Yes, sir, as I understand."[62]

A second witness, Oregon sheriff Harvey Brown, transferred his loyalties from the Pinkertons to the defense. Brown, present at Steve Adams's arrest, had encouraged Adams to "'go down there [to Boise] and do what those people want you to, you will come out all right. ... I am on the inside, and know what I am talking about.'"[63] A year later,

Brown switched allegiances. At Wallace, Idaho, Brown testified on Adams's behalf.[64]

Adams's trial at Wallace resulted in a hung jury. Seven months later, less than two months before Adam's scheduled retrial at Rathdrum, Idaho, Brown died at Baker City, Oregon. "BOMB FOR THE SHERIFF," the *Coeur d'Alene Press* reported. "At 10:45 last night, ex-Sheriff Harvey K. Brown was blown almost to pieces by a heavy charge of dynamite as he entered the gate at his home in this city."[65] Brown died the next day.

Newspapers claiming that Brown had given a deathbed statement rushed to blame the WFM for Brown's death. Brown's widow gave an interview to a United Press correspondent. An Oregon paper reported: "Mrs. Harvey Brown declares the Western Federation of Miners did not have a hand in the killing of her husband, but she believes she knows who did."[66]

From Spokane came this report: "Mrs. Brown talks wildly of fearing that the men who killed her husband will also kill her if she tells what she knows. At the same time she maintains that the miners' federation had nothing to do with the killing. She declares Brown was murdered as the result of some private business and that he had not been working on federation cases for six months prior to his death."[67]

Clarence Darrow said: "'The effort to make it appear that the Western Federation of Miners is responsible for the killing of ex-Sheriff Brown is in keeping with the policy of the prosecution in these cases to make it appear that the Federation is responsible for every crime in the west.'" He added: "'Brown has always been friendly to the defense.'" Of Adams's upcoming trial, Darrow said: "'Brown was relied upon as an important witness in the case.'"[68]

Adams's trial at Rathdrum began less than one month after Brown's death, without the benefit of Brown's testimony. James McParland served as a prosecution witness. No one was ever charged in Brown's murder.

When James McParland pursued his courtroom vendetta against the Western Federation of Miners (WFM), its membership extended east to Michigan, west to the Pacific Coast, north to Alaska and British Columbia and south, in the words of its president Charles Moyer, to "a few miles from the line of Old Mexico." Moyer added: "I can also say that we have a great many members working in Old Mexico."[69] More than twenty lawyers advocated on behalf of the WFM membership, numbering forty thousand at that time. The attorneys' efforts included cases argued before the U.S. Supreme Court. WFM aims included anti-child-labor and mine safety legislation, and the election of candidates who supported those aims.

At his trial in Boise, WFM secretary-treasurer William Haywood told Clarence Darrow: "The local unions of the Western Federation of Miners have in a number of places established hospitals." Haywood added: "We have some very good libraries ... it is very general in the local unions to establish a library."[70]

At Boise, Darrow introduced the WFM constitution into evidence. Adopted May 19, 1893, at Butte, Montana, its preamble advised "that all men are created to be free and should have equal access and opportunity to the enjoyment of all benefits to be derived from their exertions in dealing with the natural resources of the earth."[71]

The sixth object of the constitution's preamble struck directly at private detective agencies. Enacted a year after the battle at Homestead and just two months after Congress passed the federal Anti-Pinkerton Act, this clause sought: "To prevent by law any mine owner, mining company or corporation, or the agents thereof, from employing detectives, or armed forces, and to provide that only the lawfully elected or appointed officers of the county, state or province, who shall be bona fide citizens thereof, shall act in any capacity in the enforcement of the law."[72]

McParland had good reason to seek the destruction of the Western Federation of Miners. The sixth object of its constitution's preamble directly threatened his livelihood.

In arguments made at Boise on behalf of William Haywood, Clarence Darrow told the court, "this evidence from beginning to end has been marshalled [sic] and arranged and procured by the Pinkerton office, the Pinkerton detectives."[73] From the beginning of Haywood's case to its end, "there is nothing of this case but Orchard ... the rotten thread of Orchard's testimony and nothing else."[74]

As soon as the Western Federation formed, Darrow said, "the mine owners set to work to destroy it, and ... as one of their chief means of destroying it they hired the Pinkerton detective agency, with one McParland at the head in the West."[75] His client Haywood, Darrow said, was not on trial. The Mine Owners Association of Colorado had extradited the WFM officers to Idaho "that they might try and hang and execute and kill forever the Western Federation of Miners, and it is that organization and through them all organizations ... that is on trial in this court."[76]

Of the particulars of Harry Orchard's testimony, Darrow said: "I think it is a lie out of whole cloth, manufactured by the chief perjury manufacturer in this case, Mr. James McPartland [sic], and manufactured in his perjury office down in Denver." Darrow added: "McPartland [sic] ... told this fellow to swear ... a piece of testimony which is as worthless, as crooked, as valueless as any figment that ever went before a jury."[77]

When Darrow cross-examined Orchard at Boise, Orchard asserted: "Hawley and McParland simply told him to go ahead and tell the truth."[78] Courtroom deputies suppressed the laughter that followed Orchard's claim.

In the second trial of Steve Adams, the court at Rathdrum, Idaho, also warned spectators against indulging in laughter. "Didn't you tell him about king David?" Darrow asked McParland of his supposed religious conversion of Orchard. McParland replied: "Oh, yes; that was the spiritual part of the matter." Courtroom observers responded as they had responded in Boise, moving prosecutor James Hawley to protest "this silly and absurd method of laughing."[79]

Defense attorney Edmund Richardson argued at Boise on Haywood's behalf. Richardson asked: "Is there any man upon this jury so insane as to believe that forty thousand citizens of the United States of America, or four thousand, or four hundred citizens, or forty citizens can be made to combine in one criminal aggregation for the purpose of destroying life and property?"[80] Every WFM member had constituted himself, Richardson said, "a committee of one to preserve the peace and quell disturbance."[81] Such violence as the depot explosion at Victor, Colorado, "was the most suicidal, the most insane, the most idiotic, the most absurd thing that could happen to the Western Federation of Miners in conducting that strike."[82]

Of McParland, Richardson asked jurors at Boise: "Where is this terror to evil doers?" Richardson added: "I would like to have him here in this court room to hear the eulogy I am about to pronounce upon him." McParland, Richardson said, had "been held up in a sort of nebulous atmosphere as 'the great I am' that was connected with this case, and that back of it somewhere he was going to produce evidence that would astound the world."[83]

Of the dearth of McParland's evidence, Richardson said: "The seas have been combed, the land has been raked, thousands and tens of thousands of dollars have been spent, and when we come to this trial there is not a single scintilla of evidence that has been gotten to sustain Mr. Orchard's original statement which was made here by him, and by Mr. McParland in the first instance."[84]

In the trial of Steve Adams at Wallace, Idaho, Richardson described McParland "as a missionary of the heathen, as king and as chief mugwump of the gumshoe sleuths." He described Orchard as "a viper whose breath ought to have been choked off long ago."[85]

Orrin Hilton defended Steve Adams at his trial in Grand Junction, Colorado. All the "'cunning and trickery of the Pinkertons,'" Hilton said, had been brought to bear against Adams. Officers of two states had banded against him, "'with the most abandoned criminal organization of the country—the Pinkertons—using their every effort to hunt him down.'"[86]

Hilton told the jury: "'From the bunch of human jackals who

have been for three years hounding this man I want to hold up to your gaze the work of the Pinkerton Detective Agency. Don't you know perjury and false witness always follows in its trail?'"[87]

Darrow told the jury at Rathdrum, Idaho: "we claim that from beginning to the end the prosecution of Steve Adams is a humbug and a fraud; that there is not a particle of honesty, a particle of conscience or a particle of justice in the prosecution, from beginning to end. ... he is placed on trial for his life before an Idaho jury because he dared go back on McParland. That is what he is on trial for, not for murder."[88]

In the trial of Haywood at Boise, Richardson spoke to the jury of Orchard. If Orchard had indeed schemed with the Pinkertons in swearing away the lives of innocent men, "well might the soul which was within him, if he had one ... say, 'Out of your mouth you have condemned innocent men and that is a burden which should rest heavy upon your soul.'"[89]

Pinkerton superintendent James McParland, a quintessential con man, spent his entire professional life selling lies. During the trials of the officers of the Western Federation of Miners (WFM), McParland's efforts, along with those of his agents, seduced even a U.S. president.

During the WFM prosecution, McParland arranged for the transmission of Pinkerton agency reports, filed by one of his undercover operatives, to be sent via Idaho's governor, Frank Gooding, to Theodore Roosevelt at the White House. These suspect documents encouraged Roosevelt to link the alleged terrorist actions of WFM officers with those of Pennsylvania's supposed "Molly Maguires."

In January 1907, Roosevelt wrote to Lyman Abbot, editor of the *Outlook* in New York. "'I think the Western Federation of Miners is a body just exactly like the Molly Maguires of Pennsylvania,'" Roosevelt told Abbot. "'That there are a number of good, honest and stupid men in their ranks I have no doubt, just as I have no doubt that this was true of the Molly Maguires.'"[90]

Ironically, Roosevelt's prejudice may have helped gain Haywood's acquittal. A spate of correspondence, some originating from the Oval Office, helped place that prejudice in public view. It ignited a national response.

The initial controversy arose from a letter sent by Roosevelt to Congressman James Sherman of New York. To Sherman, Roosevelt described his ongoing spat with railroad magnate Edward H. Harriman. The contentious matter involved claims of political favoritism, with allegations of mendacity on both sides. Of the claim made by Harriman to Roosevelt of Harriman's own ability to manipulate the supposed pervasive dissolution within the Republican Party, Roosevelt told Sherman: "'it shows a cynicism and deep-seated corruption which makes the man uttering such sentiments, and boasting, no matter how falsely, of his power to perform such crimes, at least as undesirable a citizen as Debs, or Moyer, or Haywood.'"[91]

Six months later, in April 1907, the *New York World* published a letter written by Harriman that reiterated his allegations of corruption against the president: notably, that Roosevelt had pressured prominent Republicans for campaign contributions in exchange for political favors. Stung by Harriman's actions, Roosevelt offered the press his letter to Sherman sent in October 1906 that had identified Harriman, along with Eugene Debs and WFM officers Haywood and Charles Moyer, as undesirable citizens.

The publication of Roosevelt's "undesirable citizens" letter drew a response similar to that of George Baer's "divine rights" letter, published a half decade before. "ALIENATED LABOR PEOPLE," the *Evening Star* said from Washington. "Union Labor Wants an Explanation of Remarks About Moyer, Haywood and Debs in Sherman Letter."[92]

Labor organizations all over the country issued resolutions condemning Roosevelt's choice of language. From New York, the executive committee of the Moyer-Haywood Protest Conference wrote a letter of admonishment to the president.

Haywood, incarcerated at Boise, issued this statement: "'The president says I am an "undesirable citizen," the inference being that as such I should be put out of the way. His influence is all-powerful and his statement, coming as it does, on the eve of my trial for my life, will work me an irreparable injury and do more to prevent a fair trial than everything that has been said and done against me in the past.'"[93]

Haywood's statement continued: "'President Roosevelt is the leading exponent of the doctrine of "fair play" and a "square deal," but his reference to me in his letter to Sherman demonstrates that he does not practice what he preaches.'"[94]

A few weeks after Haywood admonished Roosevelt, the president issued another damning statement. This took the form of a letter written in response to a letter from Honoré Jaxon, chairman of the Moyer-Haywood-Pettibone Defense Conference of Chicago and Cook County. Roosevelt plucked Jaxon's letter from among the volumes of outraged protest he had received from similar groups nationwide.

Roosevelt, affirming his assessment of the undesirability of the WFM leaders, said to Jaxon of Haywood and Moyer: "'They stand as representatives of these men who by their public utterances and manifestos; by the utterances of the papers they control and inspire, both by the words and the editorials of those associated with them, habitually are guilty of incitement to or [apology] for bloodshed and violence.'"[95]

"ROOSEVELT STANDS BY STATEMENT," a *Los Angeles Herald* headline ran. "Says Idaho Prisoners Are Undesirable Citizens. With Emphasis He Repeats the Words Uttered Recently."[96] From Lewiston, three hundred miles northwest of Boise, the *Evening Teller* headline ran: "REITERATES STATEMENT ABOUT MOYER AND DEBS. In Letter Maintains They and Their Ilk Are 'Undesirable Citizens,' Together With Harriman, and Tells Why."[97] From New York, the *Sun* ran this headline: "ROOSEVELT CAN CALL NAMES. *DEFENDS HIS CLASSIFICATION OF 'UNDESIRABLE CITIZENS.'*"[98]

From Milwaukee, James Sheehan of the Federated Trades Council called on the country's laboring men and women to express their outrage. The *Los Angeles Herald* reported the movement launched from Milwaukee, "national in scope to set aside a Moyer-Haywood-Pettibone day early in May on which day every union in the country is to protest against the action of President Roosevelt in calling Haywood and Moyer undesirable citizens."[99]

On Saturday, May 4, 1907, two days before the scheduled start of Haywood's trial at Boise, working people across the United States responded. An estimated forty thousand marched in New York City. Headed by more than forty brass bands, along with fife-and-drum corps, thousands wore badges, pinned to lapels or blouses, that read "I Am an Undesirable Citizen."

In Chicago, event planners banned placards attacking President Roosevelt. But they had five thousand buttons printed stating "I Am an Undesirable Citizen." Proceeds of sales of the buttons, sold for a nickel apiece, went to the WFM defense fund.

One hundred thousand marched in Boston. The parade's chief marshal, Joseph Spero, addressed the crowd at Boston Common. Spero told marchers that abolitionists Wendell Phillips and William Lloyd Garrison, along with Jesus Christ, had all been termed undesirable citizens. He continued: "'It was the "undesirable citizen" who established the American Republic and it will be the "undesirable citizen" who will yet bring freedom to the human race.'"[100]

The good will that Roosevelt had generated with labor in 1902 with his sensitive handling of the Anthracite Mine Strike Commission evaporated in 1907 with his mishandling of the WFM prosecutions. Some of the blame for Roosevelt's myopia can be laid at McParland's door.

Despite Roosevelt's intervention, McParland's caseload against the WFM officers failed. The jury at Boise acquitted Haywood. When a second Boise jury acquitted George Pettibone, the court dropped all charges against Moyer.

At Caldwell, Idaho, a grand jury dismissed the charges against Vincent St. John. Steve Adams's trial at Wallace, Idaho, resulted in a hung jury. Adams's second trial at Rathdrum, Idaho, brought the same result. At Grand Junction, Colorado, under Orrin Hilton's withering defense, the jury deliberated for less than an hour before acquitting Adams.

Harry Orchard, convicted at Caldwell of the murder of Frank Steunenberg, was sentenced to death. On July 1, 1908, the Idaho state pardon board commuted Orchard's sentence to imprisonment for life. Governor Gooding served as one of three board members to recommend the commutation.

Though McParland lost in the courtrooms of the West, his powers of persuasion had duped one of the era's most influential men. The obtrusion of Roosevelt into the WFM trials, aided by Roosevelt's willingness to believe the Pinkerton tales, remains a singular feature in McParland's long and corrupt career.

In one regard Roosevelt's instincts, though skewed, proved valid. Pennsylvania's AOH men charged as "Mollies" did share markers with the WFM men. Those similarities arose not from shared terrorist agendas, but from distinct and powerful capabilities to rouse workingmen to widespread political action. In 1875 and in 1905, Pinkerton intervention in the form of faux prosecutions interfered with two such potent movements: one national in scope, and one international.

---

1. Joseph Wanhope, "The Haywood-Moyer Outrage: The Story of Their Illegal Arrest and Deportation from Colorado to Idaho," *Wilshire Magazine*, April 1906, 4, http://moses.law.umn.edu/darrow/documents/Wilshire_Mag.pdf.
2. J. Anthony Lukas, *Big Trouble: A Murder in a Small Western Town Sets Off a Struggle for the Soul of America* (New York: Simon & Schuster, 1997), 253.
3. Ibid., 270.
4. Reported in *Evening Statesman* (Walla Walla, WA), February 19, 1906.
5. Lukas, *Big Trouble*, 272.
6. Ibid., 271.
7. *Minneapolis Journal*, February 20, 1906.
8. Mary-Joy Martin, *The Corpse on Boomerang Road: Telluride's War on Labor 1899-1908* (Lake City, CO: Western Reflections Publishing Co., 2004), 142-43.
9. *Minneapolis Journal*, February 22, 1906.
10. *Salt Lake Herald*, February 21, 1906.
11. John H. Murphy to John F. Nugent, 8 January 1906, UMN Law, Darrow Digital, Bill Haywood trial transcript, vol. 9, http://moses.law.umn.edu/darrow/

documents/Vol_9_Haywood_Transcript_p_4042_4302.pdf, 4070 (pdf 31 of 263). Darrow offered the letter of John H. Murphy to John F. Nugent, dated January 8, 1906, as Defendant's Exhibit 24 during the trial of William Haywood. For Murphy's letter entire, see ibid., 4070-4073 (pdf 31-34 of 263).
12. Ibid., 4070 (pdf 31 of 263).
13. Ibid., 4070-72 (pdf 31-33 of 263).
14. Ibid., 4072 (pdf 33 of 263).
15. Ibid., 4073 (pdf 34 of 263).
16. UMN Law, Darrow Digital, Bill Haywood Trial – 1907, Steve Adams trial transcript, vol. 4, http://moses.law.umn.edu/darrow/documents/Adams_transcript_vol_4_pp_1552_2142.pdf 1573 (pdf 25 of 509).
17. Ibid., 1577 (pdf 29 of 509). Adams does not specify where this election, no doubt for a WFM divisional leadership, took place.
18. Ibid., 1579 (pdf 31 of 509).
19. Lukas, *Big Trouble*, 230.
20. Ibid., 225.
21. UMN Law, Darrow Digital, Steve Adams trial transcript, vol. 4, 1612 (pdf 64 of 509).
22. Chris Thiele bore no relation to the Thiel detective agency.
23. UMN Law, Darrow Digital, Steve Adams trial transcript, vol. 4, 1613 (pdf 65 of 509).
24. Ibid., 1614 (pdf 66 of 509).
25. Ibid., 1616 (pdf 68 of 509).
26. Ibid., 1617 (pdf 69 of 509).
27. Ibid., 1618 (pdf 70 of 509).
28. Ibid., 1619 (pdf 71 of 509).
29. Ibid., 1627 (pdf 79 of 509).
30. Ibid.
31. Ibid.
32. Ibid., 1630 (pdf 82 of 509).
33. Ibid., 1629 (pdf 81 of 509).
34. Ibid., 1633 (pdf 85 of 509).
35. Ibid., 1634 (pdf 86 of 509).
36. Ibid., 1635 (pdf 87 of 509).
37. Ibid., 1885 (pdf 252 of 509).
38. Ibid., 1886 (pdf 253 of 509).
39. Ibid., 1886-87 (pdf 253-54 of 509)
40. Ibid., 1887 (pdf 254 of 509).
41. Ibid., 1888 (pdf 255 of 509).
42. Ibid., 1889 (pdf 256 of 509).
43. Ibid., 1898 (pdf 265 of 509).
44. Ibid., 1636 (pdf 88 of 509).
45. Ibid., 1638 (pdf 90 of 509).
46. Ibid., 1640 (pdf 92 of 509).
47. Ibid., 1642 (pdf 94 of 509).
48. Lukas, *Big Trouble*, 295.
49. *Salt Lake Tribune*, September 8, 1906.
50. Lukas, *Big Trouble*, 334.
51. UMN Law, Darrow Digital, Steve Adams trial transcript, vol. 4, 1645 (pdf 97 of 509).

52. Martin, *Boomerang Road*, 283 (reported in *Industrial Union Bulletin*, June 22, 1907).
53. *San Francisco Call*, September 9, 1906.
54. UMN Law, Darrow Digital, Steve Adams trial transcript, vol. 4, 1646 (pdf 98 of 509).
55. *Democratic Advocate* (Westminster, MD), October 18, 1907.
56. *Barre (VT) Daily Times*, October 21, 1907.
57. *Detroit Times*, February 15, 1908.
58. UMN Law, Darrow Digital, Darrow's speech in the Haywood case, http://moses.law.umn.edu/darrow/documents/Darrow_Speech_Haywood_Case.pdf, 16 (pdf 18 of 116).
59. *Daily Appeal* (Carson City, NV), May 23, 1906.
60. Lukas, *Big Trouble*, 503.
61. *Salt Lake Herald*, February 22, 1907. See also *Los Angeles Herald* and *Billings (MT) Gazette*, same date.
62. UMN Law, Darrow Digital, Bill Haywood trial transcript, vol. 8, http://moses.law.umn.edu/darrow/documents/Haywood%20Transcript.pdf, 3777 (pdf 63 of 327).
63. UMN Law, Darrow Digital, Steve Adams trial transcript, vol. 4, 1617 (pdf 69 of 509).
64. In court testimony at Rathdrum, Idaho, Adams told Darrow that he had seen Brown "at my trial in Wallace." Darrow asked: "You called him as a witness, did you, up there?" Adams replied: "Yes, sir." See ibid., 1614 (pdf 66 of 509). This author's search for Adams's trial transcript at Wallace, Idaho, (including Brown's defense testimony) yielded no results.
65. *Coeur d'Alene (ID) Press*, October 1, 1907.
66. *East Oregonian* (Pendleton, OR), October 4, 1907.
67. *Spokane Press*, October 7, 1907.
68. *East Oregonian* (Pendleton, OR), October 5, 1907.
69. UMN Law, Darrow Digital, Bill Haywood trial transcript, vol. 8, 3772 (pdf 58 of 327).
70. Ibid., 3999 (pdf 285 of 327).
71. Ibid., 3744 (pdf 30 of 327). For WFM constitution and bylaws, ibid., 3743-3770 (pdf 29-56 of 327).
72. Ibid., 3745 (pdf 31 of 327).
73. UMN Law, Darrow Digital, Bill Haywood trial transcript, vol. 11, http://moses.law.umn.edu/darrow/documents/Vol_11_Haywood_Transcript.pdf (pdf 9 of 714).
74. UMN Law, Darrow Digital, Bill Haywood trial transcript, vol. 4, http://moses.law.umn.edu/darrow/documents/Vol_4_Haywood_Transcript_p_1583_2123.pdf, 2054 (pdf 476 of 544).
75. Ibid., 2065 (pdf 486 of 544).
76. Ibid., 2121 (pdf 542 of 544).
77. UMN Law, Darrow Digital, Darrow's speech in the Haywood case, 78 (pdf 80 of 116).
78. *Daily Capital Journal* (Salem, OR), June 10, 1907.
79. UMN Law, Darrow Digital, Steve Adams trial transcript, vol. 2, http://moses.law.umn.edu/darrow/documents/Idaho_v_Adams_transcript_vol_2_pp_506_1061.pdf, 909 (pdf 404 of 556).

80. UMN Law, Darrow Digital, Bill Haywood trial transcript, vol. 11 (pdf 320-21 of 714).
81. Ibid. (pdf 377-78 of 714).
82. Ibid. (pdf 377 of 714).
83. Ibid. (pdf 506 of 714).
84. Ibid.
85. Richardson's argument given in *Salt Lake Herald*, March 3, 1907.
86. For Hilton's argument, see *Grand Junction (CO) Daily Sentinel*, July 14, 1908.
87. Ibid.
88. *Montana News* (Lewistown, MT), December 19, 1907.
89. UMN Law, Darrow Digital, Bill Haywood trial transcript, vol. 11 (pdf 510 of 714).
90. Quoted in Lukas, *Big Trouble*, 387.
91. Quoted in ibid., 394.
92. *Evening Star* (Washington, DC), April 5, 1907.
93. *Los Angeles Herald*, April 7, 1907.
94. Ibid.
95. Ibid., April 24, 1907.
96. Ibid.
97. *Lewiston (ID) Evening Teller*, April 24, 1907.
98. *New York Sun*, April 24, 1907.
99. *Los Angeles Herald*, April 24, 1907.
100. Quoted in Lukas, *Big Trouble*, 480.

15

TWO POWERFUL MOVEMENTS

"But man, proud man, drest in a little brief authority, plays such fantastic tricks before high Heaven as make the angels weep." That's the way it was in the days of old Shakespeare. But it has grown a good deal worse than that since his time.

Patrick Ford's *Irish World*
New York, November 1878

ON MARCH 25, 1907, attorneys stood before Judge Fremont Wood at Caldwell, Idaho, to argue a motion for a change of venue in a Western Federation of Miners (WFM) case. Though Edmund Richardson, for the defendants, offered six hundred affidavits "alleging that defendants could not get a fair trial in Canyon county because of prejudice, and produced numerous newspapers to show the methods used to create the prejudice," the judge denied the defense's request.[1]

James Hawley argued for the prosecution. Denying the premise that defendants could not obtain a fair trial in Caldwell, site of the bombing of former Idaho governor Frank Steunenberg, Hawley shouted: "'This is a common murder case!'"[2]

Richardson countered: "'If this is a common murder case, why have the best lawyers in Idaho been employed to prosecute it, while the regular prosecuting attorney sits silent! ... why has $104,000 of the people's money been appropriated by the state legislature to pay these lawyers? ... why has [Caldwell], a mere village, become the cynosure of the nation's eyes, filled with reporters, detectives and lawyers? ... why has yonder jail become a hallowed spot to the working class of the nation and this court room an inspiration to the novelist and historian?'"[3]

Richardson continued: "'If this is a common murder case, why were the defendants kidnaped [sic] ... in the dead of night and spirited across an imaginary line that divides two great states? This is not a common murder case and no one knows it better than Mr. Hawley. This room, crowded with the citizens of Canyon county, knows, and the wide, wide world knows, that this is not a common murder case.'"[4]

Richardson spoke three decades after the mass executions in Pennsylvania's "Molly Maguire" cases. His assertion, "'this is not a common murder case,'" described that caseload as well.

An additional factor characterized the two Pinkerton caseloads. In both Pennsylvania's Ancient Order of Hibernian (AOH) caseload from the 1870s and the WFM caseload from the early 1900s, Pinkerton intervention, exercised at a critical moment, halted the progress of two seminal political movements.

In March 1875, Pennsylvania's Irish Catholic miners, with AOH and WBA men among them, traveled to Harrisburg to attend the Anti-Monopoly Convention. Their aims included a challenge to the company charter of Franklin Gowen's Philadelphia and Reading Coal and Iron Company. At Harrisburg, delegate Jack O'Brien also issued the call for a new national political party made up of U.S. workingmen. O'Brien lived in Tamaqua in Schuylkill County. Labor Reformer James Carroll, executed as a "Molly" in

1877, kept a tavern in Tamaqua that he had christened the Union House.

The *Harrisburg Patriot* said of O'Brien's presence in Harrisburg: "He is an Irishman of the true imported type, irresistibly captious during the last evening session. He desired the adoption of the proposition for appointing a committee to invite an immense conference of workingmen to convene at Cincinnati in July for national amalgamation."[5]

Of O'Brien's call for the Cincinnati convention, the *Patriot* said: "He won his battle like a hero on the resolution."[6] Four months after O'Brien issued his call, Frank Yost was murdered at Tamaqua. Two months after that, in early September 1875, John Jones was murdered at Lansford, five miles northeast of Tamaqua. September 1875 also brought the murders of Thomas Sanger and William Uren at Raven Run, less than five miles from Girardville, home to AOH delegate Kehoe.

By the time workingmen's delegates convened at Cincinnati on September 8, 1875, in Pennsylvania the prosecution's athletic conflation of AOH membership with supposed "Molly Maguire" terrorism had taken hold. This nativist campaign scotched effective AOH participation in the "national amalgamation" of workingmen into a new political party. At that time, AOH membership nationwide was approaching more than 700,000 members.

Three decades later, a *Los Angeles Herald* headline read: "ORGANIZE NEW LABOR FACTOR … Two Hundred Delegates Gather to Perfect New International Union."[7] On June 27, 1905, WFM secretary-treasurer William Haywood addressed delegates gathered at Brand's Hall in Chicago. Other speakers included "Mother" Mary Harris Jones of the United Mine Workers of America and Lucy Parsons, whose husband, Albert Parsons, had been hanged after the Haymarket conflict. At Chicago the women joined Haywood, Socialist Party of America leader Eugene Debs, and Socialist Labor Party leader Daniel De Leon to launch the new union called the Industrial Workers of the World (IWW).

Haywood opened proceedings. "'This is the first continental

congress of the workers of the world,'" he told delegates. "'We are here to confederate the toilers of this country into a movement that shall have for its purpose the emancipation of the workingmen class from the slave bondage of capitalism.'"[8]

The IWW hoped to create a massive union of workingmen who would own the means of production and distribution. The organization sought to organize workers by industry, overcoming divisions that had traditionally hampered widespread organization. "It is to be formed on the universal industrial order to take in every class of workers in any industry without regard to trade distinction," the *Los Angeles Herald* said. "The sympathetic strike that will involve every worker in any industry to accomplish complete stagnation and paralysis of business in the enforcement of its demands is the keynote of the projected union."[9]

At the Chicago convention in 1905 Haywood and WFM president Charles Moyer served as representative delegates for twenty-seven thousand WFM members, by far the largest workingmen's group represented. Six months after the IWW organizers met in Chicago, a bomb explosion at Caldwell, Idaho, took the life of Frank Steunenberg. The *Los Angeles Herald* reported: "Crime is Charged to Inner Circle of Coeur d'Alene Dynamiters, Whom He [Steunenberg] Prosecuted in 1899."[10]

In their ongoing war against the politicization of labor, the Pinkertons used the same game plan twice. As the prosecution in Pennsylvania's "Molly Maguire" caseload had used McParland's testimony to meld AOH membership with supposed "Molly Maguire" terrorism, three decades later McParland used Orchard's testimony to identify WFM leadership with supposed violence, anarchy, and dynamiting. Both Pinkerton caseloads, with their arrests, prosecutions, and lengthy incarcerations, halted massive, dramatic efforts at political organization by union men.

The net McParland dropped over the WFM officers effectively ended their organizing capabilities for a prolonged period of time. Haywood remained imprisoned from his arrest in mid-February 1906 through his acquittal in late July 1907. Moyer remained imprisoned for almost two years, through January 1908, when the charges against him were dropped. The twenty-one hangings in Pennsylvania in the late 1870s devastated AOH organization state and countrywide.

With both the murders in Pennsylvania in the 1870s and the bombing death of Steunenberg in 1906, violent death unleashed chaos that led to the arrest of influential political activists and the halting of burgeoning political movements. The timing of the deaths and the resulting, lucrative caseloads for the Pinkerton agency bolster the possibility that in these instances, Pinkertons operated not as agents of law and order, but as con men and commercial terrorists. Without violent death, the Pinkerton labor caseloads would not have existed. In these politically charged labor cases, murder-for-hire, not the provision of security services, may have been Pinkerton stock-in-trade.

As James "McParlan," the Pinkerton had operative had enjoyed spectacular success as the prosecution's star witness in Pennsylvania's "Molly Maguire" trials. There, jury after jury in five counties across the commonwealth's northeastern coal region had issued repeated verdicts of guilt against Irish Catholic men. Those verdicts had secured twenty-one executions.

Thirty years later, as "McParland," the operative used an identical plan for his western caseload. The Pinkerton scheme failed in the West as spectacularly as it had succeeded in the East. Though prejudice defined both caseloads, it took ethnic hatred to place ropes around the necks of twenty-one Irish Catholic men and strangle them to death.

"'It's prejudice that brought me where I am," Alexander Campbell told a reporter in 1876, ten months before his execution for an alleged "Molly Maguire" crime.[11]

[insert illus]

Shortly before Patrick Hester's execution, Hester told a reporter: "'my life has been sworn away to gratify a demand for blood ... the excitement against Molly Maguireism prejudiced my case beyond hope, nor can I procure a fair hearing before the Board of Pardons.'"[12]

Petitioners in 1877 said of James Carroll: "The evidence upon which he was convicted was of such doubtful character, that he would not and could not in any ordinary time have been convicted but the excitement prevailing at the time of his trial was very great against a society known as the Ancient Order of Hibernians and his conviction was procured through the prejudice and excitement against the society."[13]

[insert illus]

At his sentencing hearing in April 1877 for the supposed murder of Frank Langdon, John Kehoe told the court: "From the evidence against me I don't think it would be capable to convict me, but it was prejudice."[14]

"My Esteemed friend," Kehoe wrote to Quaker attorney Ramsay Potts one year later from Pottsville Jail. "Thinking over the Cruelties that has [sic] Befallen me.. By Bribery Perjury And Pregudise [sic]."[15]

"It has been said that corporations and railroad men are soulless men," a Richmond paper mused in March 1871.[16] Numerous observers from the era used similar language. In May 1871, the *New York Herald* printed an editorial titled "The Increasing Power and Danger of Railroad Monopolies." It said: "We have not yet seen or felt the full extent of the evils of these monstrous monopolies." Of the coal region conflict, the *Herald* noted: "The trouble between the laboring miners and their employers in Pennsylvania has thrown some light upon the grasping cupidity and oppression of the soulless railroad corporations." The column urged federal legislation "to save the country from the present evil and pending danger of railroad consolidation and monopoly."[17]

That same spring, in March 1871, AOH men in New York and Pennsylvania secured revised organizational charters. Based on a different law, their charters' preamble advised:

> These laws though human,
> Spring from Love Divine,
> Love laid the scheme—
> Love guides the whole design.[18]

In January 1875, as the region's Long Strike began, John Kehoe hosted New York's AOH officers at his tavern in Girardville. Kehoe's visitors included AOH national delegate Patrick Campbell. Thirteen months later, on Valentine's Day, Campbell gave an address from New York City. In it, Campbell said of AOH aims: "The majority of our people belong to the working classes ... they would often, when prostrated by sickness or accidental injuries, be reduced to the destitute condition of friendless strangers were it not for the intervention of benevolent associations of their fellow-workingmen, which in the hour of need come to their assistance, support them under sickness and the various trials of life, and, when the last hour approaches, consoles them with the assurance that the decent observances of Christian burial shall be provided for them, and their families, if they leave any to mourn their loss, shall not be without friends and helpers in their time of need."[19] The Irish Catholic benevolent order falsely accused of "Molly Maguire" terrorism by Pinkertons, railroad magnates, and nativist newsmen operated under this creed of brotherhood.

In March 1875 in Pennsylvania, miners' delegates gathered for the Anti-Monopoly Convention at Harrisburg. Delegate Jack O'Brien drafted a poem for the event. Harkening back to the "Sons of Liberty" who had gathered under Samuel Adams, Paul Revere, and John Hancock to plot the American Revolution at the Green Dragon Tavern in Boston, O'Brien's poem warned of two powerful forces that threatened the emerging American identity of the country's Irish Catholics: the tyranny of British capital over U.S. industry, and the destructive sway of an aristocratic Roman Catholic clergy. Conceived in Tamaqua, future burial site for Kehoe, the next-to-last line of O'Brien's poem carried a chilling presentiment. The poem urged:

> You sons of liberty awake,
> Your hearths and altars are at stake;
> Arise, arise, for freedom's sake,
> And strike against monopoly.
>
> Your American eagle is [not] dead,
> Again his giant wings are spread
> To sweep upon the tyrant's head,
> And down with usurping monopoly.
>
> What soul but scorns the coward slave;
> But liberty is for the brave;
> Our cry be Union or the grave,
> And down with usurping monopoly.[20]

---

1. *Scott County Kicker* (Benton, MO), April 13, 1907.
2. Ibid.
3. Ibid.
4. Ibid.
5. *Harrisburg Patriot*, March 5, 1875.
6. Ibid.
7. *Los Angeles Herald*, June 28, 1905.
8. Ibid.
9. Ibid.
10. Ibid., December 31, 1905.
11. *Shenandoah (PA) Herald*, August 29, 1876.
12. *New York Herald*, March 22, 1878.
13. B. F. Gickeson et al. to Pennsylvania Board of Pardons (not dated), James Carroll Case Folder. Death Warrants File, 1874-1899 (Series 15.21); RG-15, Department of Justice (Board of Pardons), Pennsylvania State Archives, Harrisburg.
14. *Miners' Journal* (Pottsville, PA), April 20, 1877.
15. John Kehoe to W. R. Potts, ca. March 1878, John Kehoe File, M 170.18 MI, Schuylkill County Historical County.
16. *Daily Dispatch* (Richmond, VA), March 6, 1871.

17. *New York Herald*, May 17, 1871.
18. *Report of the Case of the Commonwealth vs. John Kehoe et al.* (Pottsville, PA: Miners' Journal Book and Job Rooms, 1876), 167.
19. *San Francisco Monitor*, March 4, 1876.
20. *Harrisburg Patriot*, March 4, 1875.

16

OUR HEART'S BLOOD

... it would be more charitable ... to encourage brotherly love instead of sowing seeds of antagonism which sooner or later may lead to bloodshed.

John Kehoe
Girardville, Pennsylvania, October 1875

AFTER THE EXECUTION of John Kehoe at Pottsville Jail in December 1878, the Commonwealth of Pennsylvania hanged four additional Ancient Order of Hibernian (AOH) men: James McDonnell and Charles Sharpe at Mauch Chunk on January 14, 1879, Martin Bergin at Pottsville two days later, and Peter McManus at Sunbury on October 9, 1879.

The executions of McDonnell and Sharpe proved especially dramatic. In April 1878, both stood convicted for the 1863 murder of George K. Smith at Audenried. By the time of their convictions, fifteen AOH men had died on the gallows in Pennsylvania. The convictions of McDonnell and Sharpe rested on the evidence of three infamous prosecution witness: Charles Mulhearn, Daniel Kelly, aka "Kelly the Bum," and James Kerrigan, aka "Powder Keg."

At the close of Sharpe's trial, his wife sat with folded hands while the verdict was read, her lips moving in silent prayer. A Harrisburg paper reported: "On hearing the verdict, she sprang from her seat and rushed from the room crying in a loud voice, 'Oh! my [God], are you asleep?' She sat down on the back steps and repeated the exclamation while a large crowd gathered about her expressing sympathy. Her cries unnerved her husband, after awhile and he also wept."[1]

Others besides Sharpe's wife questioned the jury's judgment. The *Mauch Chunk Democrat* described McDonnell's conviction as "an outrage on justice." It added: "Because McDonnell acknowledged himself a Molly Maguire he was convicted. It is time here to call a halt. Heretofore there has been corroboration of the squealers."[2]

The *Mauch Chunk Coal Gazette* said: "The evidence against these two men was not of the character upon which men should be hanged." It reiterated: "Neither of these men ought to be hanged, and if they are it will be a stain on the great Commonwealth of Pennsylvania."[3]

Sharpe's defense attorneys, including P. J. Meehan, made strenuous efforts on his behalf. They deposed three new witnesses, presented the testimony to Judge Samuel Dreher, and requested a new trial. The *Coal Gazette* reported the outcome: "Judge Dreher, in an elaborate decision says the matter is entirely out of his hands, and he has no power now to act. He says if the affidavits had been before him when the original motion for a new trial was argued, he would have granted a continuance in order that the testimony might have been presented."[4] One week later, Meehan traveled to Philadelphia to ask Pennsylvania's supreme court to grant a special allocator to allow Sharpe's case to be brought before them. The court denied Meehan's request.

Kerrigan's testimony had already sent ten AOH men, including five officers, to their deaths. Kelly's testimony had sent three AOH men to the gallows, including two influential officers. If witnesses stepped forward now to impeach Kelly and Kerrigan's testimony, the integrity of many of Pennsylvania's "Molly" convictions and executions would be substantially challenged.

After Pennsylvania's supreme court refused to grant Sharpe's attorneys a hearing, Sharpe's counsel appealed to Governor John Hartranft. Hartranft granted both Sharpe and McDonnell a thirty-day respite. He did so, the *Mauch Chunk Democrat* said, based on Dreher's decision. Dreher commented: "'If the affidavit of [defense witnesses] Mundy, Quinn and McGill had been before the court in just their present form at the argument of the rule for a new trial, I would have continued the case to afford the defendant opportunity to take the testimony of these witnesses on rule and notice to the Commonwealth that it might be seen upon a full examination, tested by a cross examination, what weight and consideration should be given to their statements, and if the case was in my control I would do so now.'"[5]

Despite Hartranft's grant of the thirty-day reprieve, Pennsylvania's Board of Pardons refused to interfere. The *Tamaqua Courier* reported these last two "Molly" executions carried out in the interior chamber of Mauch Chunk Jail. McDonnell, white-haired and aged fifty or more, was married; as was Sharpe, aged about thirty-five. "McDonnell's neck was broken," the *Courier* said, "but Sharpe died hard. He drew his legs up till the knees rested almost against his stomach and struck out with them till the scaffold, firmly built as it was and strong, trembled. When he had done this twice, he was attacked with a tremor that shook him violently, and as he ceased and grew still the bell in the outer room began to ring fiercely. ... It was the messenger who brought good tidings, but came too late."[6]

Hartranft had granted the condemned men a second reprieve. The *Courier's* headline gave the macabre story: "McDONNELL AND SHARPE. A DOUBLE SWING INTO ETERNITY. THE REPRIEVE THAT CAME TOO LATE. *The Fatal Signal Given While the Messenger was Hammering at the Door—Consternation at the foot of the Gallows—The Innocence of the Hanged Men Strongly Affirmed.*" The *Courier* detailed the incident: "with the echo of the fall of the fatal trap there came through the long corridor the sharp ringing of the warden's bell. It was the messenger with the respite, but he came too late. ... No one inside suspected his great errand, and the dispatch was read by the Sheriff."[7]

As the sheriff read the telegram, the messenger, gasping, told the stunned crowd that it contained an order from Governor Hartranft to stay the execution. The information passed through the crowd in whispers. One of McDonnell's brothers, positioned at the foot of the gallows, cried out: "'It is murder. There hang two innocent men and their murderers are here in the crowd.'"[8]

As the bodies swayed above them, McDonnell's brothers John and Daniel, along with Charles Sharpe's brother Peter, swelled the general outcry. The *Courier* said: "they called in a loud voice that the execution was a murder, that the Sheriff knew the reprieve was near at hand and hastened his movements for that reason."[9]

"'It's not you I blame,'" one of McDonnell's brothers shouted out. "'Not you. It was the deputies, the murderers, who held the dispatch back. It's our heart's blood they're after. They want it all, and they will have it.'"[10]

Sharpe's brother said: "'there hangs as decent lad as any. He never thought of doin wrong, and there he is, murdered. Curses on them as did it.'"[11]

One of McDonnell's brothers cried out: "'Hell's curses upon Captain Linden, the murderer of my innocent brother.'" The second brother rejoined: "'They're in the bosom of God, but his soul will roast in hell.'"[12]

The *New York World* reflected: "The double execution at Mauch Chunk yesterday is a disgrace to public justice in the state of Pennsylvania. The demeanor of the men on the scaffold, their resolute and yet quiet protestations of innocence of this crime ... were things to stagger one's belief in their guilt. ... They were 'Molly Maguires,' they were arrested and arraigned at a time of great popular excitement, and they were condemned and hanged 'on general principles.'" The *World* added: "the Governor of Pennsylvania was willing in deference to one class of his constituents to see the men hanged, while in deference to another class ... he was willing to make a pretense of saving them.'"[13]

In an article headlined "THE GALLOWS HORROR AT MAUCH CHUNK," the *Boston Pilot* said that the evidence against McDonnell and Sharpe "was given by three men of notoriously bad character, each a self-confessed murderer." In their last moments, both McDonnell and Sharpe had "earnestly protested their innocence of any part in the murder of Mr. Smith." The *Pilot* added: "At the time of their conviction it was a very dangerous thing to be called a Molly Maguire—about as bad as it is for a dog to be called mad in the streets."[14]

The *Pilot's* coverage continued:

Nothing more disgraceful can be found in the annals of the gallows than the manner in which these lives were trifled with. There is blame, hot and blistering blame, to be placed somewhere. If the men were to be reprieved at all, they should have been reprieved in time. ... no attempt to execute the order was made. The whole business was a black and burning shame, a deep and lasting disgrace to all concerned in it. No right-minded man wants to apologize for the crimes of the Molly Maguires, — that is, for such crimes as they actually committed, — but are not the manner and circumstances of the last execution at Mauch Chunk a darker stain upon civilization than any outrage that the unlettered and desperate men of the coal regions ever perpetrated? And what if these two men had no part in the Smith murder at all, but were hounded down by a mob spirit as bad and as dangerous as that of the Paris Commune, simply because they were believed to have belonged to the Molly Maguire Order?[15]

---

1. *Harrisburg Telegraph*, April 22, 1878. The *Mauch Chunk (PA) Democrat*, April 27, 1878, quoted Sharpe's wife as saying: "'Oh, my God, my God, are you sleeping!'"
2. *Mauch Chunk (PA) Democrat*, April 20, 1878.
3. *Mauch Chunk (PA) Coal Gazette*, November 22, 1878.
4. Ibid., December 13, 1878.

5. Quoted in *Mauch Chunk (PA) Democrat*, December 21, 1878.
6. *Tamaqua (PA) Courier*, January 18, 1879.
7. Ibid.; italics in original.
8. Ibid.
9. Ibid.
10. Ibid.
11. Ibid.
12. This exchange reported in *Irish World* (New York), January 25, 1879.
13. *New York World*, January 15, 1879. See also Anthony Bimba, *The Molly Maguires: The true story of labor's martyred pioneers in the coalfields* (1932; repr. New York: International Publishers Co., 1950), 116-17.
14. *Boston Pilot*, January 25, 1879.
15. Ibid.

EPILOGUE

PENNSYLVANIA'S "MOLLY MAGUIRE" prosecutions unleashed far-ranging repercussions. By the mid-1870s, Franklin Gowen had destroyed all means of labor organization in Pennsylvania's anthracite coalfields. By the mid-1880s, with his conflation of the Ancient Order of Hibernians with so-called "Molly Maguire" terrorism, Gowen had decimated the organizing power of the AOH in Pennsylvania and throughout the country. Per official sources, AOH membership in Pennsylvania at the height of the 1876 "Molly" trials numbered "about 63,000 in Pennsylvania."[1] In 1880, one year after the last hanging, that number had dropped to seven thousand. Membership nationwide in 1876 numbered "over 700,000 in the United States."[2] Eight years later, the *Boston Pilot* reported: "The Order now numbers 114,698 in the United States."[3]

The effects of individual conflict, much of it tragic, also lingered. On June 27, 1877, C. Cathcart Taylor, a correspondent for the *Philadelphia Times*, interviewed John Kehoe in his cell at Pottsville Jail. The hanging of eleven alleged "Molly Maguires" had taken place six days before at Pottsville, Mauch Chunk, and Wilkes-Barre.[4] It was to Taylor that Kehoe described Gowen as a man of such grasping ambition "'that no obstacle, however sacred, was ever allowed to interpose between him and his end.'"[5]

Taylor may have witnessed Kehoe's ordeal on three additional, traumatic, occasions. On November 19, 1878, an unnamed reporter for the *Philadelphia Times* brought Kehoe the news that Governor Hartranft had signed Kehoe's third and final death warrant. On December 17, 1878, an unnamed reporter for the *Philadelphia Times* accompanied Mary Ann Kehoe, along with her children and Kehoe's father, to Kehoe's cell at Pottsville Jail, where Mary Ann informed her husband that his request for commutation of sentence had again been denied and that his execution would go forward. The next day, an unnamed reporter for the *Philadelphia Times* entered Kehoe's cell, described its contents, and recorded the details of the Masses said on Kehoe's behalf, along with Kehoe's belief in the intercessory power of the Blessed Mother. The reporter then positioned himself under the gallows to record the particulars of Kehoe's hanging.

Fifteen months later, in mid-March 1880, the *New York Times* gave this news: "A very sad case of suicide occurred here to-day, by which Philadelphia was deprived of one of its brightest journalists, and a gentleman whose reputation was more than local. About 9 o'clock this morning, Charles Cathcart Taylor, city editor of the Philadelphia *Times*, shot himself in the head, and died from the effects of the wound in a short time. Mr. Taylor had been in ill-health for a month or more, and his mind had become so much shattered that he had not been able to sleep for three months." The *Times* gave Taylor's age as "about 34 years."[6]

In late April 1878 Michael Donnelly, father of incarcerated "Molly Maguire" Christopher Donnelly, slashed his own throat with a razor. Michael Donnelly's son Christopher, a miner and AOH treasurer for Schuylkill County, had been elected school director for New Castle Township three months before his arrest for an alleged "Molly Maguire" crime. Three months after Michael Donnelly's failed suicide attempt, he died from complications from the wound. Coal and Iron police accompanied Christopher Donnelly from Pottsville Jail to visit his dying father.

In 1880 Robert Difendorfer, a Pottsville dentist and progressive politician, wrote to Pennsylvania's Board of Pardons on Christopher's Donnelly's behalf. Difendorfer had met with Donnelly frequently during his incarceration and found him "so far superior in conduct and gentlemanly bearing" that he wished to advocate on Donnelly's behalf.[7] Despite Difendorfer's appeal, Pinkerton operative Robert Linden recommended against Donnelly's commutation of sentence. Christopher Donnelly, an influential political operative and the father of a large and dependent family, remained incarcerated at Pottsville Jail for seven more years.

In early March 1875 John Swinton, chief of the editorial staff for the *New York Sun*, attended the Anti-Monopoly Convention at Harrisburg. At Harrisburg, Swinton heard the rhetoric and the resolutions, including "the abiding conviction ... [that] the potent and fruitful source of all those evils ... is that pestiferous outgrowth of brutal greed, the recognition and practice of the doctrine that money is value."[8] Swinton heard the convention's call: "'The purpose of this gathering is to give, in the very presence of our lawmakers ... organized expression to the conviction of the people of the commonwealth; that they, and not the great railroad and other corporations that have assumed it, are the rightful sovereigns in this state.'"[9]

Two years later, eleven days after the first mass "Molly Maguire" hangings, Swinton wrote to Pennsylvania's Board of Pardons. At the time, Swinton remained in his position as chief of the *Sun's* editorial staff. "I beseech you to save my country, and your state, from the terrible wrong and appalling disgrace of these executions," Swinton entreated the pardon board. "I beseech you to exercise clemency, which in this case I believe to be justice, toward the so-called 'Molly Maguires,' now under condemnation."[10]

Swinton's appeal to the Board of Pardons failed. Ten additional executions took place. Sometime after Pennsylvania hanged its last Irishman Swinton, as guest of honor, addressed his fellow pressmen at a banquet in New York. During Swinton's tenure with the *Sun*, the paper had provided some of the era's most virulent "Molly Maguire" coverage. Invited to toast an "independent press," Swinton told colleagues:

> There is no such thing in America as an independent press, unless it is in the small towns. You know it and I know it. There is not one of you who dares to write your honest opinions, and if you did you know beforehand that it would never appear in print. ... The business of the New York journalist is to destroy the truth, to lie outright, to pervert, to vilify, to fawn at the feet of Mammon, and to sell his race and his country for his daily bread. You know this and I know it, and what folly is this to be toasting an "Independent Press." We are the tools and vassals of rich men behind the scenes. We are the jumping-jacks; they pull the strings and we dance. Our talents, our possibilities and our lives are all the property of other men. We are intellectual prostitutes.[11]

Some participants from the "Molly Maguire" conflict thrived. In early 1875, Pinkerton operative Linden visited the federal arsenal at Rock Island, Illinois, to procure the explosive "Greek fire" for use in the post-midnight raid on the James brothers's family farm in Missouri. The James's eight-year-old brother died in the attack. Allan Pinkerton had verified Linden's supervision of the Missouri raid that claimed a child's life.

Four months later, Linden entered Pennsylvania's coalfields. His duties in the "Molly Maguire" caseload included drafting arrest warrants, overseeing arrests, overseeing the Coal and Iron police, overseeing the drafting of trial testimony and bogus confessions, and advising Pennsylvania's Board of Pardons. In October 1875, Linden traveled the region to inflame locals to vigilantism. When those efforts failed, the attack at Wiggan's Patch in December 1875, probably by a local militia, killed two of Kehoe's in-laws.

In August 1876, Linden gave perjured testimony during a "Molly Maguire" trial at Pottsville. In response to questioning by defense counsel, Linden stated: "I never had any oversight over the detectives that were investigating the James brothers [in the state of Missouri]."[12]

In 1878, the same year three prominent coal region AOH officers died on the gallows, Linden became superintendent of Pinkerton's Philadelphia office. Fourteen years later, Linden became superintendent of police for the city of Philadelphia. In 1898, when Linden married for the second time, Archbishop Patrick Ryan officiated at the cathedral in Philadelphia. From Bloomsburg, the *Columbian* reported Linden's remarriage. "He was one of those," it said, "who were largely instrumental in breaking up the Mollie Maguires, and bringing the guilty men to justice."[13] On Linden's death in 1904, the *New York Sun* said: "Linden's greatest exploit was the running down of the Molly Maguires, the gang of cut-throats, which for years maintained a reign of terror in the coal regions of the State."[14]

In June 1909 Alexander McClure, the Philadelphia newsman of Scotch-Irish descent who had so desired John Kehoe's execution, died at age eighty-one at his home in Wallingford, Pennsylvania. Newspapers countrywide eulogized McClure as Abraham Lincoln's ally. A notice from Colorado applauded McClure's "very purifying and beneficent influence over the country" through the pages of the *Philadelphia Times*, for that publication, the account noted, "was a paper without a muzzle."[15]

Another account of McClure's death noted his "inability to stay hitched to a party machine."[16] Vacillation also marked McClure's regional affections. A news account from Tupelo, Mississippi, lauded this Republican who had helped place Lincoln in presidential office as "a staunch republican, but ... at all times a friend to the south."[17] From Birmingham, Alabama, came a similar tribute: "Colonel McClure was always looked upon as a staunch friend of the south."[18] In his politics, his regional affiliations, and his consuming hatred for Kehoe, McClure remains an enigma.

Like McClure, James Frederick Wood, archbishop of Philadelphia, also used extreme efforts to paint anthracite region AOH men as murderous. In December 1875, two weeks after the raid at Wiggan's Patch, Wood issued his pastoral letter. Addressed from

"James Frederick, by the grace of God and the favor of the Apostolic See, Archbishop of Philadelphia *To the venerable Clergy and the beloved People of the Laity*," the document condemned by excommunication all members of numerous so-called secret societies, including "the Masons, Odd Fellows, Sons of Temperance ... the National Brotherhood ... the Fenian Brotherhood ... and the Mollie Maguires, otherwise the Ancient Order of Hibernians, or the Buckshots and various others whose spirit is equally objectionable and whose names seem to be selected rather to conceal than to indicate the object of their association."[19]

Wood's condemnation of AOH men as "Molly Maguire" terrorists greatly assisted the trials' prosecution. The archbishop's animus lasted beyond the last "Molly Maguire" hanging in October 1879. In March 1880, on the announcement that Pennsylvania's AOH men would hold their national convention in Philadelphia, Wood again issued his circular letter censuring the order. "'While the Archbishop of Philadelphia has denounced the order," AOH state delegate McCardle said of Wood's action, "'few, if any, other prelates have condemned it.'"[20]

In May 1880, a few weeks after AOH men from all over the country gathered for their convention in Philadelphia, Wood presided over the first Provincial Council of the Province of Pennsylvania, also held in Philadelphia. The council lasted a week. At its conclusion, Wood oversaw the transmission of its acts to Rome for Pope Leo XIII's approval. The council's acts included a request for papal condemnation of the AOH.

"Should the Council declare against the Hibernians," the *New York Times* said, "as it undoubtedly will, it will create great dissatisfaction among the members of the Ancient Order, who regard Archbishop Wood as their enemy. They are under the impression that his opposition to them comes from his personal prejudice rather than his ecclesiastical zeal, and this is to some extent accounted for by the fact that he is not an Irishman, and cannot sympathize with the wishes and desires of the Irish people."[21] Despite Wood's athletic efforts, no papal condemnation of the AOH ever issued from Rome.

Epilogue | 411

The *New York Tribune* reported Wood's death in 1883. An unnamed reporter said of the archbishop: "about twenty-one years ago I went to his palace, or house, after the consecration of part of the Philadelphia cathedral near Logan Square, and sat down to a good table d'hôte with priests and publicans, in which good sherry wine was a feature. Near this house was a bank for his parishioners, where they kept their savings. It now seems that he had formerly been a banker at Cincinnati. The Protestant priests had to go occasionally to this bank in Philadelphia, as executors or employers, to settle the accounts of their Irish servants, and Bishop Wood regaled them cordially as old fellow-Methodists; for he had been a convert to Rome."[22]

Parish priest Daniel McDermott, Wood's standard-bearer in the coal regions during the "Molly Maguire" trials, also nursed a life-long animus against the AOH. In 1908, almost thirty years after the last "Molly" hanging, McDermott, as pastor of St. Mary's Church in Philadelphia, refused AOH men permission to hold a funeral for an AOH member with Hibernian lodges in attendance. McDermott's action made headlines nationwide. He had in his possession, he said, important and inflammatory information gotten "directly from the condemned Molly Maguires themselves." McDermott added: "No power on earth will ever make me recede one inch from my stand against the Hibernians."[23]

In 1884, one year after Wood's death, McDermott had tried to press a case against the AOH before the Third Plenary Council of Baltimore. The council, made up of bishops from across the United States, had refused McDermott's request. Decades later, in 1908, the *Catholic Transcript* said from Hartford: "'Father McDermott ... may not be a man of one idea, but he has treasured up one idea for many long years.'" Of the Plenary Council's long-ago refusal to hear McDermott, the *Transcript* said: "'He was not permitted to make his charge before that august body and he seems to have suffered from mental indigestion ever since.'"[24]

From Minneapolis in 1908, the *Irish Standard* said of McDermott's refusal to allow the AOH burial Mass at St. Mary's Church:

"The Rev. D. L. [sic] McDermott, rector of one of the Philadelphia parishes, belongs to that class of men who have a hobby and who allow a hobby to master them."[25] From Kentucky, the *Irish American* said: "The most charitable view to take of Father McDermott is that he is laboring under a great mental hallucination, brought on perhaps by overwork.'"[26]

The animus of McDermott and Wood against the AOH stood in marked contrast to the empathy shown to the order's men by John Purcell, archbishop of Cincinnati. In 1857, Purcell had officiated at Wood's consecration as bishop. In 1865, both Wood and Purcell had issued cards condemning the Fenians.

But five months before the last "Molly Maguire" execution, when the AOH held its national convention in May 1879 in Cincinnati, Purcell celebrated a Mass for delegates at the cathedral. "After mass," the *New York Times* said, "the Archbishop addressed the delegates. He thanked God that the order, though during the past years abused, slandered, and reviled, had proved itself to be composed of true men, good and faithful members of society, as well as law-abiding citizens. The Archbishop said he had an abiding faith in the society, and was glad to see that other prominent ecclesiastics in the country were now of the same opinion."[27]

In August 1876, as "Molly" trials remained ongoing, "a clergyman connected with a prominent church in Ohio" had addressed a group of AOH men in Philadelphia. Newspaper coverage gave neither the name of the priest nor the name of his church. The *Shenandoah Herald* ran the story under the headline: "A Jolly 'Hibernian' Row in Philadelphia ... An Ohio Priest Goes for Archbishop Wood." This unnamed priest condemned Wood's excommunication of AOH men. "My bishop," the Ohio priest said, "through the official organ of his diocese, pronounced the action of the Philadelphia hierarchy as an injustice that was only worthy of the despot of Russia."[28]

Archbishop John Purcell's brother, Rev. Edward Purcell, served as an editor of the *Catholic Telegraph*, the official organ of the Archdiocese of Cincinnati. If John Purcell was the Ohio bishop who characterized Wood's actions as royally despotic, that comment would likely have appeared in Cincinnati's diocesan newspaper. Today, the *Catholic Telegraph* from that era can be viewed online. But before the newspaper was filmed, someone taped sheets of white paper over much of the newspaper's coverage from the dates surrounding the so-called "Molly Maguire" events.[29] Much of this coverage has been rendered unreadable.

Another dramatic erasure of history took place at St. Joseph's Catholic Church in Summit Hill, Pennsylvania. In 1878, local papers described the tombstone of alleged "Molly" Alexander Campbell, carved to mark his grave at St. Joseph's cemetery. "This stone," one account said, "is over seven feet in height, plain finish, with Gothic cross on the top and representation of the Crucifixion."[30] A second account said: "It bears the simple inscription of 'Campbell,' in heavy raised letters ... Campbell's monument weighs a ton."[31]

More than a century later Campbell's great-nephew, Patrick Campbell, visited St. Joseph's while working on his manuscript for *A Molly Maguire Story*. Father Jones walked Campbell through the old graveyard. No tombstones remained. Jones told Campbell: "'the graveyard was too hard to maintain, and there was vandalism. The Alec Campbell tombstone was knocked down several times, and so were the tombstones of other executed Mollies who are buried here.'" The priest added: "'We find garbage thrown here from time to time. So, one of my predecessors laid the tombstones down flat and covered everything with sod.'"[32]

A cross also marked the tombstone of alleged "Molly Maguire" Patrick Hester, buried at St. Mary's Cemetery in Mount Carmel. An account from 1878 said: "The headstone is of Gothic design, with a heavy wreath encircling a rustic cross, beneath which is the inscription in raised letter, surrounded by a heavy raised panel. On the top of the headstone is placed a Gothic cross. The stone rests on a heavy moulded base."[33]

Religious iconography also distinguished the headstone of alleged "Molly Maguire" John Kehoe at St. Jerome's Catholic Cemetery in Tamaqua. A stone carving, "Sacred to the memory of John Kehoe," depicts a hand grasping a cross. "May his soul rest in peace," the inscription reads. "Whilst in this silent grave I sleep, / My soul to God I give to keep."

On his bookshelf at Pottsville Jail, Kehoe kept a biography of St. Alphonsus Liguori, the Italian monk who founded the Redemptorist Order to minister to the poor. Alongside the biography of St. Alphonsus, Kehoe kept a treatise from the 1798 Irish Rebellion. This document, titled *The Poor Man's Catechism*, also contained articles of faith. "I BELIEVE in the IRISH UNION," the treatise began, "in the supreme majesty of the people, in the equality of man, in the lawfulness of the insurrection, and of resistance to oppression. I believe in a revolution founded on the rights of man, in the natural and imprescriptable [sic] right of *all* the Irish citizens to all the land."[34]

"The Almighty intended all mankind to lord the soil," the *Catechism* said. It added: "surely it is unfair that one or one hundred should hold in their hands those necessaries which none ought to want; it is not possible that God can be pleased to see a whole nation depending on the caprice and pride of a small faction, who can deny the common property in the land to his people, or at least tell them, how much they shall eat, and what kind; and how much they shall wear, and what kind."[35]

Less than a year after Kehoe's execution, and eight decades after the treatise's publication, Patrick Ford of the *Irish World* spoke with a *New York Herald* reporter on the issue of Home Rule in Ireland. Ford's comments to the *Herald* reporter reflect a merging of politics and religiosity; a potent and sweeping blend that if embraced by the AOH in Pennsylvania may have foretold the order's destruction on the commonwealth's gallows. Ford told the reporter: "'the Irish mind is undergoing a change on this land question. The idea is beginning to take hold of the people that the natural gifts of God—land, air, light and water—are things not to be bought or sold; that these things are the free gifts of the Creator to the whole human family; that reason and Scripture unite on this point; that nothing is a man's own property absolutely except it be the result of his labor, and that, therefore, all the improvements, all the man-created wealth in Ireland to-day is the property of the tiller of the soil.'"[36]

Ford, publisher of the *Irish World* in New York, was an AOH member. Equally revolutionary with Ford's description of God's natural gifts belonging to all of the human family were Ford's criticisms of the installment of Roman Catholic clergy in the United States with titles based on European nobility. "A true conversion to Christianity implies also a democratic spirit," Ford wrote in an editorial published in April 1875, one month after John McCloskey of New York became the first Roman Catholic U.S. cardinal. "We had hoped that here in the United States, at least,—where the Church was free from all entangling alliances with kings or hereditary aristocracies,—the Faith would flourish, and Religion would grow in purity and strength."[37]

In the same editorial, Ford asked: "Will His Eminence, Cardinal McCloskey, introduce amongst us the Old World style and fashion? It would seem this is to be. Immediately after the fact of his elevation to that dignity was made known, a pair of splendid black horses, and a magnificent coach bearing his coat-of-arms, were ordered for him. The cost was ... Five thousand five hundred dollars for a parade equipage! As much as a poor workingman, at $10 a week, could make in eleven years."[38] Given the hostility of a number of nineteenth-century clergy to the AOH, the issue of whether other AOH men shared Ford's views on the perils of an aristocratic clergy deserves consideration.

As an AOH member, Ford likely attended the 1875 national AOH meeting held in New York City. Kehoe, who hosted AOH national officers at Girardville in January 1875, attended the New York meeting that spring as delegate for Schuylkill County. Ford's passionate comments on Kehoe's case suggest the publisher may have known Kehoe personally. Unable to halt the ongoing parade of public strangulations of AOH men in Pennsylvania, and furious with the floods of sensational press coverage, Ford vented his outrage in the pages of the *Irish World*.

In October 1878, while Pennsylvania's Board of Pardons debated

Kehoe's case, Ford published the editorial "Judicial Murder Games in Pennsylvania." It said: "Now the murderous Court of Pardons holds a great many irresolute meetings—afraid to commit more judicial murders, yet their blood-thirsty natures holding on to the victim, watching the political sky to see if it will, or will not, burst on their guilty heads. There is not a State in the Union but has suffered hard and heavily by the political thieves. Pennsylvania has suffered more than them all from her political murderers."[39]

Ten days after Kehoe's execution, Ford observed: "'Jack' died with all the coolness and courage of one of the old Christian martyrs." The newsman concluded: "Never in the worst days of the dark ages did the ferocity of man's vile nature show itself more virulent than it has now shown itself in the judicial murder of this unfortunate victim, Kehoe. Victim of the atrocious Coal Corporations in order to break down all opposition to starvation wages. Every falsehood uttered by the mercenary tools of Gowen, liveried in his Coal and Iron Police, is echoed through the thousand mouths of the foul, lying, mercenary press."[40]

A few weeks later, Ford published the editorial "Judicial Murder of John Kehoe." Of the prosecution's conflation of AOH men with alleged terrorism, Ford said: "From the first it was easily seen that there was no organization except the A. O. H. to which was fastened the murderous name that brought on the hanging of so many innocent men." Of the statement of Attorney General Lear, "'My hands are washed of Kehoe's blood,'" Ford said: "Those words are a death sentence to the reputation of every official man engaged in compassing the death of John Kehoe."[41]

A few weeks after that, Ford mused on the punishment of death by hanging. "Men tell you everywhere that torture is abolished," he said. "It is not abolished. ... We have followed [England's] example in this modern crucifixion ... Here we remit the brutal work to ignorant blundering Sheriffs and Deputy Sheriffs to hang up the unfortunates whom our English system of disinheritance has made, to die almost invariably, by strangulation. What [those] unfortunates feel as an eternity of torture before they are permitted to die!"[42]

To date, no historian has documented the "Molly Maguire" cases in western Pennsylvania. In February 1878 Pinkerton's "Molly Maguire" juggernaut rolled into the bituminous coal region when the commonwealth arrested thirteen men at Westmoreland County's Irwin Station for the murder of Joseph Carroll. Carroll's body was "placed on the railroad track, where it was discovered at daylight, mangled and torn."[43] In June 1878, with the arrest of Henry Devlin on the same charge, an unnamed Pinkerton detective made the arrests.[44] Per the *New York Times*, the Carroll defendants had "organized and conducted the strikes" in area coal mines.[45] The disposition of the Joseph Carroll case is not known.

In April 1878 an almost identical script played out in Allegheny County, also in the western soft coal region. The commonwealth arrested seven miners for the 1874 murder of John Oatman, a mine superintendent from Williams Township. The *Pittsburgh Telegraph* reported: "It is alleged that the Mollie Maguires and Ancient Order of Hibernians resolved in secret session to get Oatman out of the way, and it is also claimed that the prisoners are all Mollies."[46] The jury in Oatman acquitted Robert Donegan, the first defendant tried. No additional trials appear to have taken place.

Pinkerton operative Linden continued his arrests of AOH men as supposed "Molly Maguires" into the 1880s. In 1881, Linden's detective work led to the arrests of eight Irishmen in Pennsylvania's Fayette County for the murder of Maurice Healy. In this instance, Linden's efforts secured at least one conviction, when a jury at Uniontown convicted Patrick Dolan of murder in the second degree. The judge sentenced Dolan to eleven years' imprisonment. As with all of the commonwealth's eastern "Molly Maguire" cases, the evidence against Dolan in western Pennsylvania was "entirely of a circumstantial character."[47]

In February 2021, Henry Louis Gates Jr.'s PBS program *Finding Your Roots* gave yet another clue into the Pinkertons' activity as their "Molly Maguire" caseload, and the cash it generated for the agency, shrank into nothingness. In a segment titled "No Irish Need Apply," Gates hosted comedian Jim Gaffigan. In the latter part of the segment, Gates informed Gaffigan that the show's researchers had discovered that Gaffigan's great-great-uncle, Michael Gaffigan, had been accused of a "Molly Maguire" crime.

Further research into Michael Gaffigan's case both shows the persistence of the Pinkerton campaign against Pennsylvania's AOH men and the ongoing pushback against the Pinkertons' efforts. Sometime in 1878 Pennsylvania's governor John Hartranft, firmly in the sway of the Pinkertons, requested the extradition from Illinois of two AOH men, Michael Gaffigan and William Merrick, for the 1865 murder of Michael Durkin at Saint Clair in Pennsylvania's Schuylkill County. A widely distributed news report said of the accused men: "Proof of their murdering Michael Durkin in '65 is abundant."[48]

"These are not the only Molly-Maguire murderers that are wanted," the *Chicago Tribune* reported the following month, one month after John Kehoe's execution. It added: "In Illinois, Ohio, and San Francisco, a detective force, under one of the most experienced and astute members of the corps of the Pinkerton Agency, is on the track of other red-handed Mollies. Among the detectives who have gone into that section of the country, to hunt down the infamous members of that terrible organization, is the celebrated Mollie-Maguire detective, James McParlan, otherwise known as James McKenna."[49]

The Pinkerton vendetta against Gaffigan and Merrick likely failed. A Pottsville dispatch from late December 1878 noted: "Gov. [Cullom] of Illinois, under pressure from the Ancient Order of Hibernia of the latter State, has withdrawn his order of arrest, and refuses to deliver to the Pennsylvania officers the two murderers ... for whom Gov. Hartranft issued a requisition."[50] In this instance, Illinois's AOH men may have prevailed against the dubious Pinkerton accusations.

Under Allan Pinkerton's sons William and Robert, the detective agency continued its assaults against labor. In 1890, protests rang out against Pinkerton violence committed against strikers on the New York Central Railroad. Terence Powderly, president of the Knights of Labor, said in a public appeal: "The orderly and law-abiding conduct of the men on strike has won the admiration of the public, and yet the best feelings of the community have been outraged by the introduction of an armed force under command of Robert Pinkerton, a man who holds no commission from the State or nation to recruit or arm men for military duty."[51]

Of the Pinkertons' recruitment methods, Powderly said: "During this strike Robert Pinkerton is the agent of that railroad company. He advertises for men ... Apparently the brute alone is sought for, and such creatures as will do any deed of desperation are best appreciated." Of the Pinkerton force brought in to break the railroad strike, Powderly said: "a hireling mob of the worst characters in the land have been quartered upon the people of New York to terrorize her citizens, to provoke men to anger and wrath—to shoot down those who asked for the right to be heard in their own behalf."[52]

The same week that Powderly mounted his protest, officers of the Central Labor Union in New York denounced Pinkerton operatives as "murderers, hired to shoot men at the rate of $1.14 per day." Union secretary James Archibald, the *Workmen's Advocate* reported, "said that he had affidavits from one of those men hired by Pinkerton, declaring that he received instructions to shoot down the strikers on the New York Central at Albany."[53]

Two years later Samuel Gompers, president of the American Federation of Labor, addressed delegates at Philadelphia. Gompers spoke months after violent conflict at the Homestead Steel Works had left at least ten men dead. He described the Pinkertons as "'an armed band of marauders sailing under no flag, owing allegiance to no State or country, and, consequently, by the laws of all nations, considered pirates.'"[54] At the same meeting, John Swinton said: "'Blasted be Pinkertonism, the enemy of freedom, the cut-throats of American liberty. These enemies of labor have cut their names on a gibbet that will cast its shadows over their tombstones.'"[55]

"The 'Pinkerton National Detective Agency' has been a disturbing element in politics and legislation for several years," the *New York World* said in 1892, after the bloody clash at Homestead. "There is scarcely a State in the Union that has not been distracted by excitement over the delegated and assumed powers and privileges of the Pinkertons. In the manufacturing districts, at railroad centres, in the coal regions, the presence of Pinkerton forces has always been a menace to peace. No private concern has ever agitated a country to the extent that this detective agency has done. Legislative halls have rung with the eloquence of speakers denunciatory of the growing power of this agency."[56]

The *World* added: "Legislation has not frightened them, because they know that the corporations which ordinarily ask their services will fight their battle for them. And the corporations are licensed to engage police aid."[57] Agitation by reformers finally led to the passage, in March 1893, of the federal Anti-Pinkerton Act. Its efficacy proved limited.

Mystery writer Dashiell Hammett, author of the *Maltese Falcon*, worked as a Pinkerton operative from 1915 to 1922. In 1917, Hammett was reportedly offered five thousand dollars to help lynch union activist Frank Little, a member of the Industrial Workers of the World (IWW). Hammett refused the offer.

The Anaconda company of Butte, Montana, a copper concern, employed thousands. The company sought to crush all organized labor within its ranks. After the Speculator Mine disaster at Granite Mountain in June 1917 killed almost one hundred and seventy miners, most of them by suffocation, Little traveled to Butte in hopes of recruiting new IWW members.

Shortly after three in morning on August 1, 1917, six masked men entered Little's boarding house. They roused his landlady, crashed open the door to Little's bedroom, and carried their victim, clad in his underwear and nursing a broken leg, out to their car. They tied Little to the car's rear bumper and dragged him over the city's granite blocks. At the Milwaukee bridge just outside town, the goons beat the strike organizer, then hanged him from a railroad trestle. Little died from strangulation.

Lillian Hellman, Hammett's long-time companion, considered Hammett's refusal to participate in the lynching a transformative event. She observed: "'this must have been, for Hammett, an abiding horror. I can date [his] belief that he was living in a corrupt society from Little's murder.'"[58]

On July 29, 1907, after hearing Clarence Darrow's defense, the Idaho jury at Boise acquitted William Haywood, founding member of the IWW and secretary-treasurer of the Western Federation of Miners, of the bombing death of Frank Steunenberg. Ten days later, Robert Pinkerton left New York for Germany aboard the *Bremen*, a German steamship. Four days after the steamer left New York, Pinkerton died on board of apparent heart trouble. He left an estate valued at three million dollars.

"Did the acquittal of Haywood have anything to do with Robert Pinkerton's death?" the *Miners Magazine* asked. "Some people are so sacrilegious as to intimate that poor Robert's heart was so lacerated by the verdict that he 'threw up the sponge.'"[59]

The *Sacred Heart Review*, a Catholic newspaper, said after Pinkerton's death: "It will surprise many people to know that the late Robert Pinkerton (head of the great detective agency) was a graduate of Notre Dame University. A writer in the *Notre Dame Scholastic* says of him: 'Robert Pinkerton was a just, benevolent man. He probably released and gave a new start in life to more offenders than he sent to prison.'"[60] On Robert's death, his son Allan took over the directorship of the agency's eastern division.

At their convention in Denver in late June 1907, WFM men re-elected Haywood and Charles Moyer, both still incarcerated at Boise, as WFM officers. But the same convention terminated the WFM's affiliation with the International Workers of the World (IWW).

After his acquittal at Boise, Haywood traveled extensively as a WFM representative, soliciting memberships countrywide. In 1908, the WFM removed Haywood from its executive board. Haywood's radical promotion of socialism helped lead to his ouster. Suggested that same year as presidential candidate for the Socialist Party, Haywood instead campaigned on behalf of Eugene Debs.

Haywood retained his ties to the IWW. As an IWW organizer, he helped marshal the 1912 "Bread and Roses" textile strike in Lawrence, Massachusetts. In 1913, he helped organize New Jersey's

Paterson silk strike. In 1915, Haywood became general secretary-treasurer of the IWW.

On August 30, 1918, at Chicago, federal judge K. M. Landis sentenced Haywood to twenty years' imprisonment at Leavenworth for sedition. One hundred additional IWW members received varying sentences for their opposition to U.S. involvement in World War I. In 1921, while appealing his case, Haywood fled the United States for Russia, where he served until 1923 as labor adviser to Vladimir Lenin's Bolshevik government. On May 18, 1928, Haywood died at Kremlin Hospital in Moscow from complications from diabetes.

"'Haywood had been unhappy for a good many years,'" Darrow said on hearing of Haywood's death. "'He was sentenced for nothing during the war when everybody went crazy. A lot of us suffered in those days.'"[61]

The *Daily Worker* said of Haywood: "As a young lad at the time of the hanging of the Haymarket martyrs, he followed the story of their trials avidly in the papers, and recognized the ferocity of the ruling class."[62] Haywood's will specified that he be cremated, with half of his ashes interred near the Chicago graves of those executed after the Haymarket Square conflict, and his remaining ashes interred at the Kremlin.

Allan Pinkerton flourished as a result of the "Molly Maguire" caseload. In May 1873, Pinkerton had faced bankruptcy. In a letter to his superintendent George Bangs, Pinkerton confided: "It looks as if I were going to go down, with money enough due me, to pay all my debts, and a great deal more, yet still I am unable to raise scarcely enough to buy a dinner."[63] Five months later, with Gowen's backing, Pinkerton operative James McParlan entered Pennsylvania's coal region undercover to investigate the so-called "Molly Maguires."

The same year Pinkerton escaped bankruptcy through his generation of the "Molly Maguire" caseload, he began lavish improvements to a parcel of land he had purchased nine years before in Illinois's Iroquois County. Larch Farm, a "Scottish laird's manor transplanted to the Illinois prairie,"[64] comprised more than two-hundred-and-fifty acres. On purchasing the land, Pinkerton imported thousands of larch trees from Scotland and had them planted on his domain. "Larch trees were set in orderly rows along the drives of the estate," a biographical sketch said. "Along these drives were placed thousands of flowers in beds that were always neat and orderly. Guards were stationed at the gates and visitors who drove their horses along the drive faster than a walk were fined five dollars for raising dust that would settle on the flowers." In the Snuggery, the manor's wine house, canvasses displayed portraits "of heroic Scots attired in kilts."[65]

By 1878, Pinkerton's relaxations included a companion, possibly a prostitute. A letter to his unnamed "Dear Friend" describing passage to Chicago included instructions to destroy all their correspondence and speak to no passengers or conductors en route. Pinkerton advised his unnamed correspondent: "You see in all those things I am systematic, and it is necessary for me to be so, and what is more I will be so, as its necessary to carry on business ... It is the way I manage my business both in Chicago, Philadelphia and New York for I will control all with an iron hand."[66]

Pinkerton died in 1884. The *New York Times* gave the cause: "Some time ago Mr. Pinkerton fell and bit his tongue, and gangrene, which set in, resulted in his death." Pinkerton's estate was valued at between $100,000 and $150,000. The *Times* said: "He owned the entire detective system which bears his name, and he made a great deal of money out of it, but he spent a large sum in maintaining a luxury in the shape of a model farm some miles south of the city [of Chicago]."[67] From Montana, a newspaper related that Pinkerton's will granted his widow and daughter the use of agency documents "in compiling others in the series known as 'Pinkerton's Detective Stories.'"[68]

After Pinkerton's son Robert died en route to Germany in 1907 William Pinkerton, along with Robert's son Allan, ran the firm jointly until William Pinkerton's death in 1923. Allan Pinkerton, grandson of the agency's founder, continued as president until his own death in 1930, when his son Robert Pinkerton, the founder's great-grandson, took over. When asked about his predecessors' strikebreaking activities, Robert Pinkerton said: "'That's a phase of our business that we're not particularly proud of ... we're delighted we're out of it. But there was nothing illegal about it then.'"[69] With Robert Pinkerton's death in 1967, family oversight of the agency ended.

James McParlan, aka McFarlan, aka McKenna, aka McParland, never replicated his star turn from the "Molly Maguire" trials. As McParland, he served for thirty years as superintendent of Pinkerton's Denver office. On his death from blood poisoning in 1919, the *Catholic Bulletin* in Saint Paul described McParland as a fourth-degree Knights of Columbus member and a brother-in-law to the superior of Colorado's Sisters of Mercy. McParland had, the *Bulletin* said, "performed one of the greatest services that has ever been rendered to the Catholic Church in America, when he broke up the notorious Molly Maguire movement in Pennsylvania in the seventies."[70]

In 1915, in yet another wearying example of ongoing anti-Irish-Catholic bias, a British publisher brought out Arthur Conan Doyle's *The Valley of Fear*. Conan Doyle's work, his last novel in the Sherlock Holmes series, was a thinly veiled derivative of Allan Pinkerton's *The Mollie Maguires and the Detectives*. When given the news of McParland's death in 1919, William Pinkerton praised Conan Doyle's work to a Chicago reporter.

"'To show how his [McParland's] exploits captured the imagination of genius I'll tell you about Conan Doyle,'" Pinkerton told the reporter. "'After the trouble at the coal fields my father wrote a book of memoirs in which he told of McParlan's work in the Mollie Maguires.'" Of Conan Doyle's *The Valley of Fear*, Pinkerton said: "'The first part was a regular detective story. The second part was a literal transcription of my father's book, in which only the name of McParlan was changed. That, in my estimation, was a wonderful compliment to McParlan.'"[71]

William Pinkerton described McParland as "'one of the best men we or any one else ever had. ... in his youth he was the soul of energy, tact, cleverness and ability.'"[72] Despite McParland's notable humiliation by defense counsel in the Western Federation of Miners cases and his excoriation by the citizens of Parsons, Kansas, as being "'of infamously bad character,'"[73] Pinkerton concluded: "'He worked all over the world for us and he has a reputation for never having failed.'"[74]

After the "Molly" trials ended James Kerrigan, whose testimony had sent so many Irish Catholic men to the gallows in Pennsylvania, went underground in Richmond, Virginia. He lived there with his family under his wife's name, Higgins, until his death in 1898.

After the "Molly" trials, U.S. Congressman John Killinger, Kehoe's "Good old" friend, went from extreme to extreme. In 1874, Killinger had introduced his bill on the floor of Congress calling for cooperative ownership of the country's railway system. The "Molly Maguire" prosecutions put an end to such efforts. Some time after Killinger left Congress in 1881, he became a solicitor for the Philadelphia and Reading Railroad.

Lin Bartholomew, the attorney whose defense of AOH clients had turned treacherous, traveled to Europe in August 1879 with George Kaercher, who served as district attorney for Schuylkill County during the "Molly" trials. The following year, at the oyster bar of the United States Hotel in Atlantic City, Bartholomew fell suddenly dead from an apparent heart attack.

Four years after the European tour Kaercher, Bartholomew's traveling companion and Gowen's former law student, was appointed solicitor general for the Philadelphia and Reading Railroad and Coal and Iron Company. Two years after that, in 1885, Kaercher married Annette Hughes, daughter of Francis Hughes, a lead prosecutor during the "Molly Maguire" trials.

On September 19, 1890, while traveling on the Pottsville Express, Kaercher met a tragic end. "READING'S WRECK," a Delaware paper reported. "Frightful Loss of Life Upon That Railroad. HURLED INTO THE RIVER. Thirty or Forty Persons Are Reported Dead."[75]

Three trains collided just north of Shoemakersville to produce the horrific accident that claimed dozens of lives. A broken coupling on a coal train and its subsequent crash into a freight train blocked both the northbound and southbound railway lines. The southbound passenger train from Pottsville, running ten minutes late and making up time, hurtled headlong into the wrecked coal train. The passenger train plunged, engine first, down an embankment and into the Schuylkill River. Kaercher, traveling in the train's Pullman car, drowned in a few feet of water.

Edward Siewers, the district attorney for Carbon County who ceded his authority during the "Molly" trials to "the slippery Charles Albright" of the Kansas property scam, also met a dramatic end. Two years before Siewers's election as district attorney, a Mauch Chunk newsman had described "a little episode in his bacchanalian career" where "a drunken snooze" had reportedly left Siewers asleep overnight in a local doorway.[76]

After his stint as district attorney, Siewers returned to private practice. In 1885, a failed venture into the hotel trade with Glen Onoko's Hotel Wahtenah, a Victorian extravaganza, drove Siewers to heavy borrowing from friends, then to "fraud, theft and embezzlement to raise money."[77] Those frauds included the forgery of his mother's name on ten Lehigh Valley Railroad bonds. Siewers's mother intervened to save him from criminal prosecution.

Siewers left Mauch Chunk. Sometime later, he surfaced as a financial editor in Philadelphia, where he assumed the faux title of "Judge Siewers." In June 1917, Siewers's body was found in the Delaware River near Philadelphia's Market Street Wharf, "an apparent suicide."[78]

Attorney Daniel Kalbfus, who represented alleged "Molly Maguires" Michael Doyle, Edward Kelly, and Alexander Campbell, had proven one of the most stalwart of the AOH defense team. In March 1879, two months after the botched executions of McDonnell and Sharpe at Mauch Chunk Jail, Siewers joined a commission, petitioned by Kalbfus's brother Joseph, to adjudge Daniel Kalbfus "a 'lunatic.'"[79] Judge Samuel Dreher, who presided over Carbon County's "Molly Maguire" caseload, ordered Kalbfus confined to the state hospital at Danville. Kalbfus died there in 1881 at age forty-two.

Charles Albright, who prosecuted John Kehoe along with

numerous other "Molly Maguire" defendants, died at Mauch Chunk in September 1880. "General Albright took an active and prominent part in the 'Molly Maguire' trials," the *New York Tribune* said. "He was a self-made man and won his own way in the world. His family will be left in comfortable circumstances."[80]

John Siney, founder in 1868 of Pennsylvania's Workingmen's Benevolent Association and president of the Miners' National Association, had helped elect Cyrus Pershing as president judge of Schuylkill County in 1872. Siney spent his last years at St. Clair, a few miles from the site of the largest mass hanging at Pottsville. In 1876, while "Molly" trials remained ongoing, Siney purchased Barber's Tavern. He renamed it "King George's Tavern" and hired a local artist to decorate its front wall with an enormous mural of the British king. Whatever comment Siney, an Irish Catholic, sought to make with that effort remains provocative.[81] Pershing died at his home in Pottsville at age seventy-eight. The *New York Times* described Pershing as "presiding Judge of the Schuylkill County courts during the trial of the members of the notorious Molly Maguires."[82]

Holy Rosary Catholic Church in Mahanoy Plane, where Father Daniel O'Connor had condemned Kehoe's relatives as so-called "Molly Maguires" following the murderous raid at Wiggan's Patch, closed in 1988. "Mine Collapse to Close Church," an Allentown paper reported. The article noted that the church was "structurally unsafe, apparently from the collapse of a mine shaft below."[83]

After Franklin Gowen's death by suicide in December 1889, the former railroad president's remains were interred at Ivy Hill Cemetery in Philadelphia. Today, in the city's Mount Airy neighborhood, Gowen Avenue bears his name.

In 1954 the towns of East Mauch Chunk and Mauch Chunk, witness to seven "Molly Maguire" executions, officially merged under the new name of "Jim Thorpe." The name change, the result of the bizarre confluence of the death of the famous Olympic athlete, his widow's efforts to secure his final resting place, the towns' steadily deteriorating economies, and a "nickel-a-week" program that was originated to fund a new textile plant, led to the towns' renaming. Today, the Jim Thorpe Mausoleum, initially funded by the nickel-a-week plan, serves as a tourist attraction in a town that the renowned athlete, Thorpe, had never visited. The transfer of Thorpe's body from Oklahoma to Pennsylvania's Carbon County remains a source of legal contention.

From 1877 to 1879, hundreds of spectators at Mauch Chunk Jail witnessed the seven "Molly Maguire" executions held in the building's indoor arena. On June 21, 1877, authorities hanged Alexander Campbell, John Donohue, Michael Doyle, and Edward Kelly with their legs and hands shackled in chains that rattled throughout their lengthy death struggles. January 14, 1879, saw the botched executions of James McDonnell and Charles Sharpe. On March 28, 1878, AOH delegate Thomas Fisher stood on the gallows and prayed aloud until the noose choked off his breath. All seven of the condemned Irishmen likely knew they faced death by slow strangulation before a leering crowd. All carried crucifixes as they ascended the gallows.

The old Mauch Chunk Jail remains open today as a tourist attraction. A museum that honors the depth and complexity of this history has yet to be established.

On January 20, 2021, Joseph R. Biden Jr. assumed the presidency of the United States. *Irish America* published a celebratory article. It noted: "Rumored to be a member of the Molly Maguires was Biden's great-grandfather Edward Francis Blewitt, a native of Louisiana whose parents Patrick and Catherine (nee Scanlon) Blewitt were from Ballina, Co Mayo. Blewitt was a major Irish American figure in Scranton. Not only did he win the election to the state senate, but he was also named Chairman of the Saint Patrick's Day Parade in 1897, and he became a co-founder of the Friendly Sons of St. Patrick in Scranton in 1908."[84]

Further research shows Biden's great-grandfather Blewitt as not just a state senator, but as an AOH officer, and, possibly, as AOH state delegate for Pennsylvania. Circa 1896, Blewitt relocated for a number of years from Scranton to Mexico, where he supervised an engineering project in Guadalajara. While in Mexico, Blewitt organized an AOH chapter. At the 1902 AOH national convention at Denver, though representing only eighteen members, Blewitt served as Mexico's delegate.[85]

"A HIBERNIAN MONOPOLIST," a *Denver Post* headline described Blewitt. "Delegate Edward Blewitt is a Big Chief in Mexico. A TYPICAL SON OF ERIN." Blewitt told the *Post* reporter of his AOH members in Mexico: "'Plenty of them are thoroughbreds; most of them are men at the heads of big enterprises, who, having mining interests, are introducing new things in commercialism and take a prominent part in the American competition.'"[86]

The *Denver Post* described Blewitt as head of an engineering company in Guadalajara valued at three million dollars. It added: "He was city engineer for ten years in Scranton, Penn., previous to his departure for Mexico six years ago. He was for six years, besides, state president of the Hibernians of Pennsylvania."[87] Blewitt's AOH involvement in Pennsylvania's coal region less than three decades after the commonwealth's "Molly Maguire" executions showed substantial courage.

By 1908, Blewitt had returned to Scranton. In July, he again traveled to Denver to attend the national Democratic convention, and to Indianapolis to attend the national AOH convention. At Indianapolis, the *New York Sun* took the political pulse of Pennsylvania's state senator Blewitt on the upcoming presidential contest.[88] With Blewitt's AOH leadership, the intersection between Pennsylvania's coal region AOH men and state and national politics continued.

In 1979, through the combined efforts of attorneys John Elliott and Thomas Elliott; John Kehoe's great-grandson, Joseph Wayne; and members of the Pennsylvania Labor History Society, Pennsylvania's Board of Pardons issued Kehoe a posthumous pardon. Governor Milton Shapp signed the historic document. Kehoe remains the only AOH member convicted in Pennsylvania as an alleged "Molly Maguire" to receive a posthumous pardon.

In 1974 John Elliott, en route to Penn State Hazleton to lecture on the "Molly Maguires," told a Philadelphia reporter: "'Camus tells us that every man has his own sense of injustice. The Mollies are mine.'"[89] Four decades later Wayne, former controller of Schuylkill County and a longtime proprietor of Kehoe's Hibernian House at Girardville, told a reporter of Kehoe: "'We must remember from whence we came. It's proper to recognize him for what he did and tried to do. He tried to better his fellow man.'"[90]

The Memorandum in Support of the Application of John J. Kehoe to Pennsylvania's Board of Pardons filed in 1978 by John and Thomas Elliott addressed Kehoe's capital trial, with its "atmosphere of religious, social and ethnic bigotry," its exclusion of Irish Catholics from the jury, its use of at least two non-English speakers as jurors, the punitive measures inflicted upon defense witnesses, the dungeon conditions which Kehoe endured while guarded by private Coal and Iron police, the appointment of special prosecutors with ties to railroad and coal interests, the prosecutors' conflation of the AOH with alleged "Molly Maguire" terrorism, the prosecutors' denouncement of the labor union as lawless, Judge Cyrus Pershing's nativist background, and Pershing's defeat for the governorship, in part, through AOH and union activity, as well as Pershing's "legally improper inflammatory statements to the jury," the "rancid and inflammatory press which prejudiced [Kehoe's] case and pre-ordained his verdict," and a trial which was "a farce devoid of fundamental fairness and basic Constitutional protections."[91]

Governor Shapp's letter in support of Kehoe's posthumous pardon described the so-called "Mollies" as "martyred men of labor." Shapp said: "we can be proud of the men known as the Molly Maguires because they defiantly faced allegations which attempted to make trade unionism a criminal conspiracy."[92]

In 1907, Eugene Debs said of Pennsylvania's alleged "Mollies": "All were ignorant, rough and uncouth, born of poverty and buffeted by the merciless tides of fate and chance." Debs added: "It is true that their methods were drastic, but it must be remembered that their lot was hard and brutalizing; that they were the neglected children of poverty, the products of a wretched environment."[93]

In actuality, at least five AOH men charged as "Mollies" had served as township school directors. Others had served as high constables, tax assessors, tax collectors, and township supervisors. Many had owned businesses. Many had served as political delegates. But the fictional, sensational press coverage surrounding these events, and the billows of falsehoods dispersed in 1877 by both Allan Pinkerton's dime novel and Francis Dewees's supposed authoritative account, continue to plague the integrity of this conflict's historical chronicling.

Of John and Mary Ann Kehoe's family from 1878, their son and four daughters all survived to adulthood. All five of the Kehoe children married. All four daughters bore a son they named "John."

Kehoe family papers archived at St. Charles Borromeo Seminary in Wynnewood, Pennsylvania, include a handwritten poem. Titled "To the memory of John Kehoe," its authorship is noted only "By graybeard." Its third and final stanza reads:

> His life [they] wanted and [they] have it now
>   for the hirelings Swore untrue
> By perjury they hung my John but anything
>   would do
> To please the prince great Franklin B. the
>   Liars done all [they] could
> And left a widow now of me to satisfy Rev.
>   Bishop Wood
> Had he been guilty I would not care, no nor
>   ask to set him free
> But by the evidence any Sensible man would
>   know it was downright perjury
> For poor Langdons blood he never shed
>   which his Jury ought to know
> But [his] life [they] wanted and [they] have it
>   now of my husband John Kehoe[94]

1. Ibid., May 22, 1880 (report of AOH national convention at Philadelphia).
2. Letter from William McIntyre, secretary, AOH Div. 2, Philadelphia, *Philadelphia Times*, August 28, 1876.
3. *Boston Pilot*, June 14, 1884 (reporting AOH state convention, Massachusetts).
4. Andrew Lenahan, the eleventh alleged "Molly" hanged that day, was executed at Wilkes-Barre for the murder of John Reilly on September 15, 1874. In November 1875 James McParlan, who conflated AOH membership with "Molly Maguireism," identified Lenahan as having "formerly belonged" to the AOH. See James McParlan, operative report, 8 November 1875, Reading Railroad Molly Maguire Papers, Hagley Museum and Library, Wilmington, DE.
5. *Philadelphia Times*, June 27, 1877 (Taylor signed this column "C. Cath.").
6. *New York Times*, March 15, 1880.
7. R. E. Difendorfer to Board of Pardons, 14 June 1880, Christopher Donnelly Case Folder. Clemency File, 1874-1900 (Series 15.17); RG-15, Department of Justice (Board of Pardons). Pennsylvania State Archives, Harrisburg.
8. *Harrisburg Patriot*, March 4, 1875.
9. Ibid., February 22, 1875.
10. John Swinton to Pennsylvania's Board of Pardons, 1 July 1877. Clemency File, 1874-1900 (Series 15.17); RG-15, Department of Justice (Board of Pardons). Pennsylvania State Archives, Harrisburg.
11. Richard O. Boyer and Herbert M. Morais, *Labor's Untold Story: The Adventure Story of the Battles, Betrayals and Victories of American Working Men and Women* (1955, repr. Pittsburgh: United Electrical, Radio, and Machine Workers of America, 2005), 81 (the authors give the date of Swinton's address as ca. 1880).
12. *Miners' Journal* (Pottsville, PA), August 19, 1876.
13. *Columbian* (Bloomsburg, PA), September 22, 1898.
14. *New York Sun*, April 17, 1904.
15. *Idaho Springs (CO) Siftings-News*, June 12, 1909.
16. *Evening Times-Republican* (Marshalltown, IA), June 14, 1909.
17. *Tupelo (MS) Journal*, June 11, 1909.
18. *Birmingham (AL) Age-Herald*, June 9, 1909.
19. *New York Times*, December 23, 1875; italics in original.
20. *Daily Gazette* (Wilmington, DE), March 26, 1880; reprinting *Philadelphia Times*.
21. *New York Times*, May 21, 1880.
22. *New York Tribune*, June 24, 1883.
23. "Priest on Hibernians. Threatens to Stir Up Great Scandal in the Church," ibid., January 8, 1908.
24. *Waterbury (CT) Evening Democrat*, January 9, 1908; quoting *Catholic Transcript* (Hartford, CT).
25. *Irish Standard* (Minneapolis, MN), January 25, 1908.
26. "Brazen Insult. Philadelphia Pastor Maligns the Ancient Order of Hibernians," *Kentucky Irish American* (Louisville, KY), January 11, 1908.
27. *New York Times*, May 14, 1879 (similar coverage in *Chicago Tribune*, same date).
28. *Shenandoah (PA) Herald*, August 30, 1876 (see also *Philadelphia Times*, August 29, 1876).
29. For *Catholic Telegraph*, see https://thecatholicnewsarchive.org/?a=cl&cl=CL1&sp=TCT. For obscured coverage see, for example, June 21, 1877, pp. 3-4.
30. *Mauch Chunk (PA) Democrat*, September 21, 1878; reprinting *Shamokin Times*.
31. *Tamaqua (PA) Courier*, September 21, 1878.

32. Patrick Campbell, *A Molly Maguire Story* (Jersey City, NJ: Templecrone Press, 1992), 28.
33. *Mauch Chunk (PA) Democrat*, September 21, 1878; reprinting *Shamokin Times*.
34. "The Union Doctrine, or Poor Man's Catechism: Union Creed," introduction by Kevin Whelan, *Labour History* 75 (November 1998): 33; italics in original.
35. Ibid., 35.
36. *New York Herald*, October 10, 1879.
37. "Worldliness in the Church," *Irish World* (New York), April 17, 1875.
38. Ibid.
39. Ibid., October 5, 1878.
40. Ibid., December 28, 1878.
41. Ibid., January 11, 1879.
42. "The Horrors of the Gallows," *Daily Cairo (IL) Bulletin*, January 31, 1879; reprinting *Irish World*.
43. *New York Times*, February 26, 1878.
44. *Evening Star* (Washington, DC) and *Daily Gazette* (Wilmington, DE), June 27, 1878; *Columbian* (Bloomsburg, PA), June 28, 1878.
45. *New York Times*, February 26, 1878.
46. *Pittsburgh Telegraph*, October 21, 1878.
47. *Somerset (PA) Herald*, December 14, 1881.
48. *Daily Kennebec Journal* (Augusta, ME), December 30, 1878.
49. *Chicago Tribune*, January 20, 1879.
50. *Daily Kennebec Journal* (Augusta, ME), December 30, 1878.
51. *New York Sun*, August 22, 1890.
52. Ibid.
53. *Workmen's Advocate* (New Haven, CT), August 23, 1890.
54. *Indianapolis Journal*, December 13, 1892.
55. *Gloucester County Democrat* (Woodbury, NJ), December 15, 1892.
56. *Irish Times* (Dublin), July 29, 1892; reprinting *New York World*.
57. Ibid.
58. Quoted in "Books of the Times; Society's Dark Corners Seen Through Keyholes," *New York Times*, August 27, 1999.
59. *Montana News* (Lewistown, MT), October 3 1907; reprinting *Miners Magazine*.
60. *Sacred Heart Review*, November 2, 1907, https://newspapers.bc.edu/?a=d&d=BOSTONSH19071102-01.2.4&e=-------en-20--1--txt-txIN-------.
61. *New Britain (CT) Herald*, May 18, 1928.
62. *Daily Worker* (New York), May 19, 1928.
63. Allan Pinkerton to George Bangs, 20 May 1873, Box 47, Folder 7, Pinkerton's National Detective Agency Records, Manuscript Division, Library of Congress, Washington, DC.
64. J. Anthony Lukas, *Big Trouble: A Murder in a Small Western Town Sets off a Struggle for the Soul of America* (New York: Simon & Schuster, 1997), 188.
65. Patricia Dissmeyer Goff, "A Collection of Writings Concerning Allan Pinkerton and the Larch Farm," Elgin, IL, 1966, https://iroquois.illinoisgenweb.org/photondx/pnkrtn.htm.
66. E. J. Allen [Allan Pinkerton's alias] to "My Dear Friend," 20 September 1878; underlining in original, Pinkerton's National Detective Agency Records, Manuscript Division, Library of Congress, Washington, DC.
67. *New York Times*, July 2, 1884.
68. *Daily Enterprise* (Livingston, MT), July 15, 1884.

69. "Robert A. Pinkerton, Chairman of Detective Agency, Is Dead," *New York Times*, October 12, 1967. The *Times* repeated this quote from Robert Pinkerton, given "years" after the Pinkertons stopped their strikebreaking activities, without giving its original date.
70. *Catholic Bulletin* (St. Paul, MN), May 31, 1919.
71. Reported in *Evening-Times Republican* (Marshalltown, IA), May 20, 1919.
72. Ibid.
73. "The Idaho Miner's Case. Trying to Convict on Testimony of Paid Detective," *Daily Appeal* (Carson City, NV), May 23, 1906.
74. *Evening Times-Republican* (Marshalltown, IA), May 20, 1919.
75. *Evening Journal* (Wilmington, DE), September 20, 1890.
76. *Mauch Chunk (PA) Coal Gazette*, October 4, 1872.
77. John P. Lavelle, *The Hard Coal Docket: One Hundred and Fifty Years of the Bench and Bar of Carbon County* (Lehighton, PA: Times News, 1994, 214.
78. Ibid.
79. Ibid., 209.
80. *New York Tribune*, September 29, 1880.
81. Edward Pinkowski, *John Siney: The Miners' Martyr* (Philadelphia: Sunshine Press, 1963), 216-17.
82. *New York Times*, June 30, 1903.
83. *Morning Call* (Allentown, PA), May 26, 1988.
84. Niall O'Dowd, "The Man Who Will be President," *Irish America*, January-February 2021, 36. See also Megan Smolenyak, "Joey From Scranton: VP Biden's Irish Roots," *Irish America*, April-May 2013, 56-59.
85. See "Proceedings of the A. O. H. Convention," *Irish Standard* (Minneapolis), July 26, 1902. See also Turtle Bunbury, "US Vice-President Joe Biden flies in next week to trace his rich Irish lineage," *Irish Daily Mail*, June 16, 2016.
86. *Denver Post*, July 17, 1902. Thanks to Turtle Bunbury for directing me to this source.
87. Ibid.
88. *New York Sun*, July 17, 1908.
89. *Philadelphia Daily News*, March 21, 1974.
90. *Times News Online* (Lehighton, PA), March 17, 2014.
91. John M. Elliott and Thomas J. Elliott to Board of Pardons, Commonwealth of Pennsylvania, Memorandum in Support of the Application of John J. Kehoe (not dated), private collection of author.
92. Letter of Governor Milton J. Shapp, 6 September 1978, John Kehoe File, M 170.18 MI, Schuylkill County Historical Society. See also Kevin Kenny, *Making Sense of the Molly Maguires* (New York: Oxford University Press, 1998), 284.
93. *Voices of Revolt*, vol. 9, *Speeches of Eugene V. Debs* (New York: International Publishers, 1928), 76.
94. Poem "By graybeard," dedicated "To the memory of John Kehoe," Eleanor Tighe Collection, Molly Maguire Papers, St. Charles Borromeo Seminary.

GLOSSARY

American Federation of Labor (AFL)

National federation of labor unions founded at Columbus, Ohio, in 1866; coordinated craft unions comprised of skilled workers. First president Samuel Gompers. Disaffection of craft unions with the Knights of Labor led to the AFL's formation. The largest U.S. union organization in the first half of the twentieth century, in 1955 the AFL merged with the Congress of Industrial Organizations to create the AFL-CIO, headed by George Meany and numbering, in 1955, fifteen million members. In 2014, the international federation included fifty-six member unions representing more than twelve million members. Richard Trumka, elected in 2009, serves as current president.

Ancient Order of Hibernians (AOH)

Irish Catholic benevolent society founded in 1836 in New York City and Schuylkill County, Pennsylvania, through charter granted from "'THE BRETHREN IN IRELAND AND GREAT BRITAIN.'"[1] In 1838 the society in the U.S. adopted the name "Ancient Order of

Hibernians" from the society that was first formed in Ireland. At the height of its power in 1876, the U.S. order numbered, per an official source, more than 700,000 members.[2] Most, if not all, of the "Molly Maguire" defendants belonged to the AOH. These alleged "Mollies" held numerous local officers, including high constable, tax assessor, tax collector, school director, overseer of the poor, and township supervisor. A number served as delegates to political conventions. Many alleged "Mollies" also held AOH leadership positions. Alleged "King of the Mollies" John Kehoe served as AOH delegate for Schuylkill County and high constable for Girardville.

Anti-Monopoly Movement

National movement, mid-1870s, arising out of Patrons of Husbandry [farming] agitation; joined by labor leaders, including anthracite coal region leaders John Siney and John Welsh. Directed in part against railroad monopolies; also included call for monetary reform and exclusion of British capital from U.S. industry (British capital backed much of Pennsylvania's hard coal industry). Movement included conventions at Indianapolis, 1874; Cleveland, Harrisburg, and Cincinnati, 1875; Indianapolis, 1876; and Toledo, 1878.

At the national convention in Philadelphia in 1878, special "Molly Maguire" prosecutor Francis Hughes assumed the presidency of the National Party (aka Greenback Labor Party) affiliated with this movement.

Anti-Pinkerton Act

Federal legislation enacted in 1893, driven by public outrage after Pinkerton intervention at the Homestead steel plant labor dispute led to violence. The act prohibited the employment of private detectives by the federal government and the District of Columbia.

Coal and Iron Police

Act 228, passed by Pennsylvania's General Assembly in 1865, authorized the creation of these private police forces. During Pennsylvania's anthracite region "Molly" trials from 1875 to 1880, officers employed by the Philadelphia and Reading Coal and Iron Company and the Lehigh and Wilkes-Barre Coal and Iron Company drew up arrest warrants, made arrests, patrolled courtrooms and jails, and served as prosecution witnesses.

Coal Combination

Cartel of railroad and coal interests formed in 1871 by Franklin Gowen, president of both the Philadelphia and Reading Railroad and its affiliated Coal and Iron Company. At different times, Gowen's combination included (along with the Philadelphia and Reading): the Central Railroad of New Jersey; the Delaware and Hudson Railroad; the Delaware, Lackawanna and Western Railroad; the Lehigh Coal and Navigation Company; the Lehigh Valley Railroad; the Pennsylvania Coal Company; and the Wilkes-Barre Coal and Iron Company. Described by one historian as "the first industry price-fixing device in United States history."[3]

Constitutional Convention, Philadelphia

Held in 1873 to revise Pennsylvania's constitution. Two "Molly Maguire" special prosecutors, Charles Buckalew and Franklin Gowen, served as delegates. Gowen argued successfully for the removal of the pardoning power from Pennsylvania's governor and the instatement a new four-man Board of Pardons. The new board, advised by one of Gowen's Pinkerton men, figured prominently in the subsequent "Molly Maguire" cases.

Copperheads

Term, derived from the poisonous snake, assigned to Northern Democrats who supported the Confederacy during and after the Civil War. In Pennsylvania, three successively defeated Democratic gubernatorial candidates from 1869 to 1875 who played roles in the "Molly" trials—Asa Packer, Charles Buckalew, and Cyrus Pershing; along with special "Molly" prosecutors Francis Hughes and Franklin Gowen—showed sympathy with this ideology.

Divine Right

Misguided belief held by some industrialists that God had placed the disposition of natural resources under their care. Espoused in 1902 by Reading Railroad president George Baer, who said: "The rights and interests of the laboring man will be protected and cared for – not by the labor agitators, but by the Christian men to whom God in His infinite wisdom has given the control of the property interests of the country, and upon the successful Management of which so much depends."[4] Baer's autocratic language, which closely resembled that of England's King George III during the Revolutionary War, led defense attorney Clarence Darrow to dub Baer "King George the Last."[5]

Ethnic/Racial Scapegoating

Use of labels, notably by politicians, to generate fear of "the other" for political gain. With racial or ethnic groups as targets, this strategy is especially effective during times of economic distress. The Panic of 1873 and its attendant economic depression helped the "Molly Maguire" label gain traction, clearing the path for the trials that followed.

Fenian Brotherhood

Irish nationalist society that sought independence from British rule. Founded in 1858 in Ireland by James Stephens, and in the United States by John O'Mahony. Most active in the 1860s in Ireland, Britain, and the United States.

Gilded Age (U.S.)

Era, from roughly the 1870s to the 1890s, marked by industrial growth and economic disparity. Infamous for its appallingly poor treatment of working people, including children, to pursue corporate profits.

Great Famine (also "Great Hunger")

Ireland's potato crop failure from 1845 to 1849 that led to the deaths of one million and the forced emigration of two million more. Alleged "Molly" defendants included numerous immigrants from Ireland. Their revised AOH charter, filed in Harrisburg in 1871, may have arisen in part from their shared chapter of Ireland's history. The introduction to this AOH charter stated: "the Supreme Being has implanted in our natures tender sympathies and most humane feeling towards our fellow creatures in distress, and all the happiness that human nature is capable of enjoying must flow and terminate in the love of God and our fellow creatures."[6] AOH aims included support for widows, disability support, and decent burial for all members, a goal that may also have arisen from devastation witnessed in Ireland.

Greenback Labor Party (also National Party)

Founded in 1876 as the National Independent Party at Indianapolis. Widely known as the Greenback Party or the Greenback Labor Party.

Haymarket Conflict

Chicago, Haymarket Square. On May 4, 1886, a peaceful demonstration in support of workers striking for the eight-hour day erupted in violence when an unknown attacker threw a dynamite bomb into the crowd. Police action, possibly augmented by demonstrators, killed seven policemen and at least four onlookers, and injured dozens more. Some workers, aware of the Pinkertons' unsavory history, believed them responsible for initiating the attack.

Police arrested dozens of suspects. Illinois convicted eight men, all supporters of the workingmen's aims, as accessories to murder. The convictions created storms worldwide, both of sympathy for the defendants and outraged demands for their executions. On November 11, 1887, four Haymarket defendants, dressed in white robes and hoods, were hanged. The strife surrounding these events effectively ended the workers' push for the eight-hour day.

Homestead Strike

Armed conflict, mid-1892, Homestead Steel Works, Homestead, Pennsylvania. Striking steelworkers belonging to the Amalgamated Association of Iron and Steel Workers clashed with Pinkerton agents hired by the Carnegie Steel Company. At least ten died, with many more wounded. The conflict led both to the collapse of the steelworkers' union and the passage in 1893 of the Anti-Pinkerton Act.

International Workers of the World (IWW, "Wobblies")

International labor organization founded in 1905 in Chicago by William ("Big Bill") Haywood, WFM secretary-treasurer; Daniel De Leon, Socialist Labor Party leader; and Eugene Debs, Socialist Party leader. Unlike the AFL, which supported craft unions, the IWW welcomed unskilled workers into its ranks. In 1908, De Leon and his supporters withdrew from the IWW. Debs remained active during the organization's early years. In 1907, the WFM terminated its affiliation with the IWW. Haywood eventually left the WFM but retained his loyalty to the IWW, serving at intermittent times from 1915 to 1918 as IWW general secretary-treasurer.

Iron Molders' International Union (IMIU)

Formed in 1859 as the National Union of Iron Molders. In 1863, William Sylvis was elected president. A model for national trades organizations, the IMIU laid the foundation for the eventual formation of the NLU.

Knights of Labor

Formed by Uriah Stephens in 1869 in Philadelphia as a secret society of tailors. The trade union, which eventually embraced all trades, was led by Terence Powderly from 1879 to 1893. In 1886 its membership numbered 700,000. The Knights' goals included equal pay, the eight-hour day, and the abolition of child labor. The order included members from the anthracite coalfields. It lost significant membership after hostile observers placed blame on the Knights for the 1886 Haymarket conflict.

Know Nothing Party (also American Party, Native American Party, Order of the Star-Spangled Banner)

Nativist U.S. political movement dating from the 1850s, based on fear of "the other." Anti-immigrant and anti-Catholic, the party accepted only U.S.-born Protestants into its ranks. In 1856, with its membership totaling more than one million, the American Party ran Millard Fillmore as its presidential nominee. For a brief time, the party's "dark lantern" tactics achieved gains in local, state, and national elections. After Fillmore's loss, the party lost traction. A secret organization, the exact extent of its influence remains murky.

Labor Reform Party (successor to National Labor Party)

Founded February 1872 at Columbus, Ohio, as a political arm of the National Labor Union (NLU). Richard Trevellick, Andrew Cameron, and John Siney backed its formation.

Legislative Charter Investigations – Philadelphia and Reading

In 1871 and 1875, the Pennsylvania legislature launched investigations challenging the company charter of Franklin Gowen's Philadelphia and Reading Railroad and Coal and Iron Company. Miners in Mahanoy City encouraged the 1871 investigation. The second investigation arose in part from anthracite miner delegates' attendance at the 1875 Harrisburg Anti-Monopoly Convention. Republican governors John Geary and John Hartranft authorized the investigations.

Long Strike of 1875

In December 1874, coal operators organized under Franklin Gowen announced draconian wage cuts for Pennsylvania's anthracite mineworkers. This ploy, to secure a region-wide strike in an effort to break the WBA, worked. Seven thousand mineworkers walked out and remained on strike for six months until, driven by desperation, they accepted the punitive wage terms Gowen offered. The strike and its consequences crushed the WBA.[7]

Miners' National Association (MNA)

National labor union of miners formed in 1873 and headquartered at Cleveland; John Siney, president. At its height in 1876, the MNA had 35,000-plus members from twelve states and one territory. Its strength was compromised by the failure of Pennsylvania's 1875 Long Strike and the subsequent crushing of the WBA.

Miners' and Laborers' Benevolent Association (MLBA)

New name given to the Workingmen's Benevolent Association in March 1870, when the WBA's general council received a state charter. The new MLBA continued to be known generally as the "WBA." To avoid confusion, this work also uses the appellation "WBA."

In Locust Gap in Pennsylvania's Northumberland County, post-Civil-War anthracite mineworkers formed a short-lived organization under the name "Miners' Benevolent Association."

MLBA Grand Council

Council of MLBA delegates convened at Mauch Chunk, Pennsylvania, in spring 1871, during a protracted wage dispute between mineworkers and operators. Two alleged "Mollies," Michael Lawler and Cornelius McHugh, served as delegates. Lawler served as one of four signatories to the arbitration agreement authorized by Judge William Elwell (John Morgan, a friend of John Kehoe's, served as head of the four-man arbitration committee). The *New York Herald* called the group an "Immense Politico-Industrial Organization—A New Power Forming in the Land."[8]

"Molly Maguires" (also "Buckshots")

Terms used by railroad president Franklin Gowen and Philadelphia archbishop James Frederick Wood to conflate the Ancient Order of Hibernians in Pennsylvania's anthracite coal region with supposed Irish terrorism. In the decades preceding the trials, widespread use of these terms by nativist editors helped them gain credence with the public.

Twenty-one AOH men were hanged in Pennsylvania under this label. Executions took place at Bloomsburg: Patrick Hester, Peter McHugh, and Patrick Tully; Mauch Chunk: Alexander Campbell, John Donohue (Donahue), Michael Doyle, Thomas Fisher, Edward

Kelly, James McDonnell, and Charles Sharpe; Pottsville: Martin Bergin, James Boyle, James Carroll, Dennis Donnelly, Thomas Duffy, John Kehoe, Hugh McGehan, Thomas Munley, and James Roarity; Sunbury: Peter McManus; and Wilkes-Barre: Andrew Lenahan.

Nativism

Anti-immigrant and anti-Catholic ideology. Its adherents promoted U.S.-born (native-born) Protestants for political office, and worked strenuously against foreign-born candidates, especially Irish Catholics. Noted nativist attacks include the Philadelphia Riots of 1844.

National Labor Party

Established in August, 1866, in affiliation with the NLU, by a majority delegate vote at the National Labor Congress, Baltimore. Renamed Labor Reform Party in 1872.

National Labor Union (NLU)

First U.S. national labor federation. Founded in August 1866 at the Baltimore National Labor Congress through the efforts of William Sylvis, Jonathan Fincher, others. Presidents: J. C. C. Whaley; William Sylvis; Richard Trevellick. The NLU helped secure the eight-hour day for federal workers. Membership estimates of 600,000 to 800,000 are considered greatly exaggerated (actual numbers have not been put forward). Dissolved in 1873.

Patriotic Order Sons of America

Formed in the early 1870s in Pennsylvania, the order spread to other states. During the "Molly Maguire" conflict, the order had at least five lodges in Schuylkill County. A few weeks after the mass hangings at Pottsville and Mauch Chunk, a coal region observer said: "Then we have got the 'Junior Sons of America,' 'Mechanics,' and many other secret societies, calling themselves Young Americans. The 'Junior' boys tell their fathers that *they* have not the same right here ... because they were not born in this country."[9]

Pinkerton National Detective Agency

Founded by Allan Pinkerton in Chicago in the 1850s; led after his death by his sons Robert and William. Notoriously anti-labor. Controversial early agency cases include: the supposed 1861 "Baltimore Plot" against Abraham Lincoln, the 1876 "Molly Maguire" caseload, the 1892 strike at the Homestead steel mill, and the 1905 Western Federation of Miners caseload. A thorough examination of Pinkerton activity, especially that of their "Molly Maguire" and WFM caseloads, suggests that the organization, while ostensibly a detective agency, may actually have been a commercial terrorist enterprise hired by industrial interests to destroy workingmen's combinations and their attendant political aspirations.

Railroad Strike of 1877

Strike of railroad workers that began weeks after the first "Molly Maguire" hangings. Unrest over wage cuts broke out at Martinsburg, West Virginia, and spread throughout Maryland and Pennsylvania, northeast to Albany and Buffalo, and west to Illinois and Missouri. The strike involved one hundred thousand workers of many trades, lasted more than two months, and led to intervention by federal troops. More than a thousand were jailed, more than a hundred killed, and scores injured. Millions of dollars worth of property was destroyed.

During the strike, Franklin Gowen's chief engineer and head of his Coal and Iron police, former Brigadier General Henry Pleasants, advised a district superintendent of the Philadelphia and Reading Coal and Iron Company: "if any crowds of strikers go to our

Collieries to intimidate the men from working, they must be kept off our property even if shooting them down becomes necessary instruct our men not to stop half way, because a little shooting only enrages a mob, whereas considerable execution frightens & demoralizes them."[10]

San Francisco Committee of Vigilance

Vigilante group in San Francisco active in 1851 and 1856. Members chose for their emblem the "all-seeing eye" subsequently used by the Pinkerton National Detective Agency. Historian Kevin Kenny described the San Francisco vigilance movement as "in part ... a pogrom directed at Irish Catholic immigrants."[11]

Shenandoah Herald

Virulently nativist anthracite coal region newspaper published by Thomas J. Foster. The *Herald's* coverage of the "Molly Maguire" trials skewed heavily toward the prosecution, and greatly influenced national coverage.

Silliman Guards

Militia funded by Schuylkill County bank president Edward Silliman and mustered in Mahanoy City, Pennsylvania, on November 13, 1875. On December 11, 1875, Frank Wenrich, first lieutenant in the militia, allegedly shot and killed John Kehoe's sister-in-law Ellen McAlister during an armed raid conducted by more than forty men at Wiggan's Patch (Kehoe's brother-in-law was also killed). No one was *[prosecuted for]* the killings. The militia was later admitted to the National Guard of Pennsylvania under the designation Company C, 7th Regiment.

Slate Pickers (also "Breaker Boys")

Use of these boys to separate coal from impurities by hand began in the 1860s and ended in the 1920s with the passage of national child labor laws. When necessary these boys, some as young as seven, worked ten-hour days, six days a week. Fatalities included being crushed to death or smothered through a fall down the coal chutes. Estimates of the ranks of this segment of child labor in Pennsylvania's anthracite region vary from 20,000 in 1880 to 24,000 in 1907, though historians consider these estimates conservative.

United Mine Workers of America (UMWA) and the Great Strike of 1902

Founded in 1890 by John Rea at Columbus, Ohio, the UMWA merged two groups, the Knights of Labor Trade Assembly No. 135 and the National Progressive Miners Union, to form its union. By 1902, UMWA membership numbered almost one hundred and fifty thousand anthracite and bituminous mineworkers. In 1902 John Mitchell, UMWA president from 1898 to 1907, joined with defense attorney Clarence Darrow at the Anthracite Coal Strike Commission called by President Theodore Roosevelt to mediate the dispute between mineworkers and coal operators during the Great Strike of 1902. The commission granted the mineworkers a nine-hour day and a ten percent wage increase.

Richard Trumka, current AFL-CIO president, served as UMWA president from 1982 to 1995. Today, the UMWA numbers more than seventy thousand members in mining, manufacturing, and health care industries, as well as criminal justice and public sector employees.

Western Federation of Miners (WFM)

Formed in 1893 at Butte, Montana; merged miners of copper, silver, lead, gold, and hard rock from Colorado, Idaho, Montana, South

Dakota, and Utah; first president John Gilligan. Aims included anti-child-labor and mine safety legislation. In 1905 William Haywood, WFM secretary-treasurer, played a role in the formation of the IWW at Chicago. The WFM's tumultuous history, including allegiances with other organizations, continued until 1967, when, under its newer name Mine Mill, it merged with the Canadian Auto Workers.

In early 1906 James McParland, chief prosecution witness during the "Molly Maguire" trials in the 1870s and superintendent, in 1906, of the Pinkertons' Western division at Denver, engineered the arrest of three WFM officers, including Haywood, for the bombing death of former Idaho governor Frank Steunenberg. The WFM numbered at that time forty thousand U.S. and Canadian members, with local divisions establishing hospitals and libraries. The WFM trials in Idaho and Colorado led to acquittals of the WFM men, the unmasking of Pinkerton methods, and the shredding of McParland's credibility.

Workingman's Benevolent Association (WBA)

Anthracite miners' union formed by John Siney at Saint Clair, Pennsylvania, in early 1868. By early 1869, Siney had organized WBA branches in all six anthracite counties. Officially headquartered at Hazleton on March 17, 1869, by the end of 1869 the WBA numbered 30,000 of the region's 35,000 anthracite miners.

In 1864, anthracite mineworkers in Pennsylvania's Carbon County formed a short-lived organization under the same name. Post-Civil-War mineworkers in Luzerne County did the same, with similar results.

Yellow Press (also "Yellow Journalism")

Term applied to exploitative, sensationalist newspaper coverage that distorts facts to increase sales. Pennsylvania's *Shenandoah Herald* and the *Miners' Journal* in Pottsville, along with the *New York Herald,* the *New York Sun,* and the *New York Times,* provided

Franklin Gowen with such coverage both before and during the "Molly Maguire" trials. Newspapers all over the country did the same. After the trials ended, John Swinton, a former editorial chief of staff for both the *New York Sun* and the *New York Times*, told fellow journalists: "'We are the tools and vassals of rich men behind the scenes. ... We are intellectual prostitutes.'"[12]

---

1. John O'Dea, *History of the Ancient Order of Hibernians* (New York: National Board of the AOH, 1923), 2: 884.
2. "The A. O. H. and the Mollies," *Philadelphia Times*, August 28, 1876 (account of AOH Division No. 2 meeting, Philadelphia).
3. Wayne G. Broehl Jr., *The Molly Maguires* (1964; repr., New York: Chelsea House/Vintage, 1983), 171.
4. Geo. F. Baer to Mr. Clark, 17 July 1902, University of Minnesota Law Library, Clarence Darrow Digital Collection, The Anthracite Coal Strike, Miscellaneous, George Baer's "Divine Right" Letter, http://moses.law.umn.edu/darrow/documents/Baer_letter_cropped.pdf.
5. For statement of Clarence Darrow see Ibid., Proceedings of The Anthracite Mine Strike Commission, reprinted from *Scranton Tribune*, 1902-03, http://moses.law.umn.edu/darrow/documents/Proceedings_Anthracite_Strike_Cropped_OPT_Fina_OCR.pdf, 252.
6. *Report of the Case of the Commonwealth vs. John Kehoe et al.* (Pottsville, PA: Miners' Journal Book and Job Rooms, 1876), 167.
7. See Kevin Kenny, *Making Sense of the Molly Maguires* (New York: Oxford University Press, 1998), 157-58, 168-81, 202-04.
8. *New York Herald*, April 12, 1871.
9. Letter signed "Vigilantibus," Mahanoy City, July 3, 1877, published in the *Boston Pilot* on July 14, 1877; italics in original.
10. Henry Pleasants to John Reese, 26 July 1877, Letterbook of Henry Pleasants, Reading Anthracite Company Collection, Pottsville, PA.
11. Kenny, *Making Sense*, 204, n. 57.
12. Richard O. Boyer and Herbert M. Morais, *Labor's Untold Story: The Adventure Story of the Battles, Betrayals and Victories of American Working Men and Women* (1955; repr. New York: United Electrical, Radio, and Machine Workers of America, 2005), 81.

ACKNOWLEDGMENTS

John Elliott and Philip Foner drew the map. Henry Foner started the avalanche. Howard Zinn and Seamus Heaney offered early encouragement; as did Anne Anderson, U. S. ambassador to Ireland. Eric Foner listened and encouraged. John Elliott, Thomas Elliott, Joseph Wayne, John Brennan, and the Pennsylvania Labor History Society advocated for this truth more than four decades ago.

Thanks to Joe Wayne, for everything, including a summer spent at Kehoe's Hibernian House while on the research trail; Ellen and Bill Engelhardt, who compiled the first research collection, and Ellen, for blazing the trail; Maureen and John Murphy, who helped house the second research collection; coal region guide Howard Crown, who spirited me a copy of Kehoe's trial transcript; Bill Engelhardt, for cover art; Sharon Wolf, for digitally reclaiming Kehoe's photo; Marci and Bob Webber, hosts extraordinaire.

And to Ned McGinley, former national president of the Ancient Order of Hibernians, and Charles McCollester of the Labor Studies program of Indiana University of Pennsylvania, whose grants supported this research. Thanks to Fairfield University's 2008 Irish College, Bob Wolensky of King's College, Bode Morin of Scranton's Anthracite Heritage Museum, the American Conference for Irish

Studies, and the Pennsylvania Historical Association for providing speaking venues.

To my great-aunts, who broke the code long ago; my grandmother; my mother and aunts; my sisters Susie Flaherty and Jane Lindsay, intrepid editors of early copy; and to Susie, a published author in the health sciences, for ongoing counsel. In 2008 Susie's son, my nephew Matt Dunbier, spoke the Hibernians' statements of innocence at Fairfield University. My niece Katie Dunbier made the Harrisburg trip for reconnaissance through microfilm readers.

To Lucia Dailey, poet of the coal region, for her unique insights; Rosemary Gido, professor emerita of criminology, for her staunch support; attorney Sarah Brozena, for incisive comments on this and a previous manuscript; the generosity of librarians and archivists, including Jean Dellock of Schuylkill County Historical Society; Mesa County Library in Grand Junction, Colorado, for scans of Orin Hilton's argument; Denver Public Library, for scans of Edward Blewitt's AOH involvement; sister professor Mary Grace Flaherty; others too numerous to mention; and Vellum Press.

Heartfelt gratitude to first reader Ms. sister Kathy Bone, whose help brought forth this work, and who brings lyricism to everything; Steve Bone, who does the same; the Misfits; Mr. Cat, who got me out of my chair; and the house on the hill overlooking the Chesapeake Bay where I wrote this manuscript.

ABOUT THE AUTHOR

Anne Flaherty, a great-great-granddaughter of John Kehoe, has spent two decades researching and documenting Pennsylvania's "Molly Maguire" conflict. She has presented papers through American Conference for Irish Studies (ACIS) meetings in Spokane, Boston, and at University College Cork; through the Pennsylvania Historical Association at Indiana University of Pennsylvania; and at Kings College, Wilkes-Barre. In 2013 Flaherty formed the Kehoe Foundation as a 501c3. Online publication of her work can be found at the blog "From John Kehoe's Cell."